Life Events
and
Rites of Passage

The Customs and Symbols of

Major Life-Cycle Milestones,

Including Cultural, Secular,

and Religious Traditions

Observed in the United States

Life Events
and
Rites of Passage

The Customs and Symbols of
Major Life-Cycle Milestones,
Including Cultural, Secular,
and Religious Traditions
Observed in the United States

By Jeff Hill and Peggy Daniels

Foreword by Clifton D. Bryant,
Professor, Virginia Tech University

P.O. Box 31-1640
Detroit, MI 48231-1640

Omnigraphics, Inc.

Cherie D. Abbey, *Managing Editor*
Helene Henderson, *Editor*
Allison A. Beckett and Mary Butler, *Research Staff*

* * *

Peter E. Ruffner, *Publisher*
Matthew P. Barbour, *Senior Vice President*

* * *

Elizabeth Collins, *Research and Permissions Coordinator*
Kevin M. Hayes, *Operations Manager*
Cherry Stockdale, *Permissions Assistant*
Shirley Amore, Martha Johns, and Kirk Kauffman, *Administrative Staff*

Library of Congress Cataloging-in-Publication Data

Hill, Jeff, 1962-
  Life events and rites of passage : the customs and symbols of major life-cycle milestones, including cultural, secular, and religious traditions observed in the United States / by Jeff Hill and Peggy Daniels ; foreword by Clifton D. Bryant.
     p. cm.
  Summary: "Provides information about the history, symbols, customs, and traditions of important life-cycle events within the broad range of cultural and religious groups in the United States. Entries are arranged in sections on birth and childhood, coming of age, adulthood, and death and mourning"—Provided by publisher.
  Includes bibliographical references and index.
  ISBN-13: 978-0-7808-0735-8 (hardcover : alk. paper) 1. Rites and ceremonies—United States. 2. United States—Social life and customs. I. Daniels, Peggy. II. Title.
  GN560.U6H56 2008
  306—dc22   2007035420

Table of Contents

v

Foreword

M any years ago a very old and very wise man observed that "Living is what you do while you are waiting to die!" Certainly there is great truth in this. The time between the moment you are born until the minute of your death constitutes your life with all of the events and experiences that occur within it. This is your life!

Your life, however, does not unfold as a steady and continuous stream of happenings and experiences. Rather, it is punctuated by a series of very special events that divide your existence into distinctive periods or segments during which one occupies a very special social status and has a unique categorical identity. There are numerous such special events and ceremonies that occur during the life course. Examples here might include coming of age and achieving adult status, graduations, marriage, and death, to mention but some. There are many such life-changing events that call for special ceremonies. These are known as "Rites of Passage." This label or phrase was first suggested in a book published in 1909 by the French anthropologist Arnold van Gennep. He was attempting to demonstrate that all cultures have such rituals or ceremonies to mark the transition from one social status to another.

Rites of passage are universal in the sense that they exist in all societies around the world. They have also occurred in all societies throughout history. Such ceremonies all share a unique commonality. All have three stages or phases. The first stage involves leaving behind the earlier social status. The second phase focuses on the process of transition, and the third and final stage involves the entry and incorporation into the new social status. As an example, in a marriage ceremony, the bride is escorted down the aisle by her father, signifying that she is leaving behind her status as a member of her parents' family (*leaving behind the earlier social status*). At the altar, the father steps aside, letting the groom take his place. The clergyman articulates in detail the new obligations and bonds that the couple will now assume (*process of transition*). After the vows, the couple walks back up the aisle as husband

and wife. This signifies that both the bride and groom are now entering a new social status with all that goes with it as members of their newly formed group of husband and wife (*entry and incorporation into new social status*).

In this volume, *Life Events and Rites of Passage: The Customs and Symbols of Major Life-Cycle Milestones, Including Cultural, Secular, and Religious Traditions Observed in the United States,* entries examine the special events, with the accompanying rites or ceremonies of passage, that punctuate the life course and divide it into social status segments. In order to demonstrate to the reader that rites of passage are, indeed, universal, the book leads the reader on a cultural odyssey that examines some of the special events and ceremonies in the life course in a number of different American groups—Hebrew, Hindu, Sikh, Muslim, Cajun, Native American, Chinese, Japanese, and others. This literary journey lets the reader fully share the rites of passage of those in other societies. As this volume shows, people everywhere enjoy and celebrate the very special events that make up their lives.

Clifton D. Bryant
Department of Sociology
Virginia Tech University

Preface

The term "rites of passage" sometimes conjures up images of archaic practices that occurred in wild, remote cultures a long time ago. This is not surprising, given that the concept was developed by early anthropologists who often focused on traditional cultures. But the need for rites of this kind is just as pressing in developed societies. This can be seen from the enormous number of present-day observances that allow people to adjust to new events in their lives—everything from graduation ceremonies to weddings to religious confirmations. The purpose of this book is to illuminate how these types of rituals are carried out in the United States at the beginning of the 21st century.

What exactly is meant by a "rite of passage"? Webster's Dictionary defines a rite of passage as "a ritual associated with a crisis or a change of status," and this is a good place to start. As people progress through their lives, they move from one state or status to another. Babies are born, small children become adolescents, adolescents become adults—to name just a few of many possible changes. The transition from one stage to the next can be a difficult and stressful time, both for the person undergoing the change and for that person's family and friends. Rites of passage mark these transitions, allowing the individual and their acquaintances to recognize formally the change that is taking place. For the purposes of this volume, a rite of passage is a ritual that helps people make the transition between life stages.

That raises the related question of what is meant by "ritual." Again, the dictionary defines it as an action performed according to "religious law or social custom" and as a "formal act or series of acts" that are "customarily repeated." Rituals are often thought of in terms of formal ceremonies, and many of the rites of passage discussed in this book fit that description. For instance, a wedding serves as the ceremonial means of marking the transition from life as a single person to life as part of a married couple, while a funeral is a formal means of expressing grief and marking a person's transition from life to death. Many of these rituals are based in specific religions.

But in the periods that surround life-changing events, Americans also engage in activities that are not formal ceremonies in the typical sense. For instance, when a father takes part in a childbirth-preparation class, he is involved in an activity that will help him and his partner make the transition to parenthood. Thus, this action functions as a rite of passage even though it involves few ceremonial functions. When appropriate, this book takes a broad approach to the subject of transition and adjustment. While formal, strictly prescribed observances are part of that story, less formal ceremonies are important as well.

Scope

Life Events and Rites of Passage: The Customs and Symbols of Major Life-Cycle Milestones, Including Cultural, Secular, and Religious Traditions Observed in the United States presents an introduction to many of these rites of passage. This volume covers the history, symbols, customs, and traditions of life-cycle events—including both secular and religious events. That's a vast subject, of course, one that no single book could adequately cover. This book is intended to provide an introduction to a sampling of major events, rather than an exhaustive overview of the subject.

Over 90 entries are included that emphasize practices that are now found in the United States, with coverage of the historical events that set the stage for the current situation. As is appropriate for a multicultural country, the book encompasses important events from some of the nation's major religious groups (Christian, Jewish, and Muslim) and major ethnic groups (African American, Hispanic, Asian American, and Native American). In addition, coverage is included on events by other distinctive groups, such as followers of the Hindu, Buddhist, and Sikh religions. Finally, the book also considers general life events that aren't confined to any particular religious, ethnic, or social group but that impact a broad range of U.S. residents.

Audience

Life Events and Rites of Passage is intended for a general audience. It was written with middle school and high school students in mind, but it will also be of interest to the general reader interested in information about rites and customs that are practiced in the United States.

Organization

The entries in *Life Events and Rites of Passage* are organized into four major parts, which address the significant stages of life in chronological order.

Part 1: Birth and Childhood includes the rituals surrounding conception, birth, and the early years of life. It covers the rites experienced by parents as well as those that focus on the child.

Part 2: Coming of Age addresses those practices that mark a person's growing maturity and transition from childhood to adolescence and the early stages of adulthood. Though it includes the many rites that accompany puberty, it considers some earlier events that can occur before a person reaches sexual maturity. The section also extends to the late teenage years, when events such as graduation from high school signify a young person's readiness to confront the challenges of living life on their own terms.

Part 3: Adulthood focuses on the ceremonies that occur once an individual reaches legal and social maturity. Many of the entries in this section are concerned with the wide variety of observances that accompany courtship and marriage. Other entries consider events, such as reunions, that help an individual to take stock of their experiences as they grow older.

Part 4: Death and Mourning concentrates on the many different customs that surround the end of life and the ways in which survivors cope with death.

Each major part is further divided into chapters that address individual subjects. For instance, in the first major part, Birth and Childhood, there are six chapters:

Conception and Pregnancy
Greeting the Baby
Naming the Baby
Entering the Faith
Firsts
Commemorating Birth

Each chapter is further divided into a series of entries on specific events related to that subject. Both the chapters and the entries are arranged in a roughly chronological order. For instance, the chapter on Conception and Pregnancy, which concerns pre-birth practices, precedes the chapter on Greeting the Baby, which focuses on activities at the time of birth.

Each entry begins with the following information:

1. **The entry name**, which can be a general subject (Birth Rituals for Fathers) or a specific individual rite (Baptism);

2. **Any alternate names** (where applicable) that are used for the practice or practices described; and

3. **The customs and symbols** that are covered in the entry.

The main body of the entry includes a brief introductory paragraph followed by three main sections:

1. **History and Significance**, which discusses the development of the ritual practices in question and some of their general meanings and purposes;

2. **Observance**, which provides an overview of the way that the customs are currently practiced in the United States; and

3. **Customs and Symbols**, which breaks the subject down into specific items and discusses their significance.

Each entry concludes with a list of Web Sites and/or Further Reading, where readers can find additional information on the subject.

Other Features

Cross References

Entries in *Life Events* often make reference to other entries in the book with related information, inviting cross-cultural comparisons. Such references to other entries are indicated in bold type. For example, a reader interested in **Aqiqah,** a Muslim purification ritual in which a newborn baby's hair is cut or shaved, might also be interested in **Upsherin**, a Jewish ritual that includes cutting a young boy's hair. Each entry is listed by name in the index, to enable readers to easily find this related information.

Bibliography

The Bibliography contains a complete list of the sources consulted in the preparation of this volume.

Index

The Index includes people, places, customs, symbols, foods, the titles of musical and literary works, and other subjects mentioned in the entries.

Acknowledgments

We want to express our appreciation for the assistance of our Advisory Board members. This volume was prepared in consultation with a distinguished panel comprised of scholars and educators in the field. Their comments and suggestions were invaluable throughout the production process. Any errors, of course, are ours alone. Following is a list of the advisors who contributed to *Life Events and Rites of Passage:*

Clifton D. Bryant, Professor
Department of Sociology
Virginia Tech University
Blacksburg, Virginia

Dr. Pamela R. Frese, Professor
Department of Anthropology and Sociology
College of Wooster
Wooster, Ohio

Paul Hill Jr., MSW, LISW
CEO/President, East End Neighborhood House
Founder, National Rites of Passage Institute
Cleveland, Ohio

Dr. Paul D. Numrich, Chair
Program in World Religions and Inter-Religious Dialogue
Theological Consortium of Greater Columbus
Columbus, Ohio

Jane I. Smith, Professor of Islamic Studies
Duncan Black Macdonald Center for the Study of Islam and Christian-Muslim Relations
Hartford Seminary
Hartford, Connecticut

Comments and Suggestions

We welcome your comments on *Life Events and Rites of Passage,* including suggestions for topics that you would like to see covered in future editions. Please address correspondence to:

> Editor, *Life Events*
> Omnigraphics, Inc.
> P.O. Box 31-1640
> Detroit, MI 48231-1640
> Email: editorial@omnigraphics.com

PART 1

Birth and Childhood

A beaming mother with her newborn baby.

PART 1

Birth and Childhood

INTRODUCTION

Because of its essential role in perpetuating the species, birth was probably revered from the earliest days of the human race, and countless rituals and ceremonies have surrounded the creation of life in the millennia since. For much of human history, the rites and charms that were intended to safeguard the mother and child formed a major part of natal care.

The advent of scientific medical practices has reduced the reliance on such tactics, yet traces of the old beliefs can still be seen in customs that surround birth. For instance, an ancient belief found in many cultures held that the mother and child should be separated from regular society during labor and for a certain period afterward. The separation was sometimes expressed by the idea that the mother and child had become spiritually unclean because of the birth process and could only rejoin the regular community after undergoing some type of ritual to cleanse them of impurities. Strict separation rituals are not common in the U.S. today, but purification ceremonies continue to be part of the Muslim (*see* **Aqiqah**) and Hindu faiths (*see* **Namakarna** and **Chudakarma**). Some traces of this idea can also be seen in infant baptism in the Christian faith—a ritual cleansing that shields the baby from supernatural harm (*see* **Entering the Faith**).

As these examples suggest, the many different ceremonies and activities that surround birth and childhood often share similarities with one another. This part groups them in according to subject and begins with those that address the process of conception and the months leading up to birth. This is a period of uncertainty and anxiety for most parents, which inspires a variety of approaches—from age-old folk beliefs to modern childbirth classes.

Religious ceremonies come to the forefront at the time of birth and in the period that immediately follows. In some cases, the goal is to greet the baby with a religious-related message in its first moments outside the womb because it is thought

3

that this will help influence the child to live a blessed and devout life. Soon after delivery, the child must be named, and the importance of this step is commemorated in both religious and non-religious observances, all of which emphasize the influence that a title is believed to have over a person's life.

The degree to which an infant can participate in religious activities varies according to the faith in question. While some religions hold that a person cannot officially enter the faith until later in life, others believe it essential to initiate the newborn. Among those religions that follow this practice are the Roman Catholic Church and several other Christian denominations, as well as Judaism. Because these religions have a very large membership in the U.S., baptism and bris milah are perhaps the most familiar infant rites of passage to contemporary Americans.

Many of the purification ceremonies mentioned earlier fall into the category of "firsts"—that is, ceremonies that commemorate a child's first time undergoing various experiences. The initial haircut is a topic of keen interest, with some religious traditions seeing it as a means of eliminating spiritually unclean elements from the child and others viewing the shedding of hair as a symbol of a child's commitment to religious learning. Certain "first" celebrations, such as the Roman Catholic **First Communion and Reconciliation**, are also serious spiritual events, while others provide a more lighthearted means of observing the growing process.

Growth is also judged by the birthday celebrations that continue throughout childhood and, in most cases, throughout a person's life. They become a means to reflect—sometimes in a melancholy way—upon the changes that take place with each passing year and so provide a measure of what has been gained and lost since a person's first moments of life.

Photo on facing page: A baby shower usually includes many gifts for the new baby.

BIRTH AND CHILDHOOD

Chapter 1: Conception and Pregnancy

INTRODUCTION

In previous centuries, the period before a birth was concerned with two essential goals: getting pregnant and insuring that both the mother and child survived the pregnancy. Rituals surrounded both of these pursuits. Some of the oldest known artworks in the world are 25,000-year-old sculptures of female figures that appear to be pregnant, and these objects were probably intended to increase childbirth. A huge number of other fertility rites have been employed over time, along with a vast range of ceremonies, spells, potions, and prayers that were intended to provide protection during the pregnancy.

The need for such safeguards was all too clear. Before the advent of modern medical practices childbirth could be a dangerous undertaking. To take one particularly grim example, during the 1600s, one of every five women in the colonial town of Plymouth, Massachusetts, died of childbirth-related causes. The situation improved as scientific knowledge increased in the following centuries. Still, it was only in the 1930s that sterile conditions and sophisticated procedures began to make birth the relatively safe procedure it is today.

While most parents now rely on medical science for help with the basic issues of conception and protection, they are still faced with the difficult transition to the role of parent. It is here that rites of passage prove most useful, and these observances come into play before the child is born. The **Baby Shower** is the primary American rite in this regard, offering the prospective parents both material support (in the form of baby-related gifts) and emotional support (through advice about parenting). The assistance the prospective mother and father provide to one another can also be essential, and the increased participation of dads in the pregnancy has become one of the hallmarks of modern childbearing in the United States. This has led to a variety of **Birth Rituals for Fathers** that allow them to prepare for the birth and adjust to their new responsibilities in raising a daughter or son.

The emphasis on scientific technology and up-to-date parenting hasn't eliminated all of the folk beliefs related to childbirth. This is especially true of groups who have maintained some independence from mainstream American society, which has allowed them to preserve some of their traditional **Protection Lore**. While many of these beliefs are serious (if unscientific) attempts to make childbirth safer, other folklore takes a lighter approach to the subject. The various means of guessing the sex of the baby before birth continue to fascinate expectant parents as well as their family and friends. The survival of these folkisms and the invention of new ones show that many Americans wish to maintain some of the mystery of creating new life, even as they depend on the certainties of science to make their birth a safe one.

BABY SHOWER

Alternate Names: Baby Sprinkle, Couples Shower

Customs and Symbols: Advice and Emotional Support, Couples Shower, Gifts, Guest Favors, Parental Debut, Shower Games

One of the most common birth observances in the United States, the baby shower can be seen as a secular ceremony that fulfills some of the same functions as the religious rituals surrounding birth. It celebrates the arrival of the baby and helps the parents adjust to their new roles in life. Unlike most religious rites, however, there's a strong dose of materialism in the baby shower, with gifts being the focus of the celebration.

History and Significance

The baby shower is a fairly recent invention. It emerged around the 1930s, by which time medical advances had improved both mother and infant's chances of surviving birth. Thus, a baby's birth gradually became more something to happily anticipate than to regard with apprehension. In 1937 Emily Post first included etiquette advice for baby showers in her popular guidebook, *Etiquette: The Blue Book of Social Usage*, which had been published in various editions since the 1920s.

The idea of presenting a gift in honor of a birth, however, particularly in a notable family or royalty, is not so new. This practice dates back to the ancient civilizations of Rome and Egypt, and a similar practice takes place in some religious rites. For instance, a small Bible may be presented when a Christian church recognizes a newborn in a dedication ceremony (*see* **Baptism**). Similarly, a baby born to Sikh parents may receive his or her first *kara* (a metal bracelet) shortly after birth (*see* **Nam Karan**). The baby shower takes this practice to new heights: instead of receiving a small token recognizing the new arrival, the child and parents are "showered" with presents at a party thrown in their honor. While it fulfills a practical need and represents real affection, this large-scale gift giving also speaks to the relative affluence of the United States and the American tradition of expressing congratulations in material terms.

Observance

A shower is usually given in honor of a family's first child, though showers for subsequent children are not unheard of. A gathering held for a later child is sometimes described as a "sprinkle" (as opposed to a shower), and these events usually place more emphasis on celebrating the new birth rather than giving gifts. If presents are given at the sprinkle, they tend to be practical things the parents wouldn't already have, such as diapers and baby food.

There are differing opinions on when it's appropriate to schedule a shower. The more traditional view is that it should not take place until the child is born, which is drawn from the old idea that it is unwise and unlucky to celebrate a birth too early in the process. This thinking was motivated by the danger that accompanied childbirth in previous centuries, and some believed that parents who celebrated a birth before it happened were likely to invite bad luck or the attention of harmful spirits. Similar thinking was applied to baby showers, even though they appeared in the era when childbirth was becoming a good deal safer. These ideas haven't been given as much credence in recent decades, and it has become increasingly common to hold showers prior to the birth. Orthodox Jews, on the other hand, usually refuse to have any type of shower celebration, before or after the birth.

> *A shower is usually given in honor of a family's first child, though showers for subsequent children are not unheard of.*

Because a direct plea from the parents for gifts would be in bad taste, the shower is usually organized or "thrown" by someone other than the mother and father. Usually, one or more of the family's close friends fill this role. The gathering usually takes place at a private residence or sometimes at a public venue such as a restaurant. Food and drink are provided, though it's more often snack-type refreshments rather than a full meal. Alcoholic drinks are usually avoided if the shower takes place before the birth, because most mothers abstain from drinking during pregnancy. Activities include shower games to help break the ice, conversation (which often centers on providing the new parents with advice and emotional support), and of course the gift giving. Many showers work the gifts in two directions by providing the attendees with guest favors. In some cases, the shower may be focused on the mother with the guests being primarily female, though couples showers that involve both parents and a mix of male and female guests are becoming increasingly common.

Customs and Symbols

Advice and Emotional Support

While the gifts may be the main reward for the parents, they are not the only reason for throwing a shower. The gathering often serves as a show of support. By seeing that they have a group of close friends and family that are pleased with the arrival of the child, the parents understand that they have a support system that will aid them in the challenges of parenting. Showers also serve as an advice session. Those attendees who have children often share tips on how best to cope with the new baby. This is part of the reason why showers are normally held for the first child: it is in the early days of parenting that advice and support is most needed.

Couples Shower

Initially, the baby shower was a woman's domain, with female guests gathering in honor of the mother and the baby. This is still true of many showers, but couples gatherings have become more popular in recent years. These celebrations focus on both the mother and father and are attended by both men and women. This is another sign of the changing dynamics of parenting—that fathers are taking on a larger share of the duties that were assigned to the mother in the past (*see* **Birth Rituals for Fathers** for more examples of this trend).

Gifts

Gift giving is the best known aspect of showers, and it can be a vital means of support for the parents. Having a child is an expensive undertaking, and the presents—especially practical items such as baby clothes and blankets—can help the parents defray expenses. Unlike wedding gifts, which are opened after the event, baby shower presents are usually unwrapped one at a time at the gathering with all of the guests showing appreciation for the presents.

Guest Favors

The attendees are often provided with a small gift, which might consist of chocolates, mints, candles, scented soaps, lavender-filled sachets, or similar items. While these don't have great value, they allow the party organizers and the parents to show their gratitude to those who turned out for the shower. And as with any gift, the favors help to strengthen the bonds between the giver and receiver. For the new parents, these bonds are especially important, as they help to insure that they will have the support of family and friends as they begin raising their child.

Parental Debut

Whether it's held before or after birth, the shower often serves as the first large-scale social gathering in which the mother and (sometimes) the father are formally recognized as parents. Thus, it is a means of introducing their new identities and allows them to show that they have accepted their new positions and are committed to the child. Likewise, the presence of friends and family serve to reassure the parents that their new duties are recognized and supported.

Shower Games

A variety of games take place in order to create a fun and relaxed mood for the gathering. These usually have a baby or parenthood theme. For instance, jars of baby food with the labels removed are passed around, and guests compete to see who can guess their contents from appearance alone. (The jars are left unopened so the parents can later use them.) Another favorite is "poopy diaper," in which pieces of various candy bars are placed in diapers and then melted in a microwave oven. Guests try to guess what brand they are. (No tasting allowed.)

Further Reading

Pleck, Elizabeth H. "Rites of Passage." In *Celebrating the Family: Ethnicity, Consumer Culture, and Family Rituals*. Cambridge, MA: Harvard University Press, 2000.

BIRTH RITUALS FOR FATHERS

Customs and Symbols: Childbirth Class, Childbirth Coaching, Couvade, Cutting the Umbilical Cord, Emotional Support, Physical Assistance

One of the most significant changes in birthing practices since the latter decades of the 20th century involves the greater participation of fathers in the childbearing process. This development reflects the larger changes in parenting that have taken place as strict gender roles have broken down. Fathers now play a bigger part in all aspects of raising a child—from caring for infants to nurturing adolescents. Birth is the first step in that process, signaling the father's willingness to be very involved in the life of his son or daughter.

History and Significance

Up until the early 1900s, the delivery of a baby was the domain of the mother, her female friends and family, and—in some cases—a physician. During this era fathers were involved in preparing the house for the delivery and would usually be standing by in case an emergency arose during labor, but they mostly steered clear of the room where the actual delivery took place. After hospital births became common, childbearing was left to the mother and the medical providers while the father maintained his vigil in the hospital waiting room. This separation was usually enforced by hospital rules and was justified by several theories: fathers would infect the sterile conditions of the delivery room; they would be in the way; and they wouldn't be able to bear the sight of their wives in pain.

This reasoning was shown to be false once men did begin to attend deliveries, which began in the 1960s and 1970s. The trend accompanied the natural childbirth movement that sought to reduce the reliance on doctors and medical science in childbearing. Natural childbirth methods often called for a "birthing partner" to assist the mother, with the father usually assuming that role. Today, it's more common for a father to be present in the delivery room than not to be. One study from the late 1990s showed that more than 90 percent of married fathers in the United States take part in the birth. This represents a complete reversal of the previous trend, and the switch has taken place in the span of a few decades.

Observance

Initially, most fathers find that their duties fall into two camps: education and encouragement. A childbirth class that involves both the mother and father has become the standard for many first-time parents. These classes explain what the parents can expect before and after birth and may discuss particular ways to prepare for the delivery—for instance, practicing appropriate breathing techniques and completing specific exercises to lessen the mother's discomfort and strengthen muscles that will be used during labor. Some of the preparatory activities take place outside of class, and the father typically plays a role in encouraging the mother to complete them. Thus, childbirth coaching often becomes one of the father's most active functions during the pregnancy.

Initially, most fathers find that their duties fall into two camps: education and encouragement.

However much they may enjoy offering athletic tips and enforcing training discipline, fathers often find that emotional support is more important to the mother. By giving her the sense that she's not undergoing the ordeal alone, the father helps the mother to become more comfortable with the impending delivery, which improves the chances of a successful birth. Of course, this type of assistance is especially important once labor begins, and the father may also provide some form of physical assistance during the delivery. Finally, in what has become the classic ritual of today's more active fatherhood, he often participates in cutting the umbilical cord.

In some instances, fathers may find that their involvement in the pregnancy has become especially intense. Some of them even develop physical symptoms that resemble those that the mother is experiencing, including weight gain and backaches. Though it usually happens subconsciously, this behavior is in some ways similar to the ancient practices of couvade, in which the father simulated aspects of pregnancy. The modern version practiced in the United States is often explained as a temporary emotional disorder and is termed couvade syndrome or sympathetic pregnancy.

Customs and Symbols

Childbirth Class

"Prepared childbirth" is the term that's often used to refer to the system of education and activity that surrounds many of today's pregnancies. As the name suggests, mothers and fathers are expected to prepare themselves for birth, and that process begins with formal classroom training. Multi-week childbirth classes are usually offered through hospitals or independent agencies and are taught by certified instructors affiliated with organizations such as the International Childbirth Education Association. Most of these courses are designed with the idea that each mother will be accompanied by a birthing partner, who is in most cases the father, though another person can fill the role as well.

The classes can vary depending on what program they're teaching, but they typically include discussion of the basic biology of childbirth, information on proper diet and exercise during pregnancy, and instruction in relaxation techniques and massage to help minimize and relieve discomfort. Participants also engage in role playing, where they simulate the birth and the appropriate activities for the mother and her partner. These classes prove especially valuable for men, most of whom have limited knowledge about the childbearing process. Beyond their educational value, the courses can also serve as a type of ritual for new dads, giving them a formal way to enter and become comfortable with the new surroundings of birth and fatherhood.

Childbirth Coaching

The pioneers of the natural childbirth movement realized early on that fathers could play an important role in helping mothers follow the details of their preparation programs. This function was often equated to being a sports coach. Ferdinand Lamaze, the French doctor who designed the well-known pregnancy regimen that now bears his name, told mothers that the child's father "will be able to assist you much as a swimming coach might, and will point out errors that you will never see by yourself." Another leader of the movement, Robert Bradley, even titled one of his books *Husband-Coached Childbirth*. What exactly the husband "coaches" depends on the type of program that is being followed. The Lamaze procedures call for a precise method of breathing that varies during the different stages of labor, so the father helps to insure that it is completed correctly. In the method advocated by Bradley, the father makes sure the mother completes the necessary exercises during pregnancy and helps her to relax through a combination of soothing words and touch, which is refined in the months before birth.

As these steps suggest, the coaching begins well before the woman goes into labor, and it continues through the birth of the child. One of the most active forms of coaching comes in the final stage of pregnancy, when some fathers encourage the mother to bear down and "push" the baby out. This method has been followed for decades but some authorities question its wisdom. A study published in 2005 in the *American Journal of Obstetrics and Gynecology* suggested that this type of active coaching speeded up delivery slightly but that the intensive pushing could cause some lingering difficulties for the mother in the months after birth. Several programs, including the Lamaze method, now place less emphasis on strict coaching. Instead, they stress that the father should be more of a supportive partner than stern taskmaster.

Couvade

One of the most mysterious birthing rituals, couvade (pronounced *coo-VAAD*) is usually considered a relic of the past. In some South American cultures, when a mother was about to give birth, the father would imitate her behavior—groaning as if he were experiencing labor pains and sometimes even wearing women's clothes as he did so. This behavior often continued after birth as well, with the father withdrawing from his normal activities and being doted on by friends and family as if he, too, had borne a child.

Anthropologists and psychologists have come up with numerous theories about couvade, three of which are particularly compelling. First, participants may have believed that they were transferring some of the mother's pain to the father through his symbolic labor pains. Second, couvade may have begun as a means for the father to publicly accept the child as his own. Finally, the practice of couvade might be related to the idea that harmful forces threatened the mother and child at the time of birth. By simulating pregnancy, the father may have been trying to fool the evil spirits and draw them to himself so that they wouldn't interfere with the real birth.

The classic characteristics of couvade are now found only among a few remote cultures, including several in South America. But a modern version of couvade-like behavior has developed in the United States and other Western countries. In these cases, fathers develop the same health symptoms as their pregnant partner. For instance, the man might gain weight or suffer nausea and back pain, just as the mother does. Often referred to as couvade syndrome or sympathetic pregnancy, this phenomenon seems to be fairly common: some studies suggest that it may affect as many as half the fathers in the United States, though the type and severity of the symptoms vary from person to person.

Couvade syndrome is sometimes considered a mental or emotional disorder that is caused by the stress of the pregnancy, but some analysts view it in a different way. Anthropologists such as Richard K. Reed see modern couvade as a type of ritual that allows men to participate in the pregnancy and prepare themselves for their role as fathers. There is a distinct difference between the sympathetic pregnancy symptoms common today and the traditional practice of couvade, however. When practiced by men in South America, couvade is usually described as a conscious, deliberate action. The couvade-like symptoms now experienced by men in the United States seem to more often be a product of the subconscious. Reed suggests that this happens because modern Western society doesn't provide men with enough meaningful ways to show their involvement in the pregnancy. They therefore compensate by developing the sympathetic ailments.

Cutting the Umbilical Cord

In the nine months before a baby is born, the umbilical cord serves as its lifeline, providing all of the elements needed for life. Thus, the cutting of that cord after the child has emerged has long been recognized as the proof that the baby has gone from unborn to born—becoming an individual that has, at least to some extent, become independent of the mother. This event has taken on a ritual status in many cultures, and the same is true of contemporary births in the United States. In many cases the act is performed by the child's father (with appropriate direction from the midwife or physician). Though a fairly simple procedure, the severing of the cord is a powerful symbol that allows a father to declare his responsibility for the new life and his dedication to insuring the child's well-being outside the womb.

Making the Cut

The physician held the little girl for a minute, then handed her to a nurse, and turned to Kevin. "Well, here's your part," he said with a smile, and offered the new father a pair of surgical scissors. Kevin took the scissors with a sense of detachment and found himself being ushered into place beside the kneeling obstetrician. "I was thinking, 'Oh man, I don't know,'" remembered Kevin. The doctor held the cord for few more seconds, then as the pulsing faded, he held out the section to be severed. "I did cut it. And it was a lot tougher, thicker than I thought it would be. I had to snip it twice. I kind of forgot that blood would squirt out and stuff. But I was real excited, and I was real happy."

Source: Reed, Richard K. *Birthing Fathers: The Transformation of Men in American Rites of Birth.* New Brunswick, NJ: Rutgers University Press, 2005, p. 7.

Emotional Support

Though they can carry out practical duties, fathers probably prove most useful as a familiar, reassuring presence that can help mothers relax during labor. Childbirth expert Robert Bradley began to recommend that fathers take part in labor after he "noticed how much more calm and cooperative the patient was when her husband was present. If he left the room, even temporarily, the mother became anxious and tense and relaxed poorly with contractions." This type of assistance can also be vital earlier in the pregnancy. The father's support is not only an immediate comfort to the mother but also signals that his interest and concern regarding the child will be ongoing, which promises good fortune for the family as a whole.

Physical Assistance

Childbirth-preparation methods often call on the father to carry out massage techniques as a means of relaxing the mother and relieving pain. This is especially helpful in the later months of pregnancy and also takes place during labor. In the final stages of birth, the father may become directly involved in supporting the mother in a certain position so she can more effectively "push" (constrict her abdominal muscles) to birth the baby.

Further Reading

Reed, Richard K. *Birthing Fathers: The Transformation of Men in American Rites of Birth.* New Brunswick, NJ: Rutgers University Press, 2005.

PROTECTION LORE

Alternate Name: Sou-khouanh

Customs and Symbols: Avoiding Compliments; Avoiding Light, Wind, and Cold; Avoiding Raising the Arms; Avoiding Startling or Unpleasant Sights; Binding the Spirit to the Body; Defending against the Evil Eye; Loosening Rituals

Pregnancy has always been filled with uncertainty and a certain amount of danger. As a result, an enormous number of folk beliefs have taken shape over the centuries that were intended to provide some type of protection for the mother and child. Such ideas have become less common since the advent of modern medical practices, but they continue to play a part in American childbirth.

History and Significance

Until the 1700s there were few scientific medical treatments devoted to childbirth, so parents usually relied on actions and objects that they believed had some kind of supernatural power. In Great Britain and other parts of Europe, magical charms were often employed to promote fertility and to give protection to expectant mothers. Some of the colonists who came to North America beginning in the 1600s brought these practices with them. For example, amulets made of coral were popular because they were said to increase the chances of becoming pregnant and to prevent miscarriage once a child had been conceived. But the Puritan religious leaders who came to dominate New England battled against any practices that they considered to be witchcraft, so the use of magical talismans was not as widespread in the American colonies as it had been in Europe.

Nonetheless, there was plenty of popular folklore devoted to pregnancy, and much of it was based on a concept of magic—though not necessarily the witches' spells feared by the Puritans. Instead, much of the lore surrounding childbirth can be defined as imitative magic, which means performing an action that in some way resembles the desired effect. For example, when a woman went into labor, the doors and windows of her home might be opened because it was thought that the opening of these passages might bring about a similar opening of the birth passage, allowing the child to be delivered quickly (*see* Loosening Rituals below for more examples of this widespread practice.) Magical rites of this type continue to be practiced in the United States, along with a number of other customs that fall outside the realm of medical science. Though they are sometimes derided as superstition, the survival of these customs shows that parents are willing to try a variety of practices in hopes of having a successful and healthy pregnancy.

Observance

Much of the protective lore takes the form of prohibitive guidelines that recommend that certain actions be avoided. Often, it is the mother and child who are expected to obey restrictive behavior such as avoiding light, wind, and cold and avoiding startling or unpleasant sights, though some guidelines, such as avoiding compliments are applied to the friends and family of the parents. Other lore dictates actions that are intended to speed the delivery, as is the case with loosening rituals, or to help the family recover from the trauma of the birth, as can be seen in those rites that are used in binding the spirit to the body.

Customs and Symbols

Avoiding Compliments

The idea that evil or bad luck is attracted to things that are beautiful causes some cultural groups to refrain from complimenting the baby. It's thought that doing so will attract harm to the child. Some members of the Hindu faith take this a step further. They place a black dot on the child's chin so that spirits won't be attracted to it and so that people won't be likely to compliment it. Another tactic is for relatives to make unflattering remarks about the baby. This is practiced by some Native Hawaiians and also by Hmong people, who hail from southern China and Laos and have formed large communities in the American Midwest and California in recent decades. Upon seeing the baby, relatives might comment on its big nose or unattractive hair, though it's generally understood that they mean the opposite of what they say. Similar ideas lie behind some naming customs practiced by various groups (*see* **Deceptive Naming**).

Avoiding Light, Wind, and Cold

This prohibition is found in various forms all around the world and is actually a rather logical set of ideas, as it tends to keep the mother and baby indoors and away from strenuous activity, which allows them to gather their strength after the birth. Among the groups who observe this guideline are various Native American tribes. A traditional practice of the Jicarilla Apache, for instance, is to place a blanket over the doorway of the dwelling to keep out the light and wind. (*See* **Pueblo Presentation Ceremonies** for a similar custom among the Pueblo people of the Southwest.) In general, many Native Americans see light as being a danger to the newborn child and view wind and cold as great hazards for the mother.

A similar idea is found among some Asian Americans, including tradition-minded individuals who trace their heritage to China and Vietnam. Their concern with cold is reflected in the custom of serving the mother foods associated with heat and discouraging her from showering and washing her hair in the weeks following birth (*see* **Red Egg and Ginger Party**). A similar idea has passed into general American folklore, with a quasi-medical twist. It contends that pregnant women should not take baths because bacteria can be passed through the water, into the mother's body, and then to the baby. There is no scientific truth to this notion.

> *The idea that evil or bad luck is attracted to things that are beautiful causes some cultural groups to refrain from complimenting the baby. It's thought that doing so will attract harm to the child.*

Avoiding Raising the Arms

This folk belief holds that if a pregnant woman raises her arms over her head, she risks strangling the unborn baby with the umbilical cord. There is no medical truth to the idea, but that hasn't limited its popularity: it is found throughout American society. It's related to the loosening rituals mentioned below, many of which also warn that a tied object will cause the umbilical cord to become tangled around the baby.

Avoiding Startling or Unpleasant Sights

The idea that the sensations perceived by the mother can harm the unborn baby is extremely ancient, and it remains common. The list of dangers that fall into this category is enormous, and the following is just a sampling. One widespread tale warns that bad things can happen if a pregnant woman sees a dead body. In one version of this tale, it's said if a mother encounters a corpse, she must look at it directly. If she averts her gaze, the baby will be born cross-eyed. Mothers among the Jicarilla Apache are warned to look away from people with physical disabilities for fear that the baby will be born with the same defect. This kind of direct, magical transference is found in other folk beliefs collected around the U.S. as well. For instance, it's said that a woman startled by a mouse will give birth to a baby with rodent-like features, while an expectant mother who quarrels with others during her pregnancy will find the baby "fighting" against her during delivery, causing a prolonged and painful birth. Birthmarks are often explained in this way—that a scare or a strong feeling on the mother's part caused a mark on the baby's body.

For instance, a strawberry shaped birthmark might be explained by the fact that the mother had an unsatisfied craving for strawberries during pregnancy.

Binding the Spirit to the Body

Some Buddhists from southeast Asia believe that the spirits of the baby and mother can become separated from their bodies during the birthing process. To bind them back together, ceremonial strings are tied around their wrists. Laotians living in the United States call this *sou-khouanh* (pronounced *soo-kwan*), and it usually takes place a month or more after birth. The gathering is attended by friends and family, all of whom tie a string in place while wishing the mother and child good health. A very similar ceremony is observed by the Hmong. It takes place three days after birth and is accompanied by the public announcement of the baby's name. Those who trace their heritage to Thailand have their own version of this practice, though it is usually held about a month after birth. Again, a sacred string is used to tie the spiritual elements to the body. In some cases the child is named on this same occasion and may undergo a ceremonial head shaving similar to that conducted in the Muslim **Aqiqah** and Hindu **Chudakarma** rituals.

Defending against the Evil Eye

Though belief in harmful supernatural powers is found throughout the world, the fear of the evil eye is especially widespread. Those who accept the existence of the evil eye believe that an envious person is capable of causing harm through the power of their gaze—intentionally or not. Specifically, if someone, particularly a stranger, looks upon another person with feelings of envy, the evil can be passed from the admirer to the object of his or her attention. Babies and children are thought especially vulnerable because strangers may find them attractive and wish them for their own. This folk belief is quite common in Mexico and other parts of Latin America and is therefore found among some Hispanic Americans. Americans who retain strong ties to the traditions of the Mediterranean region, including the Middle East, are also likely to believe in the evil eye.

Various tactics are used to ward off the evil eye. Parents may seek to shield their children from public view as much as possible. Amulets and icons in the shape of eyes (to reflect the evil back upon the gazer) and slippers (to "kick" the envious person) can also be placed on the child. A Muslim parent who perceives that a stranger is paying undo attention to their son or daughter or complimenting the child excessively might utter an Arabic phrase that translates as "God's blessing and grace upon the Prophet." This is believed to deflect the evil eye. Hispanic parents may approach the stranger directly and demand that he or she touch the child. By doing this, the stranger becomes known to the family and, as a result, their attention to the child is thought to no longer pose a danger.

Loosening Rituals

An ancient childbirth rite known throughout the world is to untie, open, or "undo" all kinds of things surrounding the mother, especially at the time of delivery. For instance, any knotted items—hair braids, clothes lines, and so forth—are untied, boxes are opened, and locks are unlocked. It's hoped that the action of loosening these objects will be transferred to the mother so that the baby will be more easily dislodged from the womb. In the United States, these actions are most commonly found among Native Americans and Asian Americans. For example, Navajo women commonly take their hair down when they go into labor, and the mother's friends and family may do the same if the delivery proves especially difficult. Some Asian Americans still follow the practice of forbidding people to stand in a doorway when a woman is in labor. It's thought that this "blockage" of the passageway may be duplicated in the mother, preventing the baby from being born. A slightly different take on the same idea is sometimes practiced by those who trace their heritage to India. An unopened flower is given to the mother near the expected time of delivery with the hope that its unfurling will be simulated by the mother and child.

Monday's Child

One of the simplest folk beliefs about birth is that the day or time that the child arrives will determine its character and future, an idea summed up in this familiar children's rhyme. Variations of this rhyme go back to England, at least to the early 19th century. This version from New York was collected by folklorist Fanny D. Bergen in the 1890s:

Monday's child is fair of face,
Tuesday's child is full of grace,
Wednesday's child is sour and sad,
Thursday's child is merry and glad,
Friday's child is loving and giving.
Saturday's child must work for a living;
But the child born on the Sabbath Day
is blithe and bonny and good and gay.

Further Reading

Bergen, Fanny D., ed. *Current Superstitions Collected from the Oral Tradition of English Speaking Folk.* Boston: Houghton, Mifflin and Company, published for The American Folk Lore Society, 1896. Available online at Project Gutenberg, http://www.gutenberg.org.

Dresser, Norine. *Multicultural Celebrations: Today's Rules of Etiquette for Life's Special Occasions.* New York: Three Rivers Press, 1999.

Fontanel, Béatrice, and Claire d'Harcourt. *Babies: History, Art, and Folklore.* New York: Henry N. Abrams, 1997.

GUESSING GENDER

Customs and Symbols: Area of Baby Activity, Amount of Baby Activity, Chinese Gender Chart, Counting Heartbeats, Drano Test, Ring Test, Shape of Mother's Stomach, Straight-Pin Test

Figuring out the sex of a baby before it is born is an age-old quest, and there's also a long history of people attempting to control what the sex will be. Today, ultrasound imaging and other advanced technology has given prospective parents the ability to solve the gender mystery with certainty, yet less scientific methods are as numerous as ever and seem to serve as a comforting—and sometimes fun—means of coming to terms with parenthood.

History and Significance

In centuries past, there was sometimes little difference between scientific knowledge and superstition, and this was certainly true when it came to determining the sex of the baby. For instance, the Greek physician Hippocrates argued that the gender could be read from the mother's body: if her right breast was firmer than the left, the baby was a boy; if the opposite was true, it was a girl. The inaccuracy of this method didn't seem to affect its use—it was still being followed in England in the 1600s. Some authorities went further and declared that it was possible for parents to control the sex of the child even after conception. One theory held that if a mother ate primarily cold food, the baby would develop as a girl. Warm food brought a boy. Similar claims were made about the position of the mother when she slept—lying on the one side encouraged a boy, the other a girl. Of course, these types of theories were proven false by later medical findings, but they did offer parents the reassurance that they could take actions to influence the pregnancy rather than leaving everything to chance.

A vast range of gender-guessing methods are common in the U.S. today. Most are based on some kind of direct observation of the mother or on her perceptions of the baby's movements.

Today, folk wisdom about how to figure out the baby's sex is alive and well in the United States. In fact, the growth of the Internet has probably made these ideas more widespread than ever before. However, theories about how to *control* the gender of the baby have largely faded away—perhaps because medical science has explained precisely how conception does occur. There is one prominent exception to this rule, however: the "Shettles method" put forth in the best-selling book *How to Choose the Sex of Your Baby* (2001). It calls for parents to organize their sexual intercourse in particular ways in order to increase their odds of having a girl or a boy, though the scientific merit of the plan has not been proven.

Observance

A vast range of gender-guessing methods are common in the U.S. today, with some of the more popular ones listed below. Most are based on some kind of direct observation of the mother or on her perceptions of the baby's movements, though the Chinese gender chart makes its prediction based on the mother's age and the month of conception. Because most of these methods are based on some kind of physical evidence, they have a quasi-scientific basis, but it should be remembered that there is little to no reliable data supporting their accuracy. But, as with the flip of a coin or any other prediction where there are only two choices, most of them will be accurate about 50 percent of the time.

Customs and Symbols

Area of Baby Activity

The idea that boys create certain effects on one side of the mother's body and girls on the opposite side has been around a long time (as the Hippocrates breast theory shows). One modern version contends that if the mother feels the child kick more often on her right side, it's a male; if on the left, it's a female.

Amount of Baby Activity

One of the simplest ideas about determining gender holds that an unborn child that is actively moving around in the womb (regardless of the area) is a girl while one that's relatively stable is a boy. Women often explain this by saying that males are lazy even before they're born.

Chinese Gender Chart

In this method, the child's sex is predicted by consulting a chart that was supposedly discovered in a royal tomb in China seven centuries ago. It determines the gender of the child based on the mother's age at conception and the month in which the child was conceived. (Remember that both the mother's age and the month of conception must be converted from the Gregorian calendar used in the United States to the lunar calendar used in China. The better web sites discussing the gender chart provide an automatic converter.)

Counting Heartbeats

A baby's heartbeat can be detected by medical equipment and is routinely checked during pregnancy. According to one folk theory, a baby with a heartbeat faster than 130 beats per minute is a female while those with a slower pulse are males.

Drano Test

One of the more dangerous and messy methods, this "test" is accomplished by mixing several ounces of the mother's urine with crystals of Drano drain cleaner. A chemical reaction results, and the gender of the baby is supposedly indicated by the color change of the liquid. Unfortunately, the various versions of the tale give different color codes. For instance, one version says that if the liquid darkens to a brownish color in the first 10 seconds, the baby is a boy, but another theory has it that brown signifies a girl. Yet a different explanation says that if the liquid bubbles vigorously, it's indicating a boy; if there are few bubbles, the mother is carrying a girl. One thing is fairly certain about the Drano test, however: the fumes released from the mixture can be harmful and should not be inhaled.

Ring Test

One of the spookier means of trying to figure out the baby's gender, this test supposedly operates according to the magnetic force given off by the unborn child. For the optimum symbolic effect, the mother's wedding ring should be used (assuming she's married), but another type of ring can be substituted. The ring should be tied to a thread or—for more of a witchcraft feel—a strand of the mother's hair. When suspended over the mother's stomach, the movement indicates the child's gender. Clockwise rotation (when looking down on the ring) means a girl; counterclockwise, a boy.

Shape of the Mother's Stomach

In some people's opinion, the appearance of the mother's stomach holds the clue to the baby's sex. If the stomach has a nicely rounded shape and the baby appears to be carried high in the abdomen, it's a girl; if not, it's a boy.

Straight-Pin Test

A variation on the ring test, this method replaces the ring with a straight pin. If the object has a circular motion to its swing when held over the mother's stomach, the baby is said to be a girl. If it goes back and forth in a straight line like a pendulum, the child is a boy.

Web Sites

"Chinese Gender Chart." Baby Gender Prediction, undated.
http://www.babygenderprediction.com/chinese-gender-chart.html

"Drano Test." Snopes.com, July 28, 2004.
http://www.snopes.com/pregnant/drano.htm

Photo on facing page: Muslim parents whisper the shahada to their newborn, typically the first words the infant hears from them.

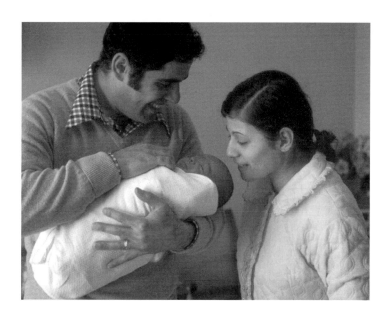

BIRTH AND CHILDHOOD

Chapter 2: Greeting the Baby

INTRODUCTION

Though all aspects of the childbearing process are loaded with meaning, the central moments when the baby is born are especially significant. There is a widespread belief that a person's first minutes outside the womb should be observed in a specific way and that doing so will have a positive effect on her or his future.

This attitude can be seen in the general birth practices that are observed in the United States. It is common for the child to be immediately given to the mother after being born so that the two can begin bonding with one another. Thus, the first impressions the baby gets of the outside world are of being nurtured by one of its parents. Fathers, too, typically play a central role by cutting the umbilical cord, an action that physically separates the mother and baby and signifies the dad's involvement with his son or daughter (*see* **Birth Rituals for Fathers**).

Recent childbirth procedures underline the concern for the baby's first experiences. In the past, newborns were often given a light spank to get them breathing. Because of concerns that this was unnecessarily violent, it's now more common for doctors or midwives to simply rub the baby's feet or chest to stimulate his or her first cry. It also used to be common for hospital personnel to quickly remove the baby from the parents for weighing, measuring, and taking foot and handprints. Many hospitals now delay these actions so that the parents and child are allowed to spend more time together immediately after birth, when the child is usually awake and alert.

While these maternity routines function as mini rituals that help the child and parents adjust to their new situations, there are also a number of more formal ceremonies that take place immediately after birth. While Christianity, the largest faith in the United States, postpones its first ritual—**Baptism**—until several weeks after the birth, other religions are much more prompt. This is particularly true of Islam, Hinduism, and Sikhism—three religions that have become more prominent in the U.S. in recent decades.

Though these faiths are quite different in many respects, their birth rituals are remarkably similar. All seek to formally introduce the newborn to the basic concept of the religion. In both **Whispering the Shahada** and **Reciting the Mool Mantra**, the basic concepts of the Muslim and Sikh faiths are spoken to the child. In the Hindu **Jatakarma** ceremony, a religious symbol may be symbolically written on the baby's tongue and a religious poem or the name of a Hindu god may be whispered to the child. In addition, all three faiths bestow a special food to the baby as its first nourishment. These similarities are partly due to geography: both Hinduism and Sikhism originated in India, and Islam also has a very large following in that region.

JATAKARMA

Alternate Name: Birth Samskara

Customs and Symbols: Aum, Ghee, Golden Utensils, Honey, Mantra, Whispering the Name of Vach

Jatakarma (pronounced *ja-tah-kar-mah*) is a Hindu life-cycle ritual (or *samskara*) performed at the time of birth. It includes several symbolic actions that introduce the baby to the Hindu faith. If conducted in the traditional manner, it is among the first experiences of the child's life, taking place in the moments after it emerges into the world.

History and Significance

Jatakarma is just one of many Hindu rituals surrounding pregnancy, birth, and early childhood. As many as nine samskaras can take place in this period (for information on some of the other rites, *see* **Namakarna**, **Chudakarma**, and **Annaprasana**). These ceremonies all have an extremely ancient history. Many of them are mentioned in the Grhya-Sutras, a collection of religious texts that dates to 500 B.C.E. Today, it's rare for Hindus to observe all of the ceremonies. The members of the faith exercise a great deal of personal choice in this regard, with some choosing to carry out a large number of rituals while others perform few or none at all. The jatakarma rite has evolved over the centuries. In the past, there was a lot of emphasis on actions that were thought to provide protection from harmful forces that threatened the baby. These preventive actions included the burning of mustard seed and rice chaff in a fire, which was believed to ward off dangerous spirits. Today, these practices are less common, and the ceremony deals more with actions that seek good fortune and intelligence for the child.

> *Jatakarma takes place at the time of birth, and if observed in the traditional manner, it occurs even before the umbilical cord is cut.*

Observance

Jatakarma takes place at the time of birth, and if observed in the traditional manner, it occurs even before the umbilical cord is cut. Honey or ghee (clarified butter) is placed in the child's mouth (or sometimes both substances are mixed together). In one interpretation of this act, a pen is dipped in honey and is then used to write the sacred word aum (also spelled "om") on the child's tongue in Sanskrit. Another way of performing this action is to use one of the golden utensils—either a spoon or a ring—to feed the baby. In addition to the food ritual, the father may recite a mantra invoking longevity as well as whisper the name of Vach, the goddess of language, in the child's ear.

Customs and Symbols

Aum

Perhaps the most important symbol in the Hindu faith, the word "aum" or "om" is considered sacred in both its written form and when spoken aloud. Aum has a wide range of meanings. It is seen as a representation of three important gods of Hinduism—Vishnu, Shiva, and Brahma—and it is also said to represent all of existence, standing for the Hindu concept that everything is connected. When spoken aloud, its deep humming tone is said to be the primal sound of the universe—the cosmic vibration out of which everything else was created. This sound is repeated by Hindu worshipers as they pray. Being such a central part of the faith, many Hindu parents believe it's appropriate to write the word in Sanskrit letters on the baby's tongue in its first moments of life, using a golden pen dipped in honey to create the word.

Ghee

An important element in Indian cooking and culture, ghee is clarified butter, which is made by taking cow's-milk butter and heating it to remove water and separate out the solid milk particles. Ghee plays a part in several Hindu rituals in addition to jatakarma and is believed to have divine qualities because it is produced

Secret Name

Some Hindus follow the ancient custom of giving the child two names: one to be used in public, one to be kept secret. In some cases the secret name is bestowed at birth but is not uttered aloud and is known only to the mother and father. Then the public name is given in the namakarna ceremony. This practice is inspired by the idea that harmful supernatural forces could be directed at the child should its "true" name become known early in life. (See **Deceptive Naming**.)

by the cow—an animal sacred to Hindus. Traditionally, ghee is said to improve the memory and intellect, and this is why it is given to the baby during jatakarma, sometimes mixed with the honey and sometimes on its own.

Golden Utensils

As with many other groups around the world, Hindus often value items made of gold, which can symbolize spiritual enlightenment, prosperity, and purity. To help impart these qualities to the newborn, a golden spoon or, in some cases, a gold ring is used to place the honey or ghee in the infant's mouth. If the parents follow the practice of writing aum on the baby's tongue, a gold pen is often used.

Honey

Honey has been highly valued for many thousands of years because its sweet taste helped liven up various dishes in the era before refined sugar was widely available. Like ghee, honey is said to promote intelligence in the child. The feeding of honey and other sweet items at birth is also found in other cultures and religions and generally serves as a symbol for the sweet gift of life that has been given to the baby (*see* **Reciting the Mool Mantra** and **Whispering the Shahada and Tahnîk**).

Mantra

The father sometimes recites a mantra—a sacred sound, phrase, or verse—to the child during the ceremony. The traditional way to do this is to whisper it in the child's right ear or near its naval (where it has been connected to the mother—and in fact may still be connected, as the ritual often takes place before the umbilical cord is cut). The mantra is intended to grant a long life to the child. An ancient poem used for this purpose lists many things that are long-lived (the gods, the ocean, and so forth) and then asks the same longevity for the child.

Whispering the Name of Vach

Another phrase that may be whispered in the baby's right ear is the name of Vach, the goddess of speech and learning. Like the use of ghee and honey, this is intended to improve the child's intellectual abilities.

Web Site

"Butter and Ghee in India." WebExhibits, undated.
      http://webexhibits.org/butter/countries-india.html

Further Reading

Knipe, David M. "Hinduism: Experiments in the Sacred." In *Religious Traditions of the World: A Journey through Africa, North America, Mesoamerica, Judaism, Christianity, Islam, Hinduism, Buddhism, China, and Japan*, edited H. Byron Earhart. New York: HarperSanFrancisco, 1993. Reprinted online at Hindu Gateway. http://www.hindugateway.com/library/rituals

Mann, Gurinder Singh, Paul David Numrich, and Raymond B. Williams. *Buddhists, Hindus, and Sikhs in America*. New York: Oxford University Press, 2001.

RECITING THE MOOL MANTRA

Alternate Name: Mool Mantra

Customs and Symbols: Honey, Mool Mantra

Members of the Sikh faith waste no time in introducing a child to their religion. Among the first sounds greeting a girl or boy after birth is a recitation of the main concepts of the Sikh faith. This is accompanied by the taste of honey, which symbolizes the sweetness that the child will hopefully enjoy as an observant Sikh.

History and Significance

The Sikh faith was founded in the early 1500s in the northwestern region of India known as the Punjab. Today, Sikhs are found not only in India but also in many other parts of the world, including the United States. Their religion stresses the believer's proper relationship to God, and this relationship begins at birth. The basic elements of the faith are announced to the child in the Mool Mantra. This religious poem makes up the first verses of the Guru Granth Sahib—a collection of hymns that serve as the Sikh scriptures. Many of the writings in the book were composed by Guru Nanak, the founder of the faith, and Sikhs consider them to be the divine message of God.

Observance

Just moments after birth, the father recites the Mool Mantra to the child. This passage from the Sikh scriptures is known to all members of the faith and explains their belief in a single god. Immediately afterward, a drop or two of honey is given to the child. Some Sikhs provide the honey in a slightly different fashion: a short time after birth, a leader of the local Sikh community visits the family and feeds the baby a mixture of honey and water while reciting the Mool Mantra and other passages from the Sikh scriptures.

Customs and Symbols

Honey

Because of its golden color and sweet taste, honey has been viewed as a divine substance by many different cultures over the course of human history. For the Sikhs, as for members of other religions, it serves as a symbol for goodness and for the rich and enjoyable existence that awaits the child.

Mool Mantra

The brief passage that sums up the central ideas of the Sikh faith, the Mool Mantra includes the following lines:

> There is One God. He
>> Is the Supreme Truth
>> Is without fear
>> Is not vindictive
>> Is Timeless, Eternal
>> Is not born, so
>> He does not die to be reborn.
>> Self-illumined,
>> By Guru's grace
>> He is revealed to the human soul,
> Truth was in the beginning, and throughout the ages.
> Truth is now and ever will be.

The mantra forms the opening verses of a longer hymn known as the Japji or Sikh Morning Prayer, which is part of the Guru Granth Sahib. Devout members of faith recite the Japji each morning, and parents who recite the Mool Mantra to their newborn are passing this tradition to their new daughter or son—allowing them to hear the hymn at the beginning of their first day outside the womb.

Further Reading

Dineen, Jacqueline. *Births*. Austin, TX: Raintree Steck-Vaughn, 2001.

Mann, Gurinder Singh, Paul David Numrich, and Raymond B. Williams. *Buddhists, Hindus, and Sikhs in America*. New York: Oxford University Press, 2001.

Singh, Rajwant, and Georgia Rangel. "Sikhism." Chapter 13 of *Sourcebook of the World's Religions: An Interfaith Guide to Religion and Spirituality*. Edited by Joel Beversluis. Novato, CA: New World Library, 2000.

WHISPERING THE SHAHADA AND TAHNÎK

Customs and Symbols: Shahada, Tahnîk

Muslims carry out two rituals that welcome the child to the world and ensure that his or her existence begins with a proper introduction to the Islamic faith. The first involves the statement of the core Muslim beliefs; the second provides the infant with a taste of a sweet substance that represents the goodness the child will know in the years to come.

History and Significance

The *shahada* (pronounced *shuh-HAHD-uh*) is the central statement of Islam—that there is only one God and that the Prophet Muhammad is his messenger. Because this phrase is so fundamental to Muslim life, parents believe that it should be among the first things that the child hears. Thus, it is recited to the baby just moments after birth. The tradition is said to have begun with Muhammad himself, who whispered the shahada to his grandson Hasan.

A second observance that occurs shortly after birth is to give the child a taste of something sweet—symbolic of the sweetness of life and also because it is said to give the child a sweet disposition. This custom is referred to as *tahnîk* (sometimes spelled *tahneek* and pronounced *ta-neek*), and it dates to ancient times in the Middle East. The traditional means of accomplishing this is to rub a bit of chewed date or some date juice on the baby's gums. In the past, a second act was also part of tahnîk: the child's father or a respected religious figure would spit into the child's mouth. The idea was that they were passing some essential element to the child that would help him or her to prosper in the world. It is said that Muhammad was frequently asked to carry out this function after he became accepted as a prophet in the seventh century C.E. The spitting portion of the ancient ritual fell into disuse, but the custom of giving the newborn something sweet is still practiced.

Observance

The infant's father is usually the central figure in both observances. In certain cases, another relative or an *imam*—a person who leads prayers at the mosque—will take the place of the father, though the person greeting the child is almost always male. In reciting the shahada, the adult figure usually whispers the words into the infant's ear. If the *adhān* and *iqāmah* are both recited (see below), they are whispered into the right and left ears, respectively. In giving the child something sweet to taste in the tahnîk rite, honey or sugar water is sometimes used, but the more traditional method is to use a date.

Customs and Symbols

Shahada

The Arabic word shahada means "affirmation." In its most basic form, the shahada simply states that "there is no god but God" and that "Muhammad is the Apostle of God" (the Arabic phrases are sometime translated in a slightly different manner). This is the foundation of the Islamic faith. The only action that is necessary to become a Muslim is to recite this statement with belief.

In whispering the shahada to their newborn, Muslim parents follow different customs. Some simply recite the basic two-part statement. Others follow the slightly more elaborate practice of repeating the traditional call to prayer that is given at mosques five times a day. This is made up of two parts. The first is the adhān, which summons the worshipers to the mosque. It includes several phrases, each of which is repeated several times: "God is greater" (sometimes translated as "God is the greatest"); "I bear witness that there is no God but God"; "I bear witness that Muhammad is the Apostle of God"; "come to prayers"; "come to salvation". (Some Muslim groups use a slightly different formula.) When recited to the newborn infant, the adhān is whispered in the child's right ear. Next, the adult recites the iqāmah in the infant's left ear. This is the statement that is made at the mosque once the worshipers have gathered together to pray. It is the same as the adhān but adds the phrase "prayers are ready." Thus, this post-birth ceremony serves as a preview of the daily prayer ritual that the child is expected to follow later in life.

Tahnîk

Date palms have been cultivated in the Middle East for thousands of years, where they are a staple part of the diet. It's little surprise, then, that they should figure in a Muslim rite that originated in the same part of the world. Several different methods can be used to give the baby a taste of the date's sweetness. Sometimes the fruit is pressed and some of the juice is rubbed on the child's gums or a date is mashed up in water and a few drops are given to the child. A more traditional practice is for an adult to first chew the date to soften it and then rub it on the child's gums. Many families observe this custom at the **Aqiqah** ceremony.

Further Reading

Gulevich, Tanya. *Understanding Islam and Muslim Traditions.* Detroit: Omnigraphics, 2004.

Holm, Jean, and John Bowker. *Rites of Passage.* London: Pinter, 1994.

Morgenstern, Julian. *Rites of Birth, Marriage, Death and Kindred Occasions among the Semites.* Cincinnati, OH: Hebrew Union College Press, 1966.

Photo on facing page: During the Sikh nam karan rite, the person leading the service uses a passage from Sikh scripture, the Guru Granth Sahib, as a guide in choosing the baby's name.

Chapter 3: Naming the Baby

INTRODUCTION

Probably the most universal belief about childbirth is that the name given to the baby can have an impact on her or his life. Today, most parents agonize over the decision for many weeks, consulting naming books and compiling lists of admired people that might serve as a namesake, be they relatives or celebrities. Certain religions place a lot of emphasis on the naming process. The Hindu **Namakarna** ceremony is specifically dedicated to revealing the child's name. Another faith that originated on the Indian subcontinent, Sikhism, has the similarly named **Nam Karan** rite, which not only announces the child's title to the fellow worshipers but requires parents to decide the name on the spot, using a passage from Sikh scripture as a guide. Ceremonies such as the Chinese American **Red Egg and Ginger Party** are a more secular means of announcing the name, making it an occasion to celebrate the mother and baby and to strengthen the bonds between the child and his or her extended family.

Many naming customs are based on the premise that the child's identity is bound up with his or her title, and they make a point of proclaiming that title to the world. But another school of thought takes the opposite approach, believing that revealing the baby's true name or giving the infant a permanent name too early in life can be dangerous. This has led to a number of **Deceptive Naming** customs. Though not widespread, these practices can still be found in the United States and provide an interesting glimpse of traditional beliefs about the magical power of names.

NAMAKARNA

Alternate Names: Namakarana, Name-giving Samskara

Customs and Symbols: Astrology, Blessing of the Newborn, New Clothes, Speaking of the Names

Namakarna (pronounced *naa-ma-kar-na*) is the Hindu name-giving ceremony. Normally observed eleven days after birth, it's a relatively simple ritual, yet it is considered important, as the selection of the proper names is thought to have a positive influence on the child's future.

History and Significance

One of the many birth samskaras (rituals), namakarna has been practiced for thousands of years. It is most commonly performed on the eleventh day after birth but can also occur on the tenth or twelfth day, depending on the custom of the family. The timing is related to traditional Hindu ideas about birth and purification. Both the mother and father were considered to be in an impure state immediately following birth. Therefore, the naming ceremony did not take place until that period came to an end. If the ceremony is not carried out on the specified early date, it can be postponed, with later observances frequently taking place on the hundredth day after birth or on the child's first birthday.

The people of India have long followed the practice of giving multiple names to the baby. In ancient times, there were usually four names. Today, three names are common: one is taken from the astrological conditions that existed at birth, a second from the god associated with the month of the child's birth, and the third is the popular name that the person will be addressed by. In addition, the number of syllables in the names is often considered important. Boys often receive names with an even number of syllables, girls an odd number. In some cases, families also follow the tradition of granting a "secret" name (*see* **Deceptive Naming**). This custom originated with the idea that an enemy could use a person's "true" name to work evil against them. To avoid this, a name was given at the time of birth but revealed to no one. Then the pub-

> *The Hindu name-giving ceremony namakarna is a relatively simple ritual, yet it is considered important, as the selection of the proper names is thought to have a positive influence on the child's future.*

licly known or popular name was granted during the namakarna ceremony for everyday use.

Observance

Though not officially revealed until the time of the namakarna observance, the parents decide upon the child's name in advance. Astrology is frequently taken into account in determining one of the names, with the child's birth date suggesting several letters that can be used to begin the name. As with many other samskaras, the ceremony takes place in the presence of a sacred fire (*see* **Jatakarma**). The mother and baby appear in new clothes, which signify their purity. In some namakarna ceremonies, a Hindu priest carries out the naming, while others leave the duties to the father. In the central action of the ceremony, the father or priest touches the nose of the child and then speaks each of the names into the child's right ear. The blessing of the newborn takes place following the naming and is carried out by senior members of the family. A feast is sometimes held after the ceremony and attended by the extended family.

Customs and Symbols

Astrology

Since ancient times, Hindus have paid great attention to the alignment of the stars and planets at the time of a person's birth, believing that it had great influence on character and destiny. The system they use to divine these conditions is known as Vedic astrology (named for the Vedic religion, which was a forerunner of Hinduism). Because the heavenly bodies are believed to have a great deal of control over a person's fate, some Hindus choose one of the child's names based on the astrological sign he or she was born under. If a family follows this custom, they refer to a chart that lists the letters associated with the child's astrological sign, then pick a name beginning with those letters.

Blessing of the Newborn

After the naming, the elder members of the family, such as the grandparents, confer their blessing upon the baby. This shows their support and good wishes for the new member of the family.

New Clothes

Both the mother and baby don brand new clothes for the ceremony. These outfits show that they are of pure spirit and ready to begin their new roles. It's also customary for each to have bathed just before the ceremony, which further underscores their purity.

Speaking of the Names

During the ceremony, the names are officially bestowed when the father or Hindu priest holds the child and speaks the titles into the baby's right ear. It's common for the speaker to give the basis for the titles as well. For instance, if the astrological conditions that existed at the time of the child's birth played a role in one of the names, the father might announce that fact aloud as he bestows the name.

Further Reading

Kalavar, Jyotsna M. "Hindu Samskāras: Milestones of Child Development." In *Rituals and Patterns in Children's Lives*, edited by Kathy Merlock Jackson. Madison: University of Wisconsin Press, 2005.

RED EGG AND GINGER PARTY

Alternate Name: Mun Yurt

Customs and Symbols: Food, Gifts, Haircut, Naming, Red Eggs

Celebrated by families of Chinese descent, the red egg and ginger party allows parents to introduce their new son or daughter to friends and family. The revealing of the child's name is an important part of the celebration, as it is believed to have a large effect on the child's fortunes. Other objects associated with good luck also figure in the party, including the red eggs and gifts of money, all of which promise good things for the child's future.

History and Significance

The timing of the ceremony—usually one month after the child is born, though sometimes held as much as three months after—stems from the high rate of infant mortality that existed in previous centuries. Because the danger was greatest during the birthing process and in the weeks that followed, families adopted the custom of waiting at least 30 days before formally recognizing the child's birth. To help protect the mother and child during this period, a tradition developed where they would observe a "sitting month" right after birth, in which they stayed at home and regained their strength. Some Chinese Americans still observe this practice; others may not confine themselves for a full month but they do follow some of the customs related to the tradition. These practices are intended to help the mother regain a balance between her internal yin and yang elements, which are often thought of in terms of temperature. The birthing process is believed to create a great deal of yin, which makes the person have a cool temperature. To bring herself back into the proper alignment, the mother is instructed to avoid cooling activities such as showering and washing her hair and to eat a lot of foods associated with warmth. Ginger is one of these foods, so it figures in her diet during the sitting month and also plays a big part of the one-month celebration.

The reason eggs are included in the party stems from the fact that they are a common fertility symbol and also because Chinese families often found themselves with a large supply of eggs shortly after a child was born. This occurred because eggs, which were considered a delicacy, were frequently brought to the family as gifts by the maternal grandmother. The eggs are dyed red because that color symbolizes luck and happiness in Chinese culture. The pickled ginger served at the party is frequently dyed red, as well.

Observance

In the past, the party would be announced by giving out the red eggs to members of the extended family and close friends. When a boy was born, an even number of eggs was given to each invitee; for a girl, an odd number was given. This practice is less common now that family members don't live so close together (eggs, even when hard-boiled, don't travel well by mail). Even if they don't serve as an invitation, the red eggs are featured at the gathering, often as table decorations and as a good luck charm directed at the baby. The wish to bring good fortune to the newborn is also seen in the gifts given by guests. This is especially true of "lucky money" (known as *li-shih* or *lai see* in Cantonese and *hong bao* in the Mandarin language).

The size of the gathering depends upon the family, but the parties can be quite large—involving all of the relatives that can attend as well as the parents' friends. In the past, the party usually took place in the parents' home. That's still true for some families, but others choose to host the party in another location, such as a restaurant. Wherever the party is held, food is a big part of the celebration. As discussed previously, favored dishes are those that are believed to promote warmth. This includes recipes that include ginger as well as pickled ginger itself.

The centerpiece of the ceremony is the naming of the child. As might be expected, the name has been chosen in advance, but the announcement of the name is the symbolic means of presenting the child to the world. In addition, a ceremonial haircut often takes place at the party. The traditional way to do this is to shave the baby's head, leaving only a small amount of hair at the crown. A modern variation is to clip a small bit of the child's hair to fulfill the custom without removing all of the child's hair. At the conclusion of the party, guests are encouraged to take home the lucky red eggs. In addition, the parents usually send a gift to each guest after the party is over. These practices help to tighten the bonds between the newborn's family and its circle of relatives and friends and suggest that the new birth will be a good thing for all.

> *Celebrated by families of Chinese descent, the red egg and ginger party allows parents to introduce their new son or daughter to friends and family. The revealing of the child's name is an important part of the celebration.*

Customs and Symbols

Food

Many of the dishes traditionally served at the gathering include ginger as an ingredient, and all are believed to help the mother adjust her internal temperature, as explained above. One of the favorite party recipes is black vinegar pig's feet, which contains a healthy dose of ginger. Gai jow, a soup with chicken, rice wine, and ginger, is also common. The most powerful zap comes from pickled ginger. Like the eggs, this food is often colored red to symbolize good luck.

Gifts

The attendees at the party are expected to bring a gift. These can be practical items similar to those given at baby showers—toys and clothing, for instance (*see* **Baby Shower**). Hats and slippers that have a tiger decoration are extremely popular because the tiger is considered a protector of children in Chinese folklore. Baby-sized gold and jade jewelry is also common. In addition, the red egg and ginger party is one of many Chinese celebrations where envelopes of "lucky money" are given as gifts. Unless the gift giver is especially close to the family, the amount of money isn't necessarily lavish, but the gift is believed to contain good fortune as well as cash—and it is considered beneficial for the one who gives the gift as well as for the person receiving it. The luck is signified by the red envelope that is always used and sometimes by the number of dollars or other currency that's inside. For instance, the numbers eight and nine are considered good. Four, however, is a bad omen. Thus, it would be better to give thirty-nine dollars rather than forty, though a double multiple such as eighty-eight or ninety-nine would be considered even luckier. Whether it is given at a red egg and ginger party or in honor of a new year or a birthday, a lucky money envelope is not to be opened until the giver has departed.

Haircut

Removing the hair of a person's head often denotes a significant change in their life, and the practice of cutting a child's hair in a ceremonial manner is found in many cultures (*see* **Aqiqah**, **Upsherin**, and **Chudakarma**). As with the other haircutting rituals, the practice of shaving the child's head at the red egg and ginger party serves as a symbolic means of separating the child from his or her previous experiences—especially life in the womb. This can be seen by the way that the shaving is performed: any hair that might have grown before birth is removed, but a small bit of hair at the crown of the child's head is usually left in place because it's believed that these strands did not appear until after the child was born. Some families have a less-symbolic reason for shaving the child: they believe it promotes the hair to grow more quickly. The hair cutting is a traditional practice, and some families no longer follow that custom. A trim of some sort, even just a few locks, usually does take place as part of the red egg and ginger party, however. It is also customary to collect whatever hair is cut and save it, usually in a package that's wrapped by a red string.

Naming

The name bestowed upon a child is thought to have a great influence on his or her life, so the choice is not taken lightly. Frequently, grandparents are involved in choosing the name and may even make the final decision. Many factors go into choosing a traditional Chinese name. Ideally the family name (which appears first) and the given name (which appears second) will complement one another, both in appearance (when written in Chinese characters) and in sound. In addition, the name should be a good match for the child's astrological chart, the animal of his or her birth year, and the elements (such as fire, water, or earth) associated with the birth date. Those families that seek to link the names of all their children also need to find a title that fits well with the names of the child's siblings. In the past, children were often given a temporary name at the red egg and ginger party, though this practice is now less common. Known as a "milk name" (because it was used during the child's early life or "milk years"), the name was chosen in order to fool the evil spirits that were thought to threaten the child (*see* **Deceptive Naming**).

Favorite Sons

In Chinese culture, it's common for families to prefer male children over females. This is partially caused by the fact that boys will grow up and continue the family legacy while girls will usually marry and leave the family. In the past, the bias against females was sometimes reflected in the red egg and ginger celebration. An elaborate celebration was held for boys, but girls usually received a simpler and smaller gathering. The distinctions between the ways that the sexes are treated are generally less severe today than they were in the past. This is especially true of Chinese Americans.

Red Eggs

Being symbols of life and good luck, the red eggs are featured prominently as table decorations at the gathering. The egg also figures in a ritual that takes place at many red egg and ginger parties. One of the child's grandmothers peels the shell off of an egg and rolls it across the infant's head and body. The idea is that this will help to transfer the egg's lucky qualities directly to the infant.

Further Reading

Gong, Rosemary. *Good Luck Life*. New York: HarperResource, 2005.

DECEPTIVE NAMING

Alternate Names: Milk Name, Secret Name

Customs and Symbols: Chinese American "Milk" Name, Native Hawaiian Nicknames, Hindu Secret Name

Names are usually chosen because they represent some kind of positive quality that the parents hope to pass on to the child. But in some cases a completely different idea goes into the selection of a title. It is used as a sort of disguise that is intended to deceive those people or supernatural forces that might harm the child. This is accomplished by choosing a name that is purposefully unpleasant or one that is a substitute for the "true" name that belongs to the child. Both tactics date to ancient times but are still practiced by some parents today.

History and Significance

Throughout history, humans have worried that harmful supernatural forces are the cause of all kinds of unfortunate events. Such ideas may be less common today, but they have by no means disappeared. Many of the people who subscribe to these beliefs are especially concerned about the period surrounding birth, when the newborn is believed to be extremely vulnerable. To reduce the danger, parents developed a wide range of preventative actions over the centuries (*see* **Protection Lore**). One of the most common tactics was to use the child's name as a means of protection, and this custom persists among some groups in the United States.

This is done in two different ways. The first is to give the child a name that makes him or her appear unattractive, which is based on the idea that harmful forces are attracted to things that are beautiful and will overlook or avoid children whose name makes them seem unappealing. The second technique draws on the concept that a person's true name is so closely tied to their being that it can be used to harm them through the use of magic. To avoid this, the child is given two or more names—one being the "true" or "secret" name that the parents keep to themselves and another that is the everyday or "popular" name by which the child will be known. Thus, an enemy is unable to work evil against the

Sometimes, a name is used as a sort of disguise that is intended to deceive those people or supernatural forces that might harm the child.

child using the popular name because it is not linked to the person's true essence in the way that the secret name is.

Observance

Though harmful spirits and other supernatural forces receive relatively little attention in mainstream American society, these subjects continue to play a part among some ethnic and religious groups in the United States. The Chinese American "milk" name is a custom that is practiced by those who maintain a close link with the traditions of China. The name comes from the practice of giving the newborn a temporary title that is used for part or all of childhood, known as the milk years. Often, the milk name is one that is thought to make the child less attractive. The same idea is found in the Native Hawaiian nicknames, which often suggest that the child is ugly or point to less flattering aspects of physical appearance. The Hindu secret name custom operates on the principle that the baby's real title should not be known to anyone except the parents and, later, the child him- or herself.

Customs and Symbols

Chinese American "Milk" Name

A practice rooted in Chinese tradition, the use of a milk name is not as common as it once was, especially in the United States, but the custom hasn't entirely disappeared. This temporary title, when given, is often bestowed during the **Red Egg and Ginger Party**, which usually takes place a month after birth. This milk name provides protection during the early years of life, when the child is thought most at risk. As with the Native Hawaiian practice described below, the idea is to give a name that will make the child less appealing and less noticeable to evil spirits. Sometimes the child's gender plays a role in these names. Traditional Chinese culture tends to favor male children over females because a boy will carry on the family lineage while a girl is likely to marry and join the family of her husband. Perhaps because boys are seen as more valuable, there is a belief that male children are more susceptible to demons. This sometimes encourages parents who have a boy baby to give him a girl's name as a temporary title. They reason that the female name will fool the spirits into avoiding the child.

Native Hawaiian Nicknames

A custom of the native Polynesian population of Hawaii is to give the child an informal name that makes him or her seem less attractive. The most common of these titles is *Pupuka*, which means "ugly." As with the milk name, the underlying idea is that harmful forces won't be drawn to a baby that's repeatedly said to be un-attractive. It might seem as if this type of name would crush the child's self-esteem, but that's generally not the case. The practice is so widespread that nicknames like Pupuka have come to take on the opposite meaning—much as "bad" is taken to mean "good" or "cool" in American English, depending on how it's used.

Hindu Secret Name

Those Hindus who follow the practice of bestowing secret and popular names to their children often designate the secret name at birth—the same time that the **Jatakarma** samskara (ritual) takes place (*see* **Greeting the Baby**). The popular name is then publicly revealed at the **Namakarna** ceremony that usually takes place eleven days after birth. The parents reveal the secret name to no one, with the exception of the child once he or she is old enough to understand. The protection offered by the secret name is thought most necessary in the early years of life. In some cases, the secret name is publicly revealed at the **Upanayana** ceremony that takes place later in childhood, usually after the child has turned eight (*see* **Religious Milestones**). By that time it's thought that the danger has passed, so the formal revelation of the child's true name becomes part of the coming-of-age ritual.

Further Reading

Dresser, Norine. *Multicultural Celebrations: Today's Rules of Etiquette for Life's Special Occasions.* New York: Three Rivers Press, 1999.

Gong, Rosemary. *Good Luck Life.* New York: HarperResource, 2005.

NAM KARAN

Alternate Name: Sikh Naming Ceremony

Customs and Symbols: Amrit, Guru Granth Sahib, Kara, Karah Prashad, Kirpan

Though many religions have a naming ceremony, the Sikh nam karan ritual is unique in that the name is chosen *during* the ceremony, with the parents responding to what they believe to be a divine message from God. In addition, several other practices take place to reinforce the family's ties to the local Sikh community.

History and Significance

Sikhs believe that the universe operates according to the divine plan of a single all-powerful god who is known by various names, including Kartar and Sahib. This idea is reinforced in the nam karan ceremony by the way in which the child's name is immediately decided by a selection from Sikh scripture. By using this method Sikhs believe that Sahib has a direct hand in choosing the child's name and is, thus, immediately involved in the child's life.

Observance

Nam karan takes place once the mother and child are well enough to attend one of the regular worship services at the *gurdwara*—the Sikh temple. During the *ardas*, a communal prayer, the child's parents are mentioned, and it is noted that they seek a letter for naming their child. The *granthi*, the person who leads the service, then randomly opens the Guru Granth Sahib, the collection of hymns that serve as Sikh scripture. The hymn that appears at the top of the left-hand page in the book is considered a divine answer to the parents' request, and the first letter in that hymn is announced to the worshipers. In response, the parents choose a name for their infant that begins with that same letter, and it is immediately announced by the granthi. In addition to the first name that is chosen by the parents, the child also receives a second name: Singh (which means lion) if it is a boy and Kaur (which means princess) if it is a girl. In the course of the ceremony, the baby may be given *amrit*, a type of sugar water that is considered sacred, and the entire congregation shares *karah prashad*, a pudding that is served as a communal food at the gurdwara. The infant may also be presented with a *kara*—a metal bracelet that is a symbol of the Sikh faith.

Customs and Symbols

Amrit

At some naming ceremonies, the child is given amrit (pronounced *am-reet*). This is a mixture of sugar and water that is prepared in a special ritual: a double-edged *kirpan* (sword) is used to mix the liquid, which is stirred in an iron bowl as recitations are made from the Guru Granth Sahib. Amrit is also part of the initiation ceremony when a person formally enters the *khalsa* or community of Sikhs. This formal initiation only takes place after a person is old enough to understand the nature of their religious commitment.

Guru Granth Sahib

The Sikh religion is based upon the teachings of Guru Nanak, the founder of the faith, whose divine message is recorded in the Guru Granth Sahib (pronounced *goo-roo-granth-sa-heeb*)—a collection of poetic hymns that's also known as the Adi Granth. The importance of this book is clearly evident at the gurdwara: it is kept on a special bed with a canopy over the top and serves as the focal point for all worship services. This book of scripture provides the letter that the parents use to name their child. A similar event takes place at all Sikh services—even when there is no naming ceremony. Before the congregation leaves, the Guru Granth Sahib is opened at random and a brief verse is read aloud. As with the naming ceremony, this passage is considered a divine message in which God directly addresses the worshipers.

Kara

Some parents follow the practice of giving the child its first kara (pronounced *ka-dha*) at the naming ceremony. This is a steel or iron bracelet that is worn as a sign of the Sikh faith. It will be replaced by larger bracelets as the child grows.

Karah Prashad

This ceremonial food is served at all Sikh services. It is a mix of flour, sugar, and ghee (clarified butter) that is cooked into a sweet pudding. Karah prashad is said to have been the food that early Sikh gurus fed to those who came to visit. When the nam karan ceremony is part of the service, the family of the child being named sometimes prepares the karah prashad. In other cases, they may make a small donation to the church to offset the cost of the preparing the dish.

Kirpan

A powerful symbol of the Sikh faith, the kirpan actually comes in two different forms. One is the large double-edged sword used to stir the amrit. The other is a

The Five Ks

The kara and the kirpan are two of the "five Ks" that distinguish the followers of Sikhism. The other three Ks are *kes* (uncut hair—which men wear knotted in a turban), *kangha* (a comb used to keep the hair clean), and *kachha* (a form of undergarment, which is similar to knee-length shorts). These symbols were adopted around 1700, when the Sikhs were being persecuted by the Mughal rulers of India. The turmoil of that era is reflected in the fact that the kara, kirpan, and kachha are all associated with warfare and show that the Sikhs were determined to fight for their religion and way of life.

smaller, curved dagger that is worn by all members of the faith. If amrit is given to the baby during the nam karan ceremony, this smaller style of kirpan is used to dribble a few drops into the child's mouth. Sikhs are expected to keep their kirpan with them at all times, which has recently created problems for some Sikh school children in North America. Certain schools that have strict bans on weapons have tried to force Sikh students to give up their kirpans. The students have protested, declaring that their swords are sacred religious icons and are not used as weapons.

Further Reading

Cole, W. Owen, and Piara Singh Sambhi. *The Sikhs: Their Religious Beliefs and Practices.* London: Routledge & Kegan Paul, 1978.

Dineen, Jacqueline. *Births.* Austin, TX: Raintree Steck-Vaughn, 2001.

Mann, Gurinder Singh, Paul David Numrich, and Raymond B. Williams. *Buddhists, Hindus, and Sikhs in America.* New York: Oxford University Press, 2001.

Photo on facing page: A baby's baptism is attended by the priest, the parents, the godparents, and the baby.

Chapter 4: Entering the Faith

INTRODUCTION

Most religions have some type of rite that is used to incorporate a new member into its community of believers, but these observances vary according to the time that they are performed. Many faiths subscribe to the idea that a person cannot become a full-fledged member of the religion until he or she attains a certain level of maturity and understands the nature of their spiritual commitment.

Judaism and certain Christian denominations have different convictions, however. For them, it is essential to perform a ceremony soon after the child is born—**Baptism** for Christian children, **Bris Milah** for Jewish males—so that the relationship between the baby and his or her god is made clear from the outset. For Christians and Jews who accept these principles, the initiation rite is seen as one of the most important events in life, and the gravity of the occasion is indicated by the elaborate procedures that surround it. A second ceremony is observed by some Jews for the first boy born to the family, though it is seen as less essential and is performed far less frequently than bris milah. Known as **Pidyon Ha-Ben**, it involves the symbolic redemption of the infant to formally excuse it from the priestly duties assigned to the eldest male child in the Jewish scriptures.

BAPTISM

Alternate Name: Christening

Customs and Symbols: Baptismal Font, Baptismal Garment, Baptismal Water, Ceremonial Candles, Chrism, Godparents, Pre-Baptismal Instruction, Silver Gifts

An essential rite for most Christian denominations, baptism is the symbolic washing away of sin with water. It simultaneously purifies the individual and signifies that they have been accepted into the Christian faith. For those denominations that baptize newborns, the ceremony usually takes place a few weeks after birth and includes the formal announcement of the child's name and the designation of godparents who are responsible for guiding the child's religious education. According to Roman Catholic Church doctrine, the infant emerges from the ritual redeemed of any sin he or she was born with and linked to the Christian community.

History and Significance

The idea of using water as a means of ritual purification predates the founding of the Christian religion. The people of Persia and Babylonia observed such rites, particularly as a means of honoring the birth of a child. The Torah—the Jewish scriptures—also refer to ceremonial cleansing, and Jews practiced a baptismal ceremony for converts (those who were not born Jewish but later adopted the faith) in the centuries just prior to the time when Jesus is said to have lived.

The biblical account of John the Baptist plays a central role in the Christian adoption of the practice. Living at the time of Jesus, John became well known in the region of Judea for convincing people to repent of their sins and to be ritually immersed in a river. According to accounts in the Bible, Jesus himself underwent John's baptism. It is written in the Gospel According to Luke that, immediately after Jesus was immersed, "the Holy Spirit descended upon him," and he began his ministry. Once adopted as a rite by the early Christians, baptism was viewed as a way for believers to receive the Holy Spirit, just as Jesus had. Early Christian leaders also took their cue from Christ's instructions to his disciples, as written in the Gospel According to Matthew: "Go, therefore, and make disciples of all nations, baptizing them in the name of the Father, and of the Son, and of the Holy Spirit."

A variety of practices developed around the baptism ritual in the early centuries of the Christian church. The rite was usually performed in a stream or river, as immersion in running water (known as "living water") was seen as the best way to cleanse a person of their sins. Some form of religious instruction always took place before the baptism. In the years when the apostles were first spreading the word of the Christian gospel, the instruction was probably rather simple, but they grew increasingly complex as time went by. By the 200s C.E., the catechumens—those hoping to be inducted into the church—spent as long as three years in study and underwent a thorough investigation and questioning. If a person passed these trials, he or she would finally be baptized by having their entire body dunked into the water three times, which symbolized the Father, the Son, and the Holy Spirit and also the three days Jesus spent in the tomb before being resurrected.

In the following centuries, the strict requirements about preparing for the ritual were eased, and people were accepted into the faith upon request. This caused baptism to lose some of the grave quality that it previously had, but it remained an essential part of the religion. Even when the Christian world was rocked by the Reformation, most of the new denominations that split off from the Roman Catholic Church retained the ritual, though some, such as the Religious Society of Friends (the Quakers), did not. Some of the newer churches did alter the ceremony, however, by delaying the ritual until a person is old enough to make their own conscious choice to accept Christ.

> Baptism is the symbolic washing away of sin with water. It simultaneously purifies the individual and signifies that they have been accepted into the Christian faith.

The idea that a newborn child needs to be redeemed comes from the Christian doctrine of original sin. This is the idea that Adam and Eve's misdeed in the Garden of Eden (eating from the tree of the knowledge of good and evil) caused all humans to inherit their sin and to be born in an unholy state. This idea is accepted by a number of denominations, including the Roman Catholic Church, but rejected by others. Those denominations that believe in the concept of original sin consider baptism absolutely necessary for eternal salvation and prefer to complete the ritual as soon as possible so that the child's soul is not at risk for an extended period.

Observance

Many churches require parents to attend pre-baptism instruction, which includes one or more meetings where church officials discuss parents' responsibility for raising the child in the Christian faith. This is to insure that those taking part in the rite seriously intend to make religion an important part of the child's life.

The exact events and order of the baptism varies among different churches and denominations, though there are some general characteristics that apply to most Christian faiths. Baptisms can take place as part of a regular church service or in a separate ceremony. Many members of the clergy prefer to perform the baptism before the full congregation because this is more in keeping with the idea that the initiate is being inducted into a religious community. The ceremony for newborns often begins with the priest or pastor asking the parents to declare their intention to baptize the child. The clergyperson then asks the parents if they are willing to fulfill their responsibility of raising the child in the Christian religion. A similar question is put to the godparents, inquiring if they are willing to support this process. In Roman Catholic churches, the priest then marks the sign of the cross on the child's forehead, stating "I claim you for Christ by the sign of the cross." In some churches the declarations by the parents and godparents take place at the beginning of the service and are performed near the entrance to the church. This

Christian Dedication Ceremonies

Not all Christian churches accept newborns as full members of their faith. These congregations believe that acceptance of the religion and its commitments must be a conscious, individual choice. Because the infant is incapable of making that decision, their acceptance must be delayed until a later date. However, many of these churches do recognize the value of having some type of ceremony to mark the birth of a child and the parents' desire to raise the child as a Christian.

Among the churches that follow this approach are the many different Baptist denominations. Their ceremony for newborns (or any child who hasn't matured enough to formally express his or her acceptance of the faith) is known as the dedication of children. Typically, it takes place as part of a regular Sunday church service and involves fewer ritual actions than most baptisms. The pastor may ask the family, including extended family members, to stand. Prayers are usually offered to thank God for the gift of the child. The parents publicly state their willingness to love and care for the child and to teach the child Christian principles. In return, the pastor and congregation declare that they will support the parents in these efforts. In some cases a Bible is given to the family for the child's later use.

symbolizes that these basic requirements must be met before the child is brought completely into the place of worship.

The actual baptism usually takes place at the church's baptismal font. The priest or pastor usually states the baby's name and then makes a statement similar to the one used in the Roman Catholic Church: "I baptize thee in the name of the Father and of the Son and of the Holy Spirit." As this is spoken, the child is washed three times with baptismal water, either by immersion (having his or her entire body submerged in the font) or by infusion (pouring water over the child's head). Next, the infant may be anointed with chrism, and a white baptismal garment may be placed on the child, which signifies his or her new status. The godfather is usually the person who takes care of the ceremonial candles, lighting the baptismal candle from the flame of the church's paschal candle. This act symbolizes the passing of the divine light of Christ to the new member of the Christian fellowship and concludes the formal ceremony of baptism. After the church service, some parents host a celebratory gathering for friends and family.

While most people associate baptisms with babies, some Christian churches will not baptize a person until they have attained enough maturity to fully confess their faith—a practice known as "believers' baptism." Among the denominations holding this position are the Baptists, Jehovah's Witnesses, Mennonites, Pentecostals, and the Church of Jesus Christ of Latter-Day Saints (the Mormons). In place of baptism, some of these churches hold Christian dedication ceremonies for newborns. The issue of original sin sometimes figures into the question of when baptism can take place. Roman Catholic, Orthodox, and other churches that uphold the idea of original sin seek to cleanse that sin as soon as possible, so they are eager to baptize infants. The churches that delay baptism generally don't believe in original sin. While many churches are flexible when it comes to the method of baptism (allowing either immersion or infusion), others are not. Many of those same faiths that reject infant baptism also reject infusion. A person who wishes to be baptized in these faiths must be fully immersed in the baptismal water.

Customs and Symbols

Baptismal Font

Though the original Christian baptisms took place in rivers, streams, and other natural bodies of water, this became less practical as time went by. Instead, churches began to use indoor receptacles of water. In the early centuries of the church, most of the people being inducted into the faith were adults, so most indoor pools were large enough to fully immerse a full-grown man or woman. After

Christianity was accepted by the leaders of the Roman Empire, there was a trend toward constructing small baptismal fonts. Large pools were difficult to build and supply with water. Also, as the religion became almost universal in Europe, most of the people being baptized were infants, so adult-sized pools were seen as less necessary. The growing practice of baptism by infusion (pouring water onto the head) also made the smaller fonts preferable. In time, churches with pools large enough to submerge an adult became rare.

This trend away from total immersion wasn't welcomed by all Christians, however. Those who examined the Bible and documents from the early history of the church noted that the original practice was to dunk the entire body into the water. Because many Christians wished to follow the example of Christ as closely as possible, they expressed a desire to conduct baptisms in this way. A growing number of people have supported this movement over the years and returned to the practice of total immersion. The construction of larger indoor fonts has become more common, and some churches even conduct the ritual in a stream or other natural body of water. This "back-to-basics" approach is especially popular among evangelical groups, but it has also been felt among the longer established denominations. Many Roman Catholic churches now contain baptismal fonts that will accommodate immersion ceremonies. Some churches have a two-level font, which includes a smaller pool where infants can be dunked into the water and a larger area for adults.

Baptismal Garment

In the early church, newly baptized members of the faith would don white robes to signify their new status and purity. This practice continues, at least in a symbolic sense. Some type of white garment is placed on the newly baptized person right after they are washed with baptismal water. In some cases, a white veil is briefly placed on the person. In other cases, there may be a full garment, such as a gown for an infant or a robe for an adult. The use of this clothing underscores the transformation that takes place in the ceremony. The person has been cleansed of sin, and the white outfit symbolizes their purity.

Baptismal Water

Though water figures in all baptisms, not all baptismal water is the same. Sometimes, regular water is used, but certain denominations prefer the use of holy water. This is particularly true of the Roman Catholic Church and other denominations that favor forms of worship that are highly symbolic and ceremonial. Water becomes holy by being consecrated (made sacred) by a member of the clergy, who asks God to impart the Holy Spirit into the water. There are actually several different kinds of holy water that are used for different purposes. Baptismal water receives a thorough blessing on Holy Saturday—the day prior to Easter Sunday. In addition to a small amount of salt, which acts as a preservative, it contains small amounts of chrism and oil of catechumens (blessed oil that was originally used to purify those awaiting initiation and is also used in the ordination of priests).

Ceremonial Candles

Light is a common symbol in Christianity, standing for the resurrection of Christ and the divine illumination of the Holy Spirit that Christians claim to receive from their faith in Jesus. (Many other religions use light in a similar manner.) Light's importance is signified at the baptism by the use of two candles. The first is the paschal candle, which is found in many churches and is symbolic of Christ's resurrection. It plays a prominent role during the Easter season, when it is kept lit any time the church is in use, and it is also lit for baptisms. Typically, the paschal candle would be burning beside the baptismal font at the point when the family and godparents join the priest or pastor there. The second candle—known as the baptismal candle—comes into play after the child has been immersed in or infused with the holy water. Someone (often the godfather) lights the baptismal candle from the lit paschal candle. This action is sometimes accompanied by a recitation from the priest or pastor, which helps explain the candle's significance. For instance: "This action is to show that you have passed from darkness to light. Shine as a light in the world to the glory of God the Father."

Chrism

The oil that is applied immediately after baptism, chrism is a mixture of olive oil and balsam, which gives it a sweet smell. More importantly, chrism is considered sacred because a member of the clergy has blessed it. The chrism used in Catholic ceremonies is blessed by a bishop rather than a lower rank of church official, and this must occur on Holy Thursday (the Thursday preceding Easter Sunday). It is also used in the confirmation rite (*see* **Religious Milestones**). Chrism serves believers as a symbol of the strength, richness, and sweetness that Christians find in their faith. Applied after the sins have been cleansed, it indicates that the person being baptized has absorbed these positive qualities. Oil of chrism is also used in the chrismation ceremony observed in the Eastern Orthodox Church, which is considered a separate rite that follows baptism.

Godparents

Usually there are at least two godparents—a man and woman—but it is possible to have more. They are intended to support the birth parents in nurturing the

The Eastern Orthodox Church: Many Rituals at the Same Time

Christians in the Eastern Orthodox Church observe two additional rituals at the time of baptism: chrismation and the Eucharist. Chrismation is similar to **Confirmation,** which is practiced by Roman Catholics and several other denominations later in childhood (usually after the child has turned 10; see **Religious Milestones**). Both chrismation and confirmation are said to impart the Holy Spirit into the child, and Orthodox Christians believe that this should take place as soon as the infant is baptized. To accomplish this, the priest lays his hands upon the baptized infant and anoints him or her with chrism.

The Eucharist, or communion, is the ceremonial sharing of bread and wine by the members of the congregation. Again, many Christian denominations don't allow children to participate in this rite until later in childhood (see **First Communion and Reconciliation**). The Eastern Orthodox Church, however, insists that baptized infants should receive communion. This is accomplished by putting the host (consecrated bread) into a chalice with the consecrated wine. A small bit of the wine is then given to the baby with a spoon. This same procedure can be used to give the wine to adults as well.

child's spiritual development. The godparents tradition is rooted in the early history of Christianity. At that time, most people joining the faith were adults. Nonetheless, church leaders realized that the new converts would benefit from having a spiritual "parent"—someone more experienced in Christian belief—to help guide their worship. This role was retained for the newborns who were inducted into the faith, but because the infants had real parents, the godparents assumed more of a support role. Some godparents are more honorary than active, but religious leaders usually discourage this type of arrangement. They stress the importance of having godparents who will encourage the child's faith. Some churches therefore require or strongly encourage the parents to choose godparents that are active worshipers in the same denomination in which the child will be baptized.

Pre-Baptismal Instruction

By requiring the parents of the newborn to attend a class on baptism, churches hope to convince them that entering a child into the Christian faith is not a casual matter. Most of these programs stress the fact that baptism is just the beginning of a lifelong process and that parents must make an ongoing effort to teach their children Christian concepts and values. Some churches also require the godparents to undergo instruction so that they can better assist in this process.

Silver Gifts

It is traditional to give the child gifts made of silver following a baptism. They are believed to bring good luck to the child. Often, these items are given to the parents at a celebratory gathering that follows the baptism ceremony.

Web Sites

"Baptism Preparation." St. Francis of Assisi Catholic Church, Ann Arbor, MI, undated.
   http://stfrancisa2.com/baptism.htm

"Holy Water." East Lewis County Catholic Community, WA, undated.
   http://landru.i-link-2.net/shnyves/holy_water2.htm

"The Sacrament of Baptism: Celebrating the Embrace of God" by Sandra DeGidio.
   Catholic Update (St. Anthony Messenger Press), undated.
   http://www.americancatholic.org/Newsletters/CU/ac0389.asp

Further Reading

Chidester, David. *Christianity: A Global History.* New York: HarperSanFrancisco, 2000.

BRIS MILAH

Alternate Names: Berit Milah, Berito shel Avraham Avinu, Brit Milah

Customs and Symbols: Candles, Chair of Elijah, Cup of Wine, Izmel, Kvaterim, Minyan, Mohel, Sandek, Seudat Mitzvah

Bris milah (pronounced *briss mee-lah*), the Jewish ritual of male circumcision, is commanded by the teachings of the Torah—the Jewish scriptures—and is considered one of the most important ceremonies of the Jewish faith. At the specific direction of the child's father, the foreskin of the infant's penis is severed. Accompanying this brief surgical procedure is a range of actions that symbolize that the boy has been pledged to the Jewish faith. In addition, his name is publicly revealed for the first time. Thus, the ceremony is designed to provide the child with both a personal and a religious identity as he begins his life's journey.

History and Significance

The essential nature of bris milah (known as *brit milah* among Sephardic Jews) is clearly stated in the Torah. The Lord speaks to Abraham, the first patriarch of the Jewish people, telling him, "This is my covenant, which you shall keep, between me and you and your descendants after you; Every male among you shall be circumcised." The Lord also tells Abraham that the circumcision will take place when each child is eight days old, and he warns that "any uncircumcised male . . . shall be cut off from his people; he has broken my covenant." (The written portions of the Torah also make up the Old Testament of the Christian Bible, with these passages being found in the Book of Genesis.) The concept of a covenant—an agreement—is central to the ritual. In fact, the term bris milah literally means "the covenant of circumcision." It signifies the compact between the Jewish people and their god—that they agree to worship no other deity and that the Lord, in return, promises that they will become a blessed people and a great nation.

The Jewish circumcision ritual was known to be widespread in the state of Judea (part of present-day Israel) in 500 B.C.E. and was likely a common practice even earlier. The ceremonial aspects of bris milah largely come from kabbalah, the mystical side of Judaism, which strives to gain some direct knowledge of God's essence. These actions in some ways resemble an animal sacrifice, which was a common practice in ancient Judaic worship. This links the bris to other post-birth ceremonies that involve a blood sacrifice, the best example being the Muslim rite of

Aqiqah. Like aqiqah, bris milah has sometimes been viewed as a means to protect the child from evil forces. Such views are less common today, but the act is still considered sacred and essential by most devout Jews.

Observance

In keeping with the commandment in the Torah, the bris milah ceremony (often simply called "the bris") is carried out on the eighth day of the child's life. The only exception to this rule is when the infant is suffering from a medical condition that makes it dangerous for him to undergo the procedure. The location of the rite varies according to custom and personal preference, with some parents opting for a synagogue and others using their own home or another private residence. According to tradition, a *minyan* (a group of ten) must be present to witness the ceremony.

Aside from the child being circumcised, the figure at the center of the ritual is the *mohel* (pronounced *moyl*)—the person who performs the surgical procedure. He or she (more often a he) begins the ceremony by calling out to the *kvaterim*—the man and woman who have agreed to assist in the religious upbringing of the child. The *kvater*—the male figure—is usually the person who brings the child into the room. At that point the attendees rise and say, "Barukh ha-ba," which translates as "Welcome! Blessed is he who comes." This is partly directed at the child but also to the arrival of Elijah the Prophet, who is said to be spiritually present at all circumcisions. The symbol of his presence is the chair of Elijah, which is placed in the room where the circumcision takes place. The infant is placed in this seat momentarily and then taken to the *sandek,* the person who is designated to hold the baby during the procedure. The sandek is often seated in a second chair near the chair of Elijah.

If the father is not performing the circumcision himself (which is now quite rare), he formally gives the mohel permission to act as his agent. The father then positions himself to the right side of the mohel as the ceremony continues. The mohel uses an *izmel* (a double-edged scalpel) to sever the foreskin and performs the *periah*—the tearing of the underlying membrane. Blood is then suctioned from the head of the penis, often by using a glass tube. All of these actions by the mohel take place quickly, usually in less than a minute.

The Jewish ritual of male circumcision is commanded by the teachings of the Torah—the Jewish scriptures—and is considered one of the most important ceremonies of the Jewish faith.

A series of blessings are recited during the ceremony, though the exact timing can vary according to custom. The mohel says, "Blessed are You, O Lord our God, king of the universe who has sanctified us with Your commandments and commanded us concerning circumcision." The father then recites, "Blessed are You, who has sanctified us by Your commandments and commanded us to enter him into the covenant of Abraham our father." The entire audience then responds, "Just as he entered into the covenant, so may he be introduced to the study of the Torah, to the nuptial canopy, and to good deeds." The severed foreskin is placed in a receptacle and covered with dirt.

Other Rites for the Newborn

Two other Jewish traditions sometimes take place in the first week of the baby's life, though these were more commonly observed in the past than they are today, especially in United States. *Shalom zachar* (meaning welcome or peace to the male child) is a gathering that takes place on the first Friday night following the child's birth, where friends and family read from the Torah and sing songs. A meal is served that includes lentils and chickpeas—foods eaten by those in mourning. This is done to express sadness for the fact that the infant has entered the world of human imperfection after his blissful time in the womb.

"Watch night" takes place on the night before bris milah. Relatives and friends visit the home and engage in a variety of activities, including dancing, singing, and reading aloud from the Zohar (an ancient text used by those who study kabbalah). These continue all night and are based on the idea that the infant needs to be watched over because he is most vulnerable to evil forces in the final hours before circumcision takes place. Various items are used to safeguard the baby. Garlic and red ribbons are sometimes attached to the crib because both are thought to ward off evil. Sweets are placed on the floor in hopes that they will distract demons away from the child, and the izmel is sometimes placed beneath the child's pillow. Also, the chair of Elijah that will be used in the bris may be brought to the parents' home in hopes that the prophet's presence will likewise insure the child's safety.

The mohel then recites a lengthy blessing over a cup of wine. It includes the phrase "in your blood shall you live," at which point a finger or a piece of gauze is dipped into the wine and placed in the infant's mouth. Sometimes the wine is also offered to others, including the sandek and the child's mother. The infant receives his name during this later part of the ceremony. The mohel performs this act by stating, "Our God and God of our fathers, preserve this child to his father and to his mother, and let his name be called in Israel [child's name], son of [father's name]." Several traditional prayers usually conclude the bris, including one directed to the child: "May God bless you and keep you. May God smile upon you and be gracious to you. May God look well upon you and grant you *shalom* [peace or wholeness]." When the ceremony concludes, the parents of the newborn often host a festive meal—the *seudat mitzvah*—for their friends and family who attended the circumcision.

Not all circumcision rituals follow this exact formula. Since the late 20th century, some Jews have opted to have the bris in a hospital or doctor's office rather than a home or synagogue. This development came about partly because so many non-Jews now have their sons circumcised that it has become a common medical procedure. In this setting, a physician rather than a mohel performs the operation. A Jewish doctor is preferred, but exceptions are sometimes made for non-Jews to perform the surgery. A rabbi takes part to carry out the religious aspects of the ritual. There is some disagreement among Jews as to whether this practice is appropriate. More conservative members of the faith tend to favor the traditional ceremony with a mohel. In another variation, some parents have their child circumcised by a physician shortly after birth with no religious ritual at all, then participate in the *hatafat dam brit* ceremony on the eighth day. This involves the drawing of blood from the penis by a small pinprick.

Customs and Symbols

Candles

Candles are lit in the room where the bris milah ceremony takes place, and they are sometimes held by those in attendance. This custom derives from a description of the birth of Moses, when the house was said to be filled with light.

Chair of Elijah

The prophet Elijah was said to have won God's favor for protesting against those who had given up the covenant of circumcision. In a midrash (an interpretation of scripture) from the eighth century C.E., it is said that God promised Elijah that he would be present at every circumcision. The symbolic means of accomplishing this is the setting aside of the chair of Elijah at each bris. In some cases, a synagogue or Jewish community has a special, elaborately carved chair that is used. Elsewhere, a regular chair is designated the chair of Elijah for a particular ceremony. Often, the seat is draped with a special piece of embroidered cloth and decorated with flowers and plants. The use of the chair during the ceremony varies. Sometimes it is used as a seat for the sandek, but in other cases it remains empty except when the infant is briefly placed in it. This creates a symbolic link to the figure who steadfastly upheld the covenant and suggests that this new addition to the Jewish community will likewise uphold the faith. Also, Elijah is recognized as a protector of the helpless, so placing the child in the chair is a way of asking Elijah to watch over him. Elijah's presence is said to benefit others at the ceremony as well. It's believed that God will forgive the sins of anyone who stands close to the chair, so most attendees pause briefly beside it before or after the ceremony.

Cup of Wine

The blessings recited at the bris are said over a ceremonial cup of wine. This same practice is part of other Jewish rituals, including the weekly observance of *Shabbat*—the day of rest and spiritual enrichment. For bris milah, the wine is usually poured into a *kiddush* cup (kiddush refers to the blessing that is said over the wine), the same type of vessel that's used on Shabbat. These are often beautifully decorated goblets made from silver or other precious metals. The blessing isn't considered complete until some of the wine is consumed. A drop or two is given to the child and then several adults may also drink from the cup, including the sandek and child's mother. The wine is usually of the sweet kosher variety that is served at most Jewish rituals. In cases where the family prefers to eliminate alcohol from the proceedings, sweet grape juice is substituted.

Izmel

The primary tool of the mohel is the izmel, a double-edged scalpel. The requirement that the cutting implement have two edges is thought to be more practical than symbolic. If foreskin proves difficult to sever and blunts one edge of the scalpel, the mohel can quickly turn the knife over and complete the operation with the other sharpened edge.

Kvaterim

Today it is common to name two kvaterim—similar to godparents in the Christian faith. One is male (the kvater) and one female (the kvaterin). In most ceremonies, the kvaterin takes the child from the mother and transfers him to the kvater, who brings him into the room where the circumcision takes place. But the real responsibility of the kvaterim extends beyond the brief ceremony. By accepting these roles, the man and woman are volunteering themselves as the child's moral protectors. Should both parents be killed or are otherwise unable to fulfill their duties, the kvaterim are responsible for the child's religious education and for his general well-being. For this reason, the kvaterim are often husband and wife; since they are already married, it is assumed that they would be better able to provide a stable home life. The kvaterim are also expected to lend support to the child in other situations, offering guidance and assisting with his education.

Minyan

A minyan is a group of 10 Jewish adults. A group of this size is required for many of the communal prayer gatherings in Jewish worship. The fact that a minyan is required to be present at the bris underscores the sacred nature of the occasion. It also indicates that the ritual is intended to be a public acknowledgement of the child's entrance into the Jewish faith. Traditionally, it took 10 men to form a minyan—women were not considered as counting toward the total. Today, most Conservative and Reform congregations have done away with this gender bias, but Orthodox Jews still observe all-male minyans.

Mohel

Bris milah is said to have originated with Abraham, who circumcised his son Isaac himself. Following this example, Jewish law makes the child's father responsible for the procedure, but few fathers feel comfortable performing the delicate surgery themselves. Thus, the father formally asks a mohel—a specialist in ritual circumcision—to carry out the procedure.

Often the mohel is a rabbi or a cantor (one who sings and leads prayers in the synagogue) who has undergone extensive hospital training. The profession is frequently handed from father to son, so many mohels hail from families that have specialized in the practice for many generations.

Sandek

The person designated to hold the infant during the circumcision, the sandek is generally an elderly figure whom the parents respect and wish to honor. The position is most often filled by the child's paternal grandfather, but the grandfather on the mother's side is also a likely candidate. If the parents have more than one son, they usually select a different person to serve as sandek for each child. Though the position seems primarily honorary, it is considered essential. Jewish law specifies that a sandek, the child's father, and—when necessary—the mohel are required to be present at the ceremony, while the other key figures (the kvaterim, the minyan, etc.) can be omitted if necessary. In more traditional ceremonies, the sandek holds the child on his knees while seated. In other cases, the child may be placed on a pillow atop a table and steadied by the sandek.

Seudat Mitzvah

The tradition of hosting a seudat mitzvah (festive meal) following the ceremony comes from a passage in the Torah that states that "Abraham made a great feast on the day that Isaac was weaned." Jewish scholars have interpreted this as meaning that a feast was held following Isaac's circumcision, though the passage does not state that directly. There are few specific guidelines as to what is to be served at this meal. Because circumcisions are traditionally observed early in the day, the food served afterward can be similar to that at a midday meal and might include lox (smoked salmon), salads, and other items. In addition to food, beverages—alcoholic and otherwise—are usually made available so that toasts can be made in honor of the child.

Further Reading

Chill, Abraham. *The Minhagim: The Customs and Ceremonies of Judaism, Their Origins and Rationale.* New York: Sepher-Hermon Press, 1979.

Goldberg, Harvey E. *Jewish Passages: Cycles of Jewish Life.* Berkeley: University of California Press, 2003.

Gollaher, David L. *Circumcision: A History of the World's Most Controversial Surgery.* New York: Basic Books, 2000.

PIDYON HA-BEN

Alternate Name: Pidyon Bekhor

Customs and Symbols: Cup of Wine, Kohen, Ornate Plate, Seudat Mitzvah, Silver Coins

A rite inspired by ancient customs and commandments from the Jewish scriptures, pidyon ha-ben (pronounced *pid-yon ha-ben*) involves the ceremonial "purchase" of a mother's first son. This is based on the idea that the first born was rightfully the property of God and was initially intended to become a priest. To release the child from this duty, the father pays a small sum of money to a religious leader. Though it has fallen out of favor with some Jews, pidyon ha-ben provides others with a strong connection to the ancient roots of their faith.

History and Significance

God's claim on the first born is made clear in the Torah (in the Book of Exodus in the Christian Bible). Speaking to Moses, the Lord commands, "Consecrate to me all the first-born; whatever is the first to open the womb among the people of Israel, both of man and of beast, is mine." A later passage explains that this command means that the first born will become priests—God's servants. As the story of Exodus continues, however, it's shown that the first-born sons are poor priests. They are involved with false worship of the golden calf, which angers God. As a result, the Lord chooses the members of the tribe of Levi to be his priests in place of the first-born sons. Later, God tells Aaron, who is one of the Levites, that "the first-born of man you shall redeem." By "redeem" he means that the first born shall be removed from the sacred status they had been granted as priests. This is to be accomplished by paying a price of "five shekels in silver," and God tells Aaron that "at a month old you shall redeem them."

Pidyon ha-ben (which translates as "the redemption of the first born") is the ceremonial means of carrying out this commandment. As the passage dictates, it is only observed for the "the first to open the womb"—that is, a woman's first child. More specifically, it applies only when the first child is male. There are also several conditions in which even the first male child is not subject to the custom. A boy born by caesarean section would not need to be redeemed because he did not "open the womb" as he would in a natural birthing process. Also, if a woman has a miscarriage after three months of pregnancy, then becomes pregnant again and gives birth to a son, the son is not subject to the ceremony because he is not considered the first product of the woman's womb.

Observance

Though the Torah explains the need to perform pidyon ha-ben, it does not say exactly how it should be carried out. The procedure that's performed today was developed between the seventh and 11th centuries C.E. In keeping with the instructions in the Book of Numbers, the ceremony takes place one month after birth (the 31st day of the child's life), though it is permissible to delay the rite until a later date. There are two central participants in pidyon ha-ben: the child's father and a *kohen* (pronounced *ko-hane*), a person who is a direct descendant of Aaron and, thus, a member of the priestly line. The ceremony begins with the kohen sitting at a table that contains hallah—traditional Jewish egg bread. The father brings his son before the kohen, holding in his hand five silver coins. He states that the child is the first born and that he is to be redeemed. In some ceremonies the child is presented upon an ornate plate, rather than simply being carried by the father.

The kohen responds with the question: "Which do you prefer? To give me your first born or to redeem him for five silver coins?" The father answers that he wishes to redeem the child. He then recites two benedictions to God before giving the coins to the kohen. The kohen holds the coins over the child and says "this instead of that, this in commutation for that, this in remission for that." He then gives the priestly blessing to the child: "May the Lord bless you and keep you; may the Lord make His countenance to shine upon you and be generous unto you; May the Lord lift up His countenance upon you and give you peace." The ceremony concludes with a blessing over a cup of wine. A seudat mitzvah (festive meal) is usually part of the observance and is attended by the parents, the kohen, and close friends and family.

Bringing Equality to the Ritual: Pidyon Ha-bat

In recent decades, some dissent has arisen over the fact that first-born females are excluded from pidyon ha-ben. This has led to the introduction of a similar ceremony for girls known as *pidyon ha-bat*. These ceremonies often include recitations that are similar to the pidyon ha-ben ritual but instead of making a payment of coins to a kohen, a *tzedakah* (charitable contribution) is made in honor of the girl. Pidyon ha-bat remains controversial. Traditional-minded Jews are generally opposed to the practice, but some more liberal Jews have adopted it.

Customs and Symbols

Cup of Wine

As in many other Jewish rituals, pidyon ha-ben includes wine. It is often poured into a ceremonial *kiddush* cup, which is a metal goblet that usually has an ornate design. A brief blessing is said over the wine, praising God, "Creator of the fruit of the vine." As is customary, once the kohen has made the blessing, some of the wine must be consumed. In most Jewish ceremonies sweet kosher wine is used, though grape juice is an acceptable substitute if the family prefers to avoid alcohol.

Kohen

A kohen (also spelled "cohen") is a person who can trace his or her heritage back to Aaron, the brother of Moses, who became the first high priest of the Jewish people. Aaron was a member of the tribe of Levi and so are his descendants, which explains the role of the kohen in pidyon ha-ben. The Levites replaced the first born as the priests of the Israelites, and God commands that they will redeem the first born. Thus, the ceremonial payment of the coins is made to a representative of this group.

Beginning with Aaron, it was the kohanim (the plural form of kohen) who carried out the actual priestly duties for the Jewish people, which included the offering of sacrifices. The influence of the kohanim was greatly reduced after the destruction of the second Jewish temple in Jerusalem in the year 70 C.E. Today, priests play a limited role in Jewish worship. In addition to taking part in pidyon ha-ben ceremonies, they make blessings and are called on to perform readings from the Torah in prayer services. Because there are both male and female descendants of Aaron, there are women kohen (known as bat kohen) as well as men. Orthodox Jews don't allow bat kohen to take part in the observance of pidyon ha-ben, but Conservative communities generally do.

Ornate Plate

Some families observe pidyon ha-ben by bringing the child to the ceremony on a large, elaborately decorated plate or platter that may also include prized items such as jewelry and sweet dessert-type foods. The plate can be quite valuable by itself; many are fashioned from silver or brass and engraved with symbols and religious scenes. One possible explanation for this custom is offered by Abraham Chill in *The Minhagim*, who suggests that it may have originally been intended to make the child more attractive to the father so that he would be more likely to redeem his son.

Some families observe pidyon ha-ben by bringing the child to the ceremony on a large, elaborately decorated plate or platter that may also include prized items such as jewelry and sweet dessert-type foods.

Seudat Mitzvah

As with many other Jewish ceremonies, pidyon ha-ben ritual is often followed by a seudat mitzvah (festive meal). In fact, the meal can be part of the ceremony. Rather than having just a symbolic hallah on the table, the family could put out a full meal, with the redemption ceremony taking place once everyone is seated.

Silver Coins

According to the commandment recorded in the Book of Numbers, the price set by God for purchasing the redemption of the first born is five shekels in silver. Shekels aren't easily found in the United States. In the interests of simplicity and of preserving the symbolic nature of the five coins, most people now substitute silver coins of another sort. Silver dollars are common. In Israel, the government has minted special silver coins to be used in the ceremony. After the coins are given to the kohen, he or she may keep them, but it is common custom to donate them as *tzedakah* (a charitable contribution). In some cases, the kohen may return the silver to the family.

Web Site

"Pidyon ha-Bat/ha-Ben (Redemption of the Firstborn)" by Rabbi Rona Shapiro. Ritualwell.org, a project of Kolot: The Center for Jewish Women's and Gender Studies, Reconstructionist Rabbinical College, Wyncote, PA, undated.
http://www.ritualwell.org/lifecycles/babieschildren/pidyonhabenhabat/pidyon2.xml

Further Reading

Chill, Abraham. *The Minhagim: The Customs and Ceremonies of Judaism, Their Origins and Rationale.* New York: Sepher-Hermon Press, 1979.

Weber, Vicki L. *The Rhythm of Jewish Time: An Introduction to Holidays and Life-Cycle Events.* West Orange, NJ: Behrman House, 1999.

Photo on facing page: Losing a first tooth—and waiting for the Tooth Fairy—is an exciting moment.

BIRTH AND CHILDHOOD

Chapter 5: Firsts

INTRODUCTION

In the first years of life a child is exposed to a huge number of new experiences. While the simple "newness" of these sights and activities can be delightful for the youngster and his or her parents, there can also be a more profound aspect to certain events. They become a means of marking the development of the child, of witnessing the fact that he or she is moving rapidly from one life stage to another. Not surprisingly, these transitions are often marked by rituals that commemorate the event and help the family come to terms with the changes.

In this process, activities that can seem mundane in later life take on a completely different character when they are observed for the first time. This is especially true when it comes to cutting the child's hair. Though mainstream American society tends to think of hair in terms of style, many groups retain traditional beliefs that uphold its religious qualities. Often, this is seen in a negative sense, which is related to the idea that the birth process is spiritually unclean. It's thought that the child's hair might harbor impure elements from before birth, or even from previous lives, and that it must therefore be removed. Both the Muslim **Aqiqah** and Hindu **Chudakarma** ceremonies fulfill this function. The Jewish **Upsherin** rite is also a ceremonial haircut, but it is focused on marking the beginning of a boy's religious education rather than removing impurities from the past.

Plenty of other "firsts" have been ritualized as well. Some have a sacred nature. These include the Hindu **Annaprasana** ceremony that honors the baby's first meal of solid food, the **Pueblo Presentation Ceremonies** that commemorate the baby's first exposure to sunlight, and **First Communion and Reconciliation** that initiates Roman Catholic children into two church sacraments. Another group of observances is less religious in nature, but they still serve as important milestones in the child's early life. The **First Day of School**, whether preschool or kindergarten, not only marks the beginning of formal education but often represents the child's first prolonged separation from her or his parents. The **First Lost Tooth**, which occurs around age six, is another symbol of maturation and shows that the commemoration of new life stages can be fun as well as solemn.

AQIQAH

Alternate Names: Akîkah, Acîca, Aqiqa, the Slaughter of the Name-giving

Customs and Symbols: Animal Sacrifice, Cutting or Shaving the Hair, Naming

Practiced by some members of the Muslim faith to commemorate the birth of a child, aqiqah (pronounced *a-KHEE-kah*) involves the ritual of the first shaving or cutting of the infant's hair and the offering of an animal sacrifice—usually by killing a sheep, ram, or goat. In addition, the naming of the child often takes place at the same time. Most commonly performed seven days after birth, these rites welcome the child as a new member of the family and the Muslim community.

History and Significance

Though associated with Islam, the aqiqah ceremony was common in the Arabian Peninsula even before the Muslim faith was founded in the early 600s C.E. In the opinion of some anthropologists, the rite was derived from a belief that is found among many cultures: that the newborn child is under the power of supernatural forces. Until the child is freed from this state, he or she is in great danger. In order to save the infant, some form of sacrifice must be offered in exchange for his or her life. This idea is expressed in a quote attributed to the Prophet Muhammad, the founder of Islam, which states that the purpose of aqiqah is "to avert evil from the child by shedding blood on his behalf." Magical elements such as this don't receive as much attention today as they did in the past, especially in the United States. Instead, parents may describe aqiqah as a means of thanking Allah for providing them a child.

The other aspect of the aqiqah ceremony—the shaving or cutting of the child's hair—also has ancient roots. The practice results from the idea that the birth process is unclean, in both a real and a spiritual sense. This uncleanness requires that the child's hair be removed so that he or she will be purified. The hair shaving also serves as a symbol of the separation that took place at birth: the child has become independent of its mother (at least to some degree) and is beginning his or her own life. Therefore, the hair that grew while the child was still part of the mother's body is removed. On a more down-to-earth note, some believe that shaving the child's head promotes the growth of hair.

Though the practice of aqiqah has been widespread among Muslims, the exact status of the ritual has been debated for many centuries. Some accounts of

Muhammad's words and actions say that the Prophet observed the rite of aqiqah for his grandsons, Hasan and Husain. However, another account indicates that Muhammad voiced displeasure at the practice even as he allowed it to continue. Because of the different tone of these statements, Islamic authorities have come to differing conclusions about the aqiqah. A small number consider it to be *wajib*, meaning that all Muslims are required perform it for their children. A larger number of scholars define it as *sunnah*, meaning that it is a recommended practice but that it is not mandatory. These mixed attitudes are reflected in the number of people who now observe aqiqah. Some Muslims perform the ritual while others do not.

Observance

The ritual of aqiqah most commonly takes place when the child is seven days old, though it may be observed earlier or later, depending on the custom of the family. If the ceremony does not take place at the appointed time, most Muslim authorities find it acceptable to do it at a later date. A wide range of practices exists regarding the animal sacrifice. Some traditions call for the father to do the killing, but it is often left to others. In a modern twist on the custom, parents can now hire a service to take care of the sacrifice and the distribution of the meat. In such cases, their only contact with the animal may be to review photos of it. The timing of the offering is sometimes important. A prayer is often recited as the sacrifice takes place asking Allah to accept the offering. The animal is then butchered and its meat is divided according to certain guidelines. One of the most prevalent customs is the distribution of meat to the poorer members of the community.

> *Aqiqah involves the ritual of the first shaving or cutting of the infant's hair and the offering of an animal sacrifice, and often the naming of the child takes place at the same time.*

After the baby's hair is cut or shaved, the locks are collected and weighed, and the value of an equivalent or greater weight of silver or gold is donated to charity. The hair is then disposed of in a ritual manner such as burying it or casting it into the water. The naming of the child often takes place as part of the aqiqah ceremony. In fact, the ceremony is sometimes referred to as "the slaughter of the name-giving." In some regions, however, the naming is treated as a separate event that can take place on a different day—either earlier or later in the child's life. There are few precise customs involved in giving the child his or her name; the parents' main duty is to publicly reveal the newborn's name and to show that careful thought has gone into choosing it.

Customs and Symbols

Animal Sacrifice

The animal most frequently chosen for the offering is a member of the sheep family—either a ram (an adult male sheep), a ewe (an adult female sheep), or a lamb (a young sheep). Goats are also frequently offered. The popularity of these species likely comes from the fact that they are common herd animals in the Middle East, the region where the aqiqah ceremony first became widespread. A sheep is not required, however, and several pronouncements note that those who cannot afford a sheep can sacrifice another animal, such as a chicken. In some communities, there seems to be an effort to match the sex of the animal to the sex of the child—for instance, a ram is offered at a boy's aqiqah, a ewe at a girl's. Some Muslims believe in offering a more valuable sacrifice for boys than for girls. In such cases, two animals may be killed for a male child and one for a female.

In many cases, very specific instructions have been attached to how the animal should be treated after it is killed. For instance, some groups specify that the hair must not be burned off of the head of the animal; if it were, no hair would grow on the head of the child. Likewise, certain communities declare that specific bones of the animal should not be broken in the slaughtering process, because it might bring harm to the child. Again, the sense is that the animal and child are linked and that careless treatment of the animal could be transferred to the human.

Sharing the meat of the animal is a standard part of the aqiqah celebration. As mentioned earlier, a portion is almost always given to the disadvantaged. One common method is to devote one third of the meat to the poor and one third to friends, while the final third is kept and consumed by the family. It is also common to use some of the meat to prepare a feast for family and friends to mark the occasion. Selling of the meat, on the other hand, is forbidden because if the family were to gain money from the animal, its killing could no longer properly be considered a sacrifice—that is, something that the family gave up in honor of the newborn.

Cutting or Shaving the Hair

The traditional practice is to shave the head completely bare, but some parents choose to cut just a few locks of the child's hair. In one variation on the ritual, everyone attending the ceremony is allowed to snip off a small bit of the child's hair—a practice that is similar to that observed at Jewish **Upsherin** celebrations. As with the distribution of the meat from the sacrificed animal, the hair-cutting ritual is used as a means of helping others. This is done by weighing the hair and calculating how much an equal or greater weight of silver or gold would be worth. That amount of money is then donated as *zakat* (pronounced *ZACK-ah*)—a charitable contribution. Zakat is one of the five "pillars of Islam" required of all Muslims, and the aqiqah donation is meant to begin the child's lifelong commitment to the giving of charity. The shorn hair is collected in a cloth or some other kind of container, which is either buried in the ground or put into the water. This derives from the ancient idea that the hair could be used to place a harmful spell upon the child, so it must be disposed of carefully. Some Muslims follow a more elaborate process by having the container transported to the holy city of Mecca, where it is deposited in the sacred Zemzem Well.

Naming

Naming isn't always recognized as being a part of the aqiqah ceremony, but because many Muslims follow the practice of giving the child a name on the seventh day after birth—the same day that aqiqah traditionally takes place—the two customs have been joined together in many communities. The task of choosing a name is not taken lightly by most Muslims. Its importance is drawn from a hadith (one of the accounts of Muhammad's words and actions) in which the Prophet states, "On the Day of Resurrection, you will be called by your names and by your fathers' names, so give yourselves good names." Muslim names often have several parts, which convey who the person's father and grandfather are in addition to the first and family names. In choosing a name, the parents are really only choosing the first name—the others are already determined. The first name is often drawn from several that were said to be recommended by Muhammad (Abdallâh and Abd al-

---

The Same Names Are the Name of the Game

The Muslim naming conventions result in a large number of people who have the same first names, but originality is considered less important than providing the child with an honorable title. An Islamic hadith notes at every gathering of Muslim men, "there is present one whose name is Muhammad or Ahmad, but God blesseth all that assemble."

Rahmān are two of these). The name of the Prophet himself, or of his family and acquaintances, are also popular.

Web Sites

"What Is Aqiqah?" by Ahmad Kutty. Islamic Institute of Toronto, September 28, 2005.
    http://www.islam.ca/answers.php?id=833

"What Is the Islamic Ruling on Aqiqah?" by Ahmad Kutty. Islamic Institute of Toronto, March 8, 2001.
    http://www.islam.ca/answers.php?id=24

Further Reading

Morgenstern, Julian. *Rites of Birth, Marriage, Death and Kindred Occasions among the Semites.* Cincinnati, Ohio: Hebrew Union College Press, 1966.

PUEBLO PRESENTATION CEREMONIES

Alternate Names: Asnaya, Pueblo Naming Ceremony

Customs and Symbols: Caregiver, Ceremonial Food, Ceremonial Washing, Cornmeal, Darkened Home, Ears of Corn, Greeting the Sun, Naming

The Native American Pueblo societies of New Mexico and Arizona retain many rites and customs that are drawn from their traditional beliefs about humans, nature, and the farming practices that have sustained them for hundreds of years. Among these is the presentation ritual in which the newborn is first exposed to sunlight and—in certain pueblos—receives his or her name.

History and Significance

There are more than 20 different Pueblo groups in the American Southwest. They are different from one another in certain respects—speaking several distinct native languages, for instance, and following somewhat different customs. But all have traditionally relied on agriculture for survival, and their focus on corn, their staple crop, is reflected in the presentation ceremony that occurs shortly after a child is born. In a sense, the ritual treats the baby as if he or she is similar to a corn plant. The child is kept in a dimly lit house for a precise number of days, which suggests the time that the corn germinates and grows underground. The baby is then brought out into the sunlight, which symbolizes the plant's emergence above the soil. The ritual also reenacts the creation myth that is common to the Pueblo groups. These stories tell how the people lived in several darkened underworlds before emerging to the present world, which is lit by sunlight.

Observance

As with many other distinctive customs, the Pueblo presentation ceremonies are not as widely observed as they were in the past. But the observances continue among certain members of the Pueblo population who have maintained their cultural heritage, particularly those living in the more tradition-bound Hopi communities. The individual pueblos carry out the ceremony in slightly different ways, though the main elements are similar.

Following birth, the child is kept in a darkened home, with the sunlight screened by blankets placed over the doors and windows. The child remains in this dim environment for a certain number of days (for instance, four days for the people of the Acoma Pueblo, eight days for the Zuni, and 20 days for the Hopi). The mother also may be confined to the home, though this tends to be more true for a first-time mom than for a woman who had already given birth.

A caregiver—usually one or more members of the father's family—is appointed to attend to the mother and child. This person carries out the ceremonial washing of the baby, which may take place soon after the birth (as among the Hopi) or after the seclusion ends (as among the Tewa).

Corn is used in various ways during and after the confinement, depending on the group. The Hopi use cornmeal to mark four sacred lines on the walls of the home. Every five days a line is wiped off so that the final line is removed on the 20th day, when the ceremony concludes. In addition, the Hopi and other Pueblo groups use specially selected ears of corn, placing them alongside the baby's crib and also holding them near the baby during the later sun-greeting ceremony. That act of greeting the sun takes place in the early-morning hours of the day when the confinement ends.

If naming is part of the ceremony, it is usually done on this same day, either as the sun breaks the horizon or just prior. After the child has been presented, a breakfast feast takes place, which draws together the child's extended family.

The Native American Pueblo societies have traditionally relied on agriculture for survival, and their focus on corn, their staple crop, is reflected in the presentation ceremony that occurs shortly after a child is born. In a sense, the ritual treats the baby as if he or she is similar to a corn plant.

Customs and Symbols

Caregiver

In many cases the person or persons who look after the mother and child following birth are members of the father's family. The father's mother (the baby's grandmother) is the most common person to fill this role, though the father's sisters may also be involved. Their duties are to insure that the light is subdued in the home, to bathe the mother and child as needed, and to prepare food and drink for the mother.

Ceremonial Food

Some Pueblos observe certain requirements regarding food during the time of confinement. The traditional Hopi practices call for the mother to eat no meat or salt during the 20 days following birth and instead to consume only cornmeal mush and tea made from the juniper bush. Once the child has been presented to the sun, it is common for a breakfast feast to be held, which is usually prepared by the maternal grandmother and other members of the mother's family. Thus, this final part of the birth observance draws in the maternal side of the family, while the paternal relatives managed the previous activities. When both families gather for the feast, the baby's extended family is linked together, which helps them to create strong interfamily bonds.

Ceremonial Washing

Most groups wash the baby shortly after birth and may repeat the bath several times during the confinement, including a washing just prior to the sun presentation activities. The Tewa, however, only bathe the child after the presentation to the sun on the fourth day after birth. The Hopi follow some very particular practices. The baby is first rubbed with ashes from burned sage, then washed in water mixed with yucca. The Hopi also bathe the new mother every five days during the 20-day separation, which coincides with the wiping away of the cornmeal marks. Some of the other Pueblos bathe the father as well as the mother, especially just prior to the presentation.

Cornmeal

Most of the Pueblos use ground corn in some fashion during the birth observances. It's frequently presented as an offering to the rising sun during the presentation

A Hopi Explains the Need for Post-Birth Darkness

If you plant a seed in the ground . . . it will be about ten days before the little plant first shows above the surface. . . .

But it must be protected. The hot sun must not shine on it while it is so little and tender. Otherwise it may die.

A baby is like a plant that has started to grow from a seed. It must be protected in just the same way. . . . For twenty days the sun must not shine on it. . . .

This . . . is the reason why windows of a house are covered where a baby has just been born.

—quoted in John Loftin's *Religion and Hopi Life in the Twentieth Century* ceremony, and the Hopi rub the cornmeal on the baby prior to taking him or her outside. The Hopi also use cornmeal—or, in some cases, ashes—to mark the four sacred lines on the wall of the home. Each line stands for one of the worlds in the Hopi creation myth—three underworlds and the present earth they now inhabit. So, as the lines are removed from the wall in five-day intervals, it suggests that the newborn is likewise passing through these stages.

Darkened Home

The Pueblo people believe that a newborn is not ready to face the elements of the outside world immediately after birth. Therefore, the subdued light in the home is seen as a means of protecting the baby in addition to symbolizing elements of Pueblo myths.

Ears of Corn

Prior to the birth, the father selects several ears of corn that have a perfect shape. These are held along with the baby during the sunrise presentation ceremony and are also placed alongside the child's crib either before or after the presentation. The ears are referred to as corn "mothers," and they usually remain with the child's crib for a certain amount of time, then the kernels may be saved to be planted the following year. The Tewa also use the corn to signify the social structure of the Pueblo. Their communities are divided into two clan-like groups, one associated with summer, one with winter. These derive from two mother goddesses—Blue Corn Woman and White Corn Maiden. To represent the two goddesses and the two groups, the Tewa employ one ear of blue corn and one ear of white corn.

Greeting the Sun

The post-birth activities reach their peak when the baby is finally presented to the sun. This takes place at dawn on the prescribed day. Usually, it is the primary caregiver, frequently the baby's paternal grandmother, who carries the child and the ears of corn outside, though she is often accompanied by an assistant and sometimes by the infant's mother. The group walks to a certain spot and waits there as the sun comes over the horizon. The assistant may take a small hand broom and make sweeping motions over the baby, as this is intended to gather blessings to the child. Often the baby and the corn will be held out to the four directions—east, west, north, south, as well as up and down—as a prayer is recited.

Naming

Many, though not all, Pueblos grant the child a name during the presentation ceremony. The name is often given by the same person who presents the baby to the

Tewa Presentation Prayer

Alfonso Ortiz included this prayer in his book *The Tewa World:*

Here is a child who has been given to us
Let us bring [him/her] to [manhood/womanhood]
You who are dawn youths and dawn maidens
You who are winter spirits
You who are summer spirits
We have brought out a child that you may bring [him/her] to [manhood/womanhood]
That you may give [him/her] life
And not let [him/her] become alienated
Take, therefore [proffering the child and the corn], dawn beings, winter spirits, summer spirits
Give [him/her] good fortune we ask of you.

sun, and in many cases this is the paternal grandmother. The Hopi, however, follow a different method. The paternal grandmother and each paternal aunt gives the baby a different name, all of which make reference to the father's clan. One of these will become the child's primary name early in childhood, and the others will fall into disuse. Later, at around age eight, the child will receive yet another name when he or she is initiated into the Kachina cult (*see* **Hopi Initiation Ceremonies**).

Web Site

Indian Pueblo Cultural Center, undated.
    http://www.indianpueblo.org

Further Reading

Loftin, John D. *Religion and Hopi Life in the Twentieth Century.* Bloomington: Indiana University Press, 1991

Ortiz, Alfonso. *The Tewa World: Space, Time, Being, and Becoming in a Pueblo Society.* Chicago: University of Chicago Press, 1969.

ANNAPRASANA

Alternate Names: Anaprasana, First-solid-food Samskara

Customs and Symbols: Cow's Milk, Ghee, Guru, Rice

Another of the early childhood samskaras (rituals) practiced by some members of the Hindu faith, annaprasana (pronounced *uh-na-praa-sh-na*) marks an important early event in the child's life—when he or she is weaned from a milk-only diet and begins to eat other food.

History and Significance

As with other samskaras, the custom of celebrating annaprasana dates back at least 2,500 years. In the past, parents paid a great deal of attention to the food that was served to the baby during the ceremony because they believed that this first meal of solid food could affect his or her future. For instance, it was thought that if the child ate fish during annaprasana, she would become swift, or if he had partridge meat, he was likely to become a religious leader later in life. Some parents would prepare an unappetizing mixture of fish, fowl, honey, cheese curd, and more in hopes of giving the child as many gifts as possible (which may have convinced more than a few babies that they should stick with their mother's milk). Today, these beliefs are not followed so closely, though the frequent use of ghee, as explained below, can be seen as a way of improving the child's fortunes.

Observance

Annaprasana usually takes place when the baby is about six months old. Essentially, it's a ceremonial meal where the proceedings surround the preparing of the food and the feeding of the child. The ceremony can take place at home or at a temple. Today, the typical food is sweetened rice, perhaps moistened with ghee (clarified butter) and cow's milk. Mantras (religious poems) are recited as the food is prepared. The feeding is usually done by the child's father or, in certain cases, by the guru the family follows. Food offerings may also be made to the sacred fire that figures in most Hindu rituals.

Annaprasana marks an important early event in the child's life—when he or she is weaned from a milk-only diet and begins to eat other food.

Customs and Symbols

Cow's Milk

Milk from cows plays a large role in the diet of many Hindus. Milk cows have long been important to India's farming economy, and there is also a religious aspect to milk consumption because Hindus consider cows to be holy animals. Mixing cow's milk with the rice in the annaprasana ceremony introduces the child to this staple food and also helps to soften the rice and make it a bit more like the liquid diet that the baby has known in his or her first months.

Ghee

A type of clarified butter made from cow's milk, ghee is believed to have divine qualities and is used in various Hindu rituals, including **Jatakarma** (*see* **Greeting the Baby**). Among its other qualities, ghee is said to improve a person's intellectual abilities, and this is why many parents include it in the rice that is served to the baby during the annaprasana ceremony.

Guru

A guru is a religious teacher in the Hindu faith. Those who study with a guru are known as disciples, and they follow the path of study laid out by the guru in hopes of attaining spiritual enlightenment. In performing the annaprasana ceremony, some parents choose to allow their guru to recite the mantras and feed the child, believing that the presence of the exalted teacher will give more meaning to the ceremony.

Rice

The primary grain raised in Asia, rice is a staple of the Indian diet, especially among Hindus who follow a vegetarian diet. The soft texture of rice, especially when moistened with milk, also makes it a natural choice for the baby's first food.

Web Site

"Healing—A Contented Cow's Milk: Part 1" by Dr. Devananda Tandavan. *Hinduism Today*, December 1995.
http://www.hinduismtoday.com/archives/1995/12/11_healing_cows_milk.shtml

Further Reading

Kalavar, Jyotsna M. "Hindu Samskāras: Milestones of Child Development." In *Rituals and Patterns in Children's Lives*, edited by Kathy Merlock Jackson. Madison: University of Wisconsin Press, 2005.

UPSHERIN

Alternate Names: Halaqa, Upsheren, Upsherinish

Customs and Symbols: Aleph-bet Card, Haircut, Peyos, Spiritual Landmark, Tallit-kattan, Weighing of the Hair, Yarmulke

Observed by some members of the Jewish faith, the upsherin ceremony revolves around a ritual first haircut that is given to boys at about the time of their third birthday. It marks the child's transition from the period when he was totally dependent on his parents to the period when he starts to act somewhat independently and begins his religious education. Meaning "to shear off," upsherin symbolizes the fact that the boy is being cut loose from infancy and taking the initial steps toward becoming an observant member of the Judaic community.

History and Significance

The origins of upsherin are not completely clear. One of the earliest references to the practice was made in the 1500s by Rabbi Chaim Vital, who observed an upsherin ceremony in Palestine—the area that's now the nation of Israel. Upsherin has been strongly influenced by kabbalah—the study of the mystical elements of Judaism in an effort to gain some direct knowledge of God's essence. Jews who place strong emphasis on the mystical elements of worship have been inclined toward adopting the hair-cutting ritual. Hasidic Jews are the most important group in this regard. This school of belief originated in eastern Europe in the 1700s and then spread throughout Europe and to the Americas in the following century.

The fact that the ritual is observed near the child's third birthday can be traced to a passage from the Book of Leviticus (which is part of both the Jewish Torah and the Old Testament of Christian Bible). Speaking of newly planted fruit trees, it declares that "you shall count their fruit as forbidden; three years it shall be forbidden to you." This idea was later applied to people: like the fruit of the newly planted tree, the child's hair was "*orlah*"—off limits—for three years. Therefore, families who observe upsherin do not cut the child's hair until the time of the ceremony, by which time it is very long. The number three also figures into the idea that upsherin is the third "cut" of the child's life: the first occurred when the umbilical cord was cut at birth; the second took place when his foreskin was severed in the **Bris Milah** circumcision ceremony.

Because upsherin represents the beginning of the child's formal religious education, some families provide their son with several items used in Jewish study and worship.

The connection between bris milah and upsherin is part of the reason that the hair-cutting ceremony is traditionally observed only for three-year-old boys and not for girls. According to this way of thinking, only males are circumcised, so only males should take part in the related severing of the hair. Another factor is that formal study of the Torah is traditionally limited to males, and upsherin marks the beginning of that process. Jews opposed to gender discrimination have attempted to create a female equivalent to upsherin in recent decades. One example includes a ritual hair-braiding on a girl's third birthday. Such activities are quite limited, however, and for the most part the ceremony is observed only for boys.

Not *all* Jewish boys undergo the custom, however. Compared with other Judaic rites of passage such as bris milah, **Bar Mitzvah**, and **Bat Mitzvah**, upsherin is rather rare. It's most commonly found among the followers of Hasidism and among those who have a strong connection to the traditional practices of the Jewish faith.

Observance

There are relatively few guidelines in how a family is to observe upsherin. Because the ritual marks the beginning of a child's religious education, many parents believe that it is appropriate to mark the occasion at a spiritual landmark. Wherever the gathering takes place, the central feature is, of course, the haircut. The weighing of the hair then takes place and an equal amount of gold or silver (or its equivalent in cash) is donated as *tzedakah*—a charitable contribution.

Because upsherin represents the beginning of the child's formal religious education, some families provide their son with several items used in Jewish study and worship. These might include the boy's first *yarmulke* (skullcap head covering) and *tallit* (undergarment with *tzitzit* fringe). Also, to aid the child in learning the Hebrew alphabet, an aleph-bet card is often provided. The *Torah tzivah,* a well-known passage from the Book of Deuteronomy, may be recited by the child.

As with most festive gatherings, upsherin activities often include food and drink. Though there are no definite guidelines, the refreshments generally include relatively simple items such as pastries and beverages. Adults are offered alcoholic drinks (usually wine or vodka) so that they can offer *l'chayims*—toasts—to mark the occasion.

Customs and Symbols

Aleph-bet Card

The process of teaching the child the Hebrew alphabet (the aleph-bet) often begins at the upsherin gathering. One way parents do this is to buy a plastic-coated card with the Hebrew letters printed on it. Some honey is placed on each letter, and the child is encouraged to pronounce each letter, and then lick the honey from the card. A variation on this practice has the parents giving the child a slip of paper that has been dabbed with honey. Rather than the letters of the alphabet, the paper contains a passage from the Torah, so that the child can begin learning the scriptures. Another, less messy, alternative is to give the boy the aleph-bet card along with a packaged treat such as a lollipop.

Haircut

Typically, a pair of scissors is passed among the friends and family members who are present, and each takes a turn at clipping off a small bit of the child's hair. In some cases, a prominent religious figure from the community is asked to take the first cutting. Exactly where the first snips take place can be important. Some Jews follow the practice of beginning at the top of the forehead because this is the place where the boy will one day wear his *tefilin*—a small box containing Torah passages that is donned during morning prayer services. Another custom holds that the first cuts are made to the hair that falls just in front of the ears—the location of the *peyos* or sidelocks that some Jews wear. After the ritual trimming has taken place, a professional barber or hair stylist is often utilized to give the boy a full haircut.

Peyos

Also known as peot and payot, these long locks of hair are worn by some Jews as a sign of religious devotion. Those members of the faith who follow this custom often use the initial haircut at the upsherin ceremony to create these sidelocks. This practice is rooted in the Lord's commandment to Moses in the Book of Leviticus that states that the people of Israel "shall not round off the hair on your temples." It's generally believed that a moderate sideburn that extends to the middle of the ear is sufficient to fulfill this commandment, but some Jews, such as those of the Hasidic tradition, wear longer locks and sometimes curl them.

Spiritual Landmark

Many Jews hold the upsherin ceremony at a place that underscores the religious significance of the ritual. Synagogues are one option. Others seek out a site that is

Lag B'Omer

Omer is the forty-nine-day period that falls between the Jewish holidays of Passover and Shavuot. It is considered a time to mourn the tragic events that have occurred in Jewish history, including the death of more than 20,000 Talmudic students who perished in a plague at about the time of the second century C.E. On Lag B'Omer (meaning the thirty-third day of Omer), the mourning is suspended. Joyous festivities take place, including bonfires and other gatherings that feature singing and dancing. The day celebrates Rabbi Shimon Bar Yochai, or "Rashbi," who is considered to be the author of the Zohar, the principal book of kabbalah.

associated with some aspect of the Jewish tradition. The practice is especially popular among Jews who are living in or visiting Israel, where there are many significant landmarks. One of the most popular is the ancient site of Meiron (also spelled Meron), where on the holiday of Lag B'Omer, thousands of Jews observe upsherin at the tomb of Rabbi Shimon Bar Yochai, an important figure in kabbalistic studies.

Tallit-kattan

This garment is a lightweight version of the tallit—the Jewish prayer shawl (also spelled tallith). Like the shawl, the tallit-kattan is adorned with tassels of white knotted fringe, which are known as tzitzit. (In fact, the entire garment is often referred to as a tzitzit.) The fringe, which is tied with a specific number of strings and knots, is derived from a passage in the Book of Numbers, where God instructs Moses to "speak to the people of Israel and bid them to make tassels on the corners of their garments throughout their generations. . . ." The tallit-kattan is usually donned as an undergarment. Very observant Jews put one on each morning with the idea that it will provide a constant reminder of their faith. Many parents believe that their child should be introduced to this custom early on, so they give their sons their first tallit-kattan as part of the upsherin ceremony.

Weighing of the Hair

Once the hair is cut, it is weighed. The value of an equal weight of gold or silver is calculated, and the parents donate this as a charitable contribution, or tzedakah. Sometimes the money goes to a charity that aids the needy, or it may be donated to the religious shrine where the upsherin ceremony is held. A new twist on this idea is to offer the hair itself to one of the organizations that provides wigs to children who have lost their hair because of cancer treatments.

Yarmulke

Also known as a *kippah*, the yarmulke (pronounced *yar-muh-ka*) is a small beanie-style cap worn by some Jews. As with the tallit-kattan, parents may wish to provide their son with his first yarmulke at the time of the upsherin ceremony. Some Jews wear the yarmulke only while at synagogue or while making blessings at home. Others wear it at all times, as a constantly visible symbol of their faith. Still others, especially Reform Jews who have given up many traditional practices, don't wear the yarmulke at any time.

Web Sites

"Tallit, Tephillin & Kippah." Reclaiming Judaism.org, undated.
    http://www.reclaimingjudaism.org/bmitzvah/Tallit.htm#The%20Meaning

"Upsherin" by Rabbi Shraqa Simmons. Aish.com, June 30, 2002.
    http://www.aish.com/literacy/lifecycle/Upsherin.asp

"Upsherin: A Coming of Age Ritual for Toddlers and their Families" by Rabbi Goldie Milgram. Reclaiming Judaism as Spiritual Practice, 2004.
    http://www.rebgoldie.com/upsherin.htm

CHUDAKARMA

Alternate Names: Chudakarana, Cudakarana, Mundan, Head-shaving Samskara, Tonsure

Customs and Symbols: Hair Shaving or Cutting, Ritual Phrases, Top Hair, Water

Chudakarma (pronounced *choo-da-kar-ma*) is one of the samskaras (rituals) observed by certain members of the Hindu faith. A head-shaving ceremony that usually takes place in the early years of life, chudakarma serves as a means of cleansing impurities that may remain from the child's past, and it is also intended to promote humility and a reverence for spiritual devotion.

History and Significance

The ceremony is rooted in the idea that a person's hair can exercise a great deal of influence over their lives—especially in a negative sense. The hair is believed to harbor impurities from the prebirth period and—because Hindus believe that each person is reborn numerous times—it may even contain harmful elements from previous lives. Thus, the head-shaving ceremony is a means of purifying the child.

An ancient belief held that the supernatural power of the hair continued even after it was cut off, and there was a fear that the shorn locks could be used to cast evil spells on the child. To prevent this, parents would mix the hair with bull dung, which was then hidden or cast into the water. Magical elements such as this are given less heed today, but the hair-cutting ritual remains important for many Hindus. It is often viewed as a means of keeping a proper spiritual balance in the child's life. Paying too much attention to the hair or other elements of external appearance can lead to vanity, which distracts the individual from higher, spiritual matters. By removing their hair, a person shows their humility before the gods and signals that their first concern is spiritual enlightenment rather than personal glorification.

Observance

Unlike most other early-childhood samskaras, which take place at home, chudakarma is frequently celebrated at a Hindu temple. The ceremony is often scheduled when the child is three years old but can also occur earlier, with some parents opting to observe it when the child is ten months old. The father is often a key player in the rite. He may perform the hair shaving or cutting himself, or he may employ a barber. The father recites various ritual phrases designed to protect the child and grant good fortune. Water is drawn and is used to wet the child's hair. If carried out in the traditional manner, all of the child's head is shaved bare with the exception of the top hair—a small tuft that's often located at the crown of the head. Many Hindus in the United States instead opt to cut only a small amount of hair. In that way they symbolically carry out the samskara, but the child's appearance is not greatly different from most other American boys and girls of their age.

Customs and Symbols

Hair Shaving or Cutting

If the child's head is being completely shaven, a straight razor is often used. Some parents prefer to trust this cutlery to a professional, so they allow a barber to do the shaving, and some temples have staff people appointed for this task. (In India, there are particular temples that specialize in the process, where thousands of people have their heads shaved each day.) If only a small amount of hair is being removed, regular scissors are the more practical tool. Whether they prefer a trim or a full shave, many Hindus choose to repeat the process of the ritual haircut at other points in their lives. This serves as a reaffirmation of their spiritual devotion and is usually performed at a temple.

Hair is believed to harbor impurities from the prebirth period and—because Hindus believe that each person is reborn numerous times—it may even contain harmful elements from previous lives.

Ritual Phrases

If performed according to traditional guidelines, the father will ask for protection for the child and also declare the intention of the ceremony. In one version of these events, the father addresses the razor that is used for the shaving, stating that "thy father is iron; Salutation be to thee. Do not hurt the child." As the shaving is about to take place, he may announce that he is cutting off the hair to bring the child "long life" as well as "productivity, prosperity, good progeny [children], and valor."

Top Hair

Traditionally, children participating in Chudakarma would be left bald except for the tuft of top hair. Today, the tuft has become less common, especially among Hindus in the United States.

Water

On one hand, the water is functional—it moistens the hair so it can be shaved. But it also has a ritual purpose, reinforcing the idea that the child is being cleansed by the ceremony. In some instances, ghee (clarified butter) is mixed with the water. Ghee is said to have divine qualities such as improving a person's intellect and memory. It plays a part in other Hindu rituals as well (*see* **Jatakarma** and **Annaprasana**).

Further Reading

Kalavar, Jyotsna M. "Hindu Samskaras: Milestones of Child Development." In *Rituals and Patterns in Children's Lives*, edited by Kathy Merlock Jackson. Madison: University of Wisconsin Press, 2005.

FIRST DAY OF SCHOOL

Customs and Symbols: Backpack, Preparation, School Clothes, Tearful Parting

An important milestone in the growing-up process, the first day of school requires a child to function independently of her or his parents, which often results in a mixture of fear, sadness, excitement, and pride. Though the transition can be difficult, the child usually emerges as a more confident and self-assured individual ready to take on more challenges.

History and Significance

Up until they begin their education, many children have spent almost all of their lives in the presence of their parents or another relative. The first day of school therefore becomes a powerful reminder that the child is no longer a helpless infant but has matured into early childhood, where she or he begins to act independently of mom and dad. In many cases, the child's initial school experience, be it preschool or kindergarten, lasts for just a few hours a day, but even this period of parental separation can seem a huge undertaking, both to the youngster and to the parents. Of course, the first school day is also significant because it is the first of many steps that will steadily separate the parent and child until the point when the son or daughter becomes a fully independent adult in their own right.

Observance

Many parents find that advance preparation helps ease the transition to school life. In addition, outfitting the child with the proper gear, including a backpack and new school clothes helps to make the child feel more confident as they undertake their new challenge. Nonetheless, both the child and the parents often shed tears when the crucial day arrives.

Customs and Symbols

Backpack

The youngster will be hauling a new kind of load now that she or he is a student, and nothing conveys that better than a backpack to carry school materials. Those materials may be fairly light for a preschooler or kindergartner, but the backpack often becomes a source of pride and helps the child to feel that he or she belongs in the school environment.

Preparation

Though the initial day of school is the dramatic moment of focus, wise parents begin laying the groundwork for that event well in advance. Even a year or more beforehand, they may begin introducing the child to situations where they are separated from mom and dad for longer and longer periods. Sharing some of the many children's books about the first day of school is a favorite means of preparing the girl or boy for what they'll encounter. Better yet, the parents may be able to bring the child to the school for an orientation session in advance of the first day, where they will be able to see their classroom and possibly meet their teacher. All of these steps can help both the child and the parent become comfortable with the new situation and improve the odds that the first day of school will be a happy one.

School Clothes

As with many other rites, special clothing often plays a part in the first day of school. Whether or not the school has a strict dress code, the outfit a child dons for this day can serve some of the same functions as a uniform. First, it sets the child apart and allows them to better realize that this isn't like any other day. Second, by dressing themselves in their new clothing, the boy or girl hopefully comes to feel that they are prepared to face the new challenges of school life.

Tearful Parting

A not-uncommon occurrence on the first day of class is that the child begins crying when it's time to say goodbye to the parents, whether outside the school or in the classroom. Many authorities suggest that the parent only comfort the child momentarily and then leave, and that most children will adjust to the absence of the mother or father fairly quickly. Of course, parents may shed their own tears as they see their boy or girl move a little closer to the grown-up world.

Web Sites

"Life Advice about Your Child's First Day at School." Federal Citizen Information Center, January 2006.
> http://www.pueblo.gsa.gov/cic_text/family/firstday/firstday.htm

"The First Day of School: Preparing Your Kindergarten or Preschool Student." Chicago Public Schools, undated.
> http://www.cps.k12.il.us/Parent/EdChild/First_Day/first_day.html

FIRST LOST TOOTH

Customs and Symbols: Throwing the Tooth, Tooth Fairy, Tooth Keepsake

Occurring around the age of six or seven, the loss of a child's first baby tooth is recognized as an important sign that a girl or boy is growing. Several folk traditions serve to commemorate the occasion. The most famous is the tooth fairy, and the child's eventual discovery of the fairy's true nature leads to maturation of a different sort.

History and Significance

The fact that the lost tooth was an actual part of the person's body was of particular importance in the past. Fears that the tooth could be used to work harmful magic against the child caused the parents to make sure that the tooth was either kept or disposed of in a way that would prevent it from falling into the hands of an enemy. This led to folk beliefs where the method of disposal had an effect on the child. For instance, the tooth was sometimes fed to an animal (a pig or dog, for instance), and the legend arose that this would make the child's new teeth take on the characteristics of that animal. Usually, this was meant in a positive sense—that the child's teeth would be strong and sharp.

The loss of a child's first baby tooth is recognized as an important sign that a girl or boy is growing, and several folk traditions serve to commemorate the occasion.

The origins of the tooth fairy are somewhat hazy but many folklorists point to a French story from the 1700s entitled "La Bonne Petite Souris" (The Good Little Mouse) by Madame D'Aulnoy, in which a fairy is transformed into a mouse and battles against an evil king by knocking out his teeth as he sleeps. The fairy who exchanges money or gifts for the lost tooth became a part of American folklore in the early 1900s. The custom gained prominence following World War II, helped along by a children's story by Lee Rogow, "The Tooth Fairy," published in the popular magazine *Colliers* in 1949.

Observance

The first baby tooth to be lost is the most significant, and some families choose to preserve it as a tooth keepsake. The other customs are often applied not only to the initial tooth but also to the subsequent ones that are lost. In the United States, the tooth fairy is by far the most popular of these practices. In this observance, the child is told to put the dislodged tooth under their pillow when they go to sleep at night. The next morning the boy or girl finds that the tooth has been exchanged for money or a small gift. This act is attributed to the tooth fairy, though the child eventually learns the truth. A less common practice is throwing the tooth, where it is tossed either over or under the family home in hopes that the replacement tooth will grow properly.

Customs and Symbols

Throwing the Tooth

In this custom the tooth is taken outside the family home and thrown either over the house (if it was a lower tooth) or under the house (if was an upper tooth). The idea is that this action will cause the new tooth to grow straight in the direction the old tooth was tossed. Thus, an upper tooth will grow straight down because the old tooth was thrown down—under the house. This folk belief is popular among some Asian Americans and is derived from the old idea that the treatment of the lost tooth can affect the child.

Tooth Fairy

The tooth fairy custom is fairly widespread in the Americas and western Europe, and especially so in the United States. Part of its appeal is that it allows the child to believe in a magical being—and the fact that this particular being is good-natured and hands out cash or presents certainly adds to the appeal. In addition, the tooth fairy serves as a way to calm the boy or girl and prevent them from being alarmed at the loss of a body part. On a deeper level, the custom helps the child to see growing up as a positive experience rather than something to be feared.

While make-believe may be part of the tooth fairy's charm, it also leads to a day of reckoning when the boy or girl realizes that this wondrous figure is not real. Accepting the truth about the fairy—not to mention Santa Claus and the Easter Bunny—becomes yet another milestone in growing up. Interestingly, children often show a willingness to have fun (and make money) with the tooth fairy even after the truth becomes known. The custom of exchanging enamel for gifts often continues on until the last of the baby teeth fall out (around age eleven), which is usually well after the truth has become known.

Tooth Keepsake

Many parents choose to preserve the first baby tooth that the child loses, usually turning it over to the child at some later point in his or her life. Special keepsake boxes are sometimes used, which can be inscribed with the date that the tooth was lost.

Web Site

"What's the Origin of the Tooth Fairy?" The Straight Dope, July 20, 2004. http://www.straightdope.com/mailbag/mtoothfairy.html

Further Reading

D'Aulnoy, Madame (Marie-Catherine). *The White Cat and Other Old French Fairy Tales.* Translated by M. Planche. New York: Macmillan, 1928.

Tuleja, Tad. "The Tooth Fairy: Perspectives on Money and Magic." In *The Good People: New Fairylore Essays.* Edited by Peter Naváez. Lexington: University Press of Kentucky, 1997.

Wells, Rosemary. "The Making of an Icon: The Tooth Fairy in North American Folklore and Popular Culture." In *The Good People: New Fairylore Essays.* Edited by Peter Naváez. Lexington: University Press of Kentucky, 1997.

FIRST COMMUNION AND RECONCILIATION

Alternate Names: First Eucharist, First Confession

Customs and Symbols: Communion Clothing, Communion Host, Communion Wine, First Communion Party, Preparation Sessions, Reconciliation

Confession, formally known as reconciliation, and the Eucharist are two of the seven sacraments practiced by Roman Catholics. A child's first participation in these ceremonies, which usually occurs around age seven, is a rite of passage that marks their growing maturity and fuller participation in the Christian faith.

History and Significance

The Eucharist—the ceremonial sharing of bread and wine by the members of the congregation—is an essential rite for most Christians. The ceremony developed from the accounts of Jesus Christ's time on earth. For instance, in the Gospel According to John, Jesus states, "I am the living bread which came down from heaven. . . . he who eats my flesh and drinks my blood has eternal life, and I will raise him up on the last day. For my flesh is food indeed, and my blood is drink indeed."

Though many Christian denominations observe the ritual consumption of bread and wine, the Roman Catholic Church places special emphasis on the worshiper's first communion. This has to do with the different customs and beliefs that have developed over the centuries. For instance, the Eastern Orthodox Church observes many rites that are similar to those in the Roman Catholic faith, but they do not celebrate first communion because Orthodox doctrine holds that believers, including infants, participate in communion from the time of baptism, so no separate communion ceremony is necessary. Roman Catholics, on the other hand, prevent children from participating in the Eucharist until they have achieved a certain degree of maturity and better understand the ideas it encompasses. Certain denominations such as Lutheran churches do follow communion guidelines that are similar to those of the Roman Catholics, but these faiths generally don't view first communion as a rite of passage in the same way that Catholics do and usually forego special gatherings in honor of the event.

The ritual of reconciliation or confession is linked to the Eucharist, so a child's participation in this sacrament usually begins at about the same time as first communion. Reconciliation requires the believer to tell a priest their sins—those ways in which they have failed to fulfill the moral teachings specified in the Bible and taught by the Church. The priest then imposes a penance that the person must perform to show their sorrow for the sin and their wish to turn away from moral lapses in the future. This might consist of special prayers, work in service of others, or an offering. The sacrament concludes with the priest reciting the words of absolution, which frees the person of their sin. The rite of confession has changed in recent decades. Instead of the small booths that used to provide some anonymity to the confessor, the sacrament now takes place in special reconciliation rooms and may involve a face-to-face meeting with a clergyman. Also, most Catholics don't participate in the sacrament on a weekly basis, as used to be common. Many priests now recommend that that believers participate in reconciliation at least once a year, but those who are guilty of mortal sins—transgressions that place their salvation in doubt—should address them immediately.

Observance

The age at which the child undertakes these rites can vary, but many Catholic dioceses follow the papal declaration made in the early 1900s, which allowed children to receive the Eucharist beginning at age seven. Some Catholic dioceses combine the first communion and first reconciliation ceremonies together and allow the child to prepare for them simultaneously. More often, however, they are treated as separate rites, and must be completed in a specified order (reconciliation before communion or vice-versa). Formal preparation sessions begin the process for both rites, providing instruction in the spiritual and practical aspects of the ceremonies.

The child's first reconciliation usually takes place as part of a communal penance service, which is followed by a one-on-one meeting between the child and a confessor. This rite is generally treated as a serious undertaking and isn't accompanied by elaborate celebration.

The first communion observance, in contrast, is treated as a more public special occasion. Churches usually hold their first communion ceremonies once a year in a separate Sunday mass that's attended by the family members of the participants. The boys and girls undergoing the rite are attired in appropriate communion clothing, and the ceremony essentially follows the typical actions that take place in the celebration of the Eucharist. This involves the Eucharistic prayer and the consumption of the communion host (the bread believed to contain the body of Christ) and perhaps

Families frequently commemorate the first communion by hosting a gathering of family and friends after the church service.

the communion wine (which is believed to contain the blood of Christ). A church-sponsored reception may follow the ceremony, and many families also host a first communion party, where the boy or girl receives gifts.

Customs and Symbols

Communion Clothing

First communion is a formal occasion, and the children are expected to dress appropriately. Girls frequently wear white dresses selected especially for the occasion, often with a matching white veil. Boys usually wear either a suit or dress pants and a dress shirt with a tie.

Communion Host

These small wafers of bread are the centerpiece of the Eucharist—and, in a sense, the center of the Roman Catholic faith. Once they have been consecrated by the priest's recitation of the Eucharistic Prayer, the hosts are believed to be the true body of Christ—a physical source of spiritual nourishment. The consumption of the host is among the most meaningful acts of Catholic worship. To receive the host, the worshipers move to the front of the church when directed during mass. When they come before the priest, the worshipers kneel or bow briefly, then receive the host in one of two ways. If they wish it to be placed directly on their tongue, they open their mouth; if they wish to have it placed in their hands, they place them one atop the other in the shape of a cross. Once the host is in the worshiper's mouth, he or she faces the altar and may make the sign of the cross.

Communion Wine

Just as Christ's body is believed to be present in the communion host, his blood is believed to be present in communion wine. Worshipers are usually offered the option of drinking the wine from a communal chalice, but participation is optional. This part of the sacrament has changed over time. For many centuries, only the priest consumed communion wine during the Eucharist, but beginning in the 1960s the wine was also made available to the laity (the non-clergy worshipers). Roman Catholic doctrine states that the whole Christ is present in both the host and the wine, so some worshipers choose to only take the host.

First Communion Party

Families frequently commemorate the communion by hosting a gathering of family and friends after the church service. These parties range from simple affairs that may include only dessert to extravagant catered dinners with entertainment. It's customary for guests to give the boy or girl a present. Religious-oriented gifts such as medals or rosaries are common, as are presents of cash.

Preparation Sessions

If a child doesn't receive instruction in both rites as part of a Catholic school education, she or he will usually attend classes sponsored by the parish Confraternity of Christian Doctrine (CCD). These classes extend over several weeks and are intended to provide the child with a thorough understanding of the spiritual aspects of the rites. They also give each boy and girl the nuts-and-bolts details of what they will need to do during their first communion and those that follow. Parents, too, may be required to attend a preparation class so that they can help prepare their son or daughter. The main idea behind all of these sessions is that the child should fully understand the implications and meaning behind communion and confession and should not consider it an empty routine that they are required to perform.

Reconciliation

For a child's first reconciliation, they often participate in a communal penance service, where they are in the company of others experiencing their first reconciliation. Parents attend as well. The communal service includes songs, prayers, and discussion of the meaning of reconciliation. Afterward, each child meets with a priest to make a private confession. (Similar services are offered to all members of the church at certain times of year, such as during Lent—the 40-day period that precedes Easter.)

Further Reading

Isca, Kay Lynn. *Catholic Etiquette: What You Need to Know about Catholic Rites and Wrongs.* Huntington, IN: Our Sunday Visitor, 1997.

Photo on facing page: Cake and presents are important parts of every good birthday celebration.

Chapter 6: Commemorating Birth

INTRODUCTION

The importance of birth as a life event can be judged by its long-lasting effects. Though many rites of passage are one-time affairs meant to commemorate a particular moment, an individual's birth—and the time that has passed since that birth—continue to be memorialized throughout their life in the form of birthday celebrations. In fact, the **Birthday** often becomes the essential event that family and friends use to show their appreciation for an individual. These birth festivities sometimes begin even before a child is old enough to retain a memory of them (birthday parties for one-year-olds, for instance, have become increasingly popular in recent years). And they are likely to continue in some form until death.

As universal as the birthday is in the U.S., it is not the only means of remembering the beginning of a person's life. The tradition of observing a **Saint's Day** or name day is practiced by some Catholics and Orthodox Christians. This custom is a holdover from the Middle Ages, a time when the birthdays of commoners were seldom noted. Instead, the good tidings that most people received each year were partly focused on the Christian saint he or she was named for. While the saint's day survives, it now is usually held in addition to—not instead of—a typical birthday celebration. Most Americans expect each year to include a birthday observance that makes them, not a religious figure, the center of attention. In this sense the birthday is well suited to the U.S.—a country where individual achievement and personal preferences are highly valued.

BIRTHDAY

Alternate Name: Tol

Customs and Symbols: Birthday Cake, Birthday Greetings, Birthday Party, Candles, Chinese-American Celebrations, Korean-American Tol Celebration, Mexican-American Celebrations, Reflection

A birthday simultaneously serves as the primary celebration of a person's existence and a constant reminder that life is ever changing. While the symbols and ceremonies sometimes refer to—and make fun of—the aging process, birthdays are also focused on personal enjoyment, allowing the celebrant to spend at least one day each year doing what he or she most enjoys. Nonetheless, because birthdays are partly about the passage of time, a certain amount of wistful reflection sooner or later becomes part of most birth anniversaries.

History and Significance

Though everyone has a birth, not everyone celebrates a birthday. This was particularly true in ancient times, when birthday festivities were usually reserved for the elite. Egyptian pharaohs and Roman emperors, for instance, were honored with lavish feasts, but those who weren't wealthy or powerful usually received no special consideration on their birthday. In the periods when there were no written birth records, many of them didn't even know the exact date of their birth.

When records were kept, the newborn was often associated with a particular god that was said to be born on the same day. The Greeks and Romans believed that this god became the person's protector, and a similar idea came into use in the Middle Ages, when children were named for Christian saints—a practice that continues among some groups (*see* **Saint's Day**). The Greek commemorations of the gods' birthdays also started the tradition of the birthday cake. Round lunar-shaped cakes were baked as offerings to the moon goddess Artemis on her monthly celebration day, with burning candles placed on top to resemble the moon's glow. This custom was later adapted to celebrate the birthdays of mortals, particularly by the Germans, who specialized in making sweet cakes in honor of the special day. Germans were also the innovators of the birthday party for children, which they called *kinderfeste*. The American version with games, hats, and entertainment became common in the 20th century.

Observance

On one level, birthdays are about being recognized. Whether they are receiving simple birthday greetings or are being fawned over in an elaborate birthday party, the person whose birthday is being celebrated receives a great deal of attention. Children are usually overjoyed at this and also by the fact that the normal limitations that are placed upon them are lifted for a day. They are allowed to eat what they like, do what they like, and lay their hands on some of the gifts that they previously desired but were denied. Adults, too, may enjoy some of this freedom. A quick browse through a store greeting-card display shows that most birthday sentiments aimed at adults urge them to spend the day eating, drinking, and enjoying other activities in excess. Nonetheless, age tends to temper birthday enthusiasm to some extent, and contemplation about the passing of time begins to replace the joys of gratification.

Appreciation of the person and their past deeds is one part of the birthday celebration, but the rituals also look forward. Many of the events and actions are meant to confer some type of blessing upon the honoree. Birthday greetings from others and the candles atop the birthday cake are both meant to grant good fortune in the days ahead. A similar idea underlies some of the rituals that are found in ethnic communities in the U.S. For example, the "lucky money" gifts that are part of the Chinese-American birth celebrations and the clothing and activities in the Korean-American Tol celebration are all intended to bring a happy and prosperous future to the birthday celebrant.

Customs and Symbols

Birthday Cake

Though cakes have been around for thousands of years, it wasn't until the 1600s that they took on the precise molded shapes and lighter texture that's common today. The precursor of the American birthday cake was the German *geburtstagorten*, a layered cake with glazed icing that was prepared for very special birthdays. The reason that cake became the traditional food of the birthday is not entirely clear. One possibility is that a dessert of this type was elaborate and somewhat expensive, so it was well suited to being a special treat that was enjoyed just once a year.

Symbolically, some see a connection between cakes and birth, with the oven representing the womb and the cake representing the baby. (The same idea is expressed in the phrase "she's got one in the oven," to indicate that a woman is pregnant.)

Also, the round shape of the traditional birthday cake makes it a symbol for the circle of life, which includes the aging process denoted by birthdays.

Birthday Greetings

There's an old belief that a person is more susceptible to supernatural forces at the time of their birthday and that any sentiments, positive or negative, directed at the birthday celebrant have great power on that day. For that reason, it was considered important to greet the birthday person with good wishes—partly for the blessings it could bring, and partly because those who weren't wishing a person well might be thought to be wishing them ill.

Traditional lore also held that the greeting had to be delivered on the birthday itself. If it was given afterward, it counted for bad luck, even if the wish was "happy birthday." The modern turn on this tradition is the birthday card, which first appeared in England in 1850. More than 1.2 billion cards are now given each year, according to the Hallmark greeting card company, and two-thirds of them are sent by mail rather than delivered in person (which no doubt increases the odds that the greeting *will* arrive late).

The other classic birthday greeting in the United States is the singing of "Happy Birthday to You." This tradition began early in the 1900s, when some unknown person put the famous lyrics to the melody of an existing song entitled "Good Morning to All." The traditional way to observe the custom is to sing the song as the birthday cake is brought into the room.

> *There's an old belief that a person is more susceptible to supernatural forces at the time of their birthday and that any sentiments, positive or negative, directed at the birthday celebrant have great power on that day.*

Birthday Party

The oldest of birthday customs, the festive gathering in honor of a birthday has been around at least since the time of the Egyptian pharaohs. In the United States, the custom is especially common for children and serves to underscore the idea that a child's birthday is her or his special day—a time when they are the center of attention and able to have many of their desires met. Various games, such as "pin the tail on the donkey," are usually part of the children's gatherings, and more elaborate parties might feature clowns, musicians, or other professional entertainers. Birthday parties for adults are also fairly common, especially on birthdays that are considered milestones, such as the 30th, 40th, and 50th.

Candles

Candles are probably the most superstitious element of birthdays. Germans in the 1800s observed the birthday custom of keeping candles burning from morning until the time the cake was eaten, replacing them as they burned down. Doing so insured good luck for the coming year. The well-known custom today is to place one candle on the birthday cake for each year being celebrated. The honoree makes a secret wish and then attempts to blow out all the candles in one breath. It's believed that if he or she succeeds, their wish will come true. A less common but more communal ritual has all members of the gathering make a wish and each blow out a single candle. Candles are part of many rituals. As the principal light source in the pre-electricity era, they became a symbol of spiritual enlightenment and hope. As far as wishing goes, they even seem to have a mechanical function, as it's said that the smoke rising from the extinguished candle carries the wish to the sky.

Chinese-American Celebrations

In traditional Chinese culture, individual birthdays were not celebrated. Instead, everyone celebrated a birthday together on the seventh day of the new year. Most Chinese Americans have given up this custom and instead honor a person on the date that they were born. Nonetheless, many of them still follow the practice of giving the birthday celebrant "lucky money," which is a popular gift for all kinds of Chinese celebrations (*see* **Red Egg and Ginger Party**). Known as *li-shih* or *lai see* in Cantonese and *hong bao* in Mandarin, lucky money is cash that is placed in a red envelope to be given as a gift. When presented to the birthday celebrant, good fortune is said to flow to both the recipient and to the person who gives the money, but the effect can be altered depending on the number of dollars given. The number four (a bad omen) should be avoided in the total amount of currency, while eights and nines are thought auspicious. Like other Americans of Asian descent, Chinese Americans place great emphasis on the 60th birthday (*see* **Asian American 60th Birthday**).

Korean-American Tol Celebration

Many Americans of Korean descent hold a special celebration in honor of the child's first birthday. Known as *tol* (pronounced *tull*), the tradition dates from the period when there was a high rate of infant mortality in Korea, which led parents to wait until the end of the first year before holding a lavish celebration. Both girls and boys are dressed in bright clothing for the occasion, and their outfit includes a pouch that symbolizes good luck and a belt that signifies long life.

The highlight of the gathering is the *toljabee*, where various items are placed on a table, and the child is allowed to pick up whatever catches his or her attention. The first item chosen is said to indicate the child's future. For instance, picking a pencil denotes a writer, while choosing a book signifies a scholar. Guests offer presents and good wishes for the child and then partake of various traditional foods that are intended to exert influence on the infant's fate. These include noodles that represent a long life, white rice cakes that signify a clean spirit, and jujubes and fruit that symbolize the many descendants that the child will one day have.

Mexican-American Celebrations

The best known of the Mexican birthday customs is the piñata, which has been adopted by American children in general, regardless if they have any Mexican heritage. These papier-mâché figures are usually made in the shape of animals and filled with candy and other treats. After being blindfolded, the birthday boy or girl tries to whack the suspended piñata with a stick. When the animal splits open, all the children present scramble for the spilled treats.

Las Mañanitas

The following English translations, published in Ralph and Adelin Linton's *The Lore of Birthdays*, present a few of the many verses that can be sung to "Las Mañanitas."

The day when you were born
Were born all the flowers.
The day when you were born
The nightingales sang

Now the dawn is coming
Now the light has seen us
Awake, my friend
Look, it has dawned.

I wish I were a sunbeam
To be able to enter your window
And say good morning to you
Lying in your bed.

Some Mexican Americans observe an adult's birthday by serenading the honoree with "Las Mañanitas," a folk song that has many different versions and is used to honor someone on a special day (it is also sung on wedding anniversaries, for instance). Preferably, the singing is done by professional mariachi musicians. The traditional way of accomplishing this is to hire the mariachis to arrive at the honoree's house in the predawn hours on the person's birthday. The band sings in the street outside the house until the honoree awakens. Then the mariachis are invited inside for food and drink, and various neighbors and friends may join in the fun.

Reflection

Because birthdays draw attention to the amount of time that has passed since a person was born, they become a natural time to take stock of what has and has not occurred during those years. As might be expected, this process tends to become more profound as a person ages. For most people, this looking back involves a mix of happiness over fond memories and happy outcomes and sadness over missed opportunities.

Web Site

"Birthday Trends and Statistics." Hallmark, March 2005.
    http://pressroom.hallmark.com/birthday_trends_stats.html

Further Reading

Linton, Ralph, and Adelin Linton. *The Lore of Birthdays*. 1952. Reprint, Detroit: Omnigraphics, 1998.

Pleck, Elizabeth H. "Cakes and Candles." In *Celebrating the Family: Ethnicity, Consumer Culture, and Family Rituals*. Cambridge, MA: Harvard University Press, 2000.

SAINT'S DAYS

Alternate Names: El Dia del Santo, El Dia del Nombre, Name Day

Customs and Symbols: Church Service, Festive Gathering, Gifts, Greetings, Icon, Prayers

A saint's day—also known as a name day—is a custom followed by some members of the Roman Catholic and Orthodox Christian churches. It simultaneously honors a person's birth and also pays tribute to the Christian saint that they are named for. Though it's often compared to a birthday, a saint's day or name day has a more spiritual quality and serves as a way to link an individual to their Christian heritage.

History and Significance

By the Middle Ages, Christianity was the dominant religion in Europe, and it became common practice to name children after saints—figures who displayed exceptional religious devotion during their lifetimes. A special relationship was believed to exist between a child and the saint he or she was named for. The saint became the child's protector or patron and was capable of fending off harm. Each saint is commemorated on a particular day—which is known as the saint's feast day—so it became customary to celebrate the child's birth on the day devoted to his or her patron saint. During medieval times, birthdays—the anniversary of the actual date a person was born on—were not widely celebrated, so the saint's day observance served as the primary way to honor an individual's existence. After the Reformation, the saint's day custom fell into disuse among Protestants, but it remained firmly rooted in most countries with a large Roman Catholic or Eastern Orthodox population. This was less true in the U.S., however, where non-religious birthday celebrations became very popular even among Catholics and members of the Orthodox faith. Today the saint's day tradition remains strongest among some Catholics of Hispanic descent and among certain Orthodox Christians.

A saint's day is often compared to a birthday, but there are some distinct differences. A person may receive a fair amount of attention and greetings on their saint's day, but the activities are partly directed toward the saint rather than

Though it's often compared to a birthday, a saint's day or name day has a more spiritual quality and serves as a way to link an individual to their Christian heritage.

Letting the Baby Select Its Name

One potentially confusing aspect of a saint's day is that it can be the same day as a person's birthday, or it can be an entirely different day. When the days coincide it's because the parents decide to let the day of birth dictate the child's name. They simply wait until the birth occurs, then choose a name from one of the saints whose feast day falls on the birth date. This practice is sometimes referred to as giving the child the name it "brought with it in its fist" because, in a sense, the baby helped decide its own name by choosing the day on which he or she would be born.

being fully focused on the individual. Thus, the honoree is better able to see himself or herself as part of a religious tradition that extends back many centuries. Also, there are fewer gifts and treats involved in the typical saint's day observance, so material elements aren't allowed to overshadow the religious meaning of the occasion. This does not necessarily mean that people in these communities never get a birthday party. The tradition of the birthday is so strong in the U.S. that it is usually observed in addition to the saint's day activities.

Observance

Since the primary purpose of the name day rite is to connect the celebrant to their faith, they are expected to participate in a church service. That's generally the only part of the observance that needs to take place outside the home, and the rest of the activities are centered around the family. An icon of the saint is often displayed in a central location at the house and appropriately decorated. A festive gathering is usually hosted, where greetings are expressed and refreshments served. Gifts may or may not be given—and, in some cases, the person celebrating their saint's day may be giving presents to others rather than receiving them.

Customs and Symbols

Church Service

The religious nature of the day is usually reinforced by a visit to the family's church, preferably to attend a service of the Eucharist (the communal sharing of bread and wine). If the service is not offered on the day in question, the celebrant is expected to attend as near to the date as possible.

Festive Gathering

A get-together of friends and family often takes place on the saint's day. When held for a young boy or girl, this gathering is usually less involved than the typical children's birthday party, and the number of children may be limited so that rough-housing doesn't disrupt the intimate, family-oriented atmosphere. One particularly popular way to observe the date is to have visitors over for some type of dessert.

Gifts

In general, gifts do not play a large role in the observance, but this varies depending on the custom of the family. Children sometimes receive small gifts from their parents or close family members. On the other hand, there is another tradition where the person who is celebrating the saint's day provides small gifts for others. These are usually small tokens of affection or simply the sweet treats served as part of the festive gathering.

Greetings

As with a birthday, a person usually receives greetings from their friends and family on their saint's day. And as with most modern-day rites, these may arrive by telephone or mail as well as in person. By whatever means, it's customary for close friends and relatives to wish the celebrant a "happy name day" or "happy saint's day."

Icon

An icon is a picture of the saint. Many families keep an icon of the children's patron saint on display in the home all year round. To denote the special status of the saint's day, it is usually moved to a prominent place in the home and surrounded by flowers and candles.

Prayers

A blessing is often recited as part of the observance, and may take place before the serving of food at the festive gathering. A prayer to the saint is considered especially fitting. If the gathering is in honor of a child, he or she is usually encouraged to recite the blessing.

Web Site

"Celebrating Your Patron's Saint Day," by Phyllis Meshel Onest. Theologic Systems, undated. http://www.theologic.com/oflweb/inhome/nameday1.htm

Further Reading

Linton, Ralph, and Adelin Linton. *The Lore of Birthdays*. 1952. Reprint, Detroit: Omnigraphics, 1998.

Rouvelas, Marilyn. *A Guide to Greek Traditions and Customs in America*. Bethesda, MD: Nea Attiki Press, 1993.

PART 2

Coming of Age

The bar and bat mitzvah is a significant milestone in a Jewish child's life.

PART 2

Coming of Age

INTRODUCTION

For most people, the transition from childhood to greater maturity is one of the most poignant periods of life, perhaps because it encompasses so many different experiences. It is, first, an educational undertaking in which an individual learns that the world is not the idealized place they may have previously thought it to be. This realization takes place as they progress from the dependant period, when they rely upon their parents for nearly everything, to a more autonomous stage, when they assume responsibility for their actions and take a larger role in caring for themselves, both emotionally and economically. Tossed into this already complicated situation is the onset of puberty and the resulting confusion of emotions, hormones, and romantic entanglements.

With so many changes taking place, "coming of age" is usually a protracted process. As a result, the rituals that recognize and facilitate a young person's growing maturity take place at various points over a wide time span: certain religious rites may occur before age 10; the many ceremonies that coincide with the arrival of sexual maturity take place near the beginning of the teen years; and the conferring of adult-style freedom tends to occur in the later teens. In fact, the process of growing up has gotten longer in modern times, at least in the U.S. and other developed countries. Previously, young men and women took on many of their adult responsibilities, including working and raising a family, closer to the time they reached sexual maturity. Now, they spend considerably more years in school, which delays some aspects of adulthood.

Though all coming-of-age rites allow or commemorate some type of greater responsibility, they cover a broad range of activities. To group them in general terms, there are, first, the many observances that result from religious beliefs. These often ask the young person to make some type of definitive commitment to the faith and, in return, they are given the status of an adult within the faith community. In some cases, this new religious status also applies to social interactions—allowing the person to date and take part in romantic relationships, for instance, as occurs with the **Quinceañera** rite and the **Lakota Awicalowanpi Ceremony**. Many of the religious ceremonies also invoke the protection of some type of spiritual force for the young person, which is intended to guide them in their new stage of life.

A number of secular events also serve as rites of passage. The first attempts at adult-hood-related activities such as **Driving** and the **First Date** serve as tests where the youth must show that they are capable of handling the privileges and responsibilities of being a grown-up. And when the end of secondary education arrives at about the age of 18, **Graduation** provides a way for the young person to formally conclude the school days of childhood and adolescence and to anticipate the events of the adult world.

Finally, recent developments have shown that rituals can be purposefully re-designed to meet new needs. Often, these "reinvented" observances are a mixture of spiritual elements and practical advice, and they draw in ceremonial activities from African, Native American, and other traditions. Such "mix-and-match" ap-proaches are well suited to modern American society, where various cultures exist side by side and young people are exposed to a wide range of ideas through the media and their educational studies.

Despite the vast range of ages and activities encompassed in the coming-of-age period, most of the rites do share one characteristic: they incorporate some type of older mentor to assist the young person in their transition. From the sponsor of Roman Catholic **Confirmation** to the ceremonial parent of **Hopi Initiation Ceremonies** to the Hindu guru of the **Upanayana** *samskara*, these figures address a widespread need for adult guidance.

Photo on facing page: This Apache puberty rite includes painting the girl white to link her to the Apache holy woman, the White Painted Woman.

COMING OF AGE

Chapter 7: Religious Milestones

INTRODUCTION

As with other major life events, coming of age is addressed in religious rites, which usually serve two purposes: first, to allow the young man or woman to manage the transition to a more mature phase of life and, second, to provide them a means to affirm or strengthen their faith. This second function is important because, previously, the person's spiritual activities were largely directed by their parents. Without a rite that allows them to make a personal declaration of faith, there's a danger that they may drift away from the religion as adults or simply follow its precepts without gaining any real fulfillment or understanding of its meaning.

Such rites generally coincide with the onset of puberty—partly because this is a traumatic life event that needs to be managed and also because, since ancient times, many societies conveyed the religious rites of adulthood at the time a person reached sexual maturity. This thinking underlies the timing of the Jewish **Bar Mitzvah and Bat Mitzvah** ceremonies, which take place around the age of thirteen. According to ancient Jewish religious and legal concepts, this was the beginning of adulthood, and the tradition has continued even though modern American society generally doesn't consider someone of that age to be an adult. Roman Catholic **Confirmation**, likewise, now takes place close to the onset of the teen years, though this is a development that has occurred only in the past century. Previously, Confirmation occurred earlier in childhood. Many Roman Catholics of Hispanic descent also hold a **Quinceañera** celebration at the time of a young woman's fifteenth birthday, which combines a religious ceremony with a social celebration that announces that the young woman is mature and eligible for dating. Some Eastern religions, likewise, see the early teenage years as a time when a person needs to become more fully immersed in their faith. The **Theravadin Buddhist Novice Monkhood** is one means of accomplishing this goal and is believed to impart beneficial spiritual qualities to the young men who participate in monastic life for a brief time.

Several Native American rituals also focus on the time of sexual maturity. Both the **White Mountain Apache Sunrise Ceremony** and the **Lakota Awicalowanpi Ceremony** take place near the time of a young woman's first menstrual cycle and both call on female spiritual figures and other supernatural forces to initiate her into this new stage of life. The **Vision Quest**, which is found among a variety of Native American communities, often occurs at the onset of puberty and can be undertaken by both young men and young women. In participating in the quest, the young person hopes to gain some form of spiritual insight that will help guide their future actions.

While the focus on puberty and the teenage years is widespread, other traditions emphasize an earlier time in a child's life. **Upanayana**, the Hindu rite that signifies the beginning of a boy's religious education, can take place as early as age five and usually occurs before the child turns eight. **Hopi Initiation Ceremonies**, likewise, occur around age eight. All of these rites are considered important symbols of the child's growing maturity and allow them to take a fuller role in religious worship.

UPANAYANA

Alternate Name: Sacred Thread Ceremony

Customs and Symbols: Acts of Acceptance, Gayatri Mantra, Haircut, New Clothing, Ritual Bath, Sacred Fire, Sacred Thread

A ritual or *samskara* observed by members of the Hindu faith, upanayana (pronounced *upah-naya-na*) is held for young boys, usually between the ages of five and eight, though it can also take place at an older age. It signifies that early childhood has come to an end and that the boy is beginning a period when he has more responsibilities and will be educated in Hindu religious principles. The key symbol of this transformation is the sacred thread, which indicates that the child is "twice born"—the second birth being his initiation into religious knowledge, which begins with the upanayana ceremony.

History and Significance

According to traditional social and religious beliefs in India, only the three upper castes (social groups)—Brahmin, Kshatriya, and Vaishya—are eligible to participate in the upanayana ceremony. In fact, their distinction as being twice born through the ritual is one of the reasons they are considered superior to the lower castes. In addition, the rite is usually observed only for males—the traditional religious and political leaders in Hindu society. However, there are some limited examples of girls undergoing the upanayana ceremony in recent years. Those who support this practice point to passages in Hindu scripture that suggest that the sacred thread was bestowed to women in ancient times.

The ceremony is rooted in the form of education that used to be practiced in India. Rather than attending the type of schools that are common today, a boy would leave his home and go to live with a guru (religious teacher), who provided instruction in the Vedas—the ancient scripture of Hinduism. Upanayana began as the formal ceremony that marked that transition. Today, public and private schools have largely replaced this type of guru education, both in India and among Hindus in the United States. While the

The upanayana activities often involve a gathering of relatives, who offer blessings to the boy. Good fortune is also requested through prayers to Hindu deities.

child may still receive religious instruction from a guru, he is now much more likely to reside with his family until adulthood, and this has changed the upanayana ceremony. The rite has become somewhat simpler and more of a ceremonial marking of maturity rather than a commemoration of leaving the family home.

Observance

The upanayana activities often involve a gathering of relatives, who offer blessings to the boy. Good fortune is also requested through prayers to Hindu deities. The child then receives a haircut and a ritual bath to symbolically purify him. After the bath, he dons brand new clothing that likewise shows that he is in a pure state and has assumed the proper sense of seriousness about his new responsibilities. If the boy will be receiving religious education from a guru, that teacher usually plays an important role in the upanayana ceremony. He places the sacred thread on the boy, which represents various concepts in the Hindu faith. The guru may also carry out several acts of acceptance to formally initiate the instructor-student relationship. The ceremony concludes with the recitation of the Gayatri Mantra, offerings to the sacred fire, and the child's vows to observe proper behavior in the following years.

Customs and Symbols

Acts of Acceptance

Two actions are often performed by the child's religious teacher to formally accept the new pupil. First, the guru takes water in his cupped hands and sprinkles it into the child's hands, which are held in a similar fashion. The guru also touches the child's chest, which is meant to symbolize the touching of his heart. Both of these represent the wisdom that will be passed from the teacher to the boy.

Gayatri Mantra

Known as the "mother" of the Vedas, this religious poem is one of the most ancient and most important passages in Hindu scripture because it directs a person's thoughts toward the attainment of wisdom. It's said that if a worshiper firmly fixes this mantra in their mind and recites it regularly, he or she will be able to escape adversity and live a satisfying life. The following translation of the Gayatri Mantra, from the Rig Veda (III, 62, 10), was rendered by Gavin Flood in *An Introduction to Hinduism* (1996):

> Om, earth, atmosphere and sky.
> May we contemplate the desirable radiance of the god Savitri;
> May he impel our thoughts.

Haircut

As is in many other rituals, upanayana uses the cutting of the boy's hair to signify that he is entering a new phase. The underlying idea is that the hair represents the elements of his previous existence that now need to be cast off so that he will enter his new life stage in a pure frame of mind. In the past, the boy usually had his head completely shaved with the exception of top hair or *sikha*—a single tuft of hair that was usually located at the crown of the head. Today, especially in the U.S., it's more common to cut just a small amount of hair. This is considered sufficient to fulfill the symbolism of the ritual, yet doesn't greatly alter the child's appearance.

New Clothing

Though Hindu men and boys in the U.S. may wear conventional Western apparel, a boy participating in his upanayana often dons traditional Indian clothing such as the *dhoti*, a long skirt-like length of fabric that is wrapped around the hips and legs. The condition of the clothing is more important than the style: it should be a completely new outfit, which signifies that the child is in a pure, renewed state as he begins the next stage of his life.

Ritual Bath

The ceremonial bath is intended to symbolically purify the child's body and mind. In many cases this occurs after the haircut and prior to donning his new clothing.

Sacred Fire

As with most other Hindu samskaras, upanayana makes use of a small sacred fire, which is believed to be a means of communicating with the gods. In some ceremonies, the child walks in a circle around the fire. Toward the end of the proceedings, he places wood into the fire to signify that, from now on, he will be contributing to religious ceremonies.

Sacred Thread

Also known as the *yagnopavita*, the sacred thread is usually made of hand-spun cotton and is constructed in a manner that reflects many symbolic meanings. It is made from three strands that are folded three times over. The number three is very important in Hindu beliefs. It represents the primary gods—Brahma, Vishnu, and Shiva—which in turn are associated with the three qualities that created the universe: passion, reality, and darkness. The three folds can also serve as a reminder that the wearer owes debts to the gods, the sages, and his ancestors. In addition, the knots in the thread are meant to represent important family members from the past. The sacred thread is placed over the child's left shoulder and across the chest, passing beneath the right arm. Ideally, the thread should be worn for the rest of the person's life, though it is repositioned for certain activities. For instance, if he attends a funeral, the thread is hung over the right shoulder rather than the left, and if he is performing physical work, it may simply be hung around the neck. If the boy keeps to the traditional practices, he will add a second thread at the time of his wedding.

Web Site

"Starting Vedic Studies: Backed by Scripture, Girls Get Their Sacred Thread" by V. L. Manjul. *Hinduism Today*, October, November, December 2002. http://www.hinduismtoday.com/archives/2002/10-12/59-girls_thread.shtml

Further Reading

Flood, Gavin. *An Introduction to Hinduism*. Cambridge, MA: Cambridge University Press, 1996.

Kalavar, Jyotsna M. "Hindu Samskaras: Milestones of Child Development." In *Rituals and Patterns in Children's Lives*, edited by Kathy Merlock Jackson. Madison, WI: University of Wisconsin Press, 2005.

Sanford, A. Whitney. "The Hindu Ritual Calendar." In *Contemporary Hinduism: Ritual, Culture, and Practice*. Edited by Robin Rinehart. Santa Barbara, CA: ABC-CLIO, 2004.

HOPI INITIATION CEREMONIES

Alternate Names: Kachina Initiation, Powamuy Initiation

Customs and Symbols: Altars, Bean Dance, Ceremonial Parent, Cloud Kachina, Cornmeal, Kiva, Sand Mosaics, Whipping

In traditional Hopi religious beliefs, the kachinas are the god-like spirits of ancient ancestors who exercise great power over daily life. The initiation ceremonies held for children around age seven or eight introduce them to the mysteries of the kachinas and allow them to take a larger role in spiritual ceremonies.

History and Significance

According to longstanding Hopi traditions, children around the age of eight must join one of two religious societies: the Kachina or the Powamuy. Both are involved in various ceremonies that have been practiced for centuries. The Powamuy society focuses on organizing the ritual dances and other functions, while the members of the Kachina society are participants in the rites and may become dancers. The initiations for the two societies are similar, but the Kachina is somewhat more involved and includes ceremonial whipping.

At the center of both ceremonies are the kachinas, which are the supernatural spirits that are said to dwell on the San Francisco Peaks in northern Arizona that are visible from the Hopi communities. The kachinas are also believed to visit the Hopi villages on certain occasions, and this is represented by various ritual dances, where tribal members dress in masks and costumes that embody the different spirits. Small children are told that the costumed figures are the actual supernatural beings and usually have considerable fear of these strange creatures. It is only at the time of the initiation that children learn that these figures are actually members of the tribe in costume. This "unmasking" of the spirits becomes a part of growing up: after learning the true nature of the kachina dancers, children are allowed to fully participate in rituals and may even become dancers themselves. Learning the secret of the kachinas also helps children to accept the Hopi concept that sacred qualities are found in all aspects of life, even among their own relatives and neighbors.

Another important aspect of the initiation ceremonies is that they are concerned with the natural elements and with agriculture. Several different ritual acts and the appearance of the Cloud Kachina are intended to insure rainfall, which is rare and precious in the dry Southwestern region where the Hopi live. In addition, the sacred nature of plant food is alluded to in the use of the cornhusks, *cornmeal*, and ceremonial bean plants, which are distributed to the community prior to the Bean Dance that concludes the initiation.

Observance

The initiations take place during the larger winter ritual known as Powamuya. Though this observance takes place every year, the initiation ceremonies are held less regularly, usually every two or three years, when there is a sizable group of children of the appropriate age. The child is guided through the activities by a ceremonial parent, who accompanies them during a two-part ceremony.

The first part of the ritual differs depending on which society a child is entering—Powamuy or Kachina. In the Powamuy activities, the initiates and their ceremonial parents gather in a kiva that has been specially prepared for the rite with the creation of altars and sand mosaics. The elders in charge of the ceremony smoke a sacred pipe and sing sacred songs. Next, a kachina—that is, a person wearing a mask and costume that represents one of the spirits—enters the kiva. This is the Cloud Kachina that is associated with rain. This figure dances and shows the children images of clouds, rain, and lightning, and this concludes the initial part of the Powamuy initiation.

According to longstanding Hopi traditions, children around the age of eight must join one of two religious societies: the Kachina or the Powamuy. Both are involved in ceremonies that have been practiced for centuries.

For the Kachina Society, the initial stage of the initiation ceremony also takes place in a kiva that has been prepared with altars and mosaics. The activities begin with the Cloud Kachina telling the children of how the spirits came to live in the mountains and how they gave the gift of agriculture to the Hopi. This is followed by the arrival of several other kachinas known as the "Mudheads," who touch each child with a ceremonial ear of corn. Then, in the most dramatic part of the initiation, two Ho Kachinas (sometimes spelled "Hu") enter, accompanied by a female figure known as Angwusnasomtaka or the Crow Mother. The Ho Kachinas then administer the whipping that leaves most of the children wailing in terror and pain. This turbulent activity wraps up the first step of the Kachina Society initiation.

The final part of the initiation takes place two days later. This is the *bean dance*, which is attended by all of the initiates of both societies, as well as other members of the community. When the costumed kachina dancers enter the kiva for this event, they no longer wear masks. Suddenly, the children can see that the kachinas are actually members of their community who have taken on the guise of the spirits.

Customs and Symbols

Altars

Set up in the kiva, the altars contain a variety of items to be used in the ceremony, including a jug of water collected from a sacred spring, cornmeal, kachina dolls, ears of corn, and the *tiiponi*—a sacred fetish that is constructed of a corn ear, feathers, and other materials.

Bean Dance

Held three days after the first part of the Powamuy Society initiation and two days after the Kachina Society's whipping, the bean dance is the final part of the children's rite of passage. Though the dance is held every year, children are prevented from attending until they have been through the other initiation rites. Therefore, they are shocked to see the unmasked kachinas who perform at the dance. The children are warned that they must never tell younger children the secret they have learned. In this way, the mysteries of the initiation are preserved.

Ceremonial Parent

A child's ceremonial parent (a girl has a ceremonial mother, a boy has a ceremonial father) is somewhat similar to a godparent, though there are rules that require the ceremonial parent to be from a clan other than the one that the child belongs to. This serves as a means of giving the child a connection to a different part of the Hopi community. The ceremonial parent helps to prepare the child for the initiation and attends the ritual. During the whipping, they hold the child and may help the youngster by taking some of the blows.

Cloud Kachina

Known as Tcowilawu or Muy'ingwa, this figure represents rainfall, and he appears during the initial rites of both societies. In the first part of the Powamuy initiation, the costumed person representing this kachina carries a *poota*—a plaque that contains pages with sun, rain, and lightning symbols on them. He opens and closes these pages as he dances, while society elders sprinkle him with sacred water and cornmeal. In the initial Kachina Society ceremony, the Cloud Kachina sprinkles water on the initiates and tells them about the kachinas.

Cornmeal

As with many other Hopi ceremonies, cornmeal—a staple part of the tribe's diet—is used as a sacred element. The initiates sprinkle it on the altar and mosaics as a blessing, and it is also bestowed upon the kachinas.

Kiva

A kiva is a circular underground meeting place used for various ceremonial purposes, including the initiation ceremonies. The design of the kiva reflects Hopi mythology. Each contains a small hole near the fire pit called the *sipapu*, which represents the entrance place where the Hopi entered the present world from an underworld. (The myths say that the original entrance took place at the bottom of the Grand Canyon.) Likewise, the kiva is entered and exited by way of a hole in the roof, so when someone leaves the kiva, they climb a ladder and emerge through the portal into the above-ground world.

Sand Mosaics

These pictures created with colored sand are laid out on the floor of the kiva for the ceremonies. In the Powamuy Society initiation, there is a single mosaic that has a design of clouds and squash blossoms. For the Kachina Society initiation, there are two: one depicts the Ho Kachinas, the other represents the six directions (east, west, north, south, up, and down) and the "road of life" that extends to the east.

Whipping

Even before the lashing starts, the Ho Kachinas and Crow Mother attempt to make themselves as scary as possible to the children by stomping upon the roof of the kiva before they enter, then shouting and jumping once they have taken up their positions near the sand mosaics. The ceremonial parents then bring the children forward—the boys naked, the girls clothed—and hold them as the kachinas administer four lashes to each child with whips made from the blades of a yucca plant. These are by no means light beatings. Often, the ceremonial parent will lessen the boy or girl's pain by taking two of the four lashes in place of the child. Once all of the children have been whipped, the two Ho Kachinas proceed to whip one another before departing.

Further Reading

Loftin, John D. *Religion and Hopi Life in the Twentieth Century*. Bloomington: Indiana University Press, 1991.

Waters, Frank. *Book of the Hopi*. New York: Penguin, 1977.

BAR MITZVAH AND BAT MITZVAH

Customs and Symbols: Aliyah, Blessings, Celebration Party, Charitable Act, Derashah, Haftarah, Tallit, Torah Scroll, Yarmulke

The Jewish rituals that mark attainment of religious maturity, bat mitzvah and bar mitzvah take place around age 13 and are centered around the performance of synagogue religious readings that demonstrate the child's familiarity with the Torah, the Judaic scriptures. This rather straightforward religious observance is often accompanied by a social celebration—sometimes quite lavish—which allows the child's coming of age to be shared by friends and family.

History and Significance

These coming-of-age rites are based on ancient Jewish religious and legal concepts, which hold that a female is considered an adult at age 12 and a male at age 13. Upon reaching that age, the girl or boy was considered responsible for their actions and was expected to fulfill the commandments specified in the Torah. This is the basis of the terms "bat mitzvah" and "bar mitzvah," which mean "daughter of the commandments" and "son of the commandments," respectively. Thus, the terms can be applied to the person as well as the ceremony, so a young man undergoing the ceremony may himself be referred to as a "bar mitzvah."

For males in pre-modern times, reaching the age of 13 also meant that they could participate fully in religious rituals, and this formed the basis of the initial bar mitzvah observances. In traditional Jewish worship, male members of the congregation are eligible to deliver readings from the scripture during services at the synagogue, so it became customary for a boy to deliver his first reading when he turned 13. This practice is thought to have begun in the Middle Ages. At that time and for many centuries thereafter, only males conducted the readings; women had a very limited role in worship services.

Writings of the 16th century refer to a celebratory feast held at the time of the 13th birthday, and this was the beginning of the social aspects of bar and bat mitzvah. As European Jews gained greater social freedom during the Enlightenment, these celebrations became increasingly elaborate, especially among more liberal members of the faith. This custom spread to the U.S., and to other branches of Judaism, and by the 1900s, even many of the conservative Jewish congregations had adopted the bar mitzvah celebration. The creation of a religious and social observance for girls

The bat mitzvah and bar mitzvah ceremonies provide a meaningful way to mark the end of childhood and the beginning of adult responsibility and do so in a way that links the young woman or young man to Jewish values and tradition.

occurred at about the same time, with the first American bat mitzvah ceremony taking place in 1922. By the 1970s the female rite had become common in many American congregations, with the exception of Orthodox synagogues, which do not allow females to recite the Torah before the congregation. Instead, Orthodox synagogues hold a Bat Torah observance, which does not involve a public reading.

The bar mitzvah and bat mitzvah ceremonies can be significant undertakings, both for the young man or woman undergoing the rite and for their family. If the religious aspect of the observance is carried out in the traditional manner, a person needs to spend several years in study before they can successfully read from the Torah scrolls, which are written in Hebrew. (Less demanding approaches are allowed in some synagogues, such as allowing a person to read from text in which the Hebrew phrases have been rendered in the Roman alphabet.) In addition, most 12- and 13-year-olds find that the prospect of performing before a congregation calls for more than a little courage. The parents' responsibilities include getting the child properly prepared for the ceremony and also planning the celebration, which can be quite involved. Most families find the rewards to be well worth the effort, however. The ceremony provides a meaningful way to mark the end of childhood and the beginning of adult responsibility and does so in a way that links the young woman or young man to Jewish values and tradition.

Observance

Though ancient Jewish texts recognized a difference between the adult age of females (age 12) and males (age 13), most bar and bat mitzvahs now take place near the thirteenth birthday. The religious portion of the ceremony takes place at a synagogue during a regular service when a Torah reading takes place. Most bar and bat mitzvahs occur during a Saturday, or Shabbat, service, though they can also be held on a Monday, Thursday, or Friday, depending on the synagogue.

The young person's reading takes place during the Torah service—the time when a portion of the scripture is recited—but their recitation usually comes last. The earlier passages are delivered by a professional reader and are interspersed by blessings that are often given by members of the young person's family. Finally, the young man or woman is recognized for their *aliyah*. They are usually attired in the traditional *tallit* prayer shawl and *yarmulke* head covering, though members of some

Reform and Reconstructionist synagogues may not wear these items. Taking the Torah scroll in hand, they recite the appropriate Torah passages in Hebrew, followed by the appropriate *Haftarah*. In some cases, they may also present a *derashah*, or sermon, about the passages in question.

When the synagogue service concludes, there is usually a celebration party, which may be as simple as a small luncheon or as elaborate as a themed reception with entertainers and party favors. Partying is not the only way to mark the occasion, however. The family, or the young man or woman celebrating their coming of age, may carry out a charitable act in honor of the bar mitzvah or bat mitzvah.

Customs and Symbols

Aliyah

The act of going before the congregation to perform a reading is known as an aliyah, which means "to ascend." The term refers to the physical climb that the person makes to take their place on the synagogue's elevated platform, or *bimah,* and also to the spiritual elevation that results from this act. Being "called to the Torah"—that is, reading from the Hebrew version of the Judaic scriptures before the synagogue congregation—is considered a high honor, and adult members of the religious community are given this opportunity on occasions other than the bar or bat mitzvah.

If completed in the traditional manner, the Torah reading is not simply a matter of reading aloud from a text. The words are in Hebrew, which requires the young woman or man to have a command of that language. Also, the Torah scroll is rendered in its original style, with no vowels and no punctuation marks, making the reading much more difficult. In training, the individual uses a modernized version of the text that helps them to learn the proper pronunciation, but many synagogues do not allow that aid to be used during the ceremonial reading. Finally, some bar and bat mitzvah candidates don't simply speak the words, they chant them to a specific melody. In such cases, they must learn and practice the musical aspects of the Torah, as well as the words.

Blessings

The different sections of the day's Torah reading are usually preceded and followed by the recitation of a blessing. This occurs in all Torah services, but when a bar or bat mitzvah take place, these blessings are used as a way to honor certain members of the young person's family—usually the parents and sometimes grandparents, siblings, or other significant relatives. The chosen individuals carry out their own

Making Decisions

For some families, planning the party serves as the primary bar mitzvah undertaking. In the following recollection in *Bar Mitzvah Disco,* David Measer recalls his 1980s bar mitzvah and how organizing the elaborate reception became another way of gaining maturity.

"You need a theme. Everyone has one. It's kind of like your image."

The voice was my mother's, tinged with competitive vigor and a caffeinated edge. I was twelve and a half years old. My image, as far as I could tell, revolved mostly around Atari Missile Command, hating my sister, and *Dukes of Hazzard* reruns. Coming up with a theme was a difficult task. I liked ice cream, what did that say about me? I had recently started taking classical guitar lessons. Maybe my theme could have something to do with music?

"That's it!" my parents exclaimed and began writing checks.

aliyah: they ascend the bimah and recite the appropriate passage. This serves as a way to allow the larger family to commemorate this special day.

Celebration Party

The tradition of holding a *seudat mitzvah*—a festive meal—following the synagogue service has been around for centuries. Initially, this was a rather simple affair, and for some families it still is. The basic requirements are kosher wine, which is part of many Jewish rituals, and challah (egg bread), over which the motzi blessing is stated. Some families expand on this to host a simple meal (usually lunch following the morning service) that might be held in a social room at the synagogue.

Conversely, some families opt for extremely lavish productions in place of, or in addition to, the post-service meal. These might include hundreds of guests, floral arrangements, expansive buffets, an open bar, and professional entertainers. The more opulent affairs can rival large weddings in their cost and complexity and, as with weddings, may sometimes serve as a display of the family's wealth and popularity. Attendees usually bring gifts, and in the case of a large gathering, the young person may end up with a significant amount of money. More than a few young

> And I began making decisions. My mother and I went on excursions to scout locations for the reception. My father and I snuck into a few Bar Mitzvah receptions to listen to prospective bands. I picked the Sound Company because of their expertise with the Duran Duran catalog. My grandfather chipped in after he found a crate of junked 45s in a dumpster in Hollywood (Men at Work's "Overkill" must have been selling surprisingly badly) and we began to craft elaborate centerpieces from the little records. It was the most exciting time of my life. . . .
>
> After I'd decided on the theme, I began to realize something was different. I was involved. Up until then, nearly all the decisions in my life were left to the grown-ups: the schools I attended, the clothes I wore, what I ate for breakfast. But now big decisions suddenly required my input. . . . It seemed the entire community of family, friends, and party profiteers were looking at me in a whole different way. They seemed to be treating me . . . well, like a man. And they were collectively telling me: "We think you're cool."

people have relied on their bar and bat mitzvah gifts to finance a portion of their college education.

Charitable Act

There is a long history of families making the bar mitzvah or bat mitzvah an occasion for giving a contribution to help others. In some cases, a gift is given to the synagogue—either a cash contribution or a specific item such as prayer books or religious art. Money may also be donated to outside organizations. Sometimes it is the parents of the young person who make the contribution, but in other cases the young person may donate a portion of the money he or she received as gifts. This is considered significant because it may be the person's first giving of *tzedakah* (a charitable contribution), which is one of the responsibilities of being an adult member of the Jewish faith.

Derashah

In some bar mitzvah and bat mitzvah ceremonies, the young man or young woman delivers a short discussion of the Torah reading once the scriptures have been recited. Known as the derashah, or the *d'var Torah*, this commentary allows the person to display the knowledge they have gained in their religious studies and is seen as a further mark of their maturity and intelligence.

Haftarah

In addition to the Torah passages assigned to them, the bat mitzvah girl or bar mitzvah boy usually also recites the Haftarah. This is a passage from Neviim, also known as the Prophets, which forms another part of the Tanakh or Jewish Bible. While not part of the Torah itself, these passages came into use in ancient times when Jews were prohibited from reading from the Torah, and they have remained part of Jewish worship ever since. (The written portions of the Torah and much of the Prophets are also part of the Christian Bible.)

Tallit

The tallit (also spelled "tallith") is the shawl that is worn during prayer. More significantly, it is worn by adult Jews, so when the young person observing their bar mitzvah or bat mitzvah dons the tallit, they are adopting an important symbol of their mature religious status. Traditionally, only men wore the tallit, and that remains true in more conservative congregations. In such cases, the tallit would not be part of the bat mitzvah, and some conservative Jews do not observe bat mitzvah at all. Conversely, Jews on the liberal end of the spectrum may choose to not wear the prayer shawl. Tallits are available in different styles and colors, but all have four corners where tassels of white knotted fringe, known as *tzitzit*, are attached—a requirement that comes from the Torah commandment that Jews must "make tassels on the corners of their garments throughout their generations."

Torah Scroll

Each synagogue owns one or more scrolls that contain the text of the Torah written in its original Hebrew form. Known as the Sefer Torah (Torah Scroll), these are considered sacred objects of the highest order. The parchment is made from the skin of a sheep or some other animal, and the text is handwritten in natural vegetable-dye ink. The parchment is rolled onto wooden handles known as the Trees of Life. When not in use, each scroll is wrapped in embroidered fabric and stored in the Holy Ark, or *Aron Ha-Kodesh*, which is located on the synagogue bimah.

Depending on the congregation, special scroll ceremonies may be observed when a bat mitzvah or bar mitzvah is taking place. In the *l'dor va-dor* (meaning "from generation to generation"), several generations of the family gather, and the scroll is passed from one to another—for instance, the young person's grandparents hand it to the parents and the parents, in turn, hand it to the boy or girl celebrating the bar mitzvah or bat mitzvah. This symbolizes the passage of the Jewish faith through the generations. A procession then takes place, with the young person carrying the

Torah around the synagogue followed by the family as well as a rabbi and cantor (a person who leads songs and prayers in the synagogue).

Yarmulke

A yarmulke (pronounced *yar-muh-ka*) or *kippah*, is a small beanie-style cap worn by some Jews. Practices regarding the yarmulke are similar to those of the tallit: in conservative congregations only males wear them (and may wear them at all times), while some liberal Jews forego them. For those in the middle of the spectrum, the cap is worn during worship, and women, including bat mitzvah participants, are usually allowed to wear them.

Further Reading

Bennett, Roger, Jules Shell, and Nick Kroll. *Bar Mitzvah Disco: The Music May Have Stopped, but the Party's Never Over.* New York: Crown, 2005.

Diamant, Anita, and Karen Kushner. *How to Be a Jewish Parent: A Practical Handbook for Family Life.* New York: Schocken, 2000.

Moskovitz, Patti. *The Complete Bar/Bat Mitzvah Book: Everything You Need to Plan a Meaningful Celebration.* Franklin Lakes, NJ: Career Press, 2000.

Weber, Vicki L. *The Rhythm of Jewish Time: An Introduction to Holidays and Life-Cycle Events.* West Orange, NJ: Behrman House, 1999.

CONFIRMATION

Customs and Symbols: Chrism, Confirmation Name, Confirmation Party, Invocation of the Holy Spirit, Laying on of Hands, Preparation Classes, Renewal of Baptismal Vows, Service Project, Sign of Peace, Sponsor

Originating in biblical passages regarding the transference of the Holy Spirit, Roman Catholic confirmation has evolved into a ceremony that marks a young person's coming of age. Because most Catholics are baptized at birth, confirmation serves as a means for affirming the religious vows that were originally made by their parents. This marks the participants' growing maturity and allows them to explore and strengthen their faith in preparation for the responsibilities and challenges they will face as adolescents and adults.

History and Significance

The rite of confirmation has changed a great deal throughout the history of Christianity. The practice is based upon passages in the Bible that suggest that the acts of baptism and the receiving of the Holy Spirit are two different things. In a passage from the Acts of the Apostles, for instance, it is said that a group of new initiates didn't receive the Holy Spirit until the apostles Peter and John "laid their hands on them." This "laying on of hands" became a key part of being inducted into the faith, as did the practice of anointing the person with chrism, a sacred oil that is a mixture of olive oil and balsam. Both acts were practiced in the early centuries of the Christian era, but there was no separate confirmation ceremony at that time because these actions took place at the time of baptism. This was true for both infants and adults, and that practice is still observed by Eastern Orthodox Christians (*see* **Baptism**).

Originating in biblical passages regarding the transference of the Holy Spirit, confirmation has evolved into a ceremony that marks a young person's coming of age.

The Roman Catholic Church of western Europe, however, developed a distinction between baptism, which could be performed by a priest, and the giving of the Holy Spirit, which could only be performed by a bishop (a more senior member of the clergy who oversees all the churches in a particular region). Because bishops couldn't be present for every baptism in every church in their diocese, confirmation ceremonies were delayed until the bishop could visit. Initially, confirmation followed soon after baptism, usually by age two, but in later centuries the rite became a part of later childhood and served as a counterpart to infant baptism. It allowed a person to affirm their belief in Jesus once they had reached "the age of reason"—the time when they were mature enough to understand the main principles of the faith. For Roman Catholics, confirmation is one of the three essential sacraments of initiation into the faith, the other two being baptism and the Eucharist (*see* **First Communion and Reconciliation**).

The age at which confirmation takes place has varied a great deal, however, and has generally moved upward in recent times. In the 1900s, the common Catholic practice was to confirm children at age 10. Today, it is more common for a young person to be confirmed during their teenage years. The precise actions that take place during confirmation have also undergone change. Beginning in the 1500s, the rite included a light blow or tap on the cheek, which became popularly known as "the bishop's slap." This symbolized the fact that a believer must be willing to suffer for their faith. Since the 1970s, that aspect of the ceremony has been omitted.

Observance

Individuals who wish to be confirmed in the Roman Catholic Church attend a long series of preparation classes. The participants also take part in a charity service project prior to confirmation to reinforce the Christian concept of giving to others. They also may select a confirmation name. In most cases, each young man or

Confirmation among Other Christians

The churches that separated from the Roman Catholic Church during the Reformation generally do not consider confirmation to be a sacrament. However, some denominations, such as the Lutherans and Episcopalians, do conduct confirmation activities that are similar to the Roman Catholic rite and treat it as an important means of affirming a person's faith as they reach an age of greater responsibility. On the other hand, those churches that reject the idea of infant baptism do not carry out a confirmation ritual of this type. Instead, the "believer's baptism" that often takes place in later childhood or adolescence serves as the affirmation of faith.

young woman being confirmed has an older sponsor (and sometimes more than one) who is intended to guide and advise the young person, both during the confirmation process and afterward.

The confirmation ritual itself usually takes place as part of a regular church service, but it is scheduled to coincide with the visit of the bishop. Because such visits are limited, a group ceremony is conducted in which the bishop administers to all of the eligible candidates at one time. During the rite, the candidates make renewal of baptismal vows, through which they declare their belief in and dedication to Christian principles. The gift of the Holy Spirit is then conferred in two steps. The first is the invocation of the Holy Spirit, in which the bishop extends his hands above the entire group and recites a prayer. He then performs the laying on of hands to each person individually, which symbolizes that they have been sealed with the Holy Spirit. As part of this process, they are anointed with chrism. The ceremony concludes with the sign of peace, after which the newly confirmed member of the church is often honored with a confirmation party.

Customs and Symbols

Chrism

The same oil used in baptism, chrism is a mixture of olive oil and balsam that has been made sacred by being blessed by a member of the clergy. The application of chrism during the laying on of hands is symbolic of the strengthening of spirit inferred by confirmation, and the oil also stands for the richness and sweetness that believers find in the Christian faith.

Confirmation Name

Most Catholics choose an additional name for themselves that is officially bestowed at the confirmation ceremony. This is typically a Catholic saint that the person closely identifies with, and the selection of the name may play a part in the religious studies that precede the ceremony.

Confirmation Party

After the church service, the newly confirmed person is often honored at a gathering of family and friends. Usually, this takes place at the family home. The honoree receives gifts, which may consist of religious books and items (such as a rosary or crucifix), money or savings bonds, or perhaps a combination of these.

Invocation of the Holy Spirit

In this part of the ceremony, the bishop raises his hands above the group being confirmed. This gesture has been used since the earliest days of Christianity to symbolize that the Holy Spirit is being passed from a member of the clergy to a member of the laity. The bishop then speaks a prayer of invocation that asks God to grant the Holy Spirit to the confirmation group.

Laying on of Hands

In the central act of the confirmation ceremony, the bishop physically places his hands upon each person being confirmed. This is accomplished through the application of chrism. The bishop moistens his fingers with the oil, then marks the sign of the cross on the forehead of the person being confirmed. This is accompanied by the words, "Be sealed with the gift of the Holy Spirit." This act indicates that the person has been marked as belonging to Christ and can share fully in his mission and protection.

Preparation Classes

Catholics prepare for the ceremony either through their classroom studies, if they attend a Catholic school, or by attending catechism instruction organized by the parish Confraternity of Christian Doctrine (CCD). The studies are thorough: the CCD classes, for instance, usually begin a year in advance of the ceremony and involve homework assignments in addition to classroom studies. The idea is to make sure that the individual understands all of the basic theology of the faith prior to confirming their allegiance to the Church.

Renewal of Baptismal Vows

In this part of the ceremony, the candidates affirm the promises that were made by their parents at the time of baptism. Essentially, the person being confirmed must renounce Satan and affirm their belief in the Christian concepts of God, Jesus Christ, and the Holy Spirit.

Service Project

As part of their preparation, confirmation candidates are usually expected to complete some type of activity that proves their willingness to help those in need. Often, this is a group project that might include all of the young men and young women hoping to be confirmed at a particular time. In other cases, the candidate may need to compile a certain number of hours—30, for instance—on different kinds of charitable work, such as volunteering at a homeless shelter or collecting items for a charity organization.

Sign of Peace

To conclude the rite, the bishop or other presiding clergy tells the candidates, "Peace be with you." Known as the sign of peace, this phrase is also part of the Catholic mass and other Christian services, when it is usually exchanged between the members of the congregation during the worship service.

Sponsor

Just as an infant being baptized has godparents who vow to assist in their religious upbringing, the young man or young woman being confirmed has one or more sponsors who are pledged to assist them before and after the ceremony. When possible, one or more of the baptismal godparents may become a confirmation sponsor, but the restrictions on who can serve as sponsor are generally more strict than those governing the selection of godparents. The sponsor must be an active member of the church, while godparents sometimes are not. In addition, the sponsor usually needs to be age 16 or older, to have undergone their own confirmation, and to have participated in the sacrament of the Eucharist.

Web Sites

"Article 2: The Sacrament of Confirmation." United States Conference of Catholic Bishops, undated.
    http://www.usccb.org/catechism/text/pt2sect2chpt1art2.htm

"Guidelines for Preparation and Celebration of the Sacraments of Initiation for the Diocese of Fort Worth." The Catholic Diocese of Fort Worth, undated.
    http://www.fwdioc.org/img2/fFormation/SacramentalGuidelines5_29_03.pdf

Further Reading

Isca, Kay Lynn. *Catholic Etiquette: What You Need to Know about Catholic Rites and Wrongs.* Huntington, IN: Our Sunday Visitor, 1997.

QUINCEAÑERA

Alternate Names: Fiesta de Quince, Fiesta de Quince Años

Customs and Symbols: Altar Pillow, Court of Honor, Crown, Doll, Dress, Food, Medal, Missal and Rosary, Ring, Shoes, Sponsors, Toasts and Poems

An important event in Hispanic-American culture, the quinceañera marks a girl's transition to adulthood. The event takes place at the time of her 15th birthday and typically includes a church service followed by a reception. Both parts of the celebration are invested with objects and activities that symbolize the young woman's life-changing transition.

History and Significance

The word quinceañera (pronounced *keen-say-an-YER-ah*) derives from the Spanish words for 15, *quince* (pronounced *KEEN-say*), and years, *años* (pronounced *AN-yos*); it refers to both the celebration and the young woman. The exact origins of the quinceañera observance are uncertain, but these events have taken place since at least the late 19th century. Some writers have traced elements of the quinceañera back to ancient Aztec and Mayan initiation rituals as well as Christian initiation rites. Experts have also noted resemblances between the traditional first waltz of the quinceañera dance and 16th-century Spanish court dances. Yet, direct links are difficult to trace. Whatever its earlier sources, the quinceañera proper became common in Mexico and other parts of Latin America, as well as in those regions of the U.S. that had a large Hispanic population. In fact, in some areas along the U.S.-Mexico border, Anglo Americans also adopted the custom. Quinceañera celebrations have spread throughout the U.S. as the number of Latin American immigrants have grown. The tradition is strongest among the country's Mexican-American, Cuban-American, and Puerto Rican populations.

It is unclear why this coming-of-age ritual for girls occurs at age 15, rather than 16 or some other nearby age. One writer cites an old belief among indigenous people of Mexico that

The quinceañera marks a girl's transition to adulthood and typically includes a church service followed by a reception. Both parts of the celebration are invested with objects and activities that symbolize the young woman's life-changing transition.

a child does not become a person until reaching the age of 15. Another notes a Mexican law that girls were recognized as adult women at age 14, after which they could legally marry.

The quinceañera is a major event in the life of a teenage girl, marking her transformation into an adult woman. It is often compared to her wedding day in terms of its significance. She may now be allowed to partake in adult activities, as well as share in adult responsibilities. Church services often stress that the girl will henceforward be considered an adult member of the congregation. In social terms, the event has much the same symbolism as an Anglo-American **Debutante Ball.** The party serves to introduce the girl into society as an adult, and paves the way for dating. It may be the first formal event at which she is allowed to wear high-heeled shoes and make-up and dress as a woman.

Observance

Preparations for the celebration are begun many months in advance, as there are often extensive logistics to be worked out, including the coordination of the many friends and family members who take part in the activities. The observance begins with a religious ceremony. Among Roman Catholics, this is a *misa*, or mass, which may be specially scheduled for the quinceañera or may be incorporated into a regularly scheduled mass at the family's church. The mass starts with the entrance of the friends and relatives who form the Court of Honor, or *corte de honor*, who sit in the front pews. Next in procession is the *madrina de cojin*, a young girl who carries the altar pillow. Then comes the quinceañera herself, either alone, with one or both of her parents, or with her male escort. Sometimes other sponsors are also part of the procession and carry symbols of earlier sacraments, such as a baptism dress, items from the girl's first communion, or photographs of earlier sacramental occasions (*see* **Baptism** and **First Communion and Reconciliation**). The female sponsors are also known as madrinas, and they are often responsible for providing the symbolic items used in the ceremony.

The service may include a number of different themes: the beginning of adult responsibilities in the church, family, and social life; the importance of family, community, God, and religion; and gratitude for life, love, and health. Indeed, the mass is often referred to as the *misa de acción de gracias*—the mass of thanksgiving. In addition, the girl may receive the sacrament of **Confirmation** during her quinceañera.

After the religious ceremony, the party assembles at a private home or a dance or banquet hall for the reception. As at the mass, the honoree and her court, parents, and sponsors make a formal entrance. Most families retain either a musical group or a deejay, who announces the arrival of the participants and begins the music. Traditionally, the first song has been the waltz, the "Sobre las Olas"; nowadays, it may also be "A Ritmo de Bals." The quinceañera dances this first waltz with her father. The members of the court of honor join in the next dance, then all in attendance may dance. After the dancing, guests partake of the food, including cake, and there are also appropriate toasts.

Customs and Symbols

Altar Pillow (El Cojin)

During the church ceremony, the quinceañera is required to kneel at certain moments. A younger girl, in the role of the madrina de cojin, carries the pillow to the altar during the opening procession of the mass for the girl to kneel on. The pillow is specially decorated for the occasion and inscribed with the quinceañera's name.

Court of Honor (Corte de Honor)

The traditional court of honor is made up of 14 friends or relatives selected by the quinceañera so that, when counting the quinceañera, there are a total of 15 attendants. However, a girl may invite fewer attendants or elect to have no court. The young men are called *chambelánes*, or escorts, and the young women are known as *damas*, or ladies. The honoree also chooses a male friend or relative to be her personal escort. The attendants play special roles during the mass as well as the reception, including a traditional dance at the latter. They practice for the event in several rehearsals ahead of time. Many Roman Catholic dioceses require the attendants to participate in religious education classes as well as the sacraments of reconciliation and communion prior to the celebration.

Crown

As part of a traditional outfit, the quinceañera wears a crown or tiara. This headpiece can be an arrangement of artificial flowers or made of rhinestones or glass beads or—for those who can afford the expense—crystal, silver, or gold. The crown has some religious implications. According to one writer, it serves as a "symbol of sharing in the mission of Christ as Priest, Prophet and King." It's also symbolic of the fact that, for this one special day, the young woman is treated as royalty.

Doll

As a symbol of her transitional status, the quinceañera is given a last doll at the reception, which often serves as a lifelong keepsake. One of the madrinas or

> *As a symbol of her transitional status, the quinceañera is given a last doll at the reception, which often serves as a lifelong keepsake.*

sponsors, is typically responsible for selecting and purchasing this gift, which is presented to the quinceañera during the reception, usually after the formal dancing. This custom seems to have begun during the 1970s in Mexico and spread to the U.S. Sometimes delicate and large porcelain dolls, up to three feet in height, are given, though more modest Barbie dolls are also common. Whichever doll is chosen, it is dressed to closely match the quinceañera's outfit. In some cases, a large number of special ribbons printed with the girl's name and date of her celebration are attached to the doll. The honoree removes these and distributes them to the guests.

Dress

The quinceañera wears an elaborate ensemble rivaling that of a bride. In the United States, many girls wear beautifully embellished white dresses, similar to American wedding dresses. In Mexico, quinceañera dresses are more often created in pastel colors. The traditional quinceañera dress has a close-fitting bodice and a wide, belled skirt. The ladies of the court wear matching formal dresses in a color and style chosen by the quinceañera. The escorts wear matching suits or tuxedos.

Food

Traditional foods at a quinceañera feast include *pollo en mole* (chicken in a dark chili sauce), tamales, *pozole* (a stew made with corn and meat), *cabrito* (fried or roasted goat), and cake. Such foods are also standard celebratory fare for Hispanics at other special occasions, including baptisms and weddings. In past years, the meal was usually prepared by family members. Today it is more common for the meal to be catered, which means that traditional specialties are less commonly served than they used to be.

Medal

One of the important quinceañera gifts provided by the madrinas is a gold religious medal. When the celebrant is of Mexican descent, the medal usually contains an image of Virgin of Guadalupe, an apparition of the Virgin Mary who is considered a divine protector by many Mexicans and Mexican Americans. In wearing the medal on a chain around her neck, the quinceañera signifies her devotion to Mary and the Christian faith and also shows her wish for divine protection as she goes forward into adulthood. During the mass, the priest blesses the medal. Afterward, the young woman may go before a statue or image of the Virgin and make an offering of a rose—the flower that symbolizes Mary's purity. The medal is usually engraved with the young woman's name or initials and the date of the quinceañera, so that it will serve as a keepsake of the event.

Missal and Rosary

Traditional Roman Catholic devotional items, the missal, or *libro*, is a small book of selected Bible passages, and the rosary, or *rosario*, is a beaded necklace with a crucifix attached that's used in reciting the rosary prayers. In most cases, the quinceañera will already own children's versions of these items, but for her quinceañera celebration, she is given adult-style versions.

Ring

Either her parents or a madrina gives the quinceañera a ring to wear, though in some cases a bracelet is substituted. If given by the parents, the ring is usually gold and is presented as part of the religious ceremony. If a sponsor gives the ring, it may contain the celebrant's birthstone. Sometimes, grandparents pass along an heirloom ring. Regardless of its style, the ring stands for the quinceañera's new ties and responsibilities to God and her community. She traditionally wears it on her left hand until she gets engaged or married, when a new life phase begins.

Shoes

The quinceañera wears flat shoes to the religious ceremony and to the reception. At the reception she ceremoniously changes into high-heeled shoes, or *zapatillas*, before the first waltz. Often her father or a male relative will change her shoes for her, as another signal that she is now a woman.

Sponsors

Many families invite extended family members and friends to be sponsors of the young woman—a role similar to that of being a godparent in a baptism. Male sponsors are called *padrinas* and female sponsors are called madrinas. The sponsors of a quinceañera assist and welcome the girl as she enters adulthood. They also help with the often enormous cost of a quinceañera celebration by taking responsibility for arranging and paying for various elements of the event. Madrinas traditionally provide such items as the doll, medal, and altar pillow. Padrinas often assume the duties of securing the reception site and decorations, music, cake, and champagne for toasts. But sponsors of both genders can contribute to any aspect of the celebration.

Toasts and Poems

At the reception, the quinceañera's father generally begins the toasting, although this can also be done by the girl's escort or a master or mistress of ceremonies. A customary toast recognizes the girl's transition into womanhood, offers advice, and expresses best wishes for her new role. Adults drink champagne, while younger attendees usually drink sparkling water. Other family members and friends may also recite poems written in honor of the occasion, either at the mass or at the reception.

Further Reading

Alomar, Ladan, and Mary Zwolinski. "Quinceañera! A Celebration of Latina Womanhood." *Voices: The Journal of New York Folklore* 28 (Fall-Winter 2002). http://www.nyfolklore.org/pubs/voic28-3-4/onair.html

Lankford, Mary D. *Quinceañera: A Latina's Journey to Womanhood.* Brookfield, CT: Millbrook Press, 1994.

WHITE MOUNTAIN
APACHE SUNRISE CEREMONY

Alternate Names: Apache Mountain Spirit Dance, Na-ih-es, Na'ii'ees

Customs and Symbols: Blessing the Sick, Cane, Cattail Pollen, Ceremonial Dress, Crown Dancers, Molding, Running Ritual, Sponsor, Sunrise Dance, Symbolic Tipi

The multi-day sunrise ceremony observed by the White Mountain Apache of Arizona commemorates a female's attainment of sexual maturity. It involves singing, dancing, and other activities that link a young woman's coming of age to the mythical past of her people.

History and Significance

While many traditional Native American customs have disappeared in the modern era, the sunrise ceremony continues to be practiced—though it, too, is less common than it used to be. The prolonged ceremony seeks to impart beneficial qualities upon the initiate as she takes on the rights and responsibilities of an adult woman. This is accomplished by having her reenact the story of Changing Woman, a supernatural figure who plays a large role in the White Mountain creation story.

Among her other qualities, Changing Woman represents longevity because she is said to have the power to regain her youth. The activities of the sunrise ceremony are, likewise, said to grant a long life to the initiate, as well as giving her other positive qualities, such as strength, prosperity, and a positive disposition. In fact, by completing the ceremony's cycle of dances, the young woman is believed to take on the sacred powers of Changing Woman, and she is expected to use them to help others. For instance, people suffering illness may come before the girl, and she will bless them in hopes of giving them some of her healing power. Another spiritual force is invoked by the appearance of the crown dancers, who represent the *Gaan*—mountain spirits that are believed to drive away evil. Their performance is intended to create positive conditions as the girl makes her transition to womanhood.

Observance

The sunrise ceremony takes place after a girl has experienced her first menstrual cycle, though it's common to delay the ritual until a specific time of year—usually in the summer—which gives friends and family time to make plans for the gathering.

Apache Puberty Rites

The White Mountain tribe is just one of several Apache groups in the U.S. The others—the Chiricahua, Jicarilla, and Mescalero—observe a girl's coming of age with ceremonies that are similar to the White Mountain sunrise ceremony, though also distinctive in certain ways. The Chiricahua, for instance, observe many of the same activities but also paint the initiate's face white because this links her to White Painted Woman, a figure that is very similar to Changing Woman. The Mescalero observe a similar custom, but their mother figure is named Isanaklesh. In the traditional Jicarilla ceremony, the girl undergoing the ceremony is accompanied by a boy of her age group on many of the dances, which allows the ceremony to serve as a type of rite of passage for the boy as well as the girl.

The size of these ceremonies is one of their most distinctive traits: dozens of people may attend, and they must be fed for the four days that the ceremony lasts. In addition, singers, musicians, and dancers are hired, so the cost of the celebration is significant. Some families find it beyond their means, and this is one reason why the ritual is less common than it used to be. However, in many cases, the extended family will help underwrite the expense. Financial assistance may also come from the woman who serves as the initiate's sponsor. This figure is usually a mature friend of the family who aids the young woman throughout the ceremony and is somewhat similar to a godmother.

On the first day, a symbolic tipi is constructed to house the ritual activities that will take place. Soon after, a medicine man blesses the ceremonial dress that will be worn by the girl, a cane, and various other sacred items used in the ceremony. On the morning of the second day, the sunrise dance is performed by the girl and her sponsor. It is during this dance that the girl is believed to take on the powers of Changing Woman, which she then uses in blessing the sick. The initiate also receives blessings, which take place when adult guests at the ceremony sprinkle cattail pollen on her head.

Throughout the four days of the ceremony, the initiate must observe certain guidelines that are related to the sacred quality she is believed to possess. She can only drink through a straw, because if she touches water directly, it's believed that she will bring rain. If she scratches her skin with her fingernails, she will be scarred, so she is given a special scratching stick to prevent this from happening. She also must maintain a serious demeanor because if she laughs a great deal during the ceremony, she is said to become prematurely wrinkled.

Beginning on the second evening, four or more crown dancers perform a dramatic set of dances, representing the Gaan mountain spirits, who are thought to create good fortune for the girl and those attending the ceremony. The crown dancers and the girl dance on subsequent days as well, and the girl also completes a running ritual. When the ceremony concludes after four days, the initiate's supernatural powers come to an end, but she is then considered a woman and is eligible for marriage.

Customs and Symbols

Blessing the Sick

When the initiate takes on the spirit of Changing Woman during the sunrise dance, she is believed to have the power to help those who are suffering from illness or otherwise need assistance. During the ceremony, they come before the girl, and she blesses them in hopes of giving them some of her qualities of longevity and strength. The girl will usually lay her hands on the person and then turn them to each of the four directions. In this way, the girl's coming of age becomes an event that also benefits the wider community.

Cane

Representing long life, the cane is made of wood and usually has bells, feathers, and ribbons attached to it. The initiate holds it during her dances, and it is also used in the running ritual.

Cattail Pollen

The Apache consider the pollen from the cattail plant to be a sacred substance that represents the life-giving quality of the earth. To invoke its power for the young woman, guests at the ceremony sprinkle the pollen on her head.

Ceremonial Dress

The girl undergoing the ceremony dons a bright yellow dress on the first day and wears it for the remainder of the ritual. Her sponsor sometimes wears one in a similar style. Traditionally, these were made of buckskin but now are often fashioned from cloth.

Crown Dancers

Wearing elaborate costumes that include enormous wooden headdresses and black hoods, the crown dancers are the most exciting element of the ritual. There are usually four of them along with a fifth clown-like figure, and they perform a long series of athletic dances around a huge bonfire, sometimes on their own and sometimes with the initiate. Impersonating the mountain spirits known as the Gaan, they are believed to have the power to drive away evil, and so are essential to making the ceremony an auspicious event.

Molding

At one point during the ceremony, the girl lies on a piece of buckskin, and the sponsor massages her entire body. It is said that this causes the girl to be "molded" into the proper form so that she will have strength and good health.

Running Ritual

In this part of the ceremony, the girl's cane is stuck into the ground in specific places, and she runs to it and circles it, returning to her starting point. This symbolizes the different stages of life she will pass through. The girl then makes four additional runs to the four cardinal directions. Small children sometimes accompany the girl during the running.

Sponsor

As she enters adulthood, the girl has the assistance of an older female who helps her make the transition. In addition to molding the initiate and participating in the sunrise dance, the sponsor often contributes money to finance the ceremony.

Sunrise Dance

The central action on the part of the girl is the sunrise dance, which takes place early on the second day of the ceremony. Accompanied by the sponsor, the initiate faces east toward the rising sun and dances a specific program of songs, usually a total of thirty-two, with music provided by singers and drummers. The songs relate the story of Changing Woman, and in the course of this performance, the girl is believed to take on the holy powers of that figure.

Symbolic Tipi

The traditional house of the Apache people is the tipi. It is invoked in the ceremony, but rather than creating an actual tipi with walls, a ceremonial open-air structure is made lashing together four spruce poles in a tipi shape. It provides a ceremonial enclosure, but the open design allows the guests to view the ritual.

Web Site

"The Sunrise Dance." Peabody Museum of Archaeology and Ethnology, undated. http://www.peabody.harvard.edu/maria/Sunrisedance.html

Further Reading

Ganteaume, Cécile R. "White Mountain Apache Dance: Expressions of Spirituality." In *Native American Dance: Ceremonies and Social Traditions*, edited by Charlotte Heth. Washington, DC: National Museum of the American Indian, Smithsonian Institution, 1992.

LAKOTA AWICALOWANPI CEREMONY

Alternate Names: Buffalo Ceremony, Išnati Awicalowan

Customs and Symbols: Buffalo Skull, Dance, Dress Exchange, Hair Parting, Sacred Person, Sacred Pipe, Water and Chokecherries

Based in the Great Plains region, the Lakota people once relied upon hunting buffalo (bison) for their livelihood, and that heritage still plays a large role in the Awicalowanpi puberty ritual that is observed for females. Calling on the imagery and behavior of the buffalo, the rite also links a girl's sexual maturity to the sacred figure White Buffalo Calf Woman.

History and Significance

Historians believe that the Lakota, a group that is part of the Seven Fires or Great Sioux Nation, became bison hunters in the 1700s, at the same time they adopted use of the horse. Awicalowanpi, sometimes known as the Buffalo Ceremony, developed after that point and continued to be practiced even after the wild buffalo herds were destroyed in the late 1800s and the Lakota were confined to reservations. The ritual weakened in the 1900s as the tribe was subjected to greater Euro-American influences, but it underwent a resurgence in the 1980s and continues to be a part of puberty for many Lakota girls.

The buffalo's role in the ceremony stems from the fact that the spiritual force of the animal is believed to guard over a woman's chastity and her ability to have children. Thus, the ritual is intended to insure that the woman behaves properly as a sexually mature person. The ceremony also invokes White Buffalo Calf Woman—the spiritual figure who is said to have given the Lakota their seven sacred rites, including Awicalowanpi. According to Lakota tradition, White Buffalo Calf Woman also gave the people the gift of the sacred pipe, which is the means by which they communicate with the spiritual world and all creatures of the universe. As with the other seven rites, the pipe is used in the puberty ceremony.

Observance

Once a girl experiences her first menstruation, a ceremonial lodge is erected that contains an altar with various sacred items, including a buffalo skull and a sacred pipe. The ceremony is conducted by a sacred person (usually a man) who dons a buffalo headdress. At the outset, the girl who is undergoing the initiation sits cross-legged before the altar. The sacred person smokes the pipe and blows smoke into the buffalo skull. He or she then paints a red line on the forehead of the skull and recites various lessons about how the young woman should be industrious, wise, cheerful, and avoid evil influences.

The central performance of the rite is a dance in which the sacred person moves close to the initiate, imitating the behavior of a male buffalo prior to mating. Assuming the role of a female buffalo, the girl drinks from a bowl of water and chokecherries, which is then shared among the guests. Next, the dress exchange takes place, with the initiate removing her child's dress and putting on an adult-style dress. Two additional actions denote the female's new status: she now sits with both legs to one side, as is customary for adult women, and in the hair parting, her hair is arranged in an adult style and a red line is painted along her scalp. After the ceremony ends, a feast is held in the girl's honor.

Customs and Symbols

Buffalo Skull

To invoke the sacred presence of the buffalo spirits, a skull from one of the animals is placed upon the altar. By first painting a red line upon the skull and then, later, upon the initiate, it is believed that the protection of these spirits is transferred to the young woman undergoing the ceremony.

Dance

In the dance portion of the ritual, the sacred person repeatedly sidles up to the initiate in the same way that a male buffalo approaches a female during mating season. Each time this occurs, the girl's mother places pieces of sage in the girl's lap and under her arms in order to repel him.

Dress Exchange

One of the most direct symbols of the initiate's new status comes when she gives up her child's dress and puts on one that is associated with a mature woman. The child's dress is then placed on top of the buffalo skull. In doing this, the sacred person announces that the dress is an offering to White Buffalo Calf Woman, though a needy member of the community may also claim it.

One of the most direct symbols of the initiate's new status comes when she gives up her child's dress and puts on one that is associated with a mature woman.

Hair Parting

After the initiate has donned her adult dress, her mother parts her hair and arranges it so it falls in front of her shoulders, as is the adult custom. A red line is then painted on the girl's forehead and back along the part in her hair, linking her to the spiritual force symbolized by the similarly painted buffalo skull.

Sacred Person

The figure who presides over Lakota rituals, the sacred person is usually a man, though women sometimes fill the role. For the Awicalowanpi ceremony, the sacred person wears a buffalo headdress and also a buffalo tail so that he or she impersonates the buffalo spirits that interact with the initiate.

Sacred Pipe

According to Lakota tradition, the first item that White Buffalo Calf Woman bestowed upon the people was the sacred pipe. Often adorned with eagle feathers and carved with images of buffalo and other animals, the pipes can measure a foot and a half in length. When not being used, its bowl and stem are disconnected to put the pipe in a "safe" mode so that its spiritual powers won't accidentally cause harm.

Water and Chokecherries

These two items are placed in a bowl and are said to represent a buffalo watering hole. When the initiate drinks from the bowl, she symbolizes her role as the female buffalo. The bowl is then passed to all of the people attending the ceremony, and each drinks a small amount of the water. This signifies the connection between the young woman and the wider Lakota community, which will be important as she takes on greater responsibilities in the coming years.

Further Reading

Powers, William K. *Oglala Religion.* Lincoln: University of Nebraska Press, 1977.

VISION QUEST

Customs and Symbols: Directional Poles, Sacred Person, Sacred Pipe, Shelter, Sweat Lodge, Visions, Vision Interpretation

A traditional rite practiced by many Native American groups, the vision quest is often used by young people to gain spiritual guidance as they enter adolescence. As the name indicates, the person undergoing the ceremony seeks some type of prophetic vision and submits to several days of isolation, thirst, and hunger in order to achieve it.

History and Significance

The vision quest was practiced by a wide range of tribes both before and after contact with Europeans and Euro-Americans. The ritual could be used to gain insight about a variety of subjects, but it was commonly observed for the first time when a person reached puberty and sought help in coming to terms with their maturity. The vision quest became less common after the native people were forced onto reservations, but it never completely disappeared. The tradition remains particularly strong among the tribes of the Great Plains, such as the Seven Fires or Great Sioux Nation, which includes the Lakota people. The following description is based on the Lakota rite, which is sometimes known as *hanbleceya*—"crying for a vision." Other tribes that still practice the vision quest may follow somewhat different procedures, though the basic idea of undergoing isolation and deprivation in order to receive a guiding vision is common to all.

While the intention of the rite is to communicate with spiritual forces—known as *Wakantanka* among the Lakota—and to receive some type of defining vision, not every seeker is successful in this regard. Even so, the act of going through the quest can serve as an important coming-of-age ritual that shows that the boy or girl has courage and the ability to withstand hardship in pursuit of greater self-knowledge.

Though the strict practices outlined below aren't especially widespread, the basic idea behind the rite—that some kind of essential truth can be obtained through self-imposed isolation and hardship—has found a great deal of appeal in the wider American society. Many believers in New Age spiritual practices find value in vision quest-style rites. Traces of Native American practices can also be found in **African American Rites-of-Passage Programs**, **Unitarian Universalist Coming-of-Age**

Programs, and a number of other recently created activities aimed at helping adolescents come to terms with their maturity.

Observance

In the past, the ceremony was primarily practiced by boys, but since the 1970s, an increasing number of girls undertake the quest. Though the vision quest itself is experienced in solitude, the rite requires the assistance of a tribal sacred person. To formally request this guidance, the person wishing to undertake the vision quest presents a sacred pipe to a spiritual figure in the community. If the sacred person agrees to help, the pipe is smoked, and preparations for the quest are made. The sacred person, the vision seeker, and some of the seeker's relatives participate in a sweat lodge ceremony to purify themselves, then travel to a remote location, often a hillside, where the quest will take place. Directional poles are erected, and in many cases, a pit shelter is dug and covered with branches.

> *The basic idea behind the vision quest—that some kind of essential truth can be obtained through self-imposed isolation and hardship—has found a great deal of appeal in the wider American society, especially among believers in New Age spiritual practices.*

The seeker is then left alone, and if the quest is practiced in the traditional manner, they wear minimal clothing, perhaps only moccasins and undergarments, though they are often provided a buffalo robe for additional warmth. The boy or girl remains alone for a specified length of time—usually one to four days—during which time they cannot eat or drink. They are instructed to keep their sacred pipe with them at all times and to conduct prayers at regular intervals. Over the course of their sojourn, it is hoped that they will receive one or more visions, which can take many forms. At the appointed time, the sacred person returns to collect the seeker. After participating in another sweat lodge ceremony, the sacred person offers a vision interpretation, which provides the seeker with a better understanding of what he or she experienced.

Customs and Symbols

Directional Poles

Erected around the shelter, these poles indicate the four cardinal directions, which have spiritual meaning for many Native American groups. Often, strips of cloth of different colors and offerings of tobacco are attached to the poles. At dawn on each day of the quest, prayers are made at each of these poles.

Sacred Person

A sacred person acts as an intermediary between the supernatural world and the common people, and many of them often enter their calling after receiving a powerful vision of their own. In assisting a young person's quest, the sacred person (who can be a man or a woman, though is more commonly a man) performs many of the preparations for the rite and participates in the purifying visits to the sweat lodge. Once the quest concludes, the sacred person provides the all-important vision interpretation.

Sacred Pipe

Most of the religious rites of the Plains tribes involve an elaborately decorated ceremonial pipe, which is believed to have great spiritual power. In the vision quest, the pipe is used in two ways. First, it is smoked to create a bond between the sacred person and the seeker before the quest begins. Then, as the seeker sets off on the sojourn, he or she is provided with a pipe that has been loaded with tobacco and sealed with tallow. It is believed that if the seeker holds onto the pipe throughout their vision quest without smoking it, they will be protected from harm.

Shelter

In many vision quests, the seeker is provided a shallow pit covered with branches as a shelter, and he or she might be instructed to remain inside for most of the sojourn, emerging only to pray. In other cases, the seeker spends most of the quest on a bed made from sage branches that is constructed at the center point of the directional poles.

Sweat Lodge

Used as a means of purification and spiritual renewal, the sweat lodge is a circular structure made of saplings covered by animal skins. During a ceremony, the participants enter, and hot stones are placed in a pit in the center of the lodge. After the door is closed, water is poured on the stones to create steam, and prayers and songs are chanted. A person undergoing a vision quest participates in a sweat lodge ceremony both before and after their sojourn, accompanied by the sacred person and some of their relatives.

Visions

The vision or visions that a person receives during their quest can involve an endless list of elements. Often, it's said that messages are delivered by animals, especially birds. Natural forces, such as wind, rain, and lightning, may also be

A Vision Recalled

The famous Lakota (Oglala Sioux) holy man Black Elk (1862-1950) related this vision to anthropologist Joseph Epes Brown in the late 1940s. Brown included it in his volume *The Sacred Pipe: Black Elk's Account of the Seven Rites of the Oglala Sioux,* 1953.

Often during the day as I was crying and sending my voice, birds and butterflies would come to me, and once a white butterfly came and sat on the end of the pipe stem, working his beautiful wings up and down. During this day I saw no large four-leggeds, just the little peoples. Then just before the sun went down to rest, I saw that clouds were gathering and the Thunder-beings were coming. The lightning was all over the sky, and the thunder was terrifying, and I think that perhaps I was a little afraid. But I held my pipe up and continued to send my voice to *Wakan-Tanka;* and soon I heard another voice saying: 'Hee-ay-hay-ee-ee! Hee-ay-hay-ee-ee!' Four times they said this, and then all the fear left me, for I remembered what the little bird had told me, and I felt very brave. I heard other voices, also, which I could not understand. I stood there with my eyes closed—I do not know how long—and when I opened them everything was very bright, brighter even than the day; and I saw many people on horseback coming towards me, all riding horses of different colors. One of the riders even spoke to me saying: 'Young man, you are offering the pipe to *Wakan-Tanka;* we are all very happy that you are doing this!' This is all they said, and then they disappeared.

significant. In addition, some seekers speak of harmful spirits who try to scare them and force them to give up their quest. It's also possible that the person will receive no vision, but the ritual can be repeated if desired.

Vision Interpretation

Following the sojourn and the second sweat lodge ceremony, the seeker tells the sacred person their visions. The sacred person then provides the seeker with an interpretation, which may have implications for the person's future. For instance, a person who has a vision that is judged to be very powerful might be told that he or she should seek to become a sacred person. Other visions might indicate that the seeker is well suited for a particular vocation.

Further Reading

Brown, Joseph Epes, ed. *The Sacred Pipe: Black Elk's Account of the Seven Rites of the Oglala Sioux.* Norman: University of Oklahoma Press, 1953.

Powers, William K. *Oglala Religion.* Lincoln: University of Nebraska Press, 1977.

THERAVADIN BUDDHIST NOVICE MONKHOOD

Alternate Name: Temporary Ordination

Customs and Symbols: Buddhist Precepts, Departure Ceremony, Meditation and Chanting, Monastery Residence, Monk Robe, Ordination Ceremony, Serving the Buddhist Community

Becoming a monk usually means making a lifetime commitment to religious study, but for Theravadin Buddhists, this is not always the case. It is common for boys or young men raised in this tradition to become novice monks for a limited time. This step is considered a sign of greater maturity and also a way to bring spiritual merit to themselves and to members of their family.

History and Significance

Theravadin Buddhism is common in parts of south and southeast Asia, and the tradition of becoming a novice monk is strong. Because an increasing number of immigrants from these countries have arrived in the United States in recent decades, the practice has come to North America. However, the influence of Western culture and the relative lack of monasteries mean that the practice is much more limited in the U.S. than it is in Asia. Only males become novice monks. While women can become spiritual leaders in Theravadin temples, that usually only occurs after their childbearing years have come to an end. Novice ordination is the also the first step toward becoming a permanent monk.

For young men who have been raised in the U.S., the experience of becoming a novice monk is a powerful means of connecting with the Buddhist heritage of their ancestors.

The Theravadin faith places a lot of emphasis on gaining merit, which is often termed "good karma" by Westerners. The best way to do that is to observe proper behavior, and the strict regimen that must be followed at a Buddhist monastery is focused on observing appropriate actions. Because merit can be transferred from one person to another, it's believed that the young novice's presence at the monastery will benefit his parents as well as himself. Also, some Theravadins believe that a novice can aid those who have died, so a boy may enter a monastery shortly after a relative passes away.

In addition to the spiritual benefits it is thought to bring, becoming a novice monk is also considered a sign of maturity. By submitting to the restrictions of monastic life, the young man shows that he can accept responsibility and hardship. In some Theravadin communities, a person who has undergone the novice initiation is considered preferable as a marriage partner. For young men who have been raised in the U.S., the novice experience is a powerful means of connecting with the Buddhist heritage of their ancestors. In addition, older adults may also become temporary monks at certain times in their lives, for example, when starting a new job or upon entering retirement.

Observance

The age of novices varies, though many are in their early teenage years. The young man must leave his home and reside at a Buddhist monastery, with the length of the stay ranging from one day to several months. The initiate is officially brought into the monastic community through the ordination ceremony. During this rite, his head is shaved, he dons his monk robe, and he must repeat phrases in Pali—the traditional language of the Theravadin religion. Afterward, he is assigned to a monastery residence that he shares with other monks. While at the monastery, the novice must follow the specified Buddhist precepts and also take part in the daily activities. A typical routine begins before dawn, when the monks rise and conduct a meditation and chanting session. Further meditation and chanting may also take place in the evening. The novice participates in serving the Buddhist community, often by accompanying more experienced monks in their visits. In keeping with the precept on eating, the novice and all the other monks consume all their meals before noon. When the novice's stay comes to an end, he takes part in a departure ceremony before returning to his home.

Customs and Symbols

Buddhist Precepts

All Buddhists—whether monks or lay people—are expected to follow five basic precepts of proper behavior, which are known as the *panca sila*: do not kill, do not steal, do not misuse sexuality, do not lie, and do not take intoxicating substances. The novices are expected to follow these guidelines, and they may also obey additional precepts, depending on the monastery. The more common prohibitions include not eating any solid food after noon each day, avoiding worldly amusements (which can mean a ban on watching television and playing video games), and doing without a luxurious sleeping place (in some places the novices may be provided a thin mattress on the floor). Some monasteries also prohibit them from wearing personal adornments such as hats, watches, and jewelry, and from handling money. While this can be a strict regimen for the novice, it is a mere hint of the 227 precepts that full-fledged monks are expected to follow. The Buddhist tradition, however, views this discipline as a spiritually beneficial "Middle Way" between self-denial and self-indulgence.

Departure Ceremony

To commemorate their return to normal life, a departure ceremony takes place. During this observance, the novice again recites phrases in Pali and then exchanges his monk robe for his regular attire.

Meditation and Chanting

Formal meditation and chanting serve as a type of worship for many Buddhists. Monks typically engage in a group session in their residence as soon as they awaken and may repeat the process later in the day. Some monks recite phrases in Pali as part of their meditation.

Monastery Residence

At most monasteries, the novice is assigned to a communal living quarters that might house two or three other monks. These residences are generally very sparse, in keeping with the idea that the monks should devote their thoughts to spiritual matters. This is reflected in the simple sleeping mattress they are provided as their beds.

Monk Robe

The traditional attire of the monks is made from three pieces of fabric, often in a burnt-orange color. It includes an inner garment, an upper robe, and an outer robe that is wrapped around the body and draped over one shoulder. Donning this attire is one of the most prominent symbols of the novice's new status. They are usually expected to wear nothing else, though monks living in states that have severe winters are often allowed to wear warmer clothing along with their robes.

Ordination Ceremony

To mark their entrance into the life of a monk, the novice undergoes a special ceremony, which is usually attended by their family members. Their hair and eyebrows are shaved, and the parents and siblings often participate by snipping off some of the young man's hair before he is completely shaved by a monk. The novice must also repeat phrases and recite the precepts using the Pali language. During the ceremony, the novice begins by wearing white robes, which are exchanged for the monk's orange robes. Another traditional part of the ceremony has the novice throw coins to those in attendance, as an illustration of his commitment to renounce worldly values.

Serving the Buddhist Community

The novice usually assists other monks in performing blessings or other beneficial acts for the lay people who attend the monastery's temple. This is often accomplished by visiting the homes of the laity or, in some cases, their businesses. This custom comes from the idea that a lay person can gain merit by having a monk perform rites for them, and in return, the lay person usually provides the monk with food or some other gift, which helps support the temple.

Web Site

"I Was a Novice Monk," by Panrit "Gor" Daoruang. ThailandLife.com, undated.
    http://www.thailandlife.com/monk.html

Further Reading

Seager, Richard Hughes. *Buddhism in America*. New York: Columbia University Press, 1999.

Photo on facing page: For many teens, learning to drive is a critical step toward independence.

Chapter 8: New Privileges and Responsibilities

INTRODUCTION

A young person moving toward adulthood inevitably takes on more of the activities associated with being a mature, independent person, including **Driving** and going out on a **First Date**. The first experiences in these activities become important rites of passage that usually take place in the early- to mid-teenage years. While eagerly anticipated by most youths, both undertakings come with significant risk and require the young person to behave in a mature manner in order to avoid problems that can be life-changing or life-threatening.

Because of the serious consequences associated with these activities, participation is often a gradual process. Parents may require early dates to be group outings, for instance, or may ask to meet the person their son or daughter is going out with. Teens are also eased into driving, with most states requiring them to compile significant practice hours in the presence of an adult before being turned loose on their own. Such safeguards can only go so far, however. At some point each young person faces these adult activities on their own, along with all of the complicated choices they entail. At that point they usually find that the challenge isn't simply to take part in these grown-up pursuits, but to handle them as a grown up should, in a careful and responsible manner.

While dating is a self-directed means of beginning the search for an appropriate romantic companion, there are other, more controlled ways to achieve the same goal. The **Debutante Ball** is a holdover from more conservative and class-conscious times. In its traditional form, it allowed a young woman to formally present herself as a candidate for marriage and took place in an exclusive atmosphere that assured that the debutante and her audience were of the appropriate social standing. High-class affairs of this type continue today, though there tends to be less emphasis on marriage as a direct outcome. In addition, more egalitarian debutante celebrations now allow a wider range of young women to take part and may serve as a symbol of maturity more than an invitation to potential suitors.

DRIVING

Customs and Symbols: Driver Education Course, Examinations, First Car, First Traffic Crash, Solo Driving, Supervised Driving, Unlicensed Driving

For many Americans, driving an automobile is essential to their way of life and offers a sense of independence that is considered an important aspect of adulthood. In gaining the right to legally drive, many youths believe they're hitting the fast lane to maturity, but they usually find that the freedom that's available on four wheels also comes with many responsibilities.

History and Significance

The difficulty and danger involved in operating a motor vehicle has made it an activity that's off limits to children. However, driving is one the earliest adult-oriented privileges granted, with most young people earning their license in their middle teen years. This gives it a special significance as a coming-of-age rite, but the youthful age of beginning drivers also increases the odds that they will be involved in crashes. According to 2004 statistics from the Centers for Disease Control, drivers between the ages of 16 and 19 are four times more likely to be in a crash than older drivers, and two of every five teenage deaths in the United States resulted from a vehicle mishap. The high accident rate stems from several sources. Young drivers are inexperienced, of course, but also are more likely to engage in dangerous behavior, which includes everything from speeding to drinking and driving.

In seeking to reduce these dangers, many states enforce a "graduated driver license" system that places extensive restrictions upon teens during their first years on the road. The licensing systems also have precise instructional and examination requirements that must be mastered to attain a license. But becoming a driver can be viewed as a multi-part test. The second portion comes after the young person receives their license and must show that they can safely operate a car on their own. Yet another challenge involves the vehicle they drive. When they first hit the road on their own, most teens are using someone else's car, but sooner or

The youthful age of beginning drivers increases the odds that they will be involved in crashes. Drivers between the ages of 16 and 19 are four times more likely to be in a crash than older drivers, and two of every five teenage deaths in the United States resulted from a vehicle mishap.

later, they face the challenge of paying for their own ride. This becomes yet another milestone of maturity and serves as an important sign that they are capable of supporting themselves in the adult world.

Observance

Some youths are introduced to automobile operation even before they enter an instruction program, when they engage in unlicensed driving, either on their own or with the assistance of someone older. Legal vehicle operation begins with the driver education course. Upon successfully completing this instruction, the young person is usually provided with a restricted license, sometimes known as a learner's permit, which allows them to engage in supervised driving in which they are accompanied by an adult. The prospective driver usually faces several different examinations in the course of completing the license requirements. The most nerve-wracking exams come with the written and road tests that must be passed so that they can earn a less-restrictive license that allows them to engage in solo driving. Many teens view this as the culmination of the driving challenge, but further adventures lie ahead. Unless they are exceedingly lucky, they will at some point experience their first traffic crash, and the first car financed solely by the young person can be a learning experience related to judgment, financial planning, and realistic expectations.

Customs and Symbols

Driver Education Course

A general formula for driver education courses is that they provide 30 hours of classroom instruction and 6 hours of practice time behind the wheel in the presence of an instructor. States that have a graduated driver license system may divide the instruction into two portions: part one takes place before the young person receives their initial license that allows supervised driving; the rest occurs after they have gained some road experience. As part of the process of instilling responsibility in the teen, many courses require perfect attendance in order to receive a passing grade.

Examinations

Driving exams come in various forms. The driver education course will likely involve written and skills tests that must be passed prior to completion. Some states may also require one or more written exams administered by the licensing agency, in which the prospective driver must demonstrate their mastery of laws and safe-driving concepts. The most significant challenge comes with the skills test or road test that must be passed before a youth is allowed to drive on their own.

First Car

Driving a car is one challenge; paying for one is another—and perhaps a better introduction to the difficulties of adulthood. An automobile is often the first large-scale purchase that a person makes, which introduces them to the process of keeping their desires matched to their budget. Being able to afford a car usually means that the youth must be employed, which reinforces the idea that the privilege of driving has a definite cost, both in terms of money and in the time that must be devoted to earning that money.

First Traffic Crash

A person's first traffic mishap tends to teach the serious nature of driving in a way that no classroom lecture is capable of. The response to the crash is often a learning experience in itself, especially when the youth is at fault. More than a few new drivers have fled the scene of their first parking-lot fender bender, trying to evade the repercussions of their mistake. Others prove their maturity by owning up to their actions and facing the resulting penalties and parental disappointment.

Solo Driving

One of the most powerful moments of youthful freedom comes when a teen is allowed to take to the road for the first time without supervision. Previously, when they didn't have the ability to move themselves over large distances, their life had restrictive boundaries; but with license in hand, it seems they can go anywhere and do anything. What many end up doing, however, is driving in a reckless manner, and this has caused many states to keep some reins on the young motorists even after they are no longer required to have an adult supervisor. Frequently, there are limitations on the number of teenagers that may be in the car with a first-year driver, and teens may also be prohibited from operating a vehicle during certain hours—for instance, between midnight and 5 A.M.

Supervised Driving

The first restricted license or learner's permit obtained by teens allows them to drive when accompanied by an adult over age 21. The people most likely to be doing the supervising are, of course, the teen's parents. This brings the parent and teen together in a situation that often proves stressful for both but hopefully results in a stronger relationship and a more skilled driver.

Unlicensed Driving

Though authorities do not condone the practice, many young people begin their driver education in an informal manner. Often, this takes place when a parent gives their son or daughter the opportunity to pilot the family car on a remote road, perhaps limiting the danger by sitting in the driver's seat with the young person so that they can take control of the vehicle if necessary. This serves as recognition of the young person's growing maturity, and the event is likely to become a cherished memory of parent-child bonding, assuming all goes well. Far more dangerous is the practice of young people driving a car without adult supervision. In cases where the "borrowed" car belongs to a stranger, the learning experience may be deemed grand theft auto—a rite that can mark the young person's passage into a juvenile detention facility.

Web Sites

"Saving Teenage Lives: The Case for Graduated Driver Licensing." "Traditional Driver Licensing vs. Graduated Driver Licensing." National Highway Traffic Safety Administration, undated.
http://www.nhtsa.dot.gov/people/injury/newdriver/SaveTeens/toc.html

"When Kids Drive." LHJ.com (Ladies Home Journal), undated.
http://ww4.lhj.com/lhj/story.jhtml?storyid=/templatedata/bhg/story/data/10815.xml
&categoryid=/templatedata/lhj/category/data/Teens.xml

Further Reading

Finch, Christopher. *Highways to Heaven: The Auto Biography of America.* New York: Harper-Collins, 1992.

FIRST DATES

Alternate Name: Going Out

Customs and Symbols: Asking for a Date, Car Dates, Goodbye Kiss, Group Dates, Parental Meeting

A powerful milestone in growing up, the first date shows that a young man or woman has gained the confidence to undertake a potentially romantic relationship.

History and Significance

With its long and varied history of social customs, dating has become an essential part of mainstream American culture. For many modern youths, the first date stands as one of the most exciting and challenging rites of passage, partly because dating requires a significant personal investment and places an adolescent's delicate self-esteem at risk. To declare interest in another person, a teen must be willing to reveal his or her feelings, and he or she must be willing to withstand the inevitable awkwardness that can accompany initial social outings.

Observance

Many teens begin their romantic relationships through group dates, in which a number of couples go out together. When carried out in a more formal manner, however, the process begins with one of the parties asking for a date. The person who initiates the date is usually responsible for planning and paying for the outing. A successful date often requires a teen to master logistics with which they have had little experience. They may have to plan an activity that is fun and sufficiently impressive, come up with enough money to finance the outing, and arrange transportation. While the actual activities of the date can vary widely, most end with the crucial moment when the goodbye kiss takes place—or not.

A young person's first date usually involves their parents to some degree. In many cases, teens must secure their parents' permission to go on their first date, and some parents may require the youths to take part in a parental meeting before they are allowed to go out. Other parents allow only group dates or forbid car dates until their children reach a certain age. Parents may also be called upon to provide transportation for the outing, particularly if the teens are too young to drive or do not have access to an automobile.

Despite the seemingly universal practice of dating among American teens, some young people do not date at all. Certain religious and cultural traditions prohibit young people from spending any time with members of the opposite sex either in groups or alone, while others place certain restrictions around the custom of **dating**.

Customs and Symbols

Asking for a Date

Asking someone for a date is often fraught with anxiety and fear of rejection. In the past, social conventions held that males should make the request for a date. However, it has become just as common for females to ask for a date.

Car Dates

The lore surrounding "car dates" has a long and rich history, and access to an automobile is still an important factor in dating. Teens who have not yet received their driver's license are often reliant on a parent to provide transportation for the outing. This allows parents some measure of control over the date, and the ability to monitor what happens during the date. Once the teens are able to drive themselves, there is far less opportunity for parental oversight. Car dates sometimes raise parental concerns about safety, particularly regarding teenaged drivers and the possibility of undesirable situations such as underage drinking or sex.

Goodbye Kiss

The goodbye kiss at the end of a first date has become an important rite of passage all its own. Whether or not the kiss is offered and accepted, what type of kiss it is, how long the kiss lasts, and whether it is deemed to have been a good kiss are all factors that contribute to the overall success or failure of the date. A successful goodbye kiss usually also indicates that the relationship has romantic potential.

Group Dates

Many teens begin with group dates that involve several couples. This allows them to ease into the world of dating, with their friends close by to smooth over awkward moments and provide moral support. Parents often support group dates, believing that they are safer than one-on-one outings. Some parents limit their children to group dates until they reach a certain age.

Parental Meeting

Some parents require a face-to-face meeting with the person their son or daughter wishes to date. While this can occur in advance of the actual outing, it more often takes place at the time of the date. For the person undergoing the scrutiny, such meetings are usually perceived as yet another anxiety-producing test that they must pass to proceed with the relationship.

Further Reading

Campbell, Joy. "The Dating Scene: Teen Board Panelists Say Group Dating Less Stressful," *Owensboro (KY) Messenger-Inquirer*, October 24, 2006.

Fox, Annie. *Can You Relate?: Real World Advice for Teens on Guys, Girls, Growing Up, and Getting Along.* Minneapolis: Free Spirit, 2000.

Turner, Jeffrey Scott. *Dating and Sexuality in America: A Reference Handbook.* Santa Barbara, CA: ABC-Clio, 2003.

DEBUTANTE BALL

Alternate Name: Cotillion

Customs and Symbols: Ball Gown, Curtsey, Dances, Escort, Presenter, Private Party

Usually associated with the American upper class, the debutante ball was created as a means for affluent parents to formally announce that their daughters were old enough to marry and to show off the young woman's grace and wealth to suitors of the proper distinction. While such class-conscious displays have become less common, they have not disappeared, and in some cases, the basic concept of a formal debut has been adapted for use by those outside high society.

History and Significance

American debutante balls, or cotillions, became common in the late 1800s and were based on the practices of English royalty at that time. During the reign of Queen Victoria, the daughters of the newly wealthy industrialists and merchants were presented at court, with the intention that this "coming out," or debut, would allow them to marry a suitor who came from high society or nobility. The well-to-do in the U.S. borrowed the custom, but because there was no royal court, the presentation took place at a formal reception, tea, or ball. The ceremony announced that the debutante (derived from the French word *debuter*, meaning "one who begins") was available for marriage and that she expected to marry someone of the upper class. The debuts were sometimes group events sponsored by an exclusive social club, with multiple debutantes being featured. The most affluent and image-conscious families held their own extravaganzas where one daughter would be the undisputed center of attention for the evening.

The tradition of dressing the debutante in a special gown and having her perform specific curtsies and dances was originally designed to show off her beauty and grace, and some contemporary observers see this emphasis on physical attributes as demeaning.

Classic high-society debutante balls reached their peak in the U.S. during the early 1900s. They have become much less common in the decades since, though they still exist, particularly in the South. Their waning popularity results partly from the weakening of strict class distinctions and also because the debuts are often viewed as being sexist. The tradition of dressing the debutante in a special gown and having her perform specific curtsies and dances was originally designed to show off her beauty and grace, and some contemporary observers see this emphasis on physical attributes as demeaning.

Two innovations have altered the image of the debutante balls to some extent, however. First, some minority and immigrant groups sponsor debuts. Though social prestige is often a factor in who takes part, participants are sometimes selected based on other criteria. For instance, some African-American cotillions select participants based on their educational accomplishments rather than their wealth. Second, debutante gatherings now often serve as fundraising events for charity. In such cases, the exclusive nature of the old balls has eased. Participation is usually open to anyone paying the required fee, and the events tend to place less emphasis on presenting the young women as potential marriage partners.

In fact, even in the case of the more exclusive debutante presentations, marriage isn't usually a direct outcome of the ball. Like other Americans, young women in these social circles tend to delay matrimony until later in life. The person they ultimately marry may have no connection to their official debut, but the debutante ball does tend to give them a stronger connection to the social set of their parents.

Observance

The age at which a young woman becomes a debutante is variable, but usually ranges from the late teens to early 20s. The key activities of the ball revolve around the debutante's formal presentation to the attendees. Attired in a ball gown or other formal wear, she is called before the guests, accompanied by her presenter—who is usually her father. In a nod to the royal heritage of the ball, the debutante may complete a curtsey and is then escorted around the dance floor by the presenter. After all the participants have gone through this process, a series of dances takes place in which the debutante dances with both her presenter and an escort, who is a male of about her own age. Thereafter, the ball becomes a less structured party, where all the guests can take part in the dancing and where the debutantes can socialize with all of the guests. Many debutantes choose to have a separate private party of their own, which may take place several days before or after the ball itself.

The Ultimate Curtsey: The Texas Dip

Vendela Vida describes a Texas dip in her book, *Girls on the Verge:*

A Texas dip is quite literally a to-the-floor curtsey in which the debutante gets so far down on her high heels that her dress flares out around her like a marshmallow. As the coup de grâce, she lays her left ear on her lap for a moment. The reason she turns her head is to prevent getting a lipstick mark on her virginal white dress....

The point of the Texas dip is to make the debutantes look graceful, like swans. A ballet instructor attends the ball rehearsals to help the debs with their dips, and during the last rehearsal they wear heels rather than flats with their jeans.... Upon curtseying all the way to the floor in their heels and their hoops, a third of the debutantes require the help of their presenter's hand to get back to standing position. And even with assistance—or in some cases, rescue—from

Customs and Symbols

Ball Gown

Because most debutante balls are considered a means of showing off the young woman, the ball gown she wears for the ceremony becomes extremely important—a symbol of her refinement, taste, and, in some cases, her family's affluence. Not surprisingly, the choice of a gown is often treated with the same seriousness as a wedding dress, and if a designer-label dress is purchased, the cost of the gown can be one of the biggest expenses of the ball.

Curtsey

By bending their knee and lowering their bodies in a curtsey, the debutantes of the royal court showed their respect for the monarch. The tradition was continued in the non-royal debuts and is still found today, though it's mostly confined to the more formal and conservative ceremonies. As with the dances and the procession with her presenter, the curtsey can be viewed as a sign of the young woman's grace.

an extended gloved hand, they wobble and teeter like fawns standing on their legs for the very first time.

After observing several Texas dips at the River Oaks Country Club's 1997 debutante ball, I noticed a pattern: the girls who smiled widest before they curtsey are the ones who manage the Texas dip gracefully on their own. The debs with the widest smiles are smiling because they know they can do it—they've practiced for months in their sorority houses and in department store dressing rooms, in front of any full-length mirror they came across....

When done correctly, the debutante looks like a ballerina resting her head on a down pillow, prepared to dream of sugar plum fairies. When done incorrectly, she looks as though drunk and on the verge of passing out....Regardless of the outcome of the Texas dip, the audience applauds.

Dances

As at a wedding reception, a formal set of dances takes place at many balls. Their arrangement symbolizes the process that will occur in marriage, when the young woman leaves her parents and joins her husband. First, the debutante dances with her presenter, which is usually her father. Then, with a change of music, the escort replaces the presenter for a second dance, which makes for a type of "giving away" of the young woman (though the escort is usually not romantically attached to the debutante).

Escort

The sponsoring organization may arrange the escort or the young woman may choose the person herself, in which case a platonic male friend is the recommended choice, so that the debut isn't complicated by romantic entanglements. As befits the occasion, the escort is attired in a tuxedo or other formal wear.

Presenter

The person presenting the debutante is usually her father, though another male figure such as an older brother or stepfather may fill the role. In addition to their role during the dances, the presenter is formally announced, appears before the guests alongside the debutante, and escorts her in a review procession.

Private Party

Though the ball is the main occasion when the debutante is presented, many families desire a more personalized way to mark the event, so they host their own party, which may take place in a home or other venue. These can range from simple gatherings to elaborate celebrations that rival the grand debutante soirees of yesteryear. For those who wish to exhibit their wealth, the private party serves as a good way of doing so. Themed extravaganzas with multiple bands, gourmet food, and limitless alcohol can add many thousands of dollars to the significant expense of the ball itself.

Further Reading

Marling, Karal Ann. *Debutante: Rites and Regalia of American Debdom.* Lawrence: University Press of Kansas, 2004.

Vida, Vendela. *Girls on the Verge: Debutante Dips, Gang Drive-bys, and Other Initiations.* New York: St. Martin's, 1999.

Photo on facing page: On prom night, everyone wants to look their best before the pictures begin.

Chapter 9: School Events

INTRODUCTION

With the exception of college, which is considered more of an adult undertaking, school is associated with childhood. It is a time of learning and preparation when the student receives considerable support and supervision. When that period is over, young people are generally expected to behave more independently and to take a larger role in caring for themselves, which are hallmarks of being a mature person. Thus, the end of high school is often considered the beginning of adulthood, and two key events that occur during that period—**High School Graduation** and **Prom**—have become powerful coming-of-age rituals. In fact, the two activities can be viewed as different aspects of the same life-changing event—graduation being the more ceremonial activity and the prom being more social. Both signify the transition to a new, more responsible stage of life with an emotional goodbye to what came before.

SENIOR PROM

Alternate Name: Formal

Customs and Symbols: Body Enhancement, Dinner, Hair, Parties, Photographs, Prom Clothing, Prom Theme, Transportation

Serving as a more celebratory counterpart to the **High School Graduation**, the senior prom helps to mark the transition from the school years to adulthood. While it is partly about looking back and spending time with the friends made during high school, the formal attire and adult-style activities anticipate the grown-up world that lies ahead.

History and Significance

Though it's so ingrained into the American experience that it seems timeless, the prom didn't become a common high school occurrence until the 1940s, when it was adapted from formal tea dances and class banquets that had originated at colleges at the turn of 20th century. The event quickly became a crucial coming-of-age event, however, perhaps because it addresses several aspects of growing up simultaneously.

First, by donning formal clothes, confronting romance, and dining at refined, "grown-up" restaurants, the prom goers are making a sort of trial run at adulthood. The prom can even be interpreted as a type of dress rehearsal for the wedding that a young man or young woman may experience later. The second major significance of the prom is that it often serves as a farewell to the childhood school years. As such, it can be an emotionally charged parting and a celebration of release from the confines of school discipline. Some even approach the prom as a last-ditch means of improving their status, imagining that their image can be enhanced by making the proper statement in terms of their date, their clothes, and their transportation.

Such hopes are part of the romanticism of the prom experience, and there are many other similar fantasies: that the occasion will be a "perfect" evening of elegance similar to those portrayed in movies, television programs, and books; that the prom will create or strengthen a romantic relationship, hopefully leading to the "perfect" love glorified in so many songs and stories. Perhaps most importantly, many youths hope that on prom night the world will begin to acknowledge them as mature individuals and that a successful prom will be a symbol of the successful adulthood that lies before them. The reality of the event often fails to match these expectations, and learning to cope with the difficulty and disappointment of a less-than-perfect prom often becomes one of the most valuable lessons of the event.

Observance

Though the prom itself takes place on a single evening, it can involve months of preplanning as participants decide on their attire and date and undertake various forms of body enhancement so as to look their best. Most of the elements surrounding the prom symbolize the maturity of the participants. The formal prom clothing presents the young men and women as grown-ups attired in outfits associated with adult sophistication. The same is true of the hair styles worn by the attendees. Though not required, many prom goers make a statement with their transportation, as well. The special, extravagant nature of the event may also be emphasized by dinner in an upscale restaurant, either before or after the prom itself. The dance event itself is made distinctive through some type of prom theme and, in some cases, by taking place in a non-school location. Many couples attend parties after the dance ends, extending prom night into the wee hours. Some youths view the after-prom activities as an opportunity to partake in more dangerous adult activities such as drinking alcohol and having sex, which has led to efforts to create adult-supervised after-prom events.

Customs and Symbols

Body Enhancement

For many participants, looking good at the prom means more than having the right clothes. They also spend extensive time and money getting their bodies in top shape. This is more often a priority for the women than men, though both sexes may get in on the primping. Workout regimens may begin months in advance. Closer to the date, many prom-goers concentrate on achieving a good tan, employing tanning salons as needed. In the frantic last days before the prom, manicures and pedicures may be arranged, not to mention the hair styling, which is a subject in its own right.

Dinner

Some of the more elaborate proms may include a sit-down meal at the dance itself, but many prom-goers arrange their own meal. In doing so, they are reinforcing the idea that they are capable of making adult-style decisions. In keeping with the emphasis on sophistication, formal restaurants are often preferred.

Arriving at the Prom in Style

In his book *Wonderland,* journalist Michael Bamberger offers the following description of the arrival of promgoers from Pennsbury High School in Fairless Hills, Pennsylvania:

> When they arrived at the red-carpet entrance, they no longer looked like kids. They no longer resembled their everyday selves. The girls—the young *ladies*—wore gowns, their hair up and cleavage exposed. There were peach gowns and sky-blue gowns and floral gowns; the girls in them looked like bridesmaids. A half-dozen or so girls wore chic black-and-white gowns that looked like chessboards. Few of the tuxedos were plain, and some were droll. Shawn Ledger was dressed like a gangster, in a big-shouldered black double-breasted tux, with black-and-white shoes—and a date from Yardley. There was a four-some of black friends who arrived carrying canes and wearing gloves and top hats and looking spiffy.

Hair

A preoccupation for many teens, hair styles take on an even more important status for the prom. The standard procedure for women is to schedule an appointment with a professional stylist on the day of the prom (the later in the day the better, so the hairdo won't lose its shape before prom time). Styles vary tremendously, but the practice of styling their hair in an "up do"—that, is, put up rather than worn down—is popular for many women because it has connotations of elegance. The regimen for the young men is less grueling, but most have a haircut shortly before the prom night so as to look their best.

Parties

Gatherings of prom couples may take place before or after the dance. The late-night post-prom parties are more common and are usually the subject of parental concern about whether the gatherings will include alcohol and provide the teens with more opportunities to engage in sex or other illicit activities. Attempting to exert some control over the situation, schools and concerned parents sometimes host post-prom gatherings so that they can keep an eye on the activity and discourage behavior they view as inappropriate. On the other end of the spectrum,

The boys—the *men*—opened the doors for their dates and offered a hand, and then sashayed toward the entrance, into the flashing lights and the cheering throng. Many of the promgoers released orange and black helium balloons into the Fairless Hills gloaming, or handed out roses to kids standing behind the barricades, or shook hands with strangers, just as movie stars do.

They came in fire trucks and police cars. They came in UPS trucks and U.S. Mail trucks. One group came in a boat pulled by a car. One couple came on an ice-cream truck, another on a Rita's Italian Ice truck. They came in motor homes, a rescue vehicle, a tractor, a drag racer. They came in Hummers and stretch Hummers. They came in convertible Corvettes and Mustang convertibles.

Alyssa Bergman, back at her old school, was a passenger in her father's Camaro, driven by her on-hold boyfriend, Michael Castor. Alyssa's father was waiting in the wings to take the car off Michael's hands and drive it to the safety of his garage.

some teens are able to arrange hotel rooms or other private quarters where they can celebrate without adult supervision.

Photographs

Prom night is expected to be remembered forever, and to assist in that goal, the participants are usually captured on film. Parents or other relatives usually photograph the prom couple before they depart. Most schools also contract with a professional photographer to shoot pictures at the dance and provide portrait packages to the prom couples. A video keepsake of the event may also be made available.

Prom Clothing

The most visible symbol that prom night is not like other high school social occasions is the formal clothing of the participants. Female prom-goers, in particular, tend to focus heavily on their attire and, in some cases, on the attire that their date will wear, as well. Many young women spend weeks hunting through catalogs and dress shops and some undertake an even more arduous project by designing and making their own dress. The link between the prom and the wedding is most visible in the clothing. Like the male members of a wedding party, male prom-goers often wear tuxedos. Many prom dresses likewise bear a strong resemblance to bridesmaid dresses.

Prom Theme

While the number of themes is seemingly endless, most focus on creating some type of idealized fantasy atmosphere. Often this is accomplished by re-creating some type of exotic location or experience. Paris, Las Vegas, Monte Carlo, Venice, Hawaii, New Orleans Mardi Gras, the Roaring '20s, and Hollywood are some of the more popular choices. Other themes play off a fairy tale or romance such as Alice in Wonderland or Romeo and Juliet.

Transportation

In the U.S., a person's identity is often closely tied to the transportation he or she uses, and this is certainly reflected on prom night. For those who can afford it, a chauffeur-driven limousine is the preferred way to get to and from the prom. To lessen the cost, several couples often pitch in to rent a single limousine big enough for all of them. Teens with appropriate connections may be able to arrange to ride in a classic or luxury car owned by an acquaintance or member of the family. There's also a tradition of allowing the prom-goers to drive themselves in a family car that was previously off limits to them.

Web Sites

"Prom Advice." The Fashion Institute of Design and Merchandising, undated.
http://www.promadvice.com

"A Rite of Passage That Fills a Need" by Jane Eisner. *Philadelphia Inquirer*, April 11, 2005.
http://www.spokesmanreview.com/breaking/story.asp?ID=3781

Further Reading

Bamberger, Michael. *Wonderland: A Year in the Life of an American High School.* New York: Atlantic Monthly Press, 2004.

Best, Amy L. *Prom Night: Youth, Schools, and Popular Culture.* New York: Routledge, 2000.

HIGH SCHOOL GRADUATION

Alternate Name: Commencement

Customs and Symbols: Cap and Gown, Class Ring, Diploma, Exuberant Celebration, Gifts, Open House, "Pomp and Circumstance," Speeches

School is one of the most important institutions in the life of children and adolescents, and the ceremony that marks the end of the general education process in the U.S. stands as a key event that signifies the termination of childhood and the beginning of adulthood. Not surprisingly, a rich collection of symbols and traditions has developed to help young people commemorate and make sense of this momentous occasion.

History and Significance

It is only in the past century that high school became a widespread experience for Americans. Previously, moving beyond the basics of a primary education was not a priority for most. In 1910, just one of every 10 people graduated from a secondary school. Advanced education became much more highly valued in the following decades, however. By 1940, about half of the country's young adults were graduating from high school. By the 1980s the graduation rate stood at around 85 percent, where it has remained through 2005, according to the National Center for Education Statistics.

In one sense, this emphasis on more education for more people helped to create the adolescent experience. Previously, it was common for young people to assume the responsibilities of full-time employment and beginning a family while still in their early and middle teens. When school was prolonged, so was the period of dependence on one's parents. As a result, it became accepted that a person was not a full-fledged adult until they reached the age of 18—the general age of high school graduation. Thus, the commencement ceremony does more than commemorate the end of school days and the attainment of a degree—it is probably the most potent symbol that the dependant adolescent is becoming a responsible adult. And high school graduation continues to have that meaning even though a

The commencement ceremony does more than commemorate the end of school days and the attainment of a degree—it is probably the most potent symbol that the dependant adolescent is becoming a responsible adult.

growing number of young people continue their education—and often their dependence on their parents—by attending college.

Observance

Special events usually call for special attire, and for graduation, each member of the class dons a cap and gown, usually in the school colors. The ceremony often takes place in some type of large auditorium or outdoor stadium capable of handling the thousands of family members who wish to attend, which gives the commencement the feel of a spectacle. The significance of the event is noted in a series of speeches by class members, school officials, and perhaps a guest speaker. The crucial moment in the ceremony comes with the issuance of a diploma to each graduate, which is sometimes accompanied by exuberant celebration by the students and their families. After concluding remarks, the class is dismissed for a final time, which cues the celebratory cap tossing. Commemorative photographs of the grads in their gowns and caps (if successfully recovered) are taken after the ceremony.

Several associated activities also mark the high school farewell. Some graduating seniors opt for a class ring to symbolize their ties to their school. The graduate's family may host an open house with food and refreshments, which allows family and friends to relay their good wishes. Either at the open house, if there is one, or through some other contact, family members often give gifts to the graduate in honor of the occasion.

Customs and Symbols

Cap and Gown

The distinctive attire of graduation looks like something from the ancient past, and in fact it is. The cap and gown were worn in the initial graduations, which began taking place in the Middle Ages at the major European universities such as Oxford, Cambridge, and the University of Paris. The flat, four-cornered "mortarboard" cap that's common today dates to the 1500s in Britain.

A good deal of etiquette and tradition surrounds the cap and its tassel. It should be worn with one of the four corners pointing forward and the "board" flat on the head, not tilted. The tassel is made to hang on the right side of the cap prior to receiving the diploma, then is moved to the left after the official graduation document is in hand. Some irreverent grads glue small figurines to the cap's flat surface or write messages on it that can be viewed by observers sitting in elevated seats at

Other Milestones on the Road to Adulthood

In addition to graduation from high school, other marks of adulthood occur at or near age 18. All U.S. citizens may register to vote in political elections once they are 18 years old, which is a right guaranteed by the 1971 ratification of the 26th Amendment to the U.S. Constitution. Before the passage of the 26th Amendment, most states required voters to be 21 years old.

Male residents of the U.S. are required to register for possible military draft on or before their 18th birthday. The Selective Training and Service Act was first enacted in 1940, suspended in 1975, and re-enacted in 1980. Although the U.S. currently operates a volunteer military, males must still register for possible draft in case of extreme circumstances; an act of Congress is required to activate a military draft of registered males.

Another age-related rite of passage occurs at 21, the age at which people in the U.S. may legally purchase and drink alcohol. Prior to 1984, the legal drinking age was determined by each state. Due in part to a consistently large number of motor vehicle accidents involving young drivers and alcohol, the U.S. federal government enacted the National Minimum Drinking Age Act. This required all states to raise the minimum drinking age to 21 or face a reduction in federal funding for the maintenance of highways and roads. All state governments complied with the act.

the graduation venue. At many schools, the tradition is to end the graduation ceremony by flinging the caps high into the air.

Class Ring

Though usually purchased and worn before the ceremony, the class ring is strongly linked to the idea of graduation, with the year of completion being proudly advertised on the metal band. Going forward, the ring serves as a symbol of the person's high school education and their ongoing identification with their alma mater and graduating class.

Diploma

The foremost symbol of the passage out of school, the diploma becomes the central focus of the graduation ceremony. This usually takes place by announcing each graduate's name individually as they walk across the stage and receive the document from one or more of the school's top educators, usually receiving a handshake or other official acknowledgment in the process. Originally, diplomas were rolled and tied with a ribbon. Today, they're more often presented in flat document holders. In some cases, the diploma itself may not be distributed at the ceremony, though some type of commemorative object is usually handed to the graduates in recognition of graduation.

Exuberant Celebration

While some view commencement as a solemn occasion, others—both students and spectators—engage in celebratory activities that some view as disruptive, including loud cheering from the crowd and irreverent arm waving or other gestures. To keep things under control, some schools ask that the audience remain silent until all diplomas are distributed. Students are sometimes kept in check by the practice of handing out participation certificates or empty document holders at the ceremony rather than the actual diplomas. This is made known in advance, with the warning that those who behave inappropriately will have their diplomas withheld.

Gifts

Presents are often bestowed upon the graduate to congratulate them for their accomplishment and give them a boost as they enter adulthood. These are sometimes tied to future plans. For example, parents might provide a computer to their son or daughter, which will be used in their college studies. Graduation cards are extremely common, and those cards often contain money—the most popular graduation gift—which is useful regardless of the young person's upcoming endeavors.

Open House

A chance for the graduate to receive some personal attention, the open house is, as the name suggests, usually held at the family home, complete with food and refreshments. Family and friends attend to offer congratulations and perhaps gifts. Open houses typically take place on the weekends surrounding graduation rather than on the actual date of the commencement.

"Pomp and Circumstance"

Graduation is one of few rites of passage that comes complete with its own soundtrack. The official name to the song performed at so many American commencement ceremonies is "Pomp and Circumstance March No. 1," being the first of a series of five linked pieces by English composer Edward Elgar. Composed in 1901, it was first played at a graduation at Yale University in 1905 (when Elgar received an honorary degree) and was soon adopted by other major universities and, eventually, high schools. While some schools use other musical themes, many uphold the tradition of playing this march, usually for the processional, when the graduating class enters the venue, or the recessional, when they leave.

Speeches

The passage of the graduating class is marked by a number of speeches that are intended to eloquently sum up the meaning of the event and inspire the graduates to strive for further accomplishments. The choice of which students are allowed to speak differs depending on the custom of the school, but often includes the class president and the class valedictorian and salutatorian—the persons with the highest and second highest ratings in academics. In addition, school officials may speak, and a keynote address may be delivered by someone of prominence, such as a school alumnus who has attained distinction in some way.

Further Reading

Hemmings, Annette B. *Coming of Age in U.S. High Schools: Economic, Kinship, Religious, and Political Crosscurrents.* Mahwah, NJ: Lawrence Erlbaum Associates, 2004.

Photo on facing page: Young rites-of-passage initiates performing at an outdoor public ceremony in Cleveland.

COMING OF AGE

Chapter 10: Revived and Reinvented Initiation Rites

INTRODUCTION

Most coming-of-age rites either originated in the past or, as in the case of a contemporary activity such as driving, developed spontaneously. But since the latter decades of the 20th century, a number of activists have purposefully created new ceremonial activities. Some of the more prominent efforts in this regard are the various **African-American Rites-of-Passage Programs** for black youths and the **Unitarian Universalist Coming-of-Age Programs** for young members of that faith.

These programs are a response to the difficulties experienced by today's adolescents. The increase in births outside of marriage and in divorce means that many youths lack strong parental role models and may have difficulty finding other figures to provide positive guidance. Activists also argue that young people lack a meaningful way to move from childhood to adulthood. This creates confusion about their place in the world and can make some youths feel overwhelmed by the looming responsibilities of adulthood. Also, because there is little public recognition of their maturity, some youths compensate by engaging in dangerous activities that they associate with adulthood, such as sex and substance abuse.

Though they're targeted to different groups, the African-American and Unitarian Universalist programs share many concepts. They strive to provide appropriate adult mentors for the young participants, and they offer practical instruction about topics such as sexuality and finance. In addition, they create ceremonial activities that symbolize the transition to adulthood so that the youths understand and accept that change. In creating these new rituals, organizers look to the past. The ceremonies in the African-American programs draw on traditional African culture, while the Unitarian Universalist activities incorporate rites from a variety of cultural and religious groups.

AFRICAN-AMERICAN
RITES-OF-PASSAGE PROGRAMS

Alternate Name: African-American Coming-of-Age Processes

Customs and Symbols: African Proverbs, Community Activism, Completion Ceremonies, Cultural Education, Guides or Elders, Libation Pouring, Nguzo Saba, Practical Instruction, Spiritual Instruction, Wilderness Training

A trend that has emerged in recent decades, African-American rites-of-passage programs seek to give black youths positive values that are based on aspects of traditional African culture. In addition to providing education and activities, these programs also allow young men and women the chance to take part in ceremonial activities that are intended to mark their passage from childhood to adulthood.

History and Significance

Coming-of-age rituals abound throughout the many cultures in Africa. Many of the African-American rites-of-passage programs created in the U.S. draw on the heritage, customs, and values carried over by enslaved Africans. Many view these programs as a positive response to urgent social dilemmas facing the black population of the U.S. Pioneers of the programs argue that violence, unstable families, and many other problems partially result from the lack of appropriate role models for black youths and from the fact that many of these young men and women don't have a meaningful way to move from childhood to adulthood. Often given titles such as "Rites of Passage" or "Unyago" (a Swahili term meaning "tribal ritual"), the programs put young people in contact with adults who can provide meaningful instruction in black culture and instill specific values regarding appropriate behavior. The programs also involve special ceremonies and activities that are intended to serve as definite rituals that help participants manage and make sense of the adult responsibilities that await them.

The majority of the rites-of-passage programs are based on the concepts of Africentrism—a movement among American blacks that embraces African heritage and culture. As a

> *Coming-of-age rituals abound throughout the many cultures in Africa. Many of the African-American rites-of-passage programs created in the U.S. draw on the heritage, customs, and values carried over by enslaved Africans.*

result, the instruction and the ceremonies draw upon ideas and rituals found in traditional African cultures, though they are adapted to apply to American society. Supporters of the programs maintain that the focus on African heritage allows young blacks to take pride in the accomplishments of their ancestors, which in turn builds their self-esteem.

Observance

Having been developed by a variety of groups and individuals, African-American rites-of-passage programs don't follow a single plan, though they share a general set of concepts. The principles of *Nguzo Saba* underlie many of the activities, and one or more guides or elders oversee the activities. In most cases, a program is intended to extend over at least one year and many plans try to keep the members involved for several years. The ages of the participants vary, but participants are generally at least 10 years old. Many become involved when they enter adolescence. Because young black males are often viewed as being particularly at risk, some rites-of-passage programs are aimed exclusively at them. Female courses also exist, however, as do programs that serve mixed groups of young men and women.

The libation pouring ceremony serves as a means of honoring ancestors, and various forms of cultural education are also used to develop the individual's pride in their ethnicity. To provide a strong moral grounding, participants receive spiritual instruction, and values are also relayed through the study of African proverbs. Everyday issues are addressed through practical instruction.

In keeping with Africentric theories, the programs stress the need for African Americans to support one another in a variety of ways. This is accomplished through community activism and through wilderness training, which also build

Sankofa

Many African-American rites-of-passage programs incorporate the *sankofa* symbol—a flying bird turning its head around to face backward. In the pictorial writing system of the Akan/Adrinka people in Ghana, sankofa means "one must return to the past in order to move forward" or, alternately, "you can always return to the source and fetch it (learn)." Sankofa encapsulates in one image the idea of rediscovering traditions and adapting them for contemporary use.

self-discipline and problem-solving skills. Completion ceremonies mark the successful conclusion of activities, providing the participants a sense of accomplishment as they move through the different stages of the programs.

Customs and Symbols

African Proverbs

The study of ancient African sayings allows the participants to receive moral instruction while also getting a better understanding of their ancestors. For instance, one of the frequently studied proverbs states, "I am because We are, and because We are, therefore I am." In analyzing this saying, the mentor can discuss the communal nature of traditional life in Africa and how this idea of an interconnected community can be applied to African Americans in the U.S.

Completion Ceremonies

Ritual activities allow the participants to celebrate their completion of the different steps of the programs. These are usually group ceremonies involving several participants, which further underscores the communal qualities promoted by the rites-of-passage activities. Most of these observances begin with a libation pouring and usually include a feast, a public statement by the young men and women being honored, and music and dance performances. In the final ceremony that concludes many of the programs, a cornstalk is burned, which symbolizes the end of the individual's childhood and the beginning of adulthood.

Community Activism

To help fulfill Nguzo Saba principles such as unity, collective work, and responsibility, program participants often take part in projects that are designed to benefit the local community. For instance, they might conduct a neighborhood clean-up and beautification project or perform volunteer work at a shelter for the homeless.

Cultural Education

Participants complete hands-on activities such as learning traditional African dances, constructing replicas of African ceremonial masks, and studying African drumming.

Field trips to museums or historical sites related to black culture are also common. These steps are aimed at giving the young women and men a better understanding of the struggles and accomplishments of their ancestors, both in the U.S. and in Africa.

Guides or Elders

The participants are aided by mature adults who serve as role models and facilitators. In some cases, two types of guides come into play: activity leaders, who are directly responsible for working with the youths and directing the activities, and elders, who tend to be older men and women who support the activity leaders and function as respected counselors to the youths. Both types of mentors undergo training prior to taking part in the programs.

Libation Pouring

In this act, participants pour a ceremonial offering of a liquid onto the ground and recite the names of important ancestors who have passed away. The act allows the young man or woman to pay homage to their heritage and to honor the sacrifices made by African Americans in the past. The ceremonial nature of the act is reinforced by the use of a special unity cup to hold the liquid.

Nguzo Saba

Nguzo Saba (pronounced *na-GOO-zoo-SAH-bah*), or the Seven Principles, represent the essential moral values that are upheld by Africentric leaders, and most of the activities of the rites-of-passage programs are intended to reinforce these ideals. (These concepts are also central to Kwanzaa celebrations.) English and African titles are applied to the principles, which are usually listed in the following order:

Unity (Umoja): Uniting the family, the community, the African-American ethnic group, and, on a larger level, all humans.

Self-determination (Kujichagulia): Allowing African Americans to define and speak for themselves.

Collective work and responsibility (Ujima): To work with other African Americans to maintain the community and to solve problems with a group effort.

Cooperative economics (Ujamaa): To maintain and frequent African American-owned businesses so that the community as a whole benefits and profits from them.

Purpose (Nia): To develop the African-American community as a collective effort.

Creativity (Kuumba): To benefit and beautify the community in innovative ways.

Faith (Imani): Believing in the African-American people, a supreme creator, and the righteousness of black struggle.

Practical Instruction

While rites-of-passage programs are partly intended to build self-esteem, they also focus on practical matters that can be a challenge to young men and women. Instruction is often provided in topics such as basic financial management, sex education, nutrition, personal hygiene, and decision making.

Spiritual Instruction

The spiritual guidance provided in the programs is usually nondenominational, though there are also church-based programs that provide a more specific religious message. Generally, the aim is to make the participants more aware of spiritual matters and to allow them to get a better understanding of moral concepts.

Wilderness Training

Building on the Africentric idea that nature should be valued, the programs often require the participants to take part in some type of outdoor activity. These can range from simple camp-style outings to more demanding ropes courses, hiking, or rafting activities that are designed to build confidence, teamwork, and leadership.

Web Sites

National Rites of Passage Institute.
    http://www.ritesofpassage.org

Rights of Passage Youth Empowerment Foundation.
    http://www.ritesofpassageonline.org

Further Reading

"Case Study: Unyago." *Rites of Passage in America: A Traveling Exhibition Organized by the Balch Institute for Ethnic Studies*, June 22, 1992-January 2, 1995. Historical Society of Pennsylvania.
    http://www.hsp.org

Hill, Paul, Jr. *Coming of Age: African American Male Rites-of-Passage*. Chicago: African American Images, 1992.

UNITARIAN UNIVERSALIST COMING-OF-AGE PROGRAMS

Customs and Symbols: Affirmation Ceremony, Historic Study, Learning or Service Project, Mentor, Retreats

A self-described liberal faith that tends to avoid prescribed ceremonies, the Unitarian Universalist (UU) denomination has nonetheless recognized the value of providing structured programs to assist adolescents in coming to terms with young adulthood and spirituality. In keeping with the UU philosophy of openness to a wide range of beliefs and cultures, some of these programs draw upon the spiritual practices of Native Americans, Buddhists, and others.

History and Significance

The UU coming-of-age activities have become increasingly common since the 1980s. They were motivated by the same basic ideas that underlie **African-American Rites-of-Passage Programs**: that young people often lack appropriate role models and that contemporary society fails to provide a meaningful way to mark a young person's passage from childhood to young adulthood. The UU programs therefore focus on providing a suitable mentor for the young man or young woman and engaging them in instruction and activities that make them more comfortable with the mature responsibilities they will soon face. The programs also utilize ceremonial activities that help to ritualize the youth's passage to adulthood, some of which are based on the practices of a variety of traditional cultures.

UU programs focus on providing a suitable mentor for the young man or young woman and engaging them in instruction and activities that make them more comfortable with the mature responsibilities they will soon face.

Observance

Though the age requirements for the UU programs are somewhat flexible, most are aimed at youths between the ages of 12 and 15. The programs vary in length. Some follow a two-year course, while others are more concise, taking a year or less. Each youth participant is paired with an adult mentor, who provides guidance over the course of the program and perhaps beyond. To explore spiritual matters, participants attend regular meetings at the church. In addition, most programs incorporate three or four more intensive retreats, which are usually multi-day weekend excursions away from the church. In addition, the youth is usually expected to complete a learning or service project, or perhaps more than one. Certain congregations incorporate historic study activities that allow the participants to gain a better understanding of the UU church. The program concludes with an affirmation ceremony that recognizes the young person's achievement in completing the required activities.

Customs and Symbols

Affirmation Ceremony

The ceremony that closes the program is designed to acknowledge that the youths have attained a new status. In most cases, this gathering is separate from normal church worship services and is attended by parents, mentors, and other staff members. A dinner may be part of the festivities, and youth-oriented fun such as dancing may also take place.

Historic Study

Some congregations believe that young people will more easily come to terms with adulthood if they have a better grasp of the UU faith. This is accomplished through study of the church's origins, and some programs organize one or more field trips to important historic sites related to the faith. Boston, where the first American Unitarian association was founded in the early 1800s, is a particularly popular destination for these excursions.

Learning or Service Project

Participants are usually required to complete one or more projects that reinforce spiritual concepts and reflect the youth's maturity and commitment to responsible behavior. In many cases, this is a service project that expresses the UU principle of helping others. For instance, a participant might perform volunteer work for a local charity. In other cases, the service may be directed more toward the church itself, or to other members of the congregation. A youth might design a worship or religious-study service for younger children in the church, perform work in a church-run community center, or complete necessary maintenance work on church facilities. In some programs, participants are allowed to complete projects that are aimed at personal betterment. In many cases, these are in keeping with the UU appreciation for spiritual disciplines outside of Christianity—for instance, completing training in yoga or martial arts.

Retreat Programs

Retreat programs vary among UU congregations, but the Prairie Star regional district, located in the Midwest, created an influential program. Their plan calls for four separate retreats that take place over the course of a year-long program.

The series begins with the High Adventure Weekend, which involves the participants in a camping excursion and an outdoors-based activity, such as rock climbing or rappelling. The intent is to get the young men and women to take part in an experience that forces them to face new mental, physical, and emotional challenges. The outing is also designed to build team spirit, which will allow the youths to become comfortable with one another for the duration of the program.

The Wizard of Oz Weekend uses the famous movie as a metaphor for the leaving-home process that the youths will undergo as they become adults. Activities include a scavenger hunt and the search for a hidden key, which are designed to force the participants to develop their problem-solving skills and to rely on others for assistance in meeting their goals.

The Medicine Wheel Weekend focuses on the symbol of the circle divided into four parts, which is used in many cultures to represent the four directions (east, west, north, south) and four phases of life (infancy, youth, adult, elder). Building on this idea, four workshops take place during the retreat that allow the participants to explore issues related to their life cycle. In the first, they are provided a letter from their parents that relates the story of their birth and the parents' hopes for the child. In the second, they go through an exercise that relates information about the human body and sexuality. In the third, they explore the value of solitude and meditation. And in the last workshop, they are asked to analyze their hopes for the future and the means of achieving them.

In the final retreat, Vision Quest Weekend, each youth undergoes a six-hour outdoor sojourn based on the concept of the **Vision Quest**. The idea is to get the participants to spend time alone and focus on the purpose and meaning of their life. To mark the end of the quest, each person returns to the group's bonfire and is ceremonially welcomed back into the circle of participants and adults.

Mentor

In most cases, each youth has a specific adult who serves as their mentor or sponsor throughout the program. Participants are often allowed to choose their mentor themselves, subject to approval by the church leaders, though most programs provide assistance in linking the youths with a willing adult. In addition to participating in the group activities, the mentor may also work with the youth on an individual basis, helping them decide on personal projects and reviewing written assignments. In some cases, the youth is required to interview their sponsor about his or her life experiences and spiritual attitudes. This project gives the young person a detailed look at the way one UU member has coped with the adult world using their faith as a guide.

Retreats

Most programs make use of special multi-day getaways to help youths focus on a variety of themes related to coming of age.

Web Sites

"Coming of Age: Retreats." Web UUs, undated.
    http://webuus.com/coa/retreats.shtml

"Coming of Age 2006." Unitarian Universalist Community Church of Park Forest, Illinois, undated.
    http://www.uuccpf.org/coa.htm

PART 3

Adulthood

A jumping the broom ceremony, complete with decorated broom,
is part of this California beach wedding.

PART 3

Adulthood

INTRODUCTION

Nearly all cultures and communities mark important life events with special celebrations and customs that are rich with symbolism. While these events are often associated with childhood firsts and the transition to adulthood, life as an adult also includes its own set of milestones. Significant occasions in adult life may confer a change in social status or acknowledge a personal transformation. Some milestones may be associated with a particular age or specific point in time such as a birthday. Others may be celebrated at any time, often in association with a life-changing decision such as getting married or retiring from work. Still others include new social or legal privileges and responsibilities. These events, whether observed publicly or privately, serve as commemorations of an individual's progress through life's many changes.

For many Americans, adulthood is marked by milestone events that reflect unique social, cultural, and religious values. This part describes a variety of occasions, celebrations, and rites of passage that are important in the lives of adults in America. A range of customs and practices as observed by different religious and cultural groups is presented in this section, with comparisons that illustrate the contrasting social rituals currently found in the U.S. Diverse community values are perhaps most often reflected in customs surrounding courtship, **Dating**, and marriage. Various ways of ritualizing and celebrating weddings are examined, along with social customs surrounding engaged and newlywed couples. Religious and cultural observances related to significant birthdays, group reunions, **Purchasing a House**, **Retirement**, and later years are also discussed. This overview of selected adult milestone events provides a brief summary of key cultural and religious influences in the lives of modern Americans.

Finding and selecting a life partner continues to be an important part of life for many American adults. For some Americans, the dating and courtship process is heavily influenced by cultural and religious beliefs. While most Americans find marriage partners independently by dating, some rely on the services of match-makers. **Matchmaking** is the practice of introducing potentially compatible people for the purpose of marriage. In the U.S., this custom is primarily observed by Muslims, Hindus, and Orthodox Jews.

Wedding preparations are another area in which the influence of community values may be seen, particularly among certain religious and cultural groups. Marriage proposals are sometimes governed by traditional practices, such as the participation of an Islamic *wali*, who facilitates a proposal of marriage for devout Muslims. **Engagement Parties** and **Wedding Showers** are generally group celebrations involving friends, relatives, and other community members. These events can also include culturally specific practices such as the African-American tradition of **Loading the Bride** or the **Henna Body Painting** parties held by some Hindu, Islamic, and Jewish Americans. Ritual **Fasting and Bathing** are undertaken by Jewish brides and grooms prior to the wedding. These customs are all intended to help the couple prepare spiritually and emotionally for the changes marriage brings.

The rich traditions found in the ceremonies of various cultures worldwide continue to influence the weddings planned by modern American couples. From the most culturally specific ritual to an original rite, the diversity of wedding customs is reflected in **Religious Ceremonies**, **Civil Ceremonies**, and **Betrothal Rituals**. Depending on their particular religious beliefs, their families, and other factors, some couples are bound by strictly outlined wedding ceremonies. Others have more freedom to design a wedding that blends secular customs with rites borrowed from different faiths. Ultimately, every wedding is as unique as its participants, often reflecting the social, religious, or cultural values that are most important to the bride and groom. American observances of post-wedding events such as the **Honeymoon** and specific **Anniversary Customs** tend to be more secular than wedding ceremonies, although many **Recommitment Ceremonies** include religious elements similar to those of the original wedding.

Gatherings such as **Family Reunions**, **Military Reunions** and school or **Class Reunions** can also be important milestone events for American adults. These events provide an opportunity for individuals to reflect on their lives and accomplishments, as well as the personal changes they may have experienced over the years. Reunions are a way to revisit the past, renew relationships, and form or restore connections with others. For this reason, many Americans look forward to these reunions with great anticipation.

Perhaps the most significant adult milestone for American Muslims is **Performing the Hajj**. The *hajj* is an annual pilgrimage to Mecca, a city in western Saudi Arabia that is regarded by Muslims as the most holy place in the Islamic world. Every adult Muslim is required to perform the pilgrimage at least once in their lifetime, if they are physically and financially able to make the trip. It is one of the oldest spiritual duties required of Muslims, and remains an extremely important achievement for those who complete the pilgrimage.

Some notable life events are specifically associated with later adulthood. For working adults, retirement can represent a life change of great magnitude. Shifting focus away from paid employment to more leisurely pursuits is usually celebrated as the beginning of an exciting new phase of life. Similarly, **Asian-American 60th Birthday** celebrations also acknowledge a fundamental new beginning. This tradition is based on the belief that, astrologically, a new life cycle starts every 60 years. Those who celebrate their 60th birthday are said to be reborn into a new life, full of new opportunities and possibilities. Some of these possibilities might include **New Living Arrangements**, with a variety of options now chosen by Americans in their later years.

The examples presented in this part illustrate the ongoing importance of rites of passage and milestone life events for adults in modern American society. Whether small or large, elaborate or simple, highly ritualized or unstructured, these observances of specific customs and celebrations help to unify smaller groups and communities within modern American culture. By maintaining shared connections through observance of religious and cultural traditions, the rich heritage of American society's many diverse cultural groups may be preserved.

Photo on facing page: A young dating couple.

Chapter 11: Courtship

INTRODUCTION

In the 21st century, men and women who pair off to take part in social activities leading to possible engagement and marriage would probably say that they are **Dating** or "going out." In generations past, people did not "date" but instead "courted," a word seldom used in modern times. Indeed, for many, the word *courtship* calls up images of demure young women in ankle-length dresses and awkward young men in stiff shirts and suits. Under the watchful eyes of parents, such potential mates would rock on a porch swing and sip lemonade on a Sunday afternoon, or perhaps slip away from a church social for a walk and a few minutes of private conversation.

Although the language and practices regarding courtship have changed, the goal remains the same. Before marriage, people take part in social rituals that allow them to interact more intimately with members of the opposite sex, or, for gay people, of the same sex. Once two people develop a relationship, they may gauge each other's interest, possibly deepen their involvement, and finally decide to make their union permanent.

Courtship rituals vary depending on the culture in which they take place. In the U.S., dating is generally the first step toward **Getting Engaged.** Others, however, such as some Chinese, Hindu, and Muslim Americans, tend to rely more on the **Matchmaking** efforts of families and religious leaders to bring young people together.

DATING

Alternate Names: Courting, Going Out, Seeing Each Other

Customs and Symbols: Blind Dates, Double Dates, and Group Dates, Dating Services, Speed Dating

Dating is the practice of spending leisure time with another person to determine whether or not they may be an appropriate partner. Americans generally begin dating as teenagers, although single people of all ages participate in dating. Dating practices in the U.S. vary considerably according to age, local custom, and other circumstances.

History and Significance

During the 19th century, dating customs in the U.S. were formalized according to social ideas of the time. A gentleman typically visited a young woman at her home, maintaining the pretense that he was calling on the family. If the young woman's parents approved of the potential match, they might eventually allow the couple a few moments of privacy. Rarely did the couple go out alone together. Outside the woman's home, the couple might meet at church, balls (dances), community picnics, and similar social events.

The emergence of the automobile in the early 20th century changed dating behaviors and laid the foundation for modern dating practices. The independent mobility provided by the automobile gave young people far more options for going out. Dating moved from the private sphere of the home to the more public, and less supervised, sphere of theaters, restaurants, and social events.

Observances

People find dating partners in many different places, including work, school, church, or social clubs. Dating services and speed dating events can also provide assistance in finding partners. Dating usually begins informally, with one person asking another to join them in an activity of mutual interest. Asking for a date was once the exclusive domain of men, but women now initiate dating relationships just as often. It is generally assumed that the person asking for the date will pay any expenses, although costs may also be shared by the couple.

There is tremendous variation in dating activities, and much dating advice is published in magazines, books, and on the Internet. Many first dates are casual meetings

Asking for a date was once the exclusive domain of men, but women now initiate dating relationships just as often. It is generally assumed that the person asking for the date will pay any expenses, although costs may also be shared by the couple.

at a public place, giving the couple a chance to decide if they would like to spend more time together. Some first dates are blind dates, double dates, or group dates. After a successful date, one party usually contacts the other to indicate interest in further dates. If the couple continues dating frequently, they are often said to be "going out" or "seeing each other."

Some religious traditions include specific ideas about dating. The Church of Jesus Christ of Latter-Day Saints, commonly known as the Mormon Church, views dating as preparation for marriage. Mormons are strongly encouraged to seek marriage partners within the faith, and young people are encouraged to double date to prevent the development of improper situations and also to avoid pairing off with one partner too quickly. Young people are also cautioned to avoid serious relationships before completing any missionary work, which requires dedicated focus for up to two years.

The Islamic faith also disapproves of the American style of dating, believing it to be improper for unrelated young men and women to spend time alone together. Couples often meet through introduction by mutual friends or family members, although Muslims in the U.S. may also look for marriage partners at local or regional Islamic events. Depending on the customs of their families, young Muslims may be allowed to date if accompanied by a chaperone. In some Muslim communities, young women are represented by a male relative who acts in the traditional role of a *wali*, or one who helps a young woman through the process of selecting a marriage partner.

Amish dating practices traditionally include midnight visits by a young man to the home of a young woman. The woman's parents are presumably asleep by this time, but often they are only pretending to be unaware of the secret visit. The young couple spends time alone together or with another couple, talking, singing, or playing games until the early hours of the morning.

Customs and Symbols

Blind Dates, Double Dates, and Group Dates

Some couples meet each other for the first time on a blind date, which is a date arranged by a friend or relative who knows both parties and believes that they would make a good couple. In these cases, especially when the two parties continue dating, the mutual friend or relative is said to have "fixed up" the couple. Double dates involve two couples going out together. Group dates are common among teenagers, with several couples going out together.

Dating Services

Dating services allow people to create profiles outlining their physical characteristics, personality, interests and hobbies, and the qualities they are looking for in a partner. Most dating services are now available via the Internet, and some charge a fee for use. Services can be open to the general public or organized around a shared characteristic or interest such as religion, ethnicity, music, travel, hobby, or geographic area. Some dating services use computer programs to find compatible matches based on similar characteristics, while others allow members to browse the profiles in order to select dating partners that interest them. Members may contact each other to determine if there is mutual interest.

Speed Dating

Speed dating is a dating service event that allows people to meet a large number of potential partners in a very short amount of time. Typically, speed dating events occur at cafés or bars, but events may also be organized at a church, synagogue, or cultural club. Participants are given the opportunity to talk with each other for a limited amount of time, usually less than ten minutes. When the time is up, a bell rings and participants change partners and begin again. After each conversation, participants make a note indicating whether or not they are interested in meeting that person again. If mutual interest is noted, event organizers provide both parties with the other's telephone number.

Web Site

Campbell, Carolyn. "Speed Dating: A New Form of Matchmaking," Discovery Health, undated. http://health.discovery.com/centers/loverelationships/articles/speed_dating.html

Further Reading

Bailey, Beth L. *From Front Porch to Back Seat: Courtship in Twentieth-Century America.* Baltimore, MD: Johns Hopkins University Press, 1988.

Gulevich, Tanya. *Understanding Islam and Muslim Traditions.* Detroit: Omnigraphics, 2004.

Mordecai, Carolyn. *Weddings: Dating and Love Customs of Cultures Worldwide.* Phoenix, AZ: Nittany Publishers, 1999.

Turner, Jeffrey Scott. *Dating and Sexuality in America: A Reference Handbook.* Santa Barbara, CA: ABC-CLIO, 2003.

MATCHMAKING

Alternate Names: Alliance Making, Arranging a Marriage

Customs and Symbols: Astrology, Numerology

Matchmaking is the practice of introducing potentially compatible people for the purpose of marriage. Most Americans find marriage partners independently by **Dating**, however some cultural and religious groups in the U.S. rely on the services of matchmakers.

History and Significance

Matchmaking has been practiced throughout history in many parts of the world, most notably Asia, India, and parts of Africa and the Middle East. In pre-revolutionary China, marriage matches were sometimes made at birth or when the children reached school age. These couples usually met for the first time at their wedding. Matchmaking continues to be commonly practiced in India among Hindus, Christians, and followers of other faiths as well. Muslims all over the world often use matchmaking services to find marriage partners, as Islam forbids the American style of dating. As people of these cultures migrated to the U.S., they brought various matchmaking customs with them.

Observances

In pre-revolutionary China, marriage matches were sometimes made at birth or when the children reached school age. These couples usually met for the first time at their wedding.

The calculation of a good marriage match may include evaluation of astrology, numerology, family background, circumstances of birth, and other criteria. By focusing on these factors, arranged marriages are thought to ensure happiness and prosperity for husband and wife, as well as their children and extended families. While many Americans recoil from the idea of an arranged marriage, many others believe that arranged marriages produce stronger relationships that are based on mutual compatibility.

Depending on how traditional the family is, the process of matchmaking may be initiated by the parents of a marriageable young woman or by an unmarried man or woman acting on their own behalf. The search often begins by spreading the word among families of similar religious and cultural backgrounds. The assistance of a professional matchmaker may also be sought, or Internet or newspaper matchmaking services may be used. Some Muslims look for potential marriage partners at local or regional Islamic events, many of which include the opportunity to meet with professional Islamic matchmakers.

When a potential marriage candidate is found, introductions will be made and the prospective couple will meet, sometimes along with members of both of their families. Contrary to popular belief, most modern arranged marriages are not forced. Young people are often presented with a number of possible marriage partners, and they choose who they will marry. If all the candidates are rejected, the search resumes until a suitable partner is found.

Customs and Symbols

Astrology

Astrology is based on the belief that stars, planets, and other heavenly bodies can influence a person's good fortune. It plays an important role in matchmaking for many Hindu and Chinese Americans. Each person's birth date, birth time, and place of birth are evaluated and analyzed to produce natal charts, which are then compared for overall compatibility. Usually, the analysis and comparison is done by an astrologer or a professional matchmaker.

Numerology

Numerology is the study of significant numbers that are believed to influence a person's life and luck. Each number is thought to have a particular value by itself and in combination with other numbers. Letters have corresponding numeric equivalents, and so a person's name can also be represented as a number. A matchmaker or numerologist calculates the numeric values of each person's birth date and time, their first name and family surname, and other pertinent information such as

Religious Practice Meets Technology

Because traditional Muslims believe that their religion forbids private meetings or dates between unrelated men and women, many turn to the Internet for assistance in finding a marriage partner. A variety of Islamic Internet dating services allow prospective partners to become acquainted without subjecting themselves to improper situations.

the proposed wedding date. Using this analysis, the matchmaker makes predictions about the compatibility of the couple and the life they could expect to have if they marry. Numerology is particularly important for many Americans of East Indian heritage.

Web Site

"Social Interaction in Islam." Muslim Women's League, September, 1995.
    http://www.mwlusa.org/publications/essays/socialinteraction.html

Further Reading

Al-Jibaly, Muhammad. *The Quest for Love and Mercy: Regulations for Wedding and Marriage in Islam.* Beirut, Lebanon: Al-Maktab al-Islaami, 2000.

Cho, David. "For Muslims, Courtship Enabled by the Internet." *Washington Post*, June 6, 2004.

Gong, Rosemary. *Good Luck Life: The Essential Guide to Chinese American Celebrations and Culture.* New York: Harper Collins, 2005.

Gulevich, Tanya. *Understanding Islam and Muslim Traditions.* Detroit: Omnigraphics, 2004.

Jain, Anita. "Is Arranged Marriage Really Any Worse Than Craigslist?" *New York Magazine*, April 4, 2005.

Kanitkar, V. P., and W. Owen Cole. *Hinduism.* Lincolnwood, IL: NTC Publishing Group, 1995.

Pries, Allison. "Englewood Cliff, NJ, Matchmaking Business Blends Counseling, Astrology." *The Hackensack (NJ) Record*, June 12, 2002.

Photo on facing page: Marriage proposals can be in private or in public, as in this proposal on the field at the University of Southern Mississippi before the last game of the season.

Chapter 12: Getting Engaged

INTRODUCTION

An important event between courtship and marriage is the engagement, a formal promise between the parties to wed. The word engagement comes from the French word *engager*, which in turn comes from the Old French word *gage*. This word refers to any kind of a pledge or token binding a person to an obligation. In the English-American tradition, another commonly used word is betrothal, which comes from the Middle English word *trouthe*, or "truth." Both words suggest that in the past, engagements entailed more of a legal obligation than they do in modern times.

Engagement periods typically extend over some months, with *Time* magazine reporting that the average engagement period increased from eleven months in 1999 to sixteen months in 2002. This period is primarily dedicated to **Wedding Preparations**. Typically, an engagement carries little in the way of legal or moral obligation (although this was not always the case), and either party can end the engagement at any time. Thus, the engagement period can be a time for the couple to either deepen their involvement or conclude that the marriage is unlikely to be successful and cancel it.

While in recent decades it has become more common for women to make a formal **Proposal** of marriage to men, asking the other to commit to marriage has traditionally been seen as the man's responsibility. At the time of the proposal or shortly thereafter, the man traditionally presents a ring to the woman (usually a diamond ring) as a symbol of the engagement. The engagement may then be formally announced and celebrated by family and friends at an **Engagement Party**.

PROPOSAL

Customs and Symbols: Bride-Price or Dowry, Engagement Ring, Ijab and Qubul, Mahr

A proposal is an offer of marriage that one party in a couple makes to the other. In some instances, the proposal is made in an almost casual fashion, perhaps even spontaneously. Most couples, however, regard their engagement as a key life event. Accordingly, thought and preparation are put into the proposal, so as to make it a memorable, romantic event.

History and Significance

In modern American life, the marriage proposal tends to be an intimate moment between the two parties. Rarely are families directly involved. Historically, however, marriage proposals were very much family affairs, with either a bride-price or dowry being exchanged between the parents of the engaged couple. Throughout most of human history, in fact, marriages in most cultures tended to be arranged by families, and some people maintain this practice. Among Muslims, for whom parents and matchmakers often play roles in finding suitable mates (*see* **Matchmaking**), the proposal and acceptance is called *ijab* and *qubul*. A wedding gift, called the *mahr*, will also be given to the woman by the man.

Historically, marriage proposals generally entailed more of a legal and social obligation than they do in modern life. A man who withdrew an offer of marriage would face social scorn and possible legal repercussions.

Historically, marriage proposals generally entailed more of a legal and social obligation than they do in modern life. For this reason, they were often made in writing, and a man who withdrew an offer of marriage would face social scorn and possible legal repercussions, with the letter of proposal serving as evidence.

Observances

In modern America, few of these historical customs are followed. Proposals of marriage rarely involve either party's family, and while people marry for a variety of motives, most marriages tend to be based on some level of love and mutual respect rather than on the economic or social needs of the families. Accordingly, the marriage proposal for most Americans is a romantic event, one that carries with it little sense of legal or financial obligation.

Proposals of marriage traditionally come almost exclusively from the man. Although in recent decades it has become more acceptable for women to propose marriage, the original custom remains strong. The typical proposal, sometimes informally referred to as "popping the question," often involves considerable preparation on the man's part. Typically, the man takes the woman out, perhaps to an elegant restaurant, and at some point gets down on one knee, presents an engagement ring, and asks the woman, "Will you marry me?" The woman, of course, is free to decline the proposal or to ask for time to consider. In contemporary life, however, large numbers of couples live together before marriage, such that the formal proposal confirms a preexisting notion that the parties may eventually wed.

Other men (and women) find more creative and elaborate ways to propose marriage, and the methods for such proposals are limited only by the prospective groom's (or bride's) creativity. Possibilities include having a small plane fly overhead with a banner printed with a marriage proposal; or taking a seaside vacation, hiding an engagement ring and note inside a bottle buried in the sand, and arranging to "find" the bottle together. Additionally, many proposals are made during activities that the couple shares. Horseback riders, for example, might ride to a favorite spot, where the proposal is then made, or a skydiver might propose marriage while the couple is in the air plunging toward the earth. Some people involve friends and associates in the proposal. Schoolteachers have been proposed to over the school's public address system, and those dating police officers have been pulled over and proposed to. The possibilities are endless.

Poor Luck

Creative or elaborate marriage proposals occasionally do not work out as planned. Numerous people, for example, have recruited waiters in restaurants to hide engagement rings in dishes served to the woman in question. Some of these romantic plans have backfired, though, when the ring was served to the wrong patron or when the woman accidentally swallowed the ring or declined to eat the dish (and therefore did not find the ring).

Customs and Symbols

Bride-Price or Dowry

Throughout much of history and also in some contemporary cultures—for example, in India and some other south Asian countries—fathers have been eager to marry their daughters off to eligible men, such that prior to a formal engagement a father might agree to give his prospective son-in-law a dowry. A dowry consists of valued property, such as land, cattle, or other goods, that is transferred to the man's family when the couple marries. In modern America, the only vestige of the dowry is the custom of asking the father's permission to marry his daughter. In yet other cultures, the husband's family pays a bride-price to the bride's family as compensation for the loss of her labor and fertility. Such financial arrangements suggest that the proposals in question may be less affairs of the heart than affairs of the purse.

Engagement Ring

An important marker of a proposal is the engagement ring. The engagement ring represents a formal agreement to be married and is regarded as a betrothal gift from the man to the woman if she accepts his proposal. Thus, it is sometimes called a betrothal ring. The selection, purchase, and giving of the engagement ring is typically regarded as a major event in a couple's relationship. For many women, receiving an engagement ring is a cause for great excitement, and most are eager to show their ring to their friends and families. After marriage, the woman usually continues to wear her engagement ring in combination with her wedding ring. Some couples later purchase new, more valuable rings to replace the engagement ring—or have the engagement ring reset—when the couple can afford to do so.

The engagement ring is typically worn by the woman on the third finger of the left hand—the ring finger—because in ancient times it was believed that the vein in that finger, the "vein of love," connected directly to the heart. By the 19th century, various types of engagement rings were commonly used. They were typically set not with diamonds but with gemstones such as sapphires, emeralds, or pearls, or with birthstones. On many engagement rings the word "Regards" was spelled out in gemstones. Yet another common design was that of the gimmal ring. This type of ring consists of two or even three parts that come together in the shape of clasping hands. While the couple was engaged, the bride-to-be wore one part, the groom-to-be wore the second, and a witness wore the third. On the wedding day, the three parts were assembled as the bride's wedding ring.

The modern practice of giving diamond engagement rings did not begin until about the middle of the 20th century. Diamond engagement rings have become the standard for several reasons. The clarity of diamonds is symbolic of purity, and because of their durability, they also symbolize the permanence of the relationship. Most diamonds—or other stones—are set in a gold band, although silver is sometimes used; a contemporary practice is to set the stones in a titanium band because of that element's extreme durability. The two most popular diamond engagement ring designs feature either one diamond (known as a solitaire) or three diamonds. The gems in the three-diamond ring are said to represent the couple's past, present, and future together.

Some men try to surprise their partners with engagement rings, but it is quite common for the couple to shop together to pick out an engagement ring after the proposal. As far as expense is concerned, there are no formal guidelines, but the cost of the ring is likely to be a reflection of the man's means.

Few men wear anything like an engagement ring, although sometimes a woman will purchase for her fiancé a "promise ring," usually an inexpensive ring to serve as a token of her love and commitment.

Ijab and Qubul

In Islam, the proposal and acceptance is called ijab-o-qubul, where ijab is the proposal and qubul is the woman's acceptance. Ijab-o-qubul is generally followed by a written contract, in which the two parties specify the terms of their engagement. A legal guardian, called a *wali,* represents the bride-to-be during the negotiation of these terms. The contract, called the *nikah,* has to be signed in front of two competent witnesses and is then announced publicly, making the engagement official.

Mahr

Depending on the couples' cultural background, a Muslim man gives his bride-to-be the mahr, or a wedding gift, either at the time of the proposal or during the wedding ceremony. This custom is based on a passage from Islam's sacred scripture,

Wedding Costs

The total price of a U.S. wedding averages close to $30,000, making weddings a $125 billion enterprise. One of the most expensive items is the engagement ring, whose cost averages over $4,100, a 39 percent increase between 1999 and 2005.

the Qu'ran. Mahr, generally a token consisting of objects or money, is a symbol of the man's responsibility to the woman. The Qu'ran does not specify the value of mahr, but moderation is generally the rule.

Further Reading

Garrison, Graham. *Groomed: From Proposal to Vows, Wedding Planning and an Engagement from a Groom's Point of View*. Lincoln, NE: iUniverse, 2005.

Martin, Richard C., ed. *Encyclopedia of Islam and the Muslim World*. New York: Macmillan Reference USA, 2004.

Stewart, Arlene. *A Bride's Book of Wedding Traditions*. New York: William Morrow, 1995.

ENGAGEMENT PARTY

Customs and Symbols: Ham, Kola Nut, Toasts, Yak Kon Sik

Engagement parties serve several functions by providing a venue for couples to bring family and friends together. The couple can publicize and celebrate their engagement at the party. Another important role of the engagement party is that it allows the bride's family and the groom's family to meet, often for the first time. In this way the "in-laws"—families that are not genetically related but become related by the couple's marriage—can get to know each other before the commencement of other mixed-family events, such as **Wedding Showers**, **Rehearsal Dinners**, and wedding ceremonies (*see* **Wedding Preparations** and **Wedding Ceremonies**).

History and Significance

Most modern engagement parties are celebratory gatherings for the couple and their families and friends, ranging from modest home affairs to upscale restaurant dinners.

Historically, engagements carried more legal force, and in many cultures the engagement was regarded as nearly as important as the wedding itself. One way this sense of legality and obligation was demonstrated was through the engagement party, when the couple formally announced to the community that they were engaged. The involvement of the community in such a party, called a "flouncing" in England, made the couple's commitment both public and more legally binding. Thus, if one party withdrew from the agreement, the other could legally claim half of his or her property. This is no longer the case, and though engagement parties are still a way to publicly announce the betrothal, their focus has become that of celebrating the couple rather than that of binding them.

Observance

In the U.S., most modern engagement parties are celebratory gatherings for the couple and their families and friends, ranging from modest home affairs to upscale restaurant dinners. Being fairly informal, most European-American engagement parties follow no set rituals. Typically, the guest list is small, restricted to relatives and close friends. The party may be hosted by anyone, such as friends or siblings of the couple, with the hosts (and also others) often giving toasts. Traditionally, they were surprise parties for the engaged couple as well as most guests, but for most modern parties, the purpose is known in advance. According to established rules of etiquette, guests are under no obligation to bring gifts, although many do. Because not all guests bring gifts, it is customary for the couple to open those received in private after the event. Among engagement party guests who do bring gifts, many divide the planned expense of a wedding present between the engagement party gift and the wedding present itself.

Some Americans maintain more elaborate customs. Korean Americans, for example, observe a number of engagement traditions, including the presentation of a *ham* (or *hamn*), a box of gifts, to the future bride by the groom's friends. The engagement itself is then celebrated at a party known as a *Yak Kon Sik*. An African tradition still followed by some African-American couples involves a visit of the prospective groom and his family to the prospective bride's family, where the groom's family offers their hosts a kola nut.

Customs and Symbols

Ham

Engagement parties for Korean Americans are common and reflect a long and rich tradition of wedding customs in Korean society. For example, at the time of an engagement, the groom's closest friends deliver a box of betrothal gifts to the bride's home in a box called a ham. One of the items in the box is usually blue and red fabric. The bride uses this fabric to make her wedding dress.

Kola Nut

An African custom preserved by some African Americans involves the nut from a kola tree. According to this custom, the prospective groom and his family visit the home of the prospective bride and her family to propose marriage. If the woman's family agrees to the marriage, the groom and his family offer money and a kola nut. The bride then cracks open the nut and gives pieces of it to her future husband and to the other family members present. Afterwards, to announce the engagement to the community, a messenger delivers pieces of the kola nut to other families.

Toasts

A chief custom of many engagement parties is the offering of toasts. Traditionally, the first person to offer a toast is the bride-to-be's father. The groom-to-be usually offers a toast to his fiancée and her family. Other guests can then also offer toasts, which may include serious good wishes combined with light-hearted stories and jokes about the couple, their courtship, how they became engaged, and the like. The engaged couple customarily refrains from drinking during the toasts.

Yak Kon Sik

Koreans often hold a formal engagement party called a Yak Kon Sik. At this party, the families of the bride and groom often meet each other for the first time. It is thus common for one person to formally introduce each member of the family and to provide details about their lives.

An important part of the Yak Kon Sik is gift giving, for failure to give lavish gifts would entail a loss of face. Traditionally, the groom's family, if they are affluent, gives the bride three sets of jewelry, and each set traditionally features a distinct semiprecious stone. Presents from the bride and her family to the groom might include an expensive wristwatch and a suit. To the groom's mother they might give a fur coat or other expensive present.

Further Reading

The Bride's Book of Etiquette. New York: Penguin, 1999.

Dresser, Norine. *Multicultural Celebrations: Today's Rules of Etiquette for Life's Special Occasions.* New York: Three Rivers Press, 1999.

Spangenberg, Lisl M. *Timeless Traditions: A Couple's Guide to Wedding Customs around the World.* New York: Universe Publishing, 2001.

Photo on facing page: Henna body painting is typically used by Hindu and Islamic cultures to celebrate special events, especially weddings.

Chapter 13: Wedding Preparations

INTRODUCTION

During the engagement period, many couples devote considerable time and effort to wedding preparations, though many pay a professional wedding planner to tend to all the details.

Among the numerous wedding preparations that must be made, the couple first has to worry about **Setting the Date** for the event—a decision fraught with considerations ranging from the climate to cultural traditions.

Members of various religious and ethnic groups have unique pre-wedding traditions, such as the Jewish **Fasting and Ritual Bath**; the **Henna Body Painting** tradition favored by many from parts of the Middle East, Africa, and south Asia; and **Loading the Bride**, an African-American gathering adapted from African customs.

A **Wedding Shower** is likely to be held for the bride or in some instances for the couple. Gathering the proper **Attire**, most notably the bride's dress, is crucial. Both the bride and groom will also select members of the **Wedding Party**. Finally, as the date of the wedding fast approaches, many gather for a **Rehearsal Dinner** after practicing the ceremony.

SETTING THE DATE

Customs and Symbols: Avoiding Holy Days, Fortune Tellers, Specific Months or Seasons

For most Americans, setting a wedding date is often a pragmatic, rather than a religious or cultural, decision. Sometimes the date is determined by the availability of facilities: if a couple insists on a reception at a particular hotel banquet room, or if they want to hold the ceremony in a particular church or at an outdoor park, they may have to select from the dates when the location is available for use. Other factors to consider include holidays and ease of travel for guests (particularly in snowy climates). Some people avoid weekends that include a Friday the 13th, and in recent years many couples have avoided September 11, the date of the terrorist attacks on the U.S. in 2001.

History and Significance

Historically, wedding dates were not set far in advance of the engagement, in large part because wedding preparations were far less complex than they are in contemporary life. It was likely that the only people attending the wedding would be family and close friends, all from the local community, so travel plans and accommodations for guests were not a complicating factor. While in modern life weddings are generally held on a Friday evening or anytime on a Saturday, in years past weddings were held on any day of the week.

Observance

While the practice is somewhat less common today, in setting their wedding dates many religious couples still avoid holy days. Other religious groups tend to schedule weddings during specific months or seasons. People in several Asian cultures employ fortune tellers in order to determine the right dates for weddings.

Once the wedding date is selected, numerous other preparations are commenced. Typically, the bride and her family, sometimes with the help of the groom and his family, reserve time at a place of worship or another ceremonial site, arrange for the services of a photographer, book a location for the reception, find musicians for both the ceremony and reception, select floral arrangements, and make decisions about many other details. Faraway relatives and friends make travel plans, and local accommodations are found for them. While invitations are usually mailed about a month or so in advance of the wedding, in reality, couples often send out advance notices to guests to "save the date" so that they can make travel arrangements and avoid making other plans for that day.

It is generally believed that the most popular month for weddings is June, when the unpredictable weather of spring has settled into the warmth of summer but the heat of July and August has not yet arrived. In recent years, many couples have found it difficult to book reception halls, churches, photographers, and the like in June, such that they have been pushed into other months.

Customs and Symbols

Avoiding Holy Days

Jewish couples, or those who plan to invite a significant number of Jewish friends to their wedding face several considerations in selecting a date. One is to avoid the Jewish Sabbath, which begins at sundown on Friday and ends at sundown on Saturday. Thus, Friday evening weddings are avoided, and Saturday weddings are delayed until after the sun sets. Also, Jews do not marry on Rosh Hashanah (which generally falls in late September to early October), Yom Kippur, or the ten days between these two holy days (often referred to as the Days of Awe). The Feast of Passover is another time that is avoided, as is Yom HaShoah, generally late April or early May, a day set aside for Jews around the world to remember the Holocaust, when millions of Jews were murdered during World War II.

Christian couples also avoid marrying during holy days or periods, including Holy Week, which runs from Palm Sunday to Easter Sunday and falls in late March or early April. The Christmas season is also unpopular, since churches and their priests and ministers are extremely busy and often unavailable for marrying couples. Additionally, some Christian churches are happy to hold weddings on Sundays any time after morning services; yet others frown on Sunday weddings, seeing them as violating the biblical command that Sunday be a day of rest.

For Islamic weddings, the worst months are Muharram, the first month of the Islamic calendar, and Islam's ninth and holiest month, Ramadan. These months are set aside as a time for fasting and prayer rather than celebration.

Historically, in many Asian cultures, the couple did not select their own wedding date; rather, a fortune-teller was enlisted to select the most auspicious date, usually through astrological calculations, taking into account the birth dates of the couple.

Fortune Tellers

Historically, in many Asian cultures, including that of China, the couple did not select their own wedding date; rather, a fortune-teller was enlisted to select the most auspicious date, usually through astrological calculations, taking into account the birth dates of the couple. In modern America, many people of Asian descent still follow the tradition of consulting a fortune-teller. If the fortune-teller concludes that a weekday is the most auspicious date, many couples hold two ceremonies: a small one on the date selected by the fortune-teller, then a larger one on the following weekend.

Specific Months or Seasons

Most Muslims regard the month of Shawwal as a good time for a wedding. Shawwal is the tenth month of the Islamic calendar, and since the Islamic calendar is lunar, the corresponding dates on the Western calendar shift back eleven or twelve days each year. Shawwal takes place after the fasting month of Ramadan. Muslim weddings are frequently held on Sundays.

A few Jewish holidays are considered favorable dates on which to schedule weddings. The 15th day of the Jewish month of Av, which falls in either July or August, was a traditional folk festival in ancient Jerusalem. Known as Tu b'Av, young women would gather to dance in vineyards, where young bachelors would come to choose their brides. Rosh Hodesh—the day of the new moon which begins each Jewish month, is said to be a propitious day for weddings. Hanukkah weddings have also become fairly common.

Amish weddings are conducted in the months of October and November, after the fall harvest is gathered and before winter weather sets in. Amish weddings are held almost always on Tuesdays or Thursdays, though Saturdays are scrupulously avoided, as cleanup would have to take place on Sunday, the Sabbath.

Further Reading

Stewart, Arlene. *A Bride's Book of Wedding Traditions.* New York: William Morrow, 1995.

FASTING AND RITUAL BATH

Alternate Names: Mikvah, Tsuwm

Customs and Symbols: Atonement, Purification

Fasting and ritual bathing are undertaken by Jewish brides and grooms prior to the wedding. These customs are intended to help the couple prepare spiritually for the changes of marriage.

History and Significance

Jewish wedding traditions descend from ancient times. In the first five books of the Torah (Hebrew scripture consisting of the books of Genesis, Exodus, Leviticus, Numbers, and Deuteronomy), the Jewish patriarchs enacted a large number of laws governing Jewish life. While many of these laws are no longer followed literally by many Liberal and Reform Jews, others have become deeply embedded traditions; all laws are observed by Orthodox Jews. Two of these traditional laws require that couples fast and ritually bathe prior to their wedding day.

Judaism regards the wedding day as a turning point in the lives of the bride and groom. On this day, the couple begins a new life together. In this way, a Jewish wedding resembles Yom Kippur, the Day of Atonement. Spiritual preparations for marriage are similar to the customs of Yom Kippur, and include purification rituals such as fasting (*tsuwm*) and ritual bathing (*mikvah*).

> *Judaism regards the wedding day as a turning point in the lives of the bride and groom. On this day, the couple begins a new life together. Spiritual preparations for marriage include purification rituals such as fasting and ritual bathing.*

Observance

In the days leading up to the wedding, Jewish couples take steps to emphasize the religious aspect of marriage. During this time, couples undergo physical and spiritual cleansing as a means of preparing for their holy union in marriage. The mikvah is used in Jewish tradition for purification and to signify a transition from one state of being to another. Couples also seek atonement, or forgiveness of sins. Fasting is the primary way to seek forgiveness, along with reflection and prayer. Jewish brides and grooms typically practice all three prior to their wedding.

Customs and Symbols

Atonement

On the day of the wedding, the bride and groom fast and ask God for forgiveness for their sins. They also pray and recite verses from the Torah. By first seeking God's forgiveness, the couple can begin their new life together in a pure spiritual state. The bride and groom break their fast together when they share the cup of wine during the wedding ceremony. Immediately after the ceremony, it is traditional for Jewish newlyweds to have a short time alone. During this brief period of seclusion, the couple often feed each other their first meal as husband and wife.

Purification

Both the bride and groom ritually bathe before their wedding day. Entering the mikvah (ritual bath) is a private rite of purification that marks a change of status, in this case from unmarried to married. Men and women go separately to the mikvah, which can be any body of moving water outdoors or a special indoor bathing facility similar to a small swimming pool. Because individuals must enter the mikvah nude, most choose the privacy of the indoor facilities built specifically for this purpose. The individual must be totally immersed in the water two or three times. Upon rising from the water, the mikvah blessing is recited by the bather. The bride-to-be is usually assisted by an attendant called a "mikvah lady," who ensures that the woman is totally immersed in the water.

Web Site

"Planning Your Jewish Wedding: Seven Simple Steps," by Gabrielle Kaplan-Mayer. MyJewish-Learning.com, undated.
   http://www.myjewishlearning.com/lifecycle/Marriage/LiturgyRitualCustom/Modern Customs/Howto_Wedding.htm.

Further Reading

Diamant, Anita. *The New Jewish Wedding*. New York: Fireside, 2001.

Gross, David C., and Esther R. Gross. *Under the Wedding Canopy: Love and Marriage in Judaism.* New York: Hippocrene Books, 1996.

WEDDING SHOWER

Alternate Name: Bridal Shower

Customs and Symbols: Couple's Shower, Games, Gift Registry, Gifts, Ribbon Bouquet

A wedding shower is a party usually hosted by a bride's family or bridesmaids prior to the wedding. During this event, the bride is "showered" with gifts and attention by those in attendance. Customs vary according to family and cultural traditions and the wishes of the bride, but most showers are attended only by women.

History and Significance

Modern bridal showers are a combination of two pre-wedding traditions that have been practiced throughout history by many cultures worldwide: the presentation of gifts to a soon-to-be-married woman, and the gathering of female friends and relatives to celebrate and help prepare a woman for her wedding. The exact origins of these traditions are unclear; however, in parts of Europe and North and South America, the gifts were once intended to supplement a woman's dowry, thereby making her more desirable as a potential bride. In parts of Africa, India, and the Middle East, as well as Jewish and Muslim communities throughout the world, female relatives were a young woman's social group and primary source of information. Pre-wedding gatherings attended only by women allowed important advice to be shared with the bride. Even as the needs of contemporary American brides continue to evolve, the wedding shower remains an important social event that celebrates the pending marriage and helps to prepare the bride—and groom—to begin a new phase of life.

Observance

There is tremendous variation in wedding shower events, with each aspect of the party being dependent upon local custom, religious or cultural traditions, or the individual preference of the bride-to-be. Wedding showers are often hosted by the maid or matron of honor and the bridesmaids (*see* **Wedding Party**), close friends, or female relatives of the bride. Most wedding showers include the

> *The wedding shower remains an important social event that celebrates the pending marriage and helps to prepare the bride—and groom—to begin a new phase of life.*

presentation of gifts to the bride, although some are simply celebrations of her pending marriage. The event may be attended by women only, or it may be a couples' shower attended by both men and women. Depending on the type of party, games may or may not be played. It is not uncommon for more than one shower to be held, as work colleagues, neighbors, school friends and roommates, and sisters and cousins, among other groups, can each hold a shower for the bride.

Some American Muslims, Hindus, and Sephardic Jews hold *mehndi* parties in conjunction with or instead of wedding showers (*see* **Henna Body Painting**). These parties are generally attended only by women, and may or may not include gifts for the bride. The African-American ritual of **Loading the Bride** is thought of as a type of wedding shower that focuses more on intangible gifts of advice rather than material goods. This custom can be observed in conjunction with a traditional wedding shower or as a separate event.

In addition to or instead of a wedding shower, some Chinese-American brides choose to observe the ancient custom of *lai beng*, or bride's cookie day. Approximately one month before the wedding, the bride receives an assortment of fancy pastries, fruit, nuts, and other edible delicacies as well as gifts from the groom's family. The bride is expected to share her bounty with members of her family. Typically, the day is celebrated as an informal gathering at the bride's home. Some brides prefer to forego the delivery of sweets—which can total into the thousands of individual pastries—and instead "share" with family members by providing them with gift certificates for use at a local Chinese bakery. The cookie day celebration is intended for the bride and her family, consequently the groom and his family usually do not take part in the celebration.

Customs and Symbols

Couple's Shower

A couple's shower is a wedding shower that includes the bride and the groom, as well as male and female guests. At these events gifts are normally given to the couple, often in "his and hers" sets. For these showers the couple might register for gifts separately at different stores.

Games

Party games are a common feature at wedding showers. The possibilities are vast, and numerous books and Internet sites offer suggestions for suitable games. Some games are based on how well each guest knows the bride and groom, while others are games of chance such as bingo. Shower hosts may also offer door prizes, based on a drawing of guests' names.

Gift Registry

Many couples register for gifts by listing the items they would like to receive from a favorite store. Once mainly a service of large department stores and specialty home goods shops, gift registry service is now offered by a wide variety of stores. After the bride and groom make their selections, the shop keeps the registry list on file and makes it available to those who are attending the wedding shower. The gift registry makes gift giving easier for guests, for they know what the couple needs and can avoid duplicating gifts or giving mismatched items. Gift registry possibilities are nearly endless—it is even possible for the engaged couple to register for their **Honeymoon** and have guests make a gift of paying for part of the trip (*see* **Post-Wedding Events**).

Gifts

Shower gifts typically include household items such as kitchen equipment or linens. Some showers organize the gift-giving around a theme, such as gardening or leisure entertainment. For these showers, guests are asked to bring gifts that fit the stated theme. Sometimes guests are asked to share special knowledge in addition to or instead of a more traditional gift. In these instances, guests may be asked to write down a favorite recipe or their best piece of relationship advice. These are then assembled into an album as a keepsake for the bride.

Ribbon Superstitions

At a wedding shower, the bride usually opens her gifts in the presence of all the guests. One traditional belief is focused on the ribbons and bows tied around the gift packages. Some say the bride is not allowed to use scissors or a knife to cut any ribbons, but must try to remove them from the package by hand. The number of ribbons that she breaks is then thought to have significance. Some say it indicates the number of children the couple will have, while others believe it signifies the number of months or years before the first child will be born. The origin of this custom is unknown, but it continues to produce much hilarity and good-natured teasing at wedding showers.

Ribbon Bouquet

Another common wedding shower tradition involves the collection of all the ribbons and bows used to decorate the gift packages. These are then assembled into a ribbon bouquet that the bride can carry during the wedding rehearsal generally held a day or two before the wedding.

Web Site

"The Muslim Wedding Celebration" by Sharbari Bose. Brides, undated.
     http://www.brides.com/weddingstyle/traditions/feature/article/105565

Further Reading

Ball, Joanne Dubbs, and Caroline Torem-Craig. *Wedding Traditions: Here Comes the Bride.* Dubuque, IA: Antique Trader Books, 1997.

Etzioni, Amitai, and Jared Bloom, eds. *We Are What We Celebrate: Understanding Holidays and Rituals.* New York: New York University Press, 2004.

Gong, Rosemary. *Good Luck Life: The Essential Guide to Chinese American Celebrations and Culture.* New York: Harper Collins, 2005.

WEDDING ATTIRE

Alternate Names: Bridal Gown, Wedding Dress

Customs and Symbols: Dress, Garter, Tuxedo, Veil

One nearly universal element of weddings is the use of special garments for the bride and groom. Perhaps the most celebrated of these is the white wedding *dress* and *veil*, although there are many variations in wedding attire depending on cultural and religious traditions.

History and Significance

The traditional white wedding dress and veil was first worn by early Roman brides as a sign of purity. Throughout the ages, wedding attire evolved around cultural and religious traditions in different parts of the world, and varied widely depending on local customs. In the U.S. up to the mid-19th century, most people were married wearing their best or newest clothing. The white bridal gown experienced a resurgence in popularity when Britain's Queen Victoria chose all-white regalia for her marriage to Prince Albert in 1840. This fashion has since taken hold all over the world, and brides of many cultures are choosing white dresses over more culturally specific garments.

Observance

When a bride chooses a modern white wedding gown, the groom usually wears an elegant suit or a tuxedo. The majority of American couples choose these outfits for their wedding attire. However, some couples forego the white dress and tuxedo in favor of more traditional clothing that reflects their heritage.

Hindu brides may wear a brightly colored *sari* (a form of Indian women's clothing) along with many different ornaments and jewelry. Hindu grooms may choose from a variety of traditional ceremonial outfits, some of which include a gleaming sword. African-American couples sometimes wear outfits made of African *kente* cloth, a woven fabric featuring bold patterns in red, gold, and green. Jewish brides generally choose white wedding dresses, while Jewish grooms often wear a white robe called a *kittel* over their wedding suit.

Historically, Chinese brides wear red dresses to attract good luck and repel evil spirits, and some Chinese-American brides do the same. Chinese-American grooms usually choose to wear a tuxedo, although some prefer the traditional Chinese gentleman's robe which features a subtle pattern on dark silk, with a long red sash draped over one shoulder and tied at the waist.

Nontraditional wedding attire is sometimes chosen by those who have planned a wedding around a particular theme, such as a masquerade ball or historical time period. Older couples or those for whom it is not their first wedding generally do not wear formal wedding dresses or tuxedos, preferring simpler outfits instead.

In addition to the bride and groom, other participants in the wedding also wear special garments. Members of the wedding party generally wear matching attire, usually including formal dresses for the bridesmaids and tuxedos for the groomsmen. The mothers of both the bride and the groom are likely to devote considerable time and thought to the selection of their outfits. Traditionally, neither of the mothers, nor anyone in the wedding party or any of the other guests, should wear a white dress or any other attire that could compete with the bride for attention.

Customs and Symbols

Dress

Most American brides wear white wedding gowns and white veils. There is tremendous variety in the style of these dresses, ranging from very plain and simple to extremely elaborate. Some brides choose dresses with trains, which are lengths of fabric that trail along the ground behind the bride. Long trains are usually only worn for the wedding ceremony; many can be detached or draped and fastened to the back of the dress for the reception.

> *Traditionally, neither of the mothers, nor anyone in the wedding party or any of the other guests, should wear a white dress or any other attire that could compete with the bride for attention.*

Some Chinese-American brides choose to wear a traditional *hong qua* or a *cheongsam*. The hong qua is a red silk wedding suit that normally includes a long pleated skirt and a jacket embroidered with silver and gold phoenixes and dragons, the traditional Chinese symbols of the bride and groom. The cheongsam is a long, sleek, form-fitting dress that has cap sleeves or is sleeveless, with a high mandarin collar and slits up to the thigh on both sides. The cheongsam is usually made of red, pink, gold, or silver silk (colors that represent happiness and prosperity) and features intricate embroidery, beadwork, or sequins in contrasting colors. Some Chinese-American brides change clothes for different parts of the wedding, often wearing a

Something Old, Something New

A popular wedding rhyme that dates back to the folklore of Victorian England has influenced the attire of countless brides over the years:

"Something old, something new, something borrowed, something blue, and a silver sixpence in your shoe."

Wearing something old represents a connection between the bride and her family, and usually the item has special meaning for the bride. It may be a piece of heirloom family jewelry or even the wedding dress worn by her mother or grandmother. The new item, which can be anything purchased specifically to be worn on the wedding day, represents a wish for good fortune and success in the bride's new life. Borrowing a piece of jewelry or a handkerchief from a close friend or family member, usually something that was worn by a happy bride on her own wedding day, is thought to bring good luck and happiness to the marriage—provided the item is returned after the wedding. The color blue has ancient associations with purity and fidelity, and modern brides sometimes pin or sew a blue band or small blue ribbon to the lining of their wedding dress. The silver sixpence tradition has evolved to include a shiny new coin of the smallest denomination, such as a penny. It is placed in the bride's left shoe as a wish for a marriage that is rich in happiness and good luck.

white wedding dress and veil for the ceremony and red garments for the wedding banquet. Because white is the color of mourning and grief in traditional Chinese culture, many brides prefer to avoid wearing white for the entire wedding day.

Garter

A garter is an elastic band that may be embellished with lace or other decorations. Garters were originally worn by women to hold up their stockings. Although the practice of wearing garters has gone out of fashion, many brides regard the garter as an essential component of their wedding attire. Many brides choose a blue garter, to satisfy the superstitious requirement that they wear "something blue" on their wedding day.

Veiling the Bride

The custom of the groom placing the veil over his bride's face is thought to have originated from ancient times, specifically the story narrated in the Bible's book of Genesis (chapters 29 and 30) about the marriage of Jacob. Jacob had fallen in love with Rachel, but her father, Laban, deceived Jacob into marrying Rachel's sister, Leah, by covering her face in a heavy veil before the wedding. Thus, in order to ensure the bride's identity, some Jewish grooms take it upon themselves to veil their own brides in a custom called *bedaken*.

Tuxedo

A tuxedo, or tux, is the traditional choice of attire for many grooms. This formal suit is generally well tailored and includes pants, a jacket, a vest or cummerbund (a broad waistband, often with horizontal pleats), a necktie, and dress shoes. Personal flair may be incorporated into the tux through the choice of a colored or printed vest, cummerbund or necktie, or with the addition of a walking stick or cane, a top hat, cape, or gloves. The tuxedo jacket may resemble a traditional suit coat; alternately the jacket may have tails or the cut of a morning coat. Although tuxedo options are extensive, compared to the time and thought given to the bride's wedding dress, often far less attention is given to the groom's attire.

Veil

A veil is worn by brides of many different cultural traditions. Historically, the bride's veil covered her face and was a sign of modesty and purity. Sometimes the veil was used solely to prevent the groom from catching even a glimpse of his bride's face before the wedding ceremony, which was thought to be very bad luck. The bride's face would remain covered until a certain point in the wedding ceremony when the groom would lift the veil from her face. This was especially significant in cases of arranged marriages, when the bride and groom would often meet for the first time on their wedding day. Many modern brides have modified the tradition by choosing to wear a veil that does not cover the face, but instead hangs down in back. In some Jewish weddings, the groom meets the bride before the wedding ceremony to place a veil over her face.

Web Sites

"Lore and Tradition." WeddingDetails.com, undated.
http://www.weddingdetails.com/lore

"Wedding Traditions and Customs Around the World." WorldWeddingTraditions.com, 2004.
http://www.worldweddingtraditions.com

Further Reading

Emrich, Duncan. *The Folklore of Weddings and Marriage: The Traditional Beliefs, Customs, Superstitions, Charms, and Omens of Marriage and Marriage Ceremonies.* New York: American Heritage Press, 1970.

Gong, Rosemary. *Good Luck Life: The Essential Guide to Chinese American Celebrations and Culture.* New York: Harper Collins, 2005.

Jones, Leslie. *Happy Is the Bride the Sun Shines On: Wedding Beliefs, Customs, and Traditions.* Chicago: Contemporary Books, 1995.

Spangenberg, Lisl M. *Timeless Traditions: A Couple's Guide to Wedding Customs Around the World.* New York: Universe Publishing, 2001.

HENNA BODY PAINTING

Alternate Names: Lailat al-Hinna, Lal Hanna, Mehndi, Night of the Henna

Customs and Symbols: Henna Paste, Pattern, Temporary Stain

Henna has been used for centuries to temporarily adorn the body. It is a custom most often associated with Hindu and Islamic cultures, although henna is also used in Jewish and Christian communities from the Middle East and Africa.

History and Significance

The use of henna for body decoration is believed to have originated around the year 1600 B.C.E. Henna has been found on Egyptian mummies, and there is evidence of its use in other ancient societies as well. Henna continues to be used for beautification throughout the world, particularly in the cultures of India, the Middle East, and parts of Africa. The practice is not specifically a religious one, but rather represents a standard of beauty shared by these cultures.

Observance

Henna is applied in elaborate, intricate designs that vary according to local custom and personal taste. Some people prefer large, open flowery designs while others choose finely detailed, lacey patterns.

Some women use henna routinely for cosmetic purposes, however it is a custom most often reserved for special occasions such as a wedding. In the Middle East, brides of all faiths celebrate the Night of the Henna (*Lailat al-Hinna*), while Hindu, Indian, and Pakistani brides have a *mehndi* party. This is a festive event held one or two nights before the wedding and usually attended only by women. During the party, the bride's hands and feet are decorated with henna paste applied in an elaborate pattern. Henna may also be applied to other parts of the body. Traditionally, only the bride receives henna, although other women may be adorned as well. Sometimes the groom receives henna decorations to complement those worn by the bride.

Sephardic Jewish brides decorate the palms of their hands with henna during an elaborate feast shortly before the wedding. This is done to ward off the evil eye, which is believed to bring misfortune. Jewish brides with Kurdish heritage may have up to three henna parties. The first takes place at betrothal, when the marriage agreement is settled. The second is known as the "false henna night" (*lel hinne bedulge*) and is intended to trick evil spirits or demons that might bring bad luck to the bride. The "real" henna party (*lal hanna*) is held one or two nights before the wedding ceremony, with the groom receiving henna at his home. The bowl of henna paste is then taken to the bride's home so that she can be hennaed. As extra protection that evening, a young girl and boy receive henna while sitting on the laps of the bride and groom, acting as decoys to confuse any lingering evil spirits.

Customs and Symbols

Henna Paste

To apply henna to the body, a paste is made from finely ground and sifted henna leaves, water, and other ingredients. The paste is painted on the skin, producing a temporary stain which will remain for a short period of time. Henna paste can also be massaged into hair to produce highlights in varying shades of red.

Pattern

Henna is applied in elaborate, intricate designs that vary according to local custom and personal taste. Some people prefer large, open flowery designs while others choose finely detailed, lacey patterns. When the bride and groom receive complementary henna designs, they each commonly wear half of a circular medallion. Then when they stand facing each other during the wedding ceremony, their clasped hands form one completed design. These complicated patterns can take hours to apply.

Temporary Stain

As it dries, henna paste leaves an orange or reddish stain on the skin. The stain will darken over time, becoming brown-red or black within a few days. For this reason, henna is usually applied one or two days before a special occasion such as a wedding, so that the henna will have achieved its full color at the appropriate time. The henna stain will gradually fade away, usually over the course of about 10 days, depending on variables such as exposure to sunlight and harsh soaps.

Web Sites

"The History and Uses of Henna," by I. C. Abiff. IslamOnline.net, 2001.
  http://www.islamonline.net/english/Science/2001/10/article3.shtml

"Jewish Henna Traditions from Kurdistan." The Henna Page, 2005.
  http://www.hennapage.com/henna/encyclopedia/kurdjewish

"Mehndi." MyBindi.com, 2001.
    http://www.mybindi.com/weddings/festivities/mehndi.cfm

"Pearls, Henna, and Challah: Sephardic Nuptial Customs," by Brigitte Dayan. *The Jewish News Weekly of Northern California*, November 8, 1996.
    http://www.jewishsf.com/content/20/module/displaystory/story_id/4886/edition_id/89
    /format/html/displaystory.html

Further Reading

Gulevich, Tanya. *Understanding Islam and Muslim Traditions*. Detroit: Omnigraphics, 2004.

Spangenberg, Lisl M. *Timeless Traditions: A Couple's Guide to Wedding Customs Around the World*. New York: Universe Publishing, 2001.

WEDDING PARTY

Alternate Names: Attendants, Bridal Party, Unterfuhrers, Witnesses

Customs and Symbols: Bachelor and Bachelorette Parties, Witness

The wedding party refers to the attendants of the bride and groom, often also known as the bridesmaids and groomsmen. This group is usually comprised of a number of people who have been significant figures in the lives of the engaged couple.

History and Significance

The custom of having attendants for brides and grooms is one of the oldest wedding traditions still observed all over the world. A wedding is regarded as a major rite of passage in most cultures worldwide, and those who are about to be married often receive special attention and assistance from close relatives and friends in the days preceding the wedding. Members of the wedding party help the bride and groom prepare for, and also bear witness to, the wedding ceremony.

Jewish tradition holds that the marriage of Adam and Eve was witnessed by the angels Gabriel and Michael, who are still regarded as the *shushvinim* (friends) of brides and grooms. Ancient Roman brides were attended by groups of bridesmaids whose main purpose was to confuse any evil spirits and unsavory humans who might wish to harm the bride. Unlike modern bridesmaids, these women dressed in outfits identical to the bride's, in order to ensure a successful deception.

Observance

The members of a wedding party are generally people who have been important or influential figures in the lives of the bride and groom. Often these are siblings, close friends, or other relatives, although anyone can serve as a bridesmaid or groomsman. The wedding party may also include any number of attendants, but an equal number of bridesmaids and groomsmen are often chosen so that they form couples. The size of the wedding party generally varies with the formality and elaborateness of the wedding. At the least, the

> *The members of a wedding party are generally people who have been important figures in the lives of the bride and groom. Often these are siblings, close friends, or other relatives, although anyone can serve as a bridesmaid or groomsman.*

bride is accompanied by a maid of honor (who is alternately called a matron of honor if she is married), and the groom is accompanied by a best man.

A Jewish bride and groom may choose to have two best men and two maids or matrons of honor, each representing their right and left hands. These four attendants are collectively known as the *unterfuhrers* (those who escort the bride and groom to the *chuppah*, the canopy under which a Jewish wedding takes place). The unterfuhrers sometimes include two married couples, often siblings of the bride or groom. Their responsibilities during the wedding ceremony may include symbolic tasks such as holding the rings and the *ketubah* (Jewish marriage contract).

The group of male friends and relatives who attend a traditional Muslim groom is known as the *hattabin*. Traditional Muslim brides are attended by female relatives and assisted by a *wali*, a male relative who acts as the bride's representative in matters related to the wedding ceremony. An Eastern Orthodox Christian best man is known as the *koumbaro*, a role traditionally filled by the groom's godfather although any close male relative can serve in this capacity. If a female relative serves as the groom's "best man," she is known as the *koumbara*. One important duty of the koumbaro(a) is to perform the crowning ritual, an important element of traditional Orthodox Christian **Religious Wedding Ceremonies**.

In addition to bridesmaids and groomsmen, the wedding party can also include any number of others who perform specific duties. Ushers help guests find seats at the wedding ceremony and sometimes also at the reception. Younger relatives or children of the bride or groom may serve as junior attendants. Boys generally act as

"Three Times a Bridesmaid, Never a Bride"

A persistent superstitious belief asserts that if a woman is a bridesmaid three times, she will never be married herself. The origins of this "bridesmaid's curse" are unknown, but the saying has become an idiomatic figure of speech used in reference to someone who repeatedly comes close to—but never quite achieves—a goal. In these cases, the unfortunate person is said to be "always a bridesmaid, never a bride." Luckily, superstition also allows for a remedy to this situation: if a woman is a bridesmaid seven or more times, the curse will be broken.

ring bearers, carrying a small pillow holding the wedding rings (or symbolic rings). Flower girls may precede the wedding party procession, scattering flower petals before them.

The modern wedding party primarily serves a ceremonial function, although any member of the wedding party may also help with wedding preparations. Typically, members of the wedding party participate in all events associated with the wedding. Members may also be responsible for arranging pre-wedding events such as the **Wedding Shower** and the bachelor and bachelorette parties. At the wedding reception, it is customary for the bridesmaids and groomsmen to offer toasts to the couple. In a gesture of thanks for all of the support and assistance, the bride presents a gift to each of the bridesmaids, and the groom gives a gift to each of the groomsmen.

Customs and Symbols

Bachelor and Bachelorette Parties

A short time before the wedding, the groomsmen may host a bachelor party for the groom. These parties are attended by the groom's male friends and relatives, and are intended to provide the groom with an opportunity to bid farewell to life as an unmarried man. Traditionally these events were raucous affairs featuring much alcohol and sometimes a hired female exotic dancer. In recent times, many bachelor parties are much more subdued gatherings, during which the men might simply play poker or spend an afternoon playing golf.

It has become common practice for bridesmaids to arrange a similar party for the bride. Known as a bachelorette party, these events can take many forms. Some are lively outings featuring visits to nightclubs and bars, with many of the bride's female friends and relatives joining in. Others might be quiet, relaxing spa trips during which the women enjoy massages or other beauty treatments. The type of bachelorette party that is held depends largely on the personality and wishes of the bride.

The primary—although often unstated—purpose of bachelor and bachelorette parties is to allow the bride and groom some time with their friends, apart from the busy wedding plans and activities. These events can also help reassure everyone that old friendships will continue after the couple is married.

Witness

Legal weddings in the U.S. are considered to be contractual agreements between two people. Many religious leaders are authorized by the government to perform legal weddings, as are judges, justices of the peace, and in certain circumstances, sea captains. In order for a wedding to be legal, certain criteria—which vary according to the location of the wedding—must be met. A marriage certificate confirming the legal status of the wedding must be signed by two witnesses in the presence of the person who performed the wedding. Bearing witness to the wedding is usually the responsibility of the maid or matron of honor and the best man. These two members of the wedding party usually sign the marriage certificate, effectively verifying that the wedding was conducted legally.

According to Jewish law, weddings are not valid unless they have been witnessed by two observers who are unrelated to each other and are also unrelated to the bride and groom. Because the best man and maid or matron of honor are often close relatives of the bride and groom, they may not be qualified to witness the wedding in this capacity. Non-Jews are also not permitted to act as witnesses. In these cases, additional witnesses must be designated.

Web Sites

"Attendants: A Glossary of Who's Who in the Wedding Party," The Knot, undated.
 http://www.theknot.com/ch_article.html?Object=AI91217122324&keywordID=163&keywordType=2&parentID=527

"What Are the Responsibilities of the Wedding Party?," by Peggy Post. Wedding Channel, undated.
 http://www.weddingchannel.com/ui/buildArticle.action?assetUID=87490&c=87490&s=84&t=71&p=67479800&l=135864

Further Reading

Clisby, Heather. "Peach Taffeta Nightmares: The High Price of Being a Bridesmaid," *Santa Barbara Independent*, February 22, 2007.

Diamant, Anita. *The New Jewish Wedding*. New York: Fireside, 2001.

Dresser, Norine. *Multicultural Celebrations: Today's Rules of Etiquette for Life's Special Occasions*. New York: Three Rivers Press, 1999.

Lee, Vera. *Something Old, Something New: What You Didn't Know about Wedding Ceremonies, Celebrations & Customs*. Naperville, IL: Sourcebooks, 1994.

REHEARSAL DINNER

Customs and Symbols: Gifts, Queh-Queh, Toasts

Many couples incorporate a rehearsal of the wedding into their planning. A rehearsal is usually not necessary for simple civil ceremonies, but most weddings are more complicated, and a walk-through helps ensure that the **Wedding Party** and other participants know what to do and when. The wedding rehearsal is typically scheduled a day or two before the wedding, and afterward it is customary to hold a dinner for the bridal party and close relatives of the bride and groom.

History and Significance

The rehearsal dinner appears to be a relatively modern American innovation, an opportunity to bring the families together socially just before the wedding. One theory holds, however, that the rehearsal dinner may descend from supper parties thrown in ancient Greece for the groom by his friends the night before the wedding.

Observance

The rehearsal dinner is often hosted and paid for by the groom's parents, though other arrangements may be made; sometimes the couple pays for the dinner, sometimes both sets of parents share the cost. The rehearsal dinner is usually held in a banquet room, but many are held at restaurants, and some are held at the home of the bride's or groom's parents. Rehearsal dinners may be highly formal, elaborate affairs or very simple and casual. The guest list may include members of the couple's immediate families (parents and siblings) and the wedding party. Sometimes, out-of-town guests are also invited. A couple may elect to have a smaller, more intimate rehearsal dinner on, say, Thursday evening for a Saturday wedding, as followed by a larger party for out-of-town guests on Friday evening.

The rehearsal dinner is a time for toasts. The rehearsal is also unlike many wedding-related events in that the bride and groom are not the recipients of any presents. Instead, they are the ones giving out the gifts. Among many African Americans, the *queh-queh* is a celebration similar to the rehearsal dinner.

Customs and Symbols

Gifts

The rehearsal dinner is typically the time when the bride and groom give gifts to members of their wedding party. These gifts tend to be relatively inexpensive and may include personal items such as jewelry, pen sets, wristwatches, engraved key rings or money clips, and the like. Any others who have taken part in the wedding planning may also receive tokens of appreciation.

Queh-Queh

The queh-queh (sometimes spelled kwe-kwe) is an African tradition preserved by some African-American couples. It is typically held during the week before the wedding and consists primarily of dances and songs from west Africa. During the party, the couple's married friends narrate stories in song designed to give the couple some idea of what to expect in marriage. All of the guests are also introduced through song. Sometimes a dish containing black-eyed peas, symbolizing riches, is served.

Toasts

The rehearsal dinner commonly includes toasts, or the ceremonial drinking of beverages, after short speeches offering good wishes. The chief toast is offered by the groom's father to his future daughter-in-law. Otherwise, few rules govern the

Libation

Another African tradition practiced by some African-American couples is the pouring of a libation, which may occur up to a month before the wedding. Members of the wedding party and the couple's families assemble for readings, such as from Bible verses and from poems and love letters, both historical and contemporary, written by prominent Africans and African Americans. A major part of the ceremony is the libation, when an elder offers the guests a drink, which can be water or a type of liquor. The elder also offers a prayer seeking blessings from God and from ancestral spirits for the couple. At the libation, the groom traditionally asks the bride's mother for her formal permission to marry her daughter.

festivities. Anyone who wants to offer a toast may do so, and the affair typically turns into one of great hilarity as members of the wedding party share stories and memories about the couple.

Further Reading

Cole, Harriette. *Jumping the Broom: The African-American Wedding Planner.* New York: Henry Holt, 2003.

Philip Lief Group. *Going to the Chapel: The Ultimate Wedding Guide for Today's Black Couple.* New York: G.P. Putnam's Sons, 1998.

Shaw, Kim. *The New Book of Wedding Etiquette: How to Combine the Best Traditions with Today's Flair.* Roseville, CA: Prima Publishing, 2001.

LOADING THE BRIDE

Alternate Name: Sending Her Home

Customs and Symbols: Advice, Ceremonial Washing, Gifts

Loading the bride is a special gathering observed by African Americans in honor of a woman who is about to be married. To help a new bride prepare for married life, her female friends and family members offer her their best advice about love and relationships.

History and Significance

Loading the bride is one of many traditions observed in African countries to mark a rite of passage into a new phase of life. The name refers to the bride being provided ("loaded") with the wisdom she will need to make a happy home. Loading the bride is seen as a time apart from daily routines, when older women focus on a younger bride in order to give her the benefit of their knowledge and experience.

Observance

African-American women who want to incorporate African customs into their wedding preparations sometimes choose to observe loading the bride. This can be included as part of a traditional **Wedding Shower** or held as a separate event. Where the traditional wedding shower normally focuses on the items brought as gifts, loading the bride places more emphasis on the advice and words of wisdom offered to the new bride.

If loading the bride is held as a separate event, normally the bride's closest friends and relatives attend, although sometimes it is held by the women of a church community. Traditionally, the bride sits in the center of a circle formed by the other women in attendance. Each woman speaks to the bride about married life, relationships, and love. Sometimes a ceremonial washing or cleansing of the bride is included to further prepare her for the wedding.

Loading the bride takes many forms and is observed in many different ways, each as individual as the bride herself. Some observances are somber and serious, possibly held in a darkened room lit only by candles. Others are lively parties, as women discuss, debate, and evaluate the advice given by each one. Regardless of the form, loading the bride is intended to show the bride that she is loved and supported by a community of women who wish her a successful and happy marriage.

Customs and Symbols

Advice

Women offer advice to the new bride on such topics as cooperation, compromise, sharing responsibilities, working together as a couple, and getting along together in daily life. This advice can be spoken directly to the bride or written down for her future reference.

Ceremonial Washing

Some observances include a ceremonial washing of the bride. In this case, the women purify the bride to remove any lingering thoughts of past relationships so that she might begin her marriage with an open and light heart. The ceremonial washing can take many forms, depending on the preferences of the bride and the other women involved. One typical custom is for the bride to remain clothed but with her neck and shoulders exposed. Each attending woman uses a soft cloth or sponge to gently wipe the bride's shoulders with warm water. While she does this, the attending woman voices a wish for the bride, for example, "May you be cleansed of all pain from your past."

Gifts

Loading the bride sometimes includes gifts like those typically found at a wedding shower, such as items that the bride can use in her new home.

Web Site

"African-American Wedding Guide: Rites of Passage." WeddingChannel.com, 1998. http://www.weddingchannel.com/ui/buildArticle.action?assetUID=3805&c=3805&s=84&t=71&p=5630936

Further Reading

Philip Lief Group. *Going to the Chapel: The Ultimate Wedding Guide for Today's Black Couple.* New York: G. P. Putnam's Sons, 1998.

Spangenberg, Lisl M. *Timeless Traditions: A Couple's Guide to Wedding Customs Around the World.* New York: Universe Publishing, 2001.

Sturgis, Ingrid. *The Nubian Wedding Book: Words and Rituals to Celebrate and Plan an African-American Wedding.* New York: Three Rivers Press, 1997.

Photo on facing page: A Jewish wedding, with the couple standing under the chuppah.

Chapter 14: Wedding Ceremonies

INTRODUCTION

A wedding can be either a religious or civil ceremony that makes a marriage official. The core of a wedding ceremony is the exchange of vows between the couple, and the ceremony typically concludes when a licensed officiant—typically a cleric or a judge—formally proclaims that the two are married. Wedding ceremonies often also include music, prayer, readings from sacred scripture, and numerous other traditional elements. While some of these traditions had literal significance centuries ago, in contemporary life, much of that meaning may be only symbolic. One central tradition, for example, is that of the father "giving away" the bride to his son-in-law—a literal truth in times past, but a custom preserved in modern weddings largely through the father escorting his daughter down the aisle.

Wedding ceremonies are usually intricate affairs in the U.S. Some couples avoid the ceremony entirely by eloping, running off to get married without any of the usual preparations and without the participation of family and friends (although witnesses must be present for the marriage to be considered legally valid). Others opt for simple ceremonies involving only themselves and perhaps a few close relatives and friends. Most couples, however, celebrate their marriage with at least some degree of elaboration. A large number of weddings are held in places of worship, even among couples who do not practice a specific religion. Still, a considerable number are held in such places as public parks, gardens, country clubs, hotels, reception halls, or at the home of someone close to the couple.

In the 21st century, marriage customs and traditions are in a state of great flux. Some couples choose to discard what they perceive as old and meaningless traditions in favor of ceremonies that they design themselves. Particularly, these couples may exchange personalized vows (the promises bride and groom make to one another during the ceremony). Many couples, too, choose to incorporate religious and ethnic customs. "Theme weddings" can include everything from military weddings for members of the armed forces to cowboy weddings for horse enthusiasts to beach weddings for surfers. Increasingly popular are "destination weddings," where the couple, their families, and all the guests travel to an exotic locale for the event. "Double weddings" are those in which two couples marry in the same ceremony; typically, two of the four people involved are siblings or very close friends. In recent years, same-sex marriage has become a hotly debated topic. Gay and lesbian couples have fought for the right to marry, though others have argued against the legitimacy of same-sex weddings.

Many wedding ceremonies, particularly in Christian settings, proceed as follows (although any of the details can be changed to suit the couple): To the accompaniment of background organ music, the guests arrive. The men in the bridal party, functioning as ushers, escort women to their seats, with the women's male companions, if any, following behind. Those who know or are related to the bride are seated on the left side; those connected with the groom are seated on the right. Considerable thought is given to seating to ensure that closest relatives and friends are seated to the front and that no guests feel offended by their placement. When all the guests are assembled, the musicians play a wedding march, and the bridesmaids walk in procession down the aisle, followed finally by the bride, accompanied by her father, who then "gives" her to the waiting groom. A common processional is the wedding chorus from Richard Wagner's opera *Lohengrin*, popularly called "Here Comes the Bride."

The ceremony itself, which may include music, prayers, and readings from scripture, culminates in an exchange of vows, either traditional or written by the couple, and an exchange of rings. The officiant pronounces the couple married and grants the groom permission to kiss the bride. The wedding party then recesses from the church. Commonly used recessional songs include Felix Mendelssohn's "Wedding

March," originally written for a 19th-century production of *A Midsummer Night's Dream*, by William Shakespeare; "Toccata," from Charles-Marie Widor's Symphony for Organ no. 5; and segments from "Ode to Joy," from the fourth movement of Beethoven's Ninth Symphony. At a reception line, either indoors or outside when the weather is fine, the couple, their parents, and members of the wedding party greet guests as they exit. The time between the wedding ceremony and the reception is likely to be one of substantial activity, as guests proceed to the reception hall while the couple, their parents, and the bridal party pose for formal photographs.

RELIGIOUS WEDDING CEREMONIES

Alternate Names: Handfasting, Marriage, Nuptials

Customs and Symbols: Arras, Canopy, Crowning, Food, Jumping the Broom, Music, Readings, Rings, Sharing a Cup, Symbolic Joining, Unity Candle, Vows

Weddings are among the most universally recognized life events and are generally viewed as one of the most important rites of passage. The rich traditions found in the ceremonies of various religions worldwide continue to influence the weddings planned by modern couples in the U.S. From the most culturally specific ritual to an original rite, the diversity of religious wedding customs is reflected in certain common practices.

History and Significance

Throughout history, different religious groups have created various symbols and traditions in weddings, reflecting their values and cultures. While weddings are often seen as the ultimate public expression of the love shared by two people, some wedding ceremonies are an expansive inclusion of two families or an even wider community. Many religious weddings focus on the holiness and sanctity of marriage and the sacred duties of husband and wife, while other faiths view marriage as more of a contractual agreement. Despite the many variations across cultures, one significant common element of all religious wedding ceremonies is a genuine wish for happiness, success, and prosperity for the newlywed couple.

Observance

Rituals to join two people together in marriage have been occurring since the most ancient times, and ceremonies full of rich and varied traditions can be found in nearly every religion. Depending on their particular religious beliefs, their families, and other factors, some couples are bound by strictly outlined wedding ceremonies. Others have more freedom to design a wedding that blends secular customs with rites borrowed from different faiths. Ultimately, every wedding is as unique as its participants.

Christian wedding ceremonies are normally performed within the context of a special worship service. The bride and groom stand apart from those assembled to witness the wedding, and the priest or minister leads them through the ceremony. The couple exchanges vows and rings, and there will usually be music and one or more readings from scripture or other appropriate literature. Orthodox Christian weddings include an elaborate crowning ceremony, and feature the bride and groom sharing a cup. Traditional Hispanic-American couples may choose to include the passing of special gold coins known as *arras*, or a rite of symbolic joining. African-American couples who choose to perform the jumping the broom ritual might include it at the end of the wedding ceremony or during the wedding reception.

Many religious weddings focus on the holiness and sanctity of marriage and the sacred duties of husband and wife, while other faiths view marriage as more of a contractual agreement.

Jewish wedding ceremonies take place under a special canopy known as a *chuppah*. In addition to one or more scripture readings, the *ketubah* (marriage contract) will also be read aloud. This contract dates back to the earliest days of Judaism, and outlines the duties and responsibilities of the husband and wife. In Orthodox Jewish ceremonies, the bride receives a ring from the groom, but in most Jewish weddings, the bride and groom exchange rings. When the ceremony is complete the groom will shatter a wine glass by stomping on it with his foot. The origin and meaning of this tradition are unclear, but it remains a highly anticipated element of many Jewish weddings.

Hindu weddings signify the joining of not just two people, but two entire families. Before the wedding ceremony begins, the bride's hands and feet will be decorated with intricate designs in a **Henna Body Painting** ritual known as *mehndi*. Once it begins, the elaborate wedding ceremony can be quite long, even lasting a week or more, with various prayer ceremonies and rites interspersed with feasting. Once the couple has been pronounced husband and wife, the groom traditionally places a small red circle on the bride's forehead. She may wear this indication of her marital status for the rest of her life.

Islam recognizes marriage as a state blessed by Allah, however, it is seen as a contract between two people rather than a religious rite. Both marriage and the contract are referred to as *nikah*. Some Muslims choose to have their wedding ceremony performed in a mosque by an *imam* (a Muslim religious leader), but this is not required in order for the marriage to be recognized in Islam. Similarly, traditional Buddhism regards marriage as a social and civil matter, and consequently no religious wedding ceremonies are held. However, customs vary according to sect, and many Chinese-American and Korean-American Buddhists often incorporate elements such as chanting, meditation, and the use of ceremonial beads into secular wedding ceremonies. Monks may bless the newlyweds in a separate ritual, but with a clear distinction made between that ceremony and the actual wedding.

The Jewish Marriage Contract

The ketubah, or marriage contract, has been an important part of Jewish weddings since the first century B.C.E. Orthodox and traditional Jewish weddings include the same text that has been used for thousands of years, while Liberal Jewish customs allow modern ketubah language. Consequently there are many various documents in use today, but all are usually written in both Hebrew and English and signed by the bride, groom, witnesses, and rabbi. An excerpt from one modern ketubah, in Anita Diamant and Howard Cooper's *Living a Jewish Life,* reads:

> We promise to consecrate ourselves, one to the other as husband and wife, according to the tradition of Moses and Israel; to love, honor, and cherish each other; to work together to create a home faithful to the teachings of Torah, reverent of the Divine, and committed to deeds of lovingkindness. We promise to try always to bring out in ourselves and in each other qualities of forgiveness, compassion, and integrity. All this we take upon ourselves to uphold to the best of our abilities.

Although many Native American religious ceremonies have been lost over time, some elements of old wedding rites are still practiced today. Customs vary widely among the different tribes, but there are a few common elements. Wedding ceremonies, like many Native American religious rites, are usually performed outdoors. Symbolic or sacred food is usually featured in the wedding ceremony, along with symbolic joining of the bride and groom as newlyweds.

A popular Wiccan and Neopagan wedding ceremony is called handfasting, which is a type of symbolic joining. While not recognized as a legal marriage in the U.S. unless performed by a licensed, ordained priest or minister, handfasting signifies a valid union within the Neopagan community. Some Neopagans see handfasting as an extended engagement period, and will have a legal wedding ceremony after they have been handfasted for one year. Others may never seek a legal wedding. Wiccans and Neopagans who marry legally often include the handfasting rite in their secular ceremony.

Although marriage between two people of the same gender is not legally recognized in most parts of the U.S., gay and lesbian weddings known as commitment ceremonies are allowed in some American religious communities. Depending on the policies of a particular group, religious commitment ceremonies may be performed by a minister or priest and may take place in a church, temple, or other location. Faith-based commitment ceremonies often incorporate the same elements as other contemporary religious weddings, according to the beliefs and traditions observed by the participants.

Customs and Symbols

Arras

Arras (literally, "earnest money") refers to a set of 13 gold coins that the groom gives to the bride during the wedding ceremony. The custom of passing arras originated in Spain, where it symbolized the groom's promise to always provide for the bride. It is seen as a sign of fidelity. In addition, the passing of the coins seals the marriage contract. During the wedding ceremony, a box containing the coins is given to the priest. The priest slowly pours the coins out into the groom's cupped hands, and the groom lets the coins fall into the bride's hands, which she has cupped below his. The coins are then returned to their box, and the priest offers prayers for the benefit of the couple.

Canopy

Wedding ceremonies are held under a canopy in many religious traditions. Perhaps the most well known is the Jewish chuppah, which can be a cloth draped over four poles or a bower of flowers over a trellis. Hindu couples are sometimes married underneath a canopy supported by twelve pillars. A canopy made of bark called a *kappa* is used by Native Hawaiians.

Crowning

Orthodox Christian wedding ceremonies include the practice of placing crowns or wreaths known as *stephana* on the heads of the bride and groom. The design of these crowns varies according to tradition and personal taste. They may be decorated metal crowns or wreaths of flowers or olive leaves. The crowning ritual symbolizes the creation of a new household, which the bride and groom pledge to rule according to God's law.

Food

Food is sometimes used in religious wedding ceremonies to symbolize the nurturing relationship of the bride and groom. In certain Native American wedding rituals, the bride and groom feed each other a small amount of food. During Hindu

265

wedding ceremonies, guests are provided with small portions of a traditional dish in a gesture that signifies respect for community.

Jumping the Broom

The tradition of jumping the broom is believed to have started before the Civil War with African-American slaves who were not allowed to marry. Lacking access to organized wedding ceremonies and largely forbidden to practice the religious ceremonies of their native lands, many slaves devised alternate rituals to signify a marriage. Two people who wanted to marry would place a decorated broom on the ground. A few words would be spoken about their love for each other and the duties of marriage, and then the bride and groom would join hands. In a breathless moment, they would jump over the broom together, leaping as individuals but landing as husband and wife. A growing number of African-American couples are choosing to incorporate this ritual into their wedding ceremonies, using brooms decorated with ribbons, streamers, and flowers.

Music

Music is an important part of wedding ceremonies in many religious traditions. Ceremonies often begin with a special processional that is played during the entrance of the bride and her attendants. The wedding chorus from Richard Wagner's opera *Lohengrin,* popularly called "Here Comes the Bride," is commonly used as a processional in contemporary American weddings of many faiths. During the ceremony, hymns and other songs with spiritual significance may be featured, although popular secular music is sometimes also used if appropriately related to themes of marriage, love, and commitment. Special songs are often chosen by the bride and groom to accompany parts of the ceremony such as the lighting of the unity candle. If a relative or close friend of the bride or groom is a musician or singer, they may be invited to perform during the ceremony. A recessional is often played at the conclusion of the ceremony. Recessional songs commonly used in modern American religious ceremonies include Felix Mendelssohn's "Wedding March," "Toccata," from Charles-Marie Widor's Symphony for Organ no. 5, and segments from "Ode to Joy," from the fourth movement of Beethoven's Ninth Symphony.

Readings

Religious wedding ceremonies typically include one or more recitations from religious texts or appropriate secular literature that address topics related to marriage or love. Sometimes close friends or family members deliver the readings during the ceremony, or the readings may be done by church attendants or the wedding offi-

Popular Readings

Regardless of religion or cultural tradition, certain readings have become very popular for weddings. One of the most widely used wedding ceremony readings is an excerpt from *The Prophet* (1923) by Lebanese-American poet Kahlil Gibran:

> Love one another, but make not a bond of love:
> Let it rather be a moving sea between the shores of your souls . . .
> Sing and dance together and be joyous, but let each one of you be
> alone,
> Even as the strings of a lute are alone though they quiver with the
> same music . . .
> And stand together, yet not too near together:
> For the pillars of the temple stand apart,
> And the oak tree and the cypress grow not in each other's shadow.

cians. The bride and groom may also read certain passages to each other. No matter how the readings are delivered, they are generally chosen with the intention of emphasizing important aspects of married life and the lifelong devotion of the bride and groom to one another.

Rings

The bride and groom typically exchange rings during religious wedding ceremonies as a sign of their love and commitment to each other. These rings can be made of any material in any design, although many couples choose rings made of gold and, perhaps, diamonds. Jewish tradition dictates that wedding rings be plain and designed simply, without stones. Although there is some variation in different traditions, wedding rings are normally worn on the third finger of the left hand. This custom can be traced back to the ancient Roman belief that a nerve ran directly from this finger to the heart.

Sharing a Cup

Many different religious wedding ceremonies feature the bride and groom drinking a small amount of wine or other beverage from the same cup. This is done to symbolize the unity of marriage. In Jewish wedding ceremonies, the bride and groom share two cups of wine, one after each of the two different marriage blessings offered by the rabbi. In Roman Catholic weddings, the couple share a cup of wine as part of the sacrament of the Eucharist (*see* **First Communion and Reconciliation**).

Symbolic Joining

The well-known phrase "tying the knot" probably originated with the ancient practice of physically or symbolically joining the bride and groom together. This custom is still observed in many different cultures as physical evidence of the spiritual bond created in marriage, and ritual tying remains a part of many different religious weddings.

A Hindu bride and groom will have their hands joined with a piece of yellow thread. In some traditional Hispanic-American ceremonies, an ornate rosary or white rope is wound around the bride and groom in a figure-eight pattern, encircling them both and crossing between them. If a rosary is used, the wedding officiant says a special prayer of blessing, and the rosary then becomes a cherished family heirloom. Traditional Filipino-American weddings sometimes include a similar ritual using the *yugal* (a cord, garland of flowers, or string of coins), which is draped loosely around the necks of the bride and groom in a figure-eight pattern. The figure eight represents an eternal union.

For Wiccans and Neopagans, ritual tying known as handfasting is an important element of the wedding ceremony, and sometimes the only element. Two people who wish to marry participate in the handfasting rite, during which the priestess or priest binds their hands together with a rope or length of cloth to signify their union.

Some Native Americans continue an ancient tradition of braiding or tying together two locks of hair taken from the bride and groom during the wedding ceremony. Cherokee and Sioux people may observe the custom known as wrapping the blanket, in which the mothers of the bride and groom drape one blanket over the bride and groom together, representing a wish for the couple's unity and protection.

Unity Candle

Candles are used in many religious rites, but the unity candle has special significance for a wedding. Before the wedding ceremony, three candles are arranged on or near the main altar or at a side altar. These include a large candle centered between two smaller candles. The two smaller candles are lit before the ceremony begins. At some point during the wedding ceremony, the bride and groom approach the three candles. They each take one of the lit candles and use these to light the larger center candle together. This is done to symbolize the two separate lives that become one in marriage.

Vows

Nearly all couples who marry in a religious wedding ceremony exchange vows to profess their love and commitment to each other. Vows can take many forms, including simple responses to the officiant's questions or longer statements either recited from memory or composed spontaneously. Jewish weddings sometimes include a private ceremony before the public wedding, and it is during this time that the bride and groom make their vows to each other.

Web Site

"Lore and Tradition." WeddingDetails.com, undated.
    http://www.weddingdetails.com/lore

Further Reading

Diamant, Anita, and Howard Cooper. *Living a Jewish Life: Jewish Traditions, Customs and Values for Today's Families.* New York: HarperCollins, 1991.

Gourse, Leslie. *Native American Courtship and Marriage.* Summertown, TN: Native Voices, 2005.

Higginbotham, Joyce, and River Higginbotham. *Paganism: An Introduction to Earth-Centered Religions.* St. Paul, MN: Lewellyn Publications, 2002.

Jones, Leslie. *Happy Is the Bride the Sun Shines On: Wedding Beliefs, Customs, and Traditions.* Chicago: Contemporary Books, 1995.

Klausner, Abraham J. *Weddings: A Complete Guide to All Religious and Interfaith Marriage Services.* Columbus, OH: Alpha Publishing, 1986.

Spangenberg, Lisl M. *Timeless Traditions: A Couple's Guide to Wedding Customs Around the World.* New York: Universe Publishing, 2001.

CIVIL WEDDING CEREMONIES

Customs and Symbols: Elopement, Jumping the Broom, Music, Readings, Rings, Shotgun Wedding, Symbolic Joining, Vows

A civil ceremony is a wedding conducted by a judge, magistrate, justice of the peace, or other secular figure with the authority to perform a legal marriage. Civil ceremonies may be simple or elaborate and are often designed to reflect the personal tastes of the bride and groom. Although civil ceremonies are not specifically religious, spiritual practices and religious traditions are sometimes included.

History and Significance

The evolution of civil and religious wedding ceremonies through the ages has been somewhat convoluted. In some societies with little or no separation of religious and civil law, such as historically Orthodox Jewish communities, a wedding could only be performed as part of a religious rite. For others, such as primarily Buddhist cultures, legal marriage was a civil matter and religion played no part. Civil wedding ceremonies did not become popular among Christians until after the Protestant Reformation in the 16th century. The leader of the Reformation, Martin Luther (1483–1546), denied that matrimony was a sacrament and characterized it instead as a "worldly thing." Then at the end of the 18th century, the French Revolution greatly reduced the influence of the Catholic Church in daily life and marriage became a civil rather than religious institution. These two events greatly contributed to the secularization of marriage in European countries where Christianity was the primary religion.

In contemporary American society, most licensed, ordained religious leaders are authorized to perform marriages that are also legally valid. However, some religious ceremonies are not legally recognized. In addition, civil wedding ceremonies are not recognized as valid marriages within some religious traditions. In these cases, couples who wish to have their marriage recognized by the church and the government must have two separate ceremonies—one religious and one civil.

Observance

A civil ceremony is typically conducted by a judge, a justice of the peace, or a magistrate. Other governmental figures such as city mayors and commissioners may also be empowered to conduct weddings. In certain circumstances, the captain of a ship at sea may perform a civil wedding ceremony.

Civil ceremonies can take many forms. Some are simple and brief, taking place in a courtroom, judge's chambers, or wedding chapel. Others are elaborate formal events attended by hundreds of guests. Typically, the bride and groom stand apart from those assembled to witness the wedding, and the officiant leads them through the ceremony. The couple exchanges vows and rings, and there may be music and one or more readings. Civil ceremonies may include elements of **Religious Wedding Ceremonies** or cultural traditions such as symbolic joining or jumping the broom.

One type of civil wedding ceremony is an elopement. In the past, an elopement implied a wedding held in secret without the permission of parents. In modern life, couples who elope may have simply decided to forego the fuss and expense of a formal wedding.

Although marriage between two people of the same gender is not legally recognized in most parts of the U.S., some gay and lesbian couples choose to hold commitment ceremonies to publicly profess their intention to join together as partners for life. While lacking the official legal status of civil ceremonies, commitment ceremonies may incorporate the same elements as other contemporary American weddings.

Customs and Symbols

Elopement

The word elope stems from the word *lope*, meaning "to run." The practice arose at a time when family approval was typically required for marriage, such that when a couple eloped, they ran away to get married secretly. In the classic elopement scenario, the groom would arrive at the home of the bride's parents at night. He would then help the bride escape from the home and the two would flee on foot, on horseback, or in a carriage to the nearest place where they could marry, often in a civil ceremony. In modern life, the word is also used to refer to wedding ceremonies that take place more or less spontaneously, without planning, guests, formal receptions, and so on.

Jumping the Broom

The tradition of jumping the broom is believed to have started before the Civil War with African-American slaves who were not allowed to marry. Lacking access to organized wedding ceremonies and largely forbidden to practice the religious ceremonies of their native lands, many slaves devised alternate rituals to signify a marriage. Two people who wanted to marry would place a decorated broom on the ground. A few words would be spoken about their love for each other and the duties of marriage, and then the bride and groom would join hands. In a breathless moment, they would jump over the broom together, leaping as individuals but landing as husband and wife. A growing number of African-American couples are choosing to incorporate this ritual into their wedding ceremonies, using brooms decorated with ribbons, streamers, and flowers.

Music

Music is an important part of many American weddings. Ceremonies often begin with a special processional that is played during the entrance of the bride and her attendants. The wedding chorus from Richard Wagner's opera *Lohengrin*, popularly called "Here Comes the Bride," is commonly used as a processional. Special songs are often chosen by the bride and groom to accompany parts of the ceremony, and if a relative or close friend of the bride or groom is a musician or singer, they may be invited to perform. A recessional is often played at the conclusion of the ceremony. Recessional songs commonly used in modern American religious ceremonies include Felix Mendelssohn's "Wedding March," "Toccata," from Charles-Marie Widor's Symphony for Organ no. 5, and segments from "Ode to Joy," from the fourth movement of Beethoven's Ninth Symphony.

Readings

Some civil ceremonies include one or more readings of poetry or passages of literature. Readings are generally chosen with the intention of emphasizing important aspects of married life and the lifelong devotion of the bride and groom to one another.

Rings

In a civil ceremony, the bride and groom typically exchange rings as a sign of their love and commitment to each other. These rings can be made of any material in any design, although many couples choose rings made of gold and, perhaps, diamonds. Wedding rings are normally worn on the third finger of the left hand, a custom that can be traced back to the ancient Roman belief that a nerve ran directly from this finger to the heart.

Shotgun Wedding

The term "shotgun wedding" is an American colloquialism that dates to the early 19th century. It refers to a scenario in which an unplanned pregnancy forces a couple to marry in haste, usually at the urging of the young woman's father and his shotgun. While the shotgun wedding was more mythical than real, the phrase continues to be used to refer to people who marry in haste for a variety of reasons.

Symbolic Joining

The well-known phrase "tying the knot" probably originated with the ancient practice of physically or symbolically joining the bride and groom together. Some couples choose to incorporate this custom into their civil ceremony to emphasize the importance and seriousness of their commitment to each other. Symbolic joining during a wedding may take a variety of forms, typically involving a cord or length of cloth that is wound around the couples' hands or encircling them both in a figure-eight pattern. The figure eight represents an eternal union.

Vows

Couples who marry in a civil wedding ceremony exchange vows to publicly profess their love and commitment to each other. These vows can take many forms: they might follow a standard text, or they might be written by the couple to express a more personal view of their understanding of their commitment. The vows spoken in a civil ceremony are regarded by law as a binding contract between two people, who are then entitled to the rights, benefits, and protections of legal marriage in the U.S.

Further Reading

Bankhead, Donna, and Lynnette Blas. *Last Minute Weddings.* Franklin Lakes, NJ: Career Press, 1999.

Cole, Harriette. *Jumping the Broom: The African-American Wedding Planner.* New York: Holt Paperbacks, 1995.

Johnson, Judith. *The Wedding Ceremony Planner: The Essential Guide to the Most Important Part of Your Wedding Day.* Naperville, IL: Sourcebooks Casablanca, 2005.

BETROTHAL AND MARRIAGE RITUAL

Alternate Names: Betrothal and Marriage Ceremony, Erusin and Nissuin

Customs and Symbols: Breaking of the Glass, Chuppah, Ring, Second Blessing, Seven Blessings

The betrothal ritual is part of a traditional Jewish wedding. The name suggests that an explication would more properly belong in a discussion of engagements, but among many Jewish Americans today, the ritual is actually part of the wedding ceremony. Like most components of Jewish weddings, the betrothal ritual is designed to heighten the religious aspect of the ceremony and, in particular, to place the wedding ceremony within the long history of Jewish tradition.

History and Significance

Jewish weddings historically took place in stages that lasted an entire year. At the betrothal ceremony, called the *erusin*, the man and woman were engaged to be married, and from that time neither was allowed to have romantic relationships with others. In effect, the two were married, although the wedding itself took place a year later, when the bride was finally allowed to move into the groom's home and the two could consummate their relationship.

A major purpose of the betrothal ritual, as with many Jewish wedding traditions, was to emphasize that the marriage was more than a bond between two people. The Jewish community regarded weddings as very much public events, celebrated to ensure the ongoing survival of Judaism. An important theme in Jewish history, one reflected throughout the Torah, has been that of a covenant, or binding agreement, between God and the Jews, who are sometimes referred to as his "chosen people." The wedding bond is considered a reflection of that covenant.

Observance

The first part of a traditional Jewish wedding is the betrothal ceremony, the erusin, sometimes referred to as the *kiddushin*, meaning "marriage." For the betrothal ceremony, the bride and groom, led by their parents, first enter and take their place under the *chuppah*, or marriage canopy. The bride always stands at the groom's right hand, reflecting a line in the biblical book of Psalms stating that a queen always stands at a king's right hand. Typically, the bride is not ornamented (with jewelry, for example), and it is traditional for the guests to tell the groom how beautiful the bride is. The bride (the *kallah*) and the couple's families circle the groom (the *choson*, also called the *chatan*) seven times to symbolize the binding of the couple. The number seven has mystical significance in Judaism, as reflected in the seven candles of the *menorah*, the Jewish ritualistic candelabra. In the betrothal ceremony, the seven circuits around the groom signify the seven days of creation as related in the Book of Genesis, since marriage is predominantly regarded by Jews as a creative act ensuring the continuation of the Jewish nation. Holding a cup of wine, the rabbi conducting the ceremony pronounces two blessings. The first is a generic blessing, similar to one used on any ceremonial occasion, while the second blessing pertains specifically to the betrothal ceremony.

After these blessings, the bride and groom then drink wine from the cup the rabbi has been holding, signifying that they will share the cup of life during their marriage. The groom then places a ring on the index finger of the bride's right hand and says, "Behold, by this ring you are consecrated to me as my wife according to the laws of Moses and Israel." According to traditional Jewish law, the process of betrothal is not symmetrical, such that Orthodox women never pronounce the formula "Behold, by this ring . . . ," and they remain silent. In modern life, however, most Jewish communities have set aside ancient gender roles and incorporate some kind of statement from the bride, such as a prayer or a passage from scripture. In the most liberal Jewish communities, the woman does repeat the words spoken by the man.

Then follows the reading of the marriage contract, or *ketubah*, which is considered the close of the betrothal ritual. The bride then takes the marriage contract as her personal property, for it stands as a record of the promises the groom has made to her. The ketubah is in some respects similar to a prenuptial agreement, as it specifies the husband's financial obligations to his wife and family. The document itself is often written in beautiful calligraphy and may be framed and hung in the couple's home.

The acts that follow the ketubah are the reading of the seven blessings, or *Sheva Berakhot,* and the breaking of the glass. These customs constitute the marriage ceremony, or *nissuin.*

Customs and Symbols

Breaking of the Glass

One of the most recognizable Jewish wedding customs occurs when the groom breaks a glass with his foot. Typically, after the rabbi pronounces a blessing on the couple, the two drink from a shared glass. The groom then places the glass on the floor and smashes it with his right foot. This custom evokes the destruction of the Jewish temple in Jerusalem by the Roman Empire in 70 C.E. The breaking of the glass symbolizes the breaking of Jews' hearts as they remember this defining event in Jewish history, even on joyous occasions. Some Jews attach a more humorous interpretation to the glass-breaking custom: it is the last time the man will be able to "put his foot down." There are myriad other explanations for the ritual, as well as a joke stating that the couple will have to glue the pieces of the broken glass together if they wish to obtain a divorce.

Typically, not just any glass is broken. As part of the wedding preparations, many couples purchase glass-breaking "kits" that consist of a special glass that has been blessed by a rabbi and can be placed within a decorated bag. Some couples will substitute the glass with a light bulb, which is easier to break.

After the glass has been smashed, the assembled congregation shouts *mazel tov*, which roughly means "good luck," and the bride and groom leave the huppah to retire to the *yichud* room, a private room where they can be together as husband and wife for the first time. Since the two have typically fasted throughout the day, they may break their fast at this time with a small meal.

Chuppah

During both the betrothal ritual and the wedding ritual, the bride and groom stand beneath a chuppah (often spelled *huppah* or *chuppa*), a canopy supported by four poles. The chuppah symbolizes the couple's living together and the husband's taking his wife to his home. The chuppah is such a central part of Jewish weddings that the event itself is often colloquially referred to as a "chuppah."

Ring

Jewish law regulates the nature of the ring. Traditionally, the ring symbolizes the property that the groom brings to the wedding for the benefit of the bride, so the ring must actually belong to the man and must have some economic value. The ring does not bear gemstones, and decorations are not cut into the ring, as the ring symbolizes the permanence of the marriage in being an uninterrupted circle.

Second Blessing

The second blessing, the one particular to the betrothal ritual, reads as follows:

> Blessed are You . . . He, Who has commanded us concerning forbidden relations, prohibiting us the betrothed women . . . permitting us the married,

the *nesuot*, ours through *Huppah* and *Kiddushin*. Blessed are You . . . He, Who sanctifies His people Israel through Huppah and Kiddushin.

This version appears in Leo Trepp's *The Complete Book of Jewish Observance*. The word kiddushin means "marriage," but the implication is something more like "full-fledged marriage," in contrast to the bond created by the betrothal.

Seven Blessings

The seven blessings, or Sheva Berakhot, which are particular to the marriage ritual, are read by the rabbi and thank God. This version appears in Leo Trepp's *The Complete Book of Jewish Observance*:

> for the fruit of the vine;
> for creating the universe
> for creating human beings;
> for creating human beings in His image, in such fashion that they in turn can create life;
> for His grace, as He will make Zion joyful again through [the return of] her children;
>> for making groom and bride joyful; may He bring gladness to them as He brought it to His creatures in the Garden of Eden;
> for Him, who as Source of all joy is implored to restore speedily to the cities of Judah and the streets of Jerusalem
>> the voice of mirth and the voice of joy;
>> the voice of groom and the voice of bride . . .
>> Blessed are You, Lord, You are He, Who makes the groom rejoice with the bride.

Further Reading

Gross, David C., and Esther R. Gross. *Under the Wedding Canopy: Love and Marriage in Judaism.* New York: Hippocrene Books, 1996.

Monger, George P. *Marriage Customs of the World: From Henna to Honeymoons.* Santa Barbara, CA: ABC-CLIO, 2004.

Trepp, Leo. *The Complete Book of Jewish Observance.* New York: Behrman House/Summit Books, 1980.

Photo on facing page: Cutting the cake at the reception is a typical wedding ritual.

Chapter 15: Wedding Receptions

INTRODUCTION

For most newly married couples, a reception is an important part of the wedding day festivities. After the ceremony, the wedding party and all of the guests assemble at an appropriate location for what amounts to a party, usually featuring a meal, dancing, and, in many instances, the consumption of alcohol. **Wedding Receptions** can be held anywhere, but a popular location is a large banquet room. Receptions are also commonly held in church meeting rooms, at country clubs, or outdoors on the grounds where the ceremony was held, often under tents put up for the purpose.

Many wedding receptions in the U.S. have no particular significance other than to celebrate the wedding, although certain reception events may bear traditional importance, such as the second line dance among some African-American communities. For Muslims, the reception, called a **Walimah**, is an important part of the wedding itself, for it is the couple's way of making their marriage public, a requirement under Islamic law.

A traditional American wedding reception proceeds as follows, although any of these details, like any part of the wedding ceremony, can be modified to suit the tastes and preferences of the couple. Also, the order of many of these events can be modified depending on circumstances and preferences.

Some wedding receptions start with a receiving line. Often the receiving line is formed at the location where the wedding took place, but sometimes it is formed at the reception as a means of getting the site of the ceremony quickly vacated. In the receiving line, the couple and their parents greet guests as they enter. Typically, the mother of the bride is first, followed by the bride's father, the groom's mother, the groom's father, and the married couple. Members of the wedding party, especially the maid of honor, are often also part of the receiving line.

Before or during the meal, it is customary for toasts to be offered to the newlyweds. Nearly always, the groom's best man offers a toast, which is likely to be either sentimental or humorous, typically a combination of the two. Following the meal, the **Wedding Dance** begins.

Prior to the departure of the bride and groom, three rituals are customary. One is the tossing of the bouquet; the second is the tossing of the bride's garter; and the third is the couple's cutting of the cake. The newly married couple typically departs from the reception while it is still under way. At some weddings, guests attach shoes, tin cans, or other items to the car the couple will be leaving in, along with a sign that says "Just Married."

Traditionally, the bride's parents have borne most of the expenses associated with a wedding; the notable exception is the rehearsal dinner, typically paid for by the groom's parents. In the modern U.S., however, this arrangement is in a state of flux. Many parents simply cannot afford the cost of a lavish wedding, and if the groom's parents are more affluent than the bride's, they may offer to take on more of the expenses. Further, couples are marrying later than they used to, and many are already living together by the time they marry. If both are working and earning money, they may pay for much of their own wedding, demonstrating that they are no longer dependent on their parents. Thus, the division of expenses almost always varies, with both sets of parents and the couple sharing expenses based on ability to pay. These concerns with costs arise particularly in connection with the reception.

WALIMAH

Alternate Name: Muslim Wedding Feast

Customs and Symbols: Avoidance of Alcohol and Certain Foods, Gender Separation

The reception that follows an Islamic wedding, called the walimah, serves much the same purpose as other wedding receptions in the U.S. It is a time for family and friends to assemble to celebrate the wedding by sharing a feast. Islam explicitly regards weddings as community-oriented events; in fact, Islam expressly forbids secret marriages, and the walimah is the traditional setting in which the marriage is made public. While some walimah are simple, others last for days following the wedding.

A source of controversy among Islamic communities in non-Islamic countries is the nature of weddings, particularly of wedding receptions. In the United States, as well as in other countries in the West, many Islamic couples hold wedding receptions that, in the eyes of conservative Muslims, violate Islamic law. In particular, they feature improper dancing and singing, and the sexes are not duly segregated. Many conservative Muslims decry this trend, believing that the traditions and teachings of Islam are being corrupted by young people in the West.

History and Significance

Islamic marriage customs were established by the Prophet Muhammad, the founder of Islam. Some of these customs are prescribed in the Qu'ran, Islam's sacred scripture, while others derive from the hadiths, the sayings and teachings attributed to Muhammad and recorded by his followers. According to Islamic teaching, Muhammad urged his followers to hold a walimah after a wedding ceremony, and he set an example by holding one after his own wedding. Further, it is considered extremely rude to decline a wedding invitation. Muslims may decline an invitation only under extreme circumstances, including the call of a higher religious duty. Traditionally, the responsibility for holding the walimah fell to the groom, but in modern life the expenses are likely to be shared by the groom and the couple's parents.

The Muslim bride will often change into an elaborate dress adorned with gold and jewels for the occasion, and she may be carried around like royalty.

A source of discussion among some Islamic scholars is the timing of the walimah. It is usually held immediately after the wedding ceremony. Some scholars, however, believe that Islamic law requires the walimah to be held after the marriage has been consummated (that is, after the newly married pair have had sexual relations for the first time). These scholars believe that the purpose of the walimah is to celebrate not just the wedding but also the consummation of the marriage. Accordingly, some Muslims hold the walimah the day after the wedding.

Observance

As at any wedding reception, the bride and groom, along with their families, make their entrance and attempt to greet each guest individually. The feast features traditional dishes, including fish, chicken, lamb, sometimes beef, and rice dishes. The Muslim bride will often change into an elaborate dress adorned with gold and jewels for the occasion, and she may be carried around like royalty for an extended period of time before being returned to the hands of the groom.

Customs and Symbols

Avoidance of Alcohol and Certain Foods

Muslims use the terms *halal* and *haram* to refer to substances and practices that are permitted or not permitted, respectively, according to Islamic law. Things that are considered haram, or not permitted, include alcohol and pork. Any meat that has not been slaughtered according to Islamic custom is also haram.

Gender Separation

Islam strictly regulates the behavior of men and women in social situations. The avoidance of any kind of sexual temptation is strongly emphasized, and standards of modesty tend to make Islamic women feel uncomfortable when they are being looked at by men who are not their husbands or members of their family—as might be the case at a wedding reception. Accordingly, it is common at the walimah for there to be in effect two parties occurring simultaneously, one for men and one for women, each in a separate room. Sometimes members of the same sex dance together in these separate rooms. Also, it is not customary for male guests to kiss the bride, as this would be regarded as improper contact between men and women who are not married.

Further Reading

Al-Jibaly, Muhammad. *The Quest for Love & Mercy: Regulations for Marriage & Wedding in Islam.* Beirut, Lebanon: Al-Maktab Al-Islaami, 2000.

WEDDING DANCE

Alternate Name: Bridal Dance

Customs and Symbols: Broom Dance, Chair Dance, Dollar Dance, Father's Dance, First Dance, Garba, Horah, Mitzvah Tanz, Second Line Dance, Wedding March

Dancing is a common feature of many **Wedding Receptions**, with music and dance choices often being heavily influenced by religious or cultural traditions.

History and Significance

The joining of two people in marriage is cause for celebration in cultures and religious traditions all over the world. Music and dance are nearly universal elements of the wedding celebration, and there are long and varied histories of wedding dances in many societies. From the silly to the sentimental, wedding dance traditions bring people together in recognition and appreciation of the newlyweds' happiness.

Observance

Some wedding dance traditions have become fairly standard features of most American wedding receptions. At some point during the party, the bride and groom can be expected to share their first dance together. The father's dance brings the bride and her father together for a sentimental turn on the dance floor, while all the guests might take part in a wedding march or a dollar dance.

From the silly to the sentimental, wedding dance traditions bring people together in recognition and appreciation of the newlyweds' happiness.

Couples may also choose to emphasize specific customs reflecting their religious or cultural heritage by making traditional dances a part of their wedding reception. Jewish tradition is rich with special dances for wedding guests, from the *bobbes tanz*—for grandmothers only—to the *flash tanz*, during which the dancer must keep a bottle balanced on the top of their head or forehead. Perhaps the most well-known Jewish wedding dances are the *horah* and the chair dance. The *garba* is a fixture of any Indian-American celebration, especially a wedding. In some African-American traditions as well as the Cajun communities of Louisiana, wedding receptions often include the second line dance and the broom dance.

Customs and Symbols

Broom Dance

The broom dance is one wedding tradition most often found in Louisiana's Cajun community. Sometimes also called the mop dance, this dance features any older, unmarried sibling of either the bride or the groom. The person is required to dance alone, barefoot, with a broom or mop; a male dancer usually rolls up his pant legs several inches for the dance. The dancer—with the broom for a partner—gets a dose of good-natured teasing from the other guests, because their younger sibling has managed to get married before them.

Chair Dance

The chair dance is a much-anticipated feature of many Jewish wedding receptions. In this dance, the bride and groom are seated on chairs which are lifted into the air by wedding guests. The couple each holds one end of a handkerchief or scarf as they are whirled around each other to the beat of lively music. The origin of this custom is unclear, but it is believed to have started as a way for the couple to catch a glimpse of one another over the physical barrier that separated the rejoicing of male and female wedding guests in Orthodox Jewish communities. It may also be a gesture of treating the newlyweds as royalty, who in ancient times often rode on chairs borne by servants.

Dollar Dance

Some American wedding receptions feature a dollar dance, in which each wedding guest presents the bride with a cash gift as they take a turn dancing with her. The dollar bills are sometimes pinned to the bride's veil or dress, but most often they are collected in a special bag or purse. The dollar dance signifies a wish for good fortune for the newlyweds.

Father's Dance

During many American weddings, regardless of religious or cultural heritage, the bride dances with her father to a song specially chosen for its significant lyrics. After a few moments, the groom and his mother may join in, or they may dance separately to a different song chosen for the occasion. This custom is a gesture of respect to the couples' parents and is often sentimental, as parents acknowledge their child's important rite of passage into married life.

First Dance

A common custom at many American wedding receptions is for the bride and groom to enjoy their first dance as a married couple alone on the dance floor. Couples typically choose a specific song for their first dance, frequently one that has special meaning to them. After the bride and groom have danced for a few moments, the other couples in the wedding party may be invited to join them on the dance floor. The first dance is often included in contemporary American wedding receptions in addition to traditional cultural dances.

Garba

The garba is an East Indian folk dance that originated as a religious devotional practice. As a cultural tradition, the garba is usually performed at any celebratory occasion, especially a wedding. This graceful dance is taught to Indian children at a very young age, and so people of all ages participate when it is performed. There are many variations in performance style, but in general the dancers move in circles, bending sideways, sweeping their arms out, and clapping rhythmically to the beat of the music. The music can often build slowly to become quite fast-paced, making the garba an exuberant celebration of its own.

Horah

The horah is commonly performed at Jewish weddings. This traditional dance began as a Romanian folk custom and can require great physical exertion from dancers. The horah begins slowly, with dancers in a line holding hands or with arms interlocked behind their backs. Swaying in place at first, as the tempo of the music builds the dancers begin a repeating sequence: two steps to the right, then one jump on the left foot. As the music plays faster and faster, the dancers will be almost running as they stomp and kick. Most participants finish the horah exhilarated and exhausted.

Mitzvah Tanz

One tradition among Jews of Eastern European descent is the *mitzvah tanz* (literally "the dance of the commandment"). Dancing with the bride at her wedding is considered a mitzvah (a commandment), and consequently most of the wedding guests take a turn dancing for at least a moment with her. The tradition has evolved to include the groom, with everyone taking their turn to dance with him also.

Second Line Dance

The second line dance is a prominent feature of some African-American weddings, particularly those with a Cajun heritage. The second line dance begins under a large umbrella that has been lavishly decorated with streamers, lace, and flowers. The bride's father leads a procession as guests wave white handkerchiefs. The dancers strut and twirl under the umbrella to lively jazz music.

Wedding March

Another wedding custom with Cajun roots is the wedding march. To open the floor for dancing, the bride and groom begin circling the room as lively wedding march music plays. Each guest pairs up with a partner and joins in until everyone is following the bride and groom, who eventually lead the parade to the dance floor. The guests encircle the dance floor and the newlyweds then enjoy their first dance.

Web Site

"Cajun Wedding Traditions," by Jane Vidrine, *Louisiana's Living Traditions*, undated. http://www.louisianafolklife.org/LT/Articles_Essays/cajun_wed.html

Further Reading

Ancelet, Barry Jean, Jay Dearborn Edwards, and Glen Pitre. *Cajun Country*. Jackson: University Press of Mississippi, 1991.

Boehm, Yohanan. "Horah." In *Encyclopaedia Judaica*. Edited by Michael Berenbaum and Fred Skolnik. Detroit: Macmillan Reference USA, 2007

Diamant, Anita. *The New Jewish Wedding*. New York: Fireside, 2001.

Diamant, Anita, and Howard Cooper. *Living a Jewish Life: Jewish Traditions, Customs and Values for Today's Families*. New York: HarperCollins, 1991.

McBride-Mellinger, Maria. *The Perfect Wedding Reception: Stylish Ideas for Every Season*. New York: HarperResource, 2001.

WEDDING RECEPTIONS

Alternate Names: Wedding Banquet, Wedding Feast

Customs and Symbols: Cake, Father's Dance, First Dance, Food, Introduction, Receiving Line, Speeches, Throwing the Bouquet and Garter

The party that is held after a wedding ceremony is called a reception. At a wedding reception, the bride and groom are surrounded by friends, family members, and other invited guests who have come together to celebrate the new marriage in a festive atmosphere.

History and Significance

Weddings are celebrated as communal events in nearly all cultures, dating back to the earliest societies. Archaeologists have discovered historical evidence of wedding feasts held by ancient peoples across Asia, Africa, Europe, and North and South America. Perhaps the most well-documented wedding feasts and parties were those of the ancient Romans, who believed that a marriage was not legally binding until the couple shared a meal together. The parents of a groom in ancient China would host a lavish feast as a demonstration of their wealth and position in society.

Today, wedding receptions provide an opportunity for the families and friends of the bride and the groom to meet each other in a social setting. The old custom of sharing a communal meal is often combined with music and dancing, all of which signifies public acknowledgment and acceptance of the new marriage.

Observance

Contemporary American wedding receptions vary widely in style, tone, size, location, time of day, and duration. Most are held on the same day as the wedding ceremony, either immediately following the exchange of vows or a short time later. Some receptions are held days, weeks, or even months after the wedding ceremony, particularly in the case of an elopement or a wedding that took place far away from the couple's home town. Still other receptions are held over a period of several days, including various parties and feasts attended by different groups of guests.

Many American wedding receptions incorporate customs drawn from the cultural heritage of the newlywed couple, or combine elements of celebrations that have been borrowed from other cultures. Whether or not any specific cultural practices are included, most receptions feature certain customs that have become American wedding traditions. A typical wedding reception includes plenty of time for guests to relax and socialize, beginning with a cocktail hour. Members of the **Wedding Party** may hold a receiving line during this time to informally greet guests as they arrive. A formal introduction of the wedding party is usually made later in the event, either before or after food is served. Almost all wedding receptions include food, which can be as simple as an appetizer buffet or as elaborate as a full dinner presented in several courses. Speeches and toasts to the newlyweds are typically made immediately before and sometimes also during the meal.

> *Music and dancing are an important part of most American wedding receptions.*

Music and dancing are another important part of most American wedding receptions. Any number of **Wedding Dance** traditions may be included in the reception, most notably the newlyweds' first dance as husband and wife and the sentimental father's dance. While music is typically played throughout the reception, dancing usually begins after the meal.

At some point during most receptions, the bride and groom will cut the first piece from their wedding cake. This is usually a special moment, and guests often gather to watch as the couple feeds each other a bite or two. Towards the end of the reception, the custom of throwing the bouquet and garter again gathers an audience of guests. As the reception draws to a close, the bride and groom may make their grand exit, sometimes leaving immediately for their **Honeymoon**.

In some communities, male and female guests are separated at the wedding reception. This may be achieved by setting up a physical barrier such as a temporary wall or curtain to divide the room, or by holding the reception in two separate rooms. This is typically done in Orthodox Jewish or conservative Islamic communities. In their separate spaces, wedding guests enjoy many of the same customs found in other receptions, such as food, music, and dancing.

Customs and Symbols

Cake

Nearly all American wedding receptions feature some type of wedding cake. Wedding cakes are available in a seemingly endless variety of sizes, shapes, flavors, and decorative styles ranging from flat sheet cakes to towering arrangements of fancy layers. The most traditional choice for American weddings is a multi-tiered white cake decorated with white frosting.

After the bride and groom have cut the first piece of their wedding cake, the cake may be served to guests for dessert or pieces may be wrapped for guests to take home and enjoy later. According to one old superstitious belief, if an unmarried woman who was a guest at the wedding sleeps with a piece of the wedding cake under her pillow, she will dream that night of the man she will marry.

Father's Dance

During many American weddings, the bride often dances with her father to a song specially chosen for its significant lyrics. After a few moments, the groom and his mother may join in, or they may dance separately to a different song chosen for the occasion. This custom is a gesture of respect to the couple's parents and is often sentimental, as parents acknowledge their child's important rite of passage into married life.

First Dance

A common custom at many American wedding receptions is for the bride and groom to enjoy their first dance as a married couple alone on the dance floor. Couples typically choose a specific song for their first dance, frequently one that has special meaning to them. After the bride and groom have danced for a few moments, the other couples in the wedding party may be invited to join them on the dance floor.

Food

Some type of communal meal is usually served at wedding receptions. Depending on the time of day when the reception takes place, this may be breakfast, brunch, lunch, dinner, or an array of appetizers. In some communities, the wedding feast is the most important part of the reception. Traditional Asian Americans view the food served at a wedding as a gesture of gratitude and respect for the assembled guests. Consequently, large quantities of the best, most expensive, or most elaborate dishes are served. Foods with symbolic meaning are often served at Chinese-American wedding receptions, such as whole fish, which represents a wish for abundance, or sweet lotus seeds, which signify a wish for many children. Hindu and Islamic wedding celebrations typically also include an extensive feast, usually with special dishes that are normally reserved for holidays and other special times. In traditional Jewish wedding receptions, special prayers and blessings are offered before and after the wedding feast.

Introduction

At some point fairly early in the reception, the wedding party may be formally introduced. The introductions generally begin with the groom's parents, followed by the bride's parents, the members of the wedding party, and finally the bride and groom. Because this will be the first time that the newlyweds are introduced as husband and wife, their introduction is usually greeted with great enthusiasm.

Receiving Line

Parents of the newlyweds, members of the wedding party, and the bride and groom participate in the receiving line to welcome each guest personally as they arrive at the reception. This is also an opportunity for introductions to be made among guests who may not already know everyone present.

Speeches

Speeches made by the couple's close friends and relatives are another fairly common wedding reception tradition. These are usually toasts to the couple's happiness or brief anecdotes about the couple. Speeches are most often made by members of the wedding party, particularly the best man and the maid of honor. At some wedding receptions, speeches may be made by any guest.

Throwing the Bouquet and Garter

The origin of the custom of throwing the bouquet is unclear, but it has become one of the most traditional American wedding customs. At some point near the end of the reception, a group of unmarried women is assembled. The bride stands with her back to the group, and throws her bouquet over her shoulder towards them. According to an old superstition, the woman who catches the bouquet will be the next to marry.

More recently, the throwing of the bouquet has evolved to include the throwing of the garter. A garter is an undergarment that was once used by women to secure their stockings. Although garters are unnecessary for most modern brides, some choose to wear one specifically for this custom. Mimicking the throwing of the bouquet, the groom throws the garter over his shoulder to a group of unmarried male guests. The one who catches it is said to be the next man to marry.

At some receptions, a raucous exchange then occurs between the woman who caught the bouquet and the man who caught the garter. This generally involves a bit of good-natured teasing and joking.

Web Sites

Bose, Sharbari. "The Muslim Wedding Celebration," Brides.com, undated.
   http://www.brides.com/weddingstyle/traditions/feature/article/105565

"Essential Guide: Receptions." Brides.com, undated.
   http://www.brides.com/weddingstyle/receptions/guide

"Jewish Weddins: Reception Rituals." TheKnot.com, undated.
   http://www.theknot.com/ch_article.html?Object=AI91108165802

"Order of Reception Events." USABride.com, undated
   http://usabride.com/webplan/a_reception_order.html

Winikka, Anja. "Customs: Ancient Wedding Day Traditions." Chinese Weddings by The Knot, undated.
   http://www.chineseweddingsbytheknot.com/articles/article.aspx?articleid=A60919094253

Further Reading

McBride-Mellinger, Maria. *The Perfect Wedding Reception: Stylish Ideas for Every Season.* New York: HarperResource, 2001.

Photo on facing page: The 25th wedding anniversary often involves a celebration with family.

Chapter 16: Post-Wedding Events

INTRODUCTION

After the wedding, newlyweds typically take part in further rituals. Some of these rituals are designed to cement their status as a couple, while others are modern-day reflections of ancient superstitions whose original significance has been lost. In earlier centuries, it was widely believed that major life events made people susceptible to the influence of evil spirits and general bad luck. Thus, many wedding customs were designed to ward off evil spirits. The modern custom of honking car horns as the bridal party and guests travel from, say, the church to the reception is a vestige of ancient customs, such as bell ringing and the launching of fireworks, designed to scare away evil spirits.

For this reason, the passage of a newly married couple into their home was considered a time fraught with danger. Households, and especially thresholds, were believed to be dangerous for new brides. Accordingly, one custom that emerged was that of the groom carrying the bride over the threshold of the new home as a way of protecting her from evil spirits or unlucky influences. It was also a way to ensure that she did not stumble at the threshold, a sign that she would be unlucky in marriage.

In the modern U.S. many newlyweds embark on a **Honeymoon**, a vacation the couple may take immediately following the wedding reception. Another immediate, though far less common, post-wedding custom is the **Charivari**, a kind of serenade that guests perform for the newly married couple.

Over the course of married life, many couples observe various **Anniversary Customs** to mark each successive year of their marriage. Some also choose to have a **Recommitment Ceremony** at some point to reaffirm their marital bond. Unfortunately, a significant number of weddings will ultimately result in **Divorce.**

CHARIVARI

Alternate Names: Chiravari, Shivaree

Customs and Symbols: Rough Music, Wedding Vehicle

The charivari is a post-wedding custom that survives primarily among Cajuns in Louisiana. Similar events take place in certain rural areas of the U.S., although the custom is not as widespread as it was during the 19th and early 20th centuries.

History and Significance

The charivari, or shivaree, originated in France. It was then carried to North America by French immigrants to such Canadian provinces as Newfoundland and Nova Scotia. Some descendants of these immigrants, in turn, later settled in Louisiana, where they are known as Cajuns. Accordingly, the charivari is regarded as a primarily Cajun custom, although it has been practiced in Georgia and other states as well.

Observances

The charivari can be thought of as a kind of serenade. After the wedding, the bride and groom set off to their new home. The wedding guests follow to assemble around the home and beat on noisemakers, including pots and pans, tambourines, drums, and the like. Often, musical instruments such as fiddles are played. The object is to produce as much noise as possible, with a view to drawing as much attention to the wedding as possible. Generally, the wedding vehicle and compilations of sounds known as rough music may also be employed in drawing attention. Traditionally, the bride and groom put a stop to the racket by inviting the guests in for food and drink.

Customs and Symbols

Rough Music

From the 17th through the 19th centuries, British communities would collectively mete out punishment to men who were thought to be guilty of such offenses as spousal abuse or adultery. To call attention to the husband's infractions, men in the community would assemble outside his home and create noise with whistles, horns, pots and pans, and the like. They would also beat on a straw effigy of the man. All of this noise was referred to as "rough music," and the men who made it were referred to as a "rough band." Over time, rough music became part of the wedding celebration.

Wedding Vehicle

While the wedding vehicle is not part of the charivari per se, it can be part of the general noisemaking that often accompanies a wedding. Typically, members of the wedding party or other guests decorate the vehicle that the couple will use. The most common decorations include a sign that reads "Just Married" and cans and shoes tied to the back of the car. (The cans become noisemakers when the car is in motion.) After the couple leaves the reception, they drive away as the assembled guests send them off with good wishes. The noise made by the vehicle draws public attention to the wedding in much the same fashion that the charivari does.

Further Reading

Ancelet, Barry Jean, Jay Dearborn Edwards, and Glen Pitre. *Cajun Country.* Jackson: University Press of Mississippi, 1991.

Thompson, E. P. "Rough Music." In *Customs in Common: Studies in Traditional Popular Culture.* New York: The New Press, 1993.

HONEYMOON

Alternate Name: Post-Wedding Vacation

Customs and Symbols: Honeymoon Suite, Niagara Falls, Registry

A honeymoon is a private vacation that is enjoyed by many newlyweds immediately after the wedding. This time away from everyday duties is intended to provide the couple with an opportunity to relax together and savor their new status as husband and wife.

History and Significance

The origin of the term honeymoon can be traced back to early Teutonic tribes in medieval Europe. It was customary in those societies for a man to abduct his bride from a neighboring tribe, an act that forced them both into hiding for several weeks. Thus, the honeymoon referred to the mead—a sweet wine made of honey—shared by the couple as well as the lunar month during which they stayed hidden.

From the late 16th century through the 18th century, the honeymoon referred to the couple's emotions during the early days of their marriage rather than to any period of isolation. It was not until the early 19th century that the honeymoon began to refer to post-wedding travel. Through the 19th and early 20th centuries, honeymoons were primarily enjoyed only by wealthy Americans, who normally took extended tours of Europe, often accompanied by friends and relatives.

In the 20th century, travel became more affordable for middle-class couples. Honeymoon vacations grew in popularity and began to resemble those enjoyed by modern newlyweds. Honeymoons today differ from other types of vacations that a couple might take in that the newlyweds generally keep to themselves. Even if the couple chooses a destination that is crowded with others, it is typically assumed that they would prefer to enjoy each other's company privately.

> *A honeymoon is a private vacation, a time away from everyday duties intended to provide the couple with an opportunity to relax together and savor their new status as husband and wife.*

Observance

For most Americans, regardless of religious or cultural background, the expectation is that virtually every couple will take some time away from everyday life, even if only for a day or two. No particular observances are followed during honeymoons, and there are no rules governing the choice of honeymoon destinations or activities. The type of trip, the destination, and the length of the honeymoon are all determined by the couples' interests and imagination. Many hotels and vacation destinations in the U.S. and abroad offer honeymoon suites, which include special amenities for newlyweds. For many years, Niagara Falls was one of the most popular American honeymoon destinations.

Honeymoons are typically not observed by Orthodox Jewish newlyweds. Jewish tradition specifies that the couple establish themselves within the community for a period of seven days immediately after the wedding. During this week, relatives and friends may host dinners in honor of the couple, who may otherwise spend time studying the Torah or doing charitable work.

Customs and Symbols

Honeymoon Suite

A honeymoon suite is a luxury room or rooms at a hotel or resort. These rooms are designed to enhance the romantic aspect of the honeymoon, and often include special amenities such as private dinners and complimentary champagne, flowers, candies or other delicacies.

Niagara Falls

Niagara Falls, located on the border between Canada and the U.S. in New York, became a common honeymoon destination in the 1830s. By the 1930s, the Falls were marketed as "the honeymoon capital of the world," and the area remained a popular honeymoon destination through the 1950s. Niagara Falls became such a stereotypical honeymoon destination that far fewer couples went there in succeeding decades, preferring instead to visit less crowded places.

Registry

One fairly new custom is for the engaged couple to register for their honeymoon as a series of individual gifts that can be purchased by wedding guests. In this way, guests can choose to pay for all or part of the couple's airfare, hotel stay, or other expenses. Luxury extras can also be added to the couple's honeymoon as a surprise gift, for example, limousine transportation from the airport to the hotel, a massage or other spa service, or a romantic dinner. An expansion of the traditional wedding gift registry, the honeymoon registry has become a novel option for modern couples who already have all the household goods they will need.

Web Site

"The Jewish Wedding Guide," Jewish American History on the Web, undated. http://www.jewish-history.com/minhag.htm

Further Reading

Bulcroft, Kris, Linda Smeins, and Richard Bulcroft. *Romancing the Honeymoon: Consummating Marriage in Modern Society*. Thousand Oaks, CA: Sage Publications, 1999.

Lehman, Katherine. "Honeymooning." In *Encyclopedia of Recreation and Leisure in America*. Edited by Gary S. Cross. Farmington Hills, MI: Charles Scribner's Sons, 2004.

ANNIVERSARY CUSTOMS

Customs and Symbols: Announcement; Gifts; Second Honeymoon; Silver, Golden, and Diamond Anniversaries; Wedding Cake; Wedding Candle

Annual wedding anniversaries are important occasions for married couples, especially those who have been together for many years. Couples typically observe their anniversary privately, although parties involving friends and relatives may be held for particularly significant anniversaries such as the 25th, 50th, or 60th.

History and Significance

The origin of many popular wedding anniversary customs is not known. Some of the more formalized American cultural customs, such as the traditional types of anniversary gifts, are believed to have originated in England during the Victorian era in the 19th century. For most married couples in the U.S., wedding anniversaries continue to hold significance as an annual reminder of their commitment to each other. Whether the day is noted privately or with a party including many people, the wedding anniversary is a milestone occasion that marks the longevity of a couples' relationship.

Observance

Wedding anniversaries are observed with a wide variety of customs, both public and private. Some couples celebrate with a **Recommitment Ceremony** or they may enjoy a second honeymoon vacation. Others light a wedding candle or share a portion of their wedding cake which has been preserved for the occasion. It is also customary for couples to exchange personal gifts on this day. In addition, an announcement may be placed in the local newspaper. Anniversary parties are generally only held for the silver, golden, and diamond anniversaries.

Some couples mark their anniversary by making a charitable donation in gratitude for the years of happiness they have enjoyed. If the couple is religious, this donation is often given to a faith-based organization. In Jewish tradition, it is customary for couples celebrating an anniversary to make a donation known as a *nedavá* to their synagogue. This is commonly a monetary donation that is often equal to some multiple of $18, because the number 18 is similar to the Hebrew word meaning "life."

Customs and Symbols

Announcement

Many newspapers, community newsletters, and other periodicals publish free announcements of significant wedding anniversaries. These announcements are usually submitted for publication by the couple or their children, generally to note anniversaries of 25, 50, or 60 years or more. A photo of the couple is often included, which can be current or from their wedding.

Gifts

Particular types of gifts are traditionally associated with certain anniversaries. These anniversaries include the first through the 15th, followed by the anniversary for each five-year interval through the 60th, and then the 75th. The origin of these anniversary associations cannot be stated with certainty, and the gift suggestions are by no means mandatory. However, many Americans continue to incorporate these suggestions when observing a wedding anniversary.

Normally, family and friends will only give the couple a gift on significant anniversaries such as the 25th, 50th, and 60th or 75th. Couples usually give each other personal gifts on every anniversary.

Second Honeymoon

Couples who have been married for any length of time may take a romantic vacation together to celebrate a wedding anniversary. This custom is commonly known as taking a second honeymoon—although some couples enjoy a third and fourth honeymoon as well. This trip can be planned by the couple, but may also be arranged and paid for by their children or friends as a special anniversary gift.

Silver, Golden, and Diamond Anniversaries

The three anniversaries that are likely to be the most elaborately celebrated are the silver (25th), golden (50th), and diamond (60th or 75th). These anniversaries are named for the materials that serve as gifts that are traditionally associated with those years.

These anniversaries represent major milestones in the married life of a couple and stand as testimony to the couple's ability to sustain their bond through major life events. At these anniversaries, the couple's children are likely to host a party with

Traditional and Modern Gifts

Although most adhere to the traditional wedding anniversary associations, some etiquette experts agree on modern substitutions.

Anniversary Year	Traditional Gift	Modern Gift
First	Paper	Clocks
Second	Cotton	China
Third	Leather	Crystal or Glass
Fourth	Linen or Silk	Appliances
Fifth	Wood	Silverware
Sixth	Iron	Wood
Seventh	Wool or Copper	Desk Sets
Eighth	Bronze	Linen or Lace
Ninth	Pottery or China	Leather
Tenth	Tin or Aluminum	Diamond
Eleventh	Steel	Fashion Jewelry
Twelfth	Silk	Pearls or Gems
Thirteenth	Lace	Textiles or Furs
Fourteenth	Ivory	Gold Jewelry
Fifteenth	Crystal	Watches
Twentieth	China	Platinum
Twenty-Fifth	Silver	Sterling Silver
Thirtieth	Pearl	Diamond
Thirty-Fifth	Coral or Jade	Jade
Fortieth	Ruby	Ruby
Forty-Fifth	Sapphire	Sapphire
Fiftieth	Gold	Gold
Sixtieth	Diamond	Diamond
Seventy-Fifth	Diamond	Diamond

friends and other family members in attendance. The couple is also usually presented with gifts on these occasions.

The 60th wedding anniversary is a special time for Koreans and Korean Americans. At this time, the couple reenacts their original wedding ceremony in a celebration called the Huihun Festival. The "bride" and "groom" appear before the assembled guests wearing the attire they wore at their wedding, or attire very like it. The event typically takes place at a hall, a nightclub, or a restaurant and features dancing and singing. The couple's relatives serve them rice wine, and a master of ceremonies narrates the history of the couple's married life.

> *Some couples preserve the top tier of their wedding cake by freezing it. On their first anniversary, the cake is thawed and shared by the couple.*

Wedding Cake

Some couples preserve the top tier of their wedding cake by freezing it. On their first anniversary, the cake is thawed and shared by the couple as a special way of marking the date.

Wedding Candle

One custom that some couples follow is that of lighting a wedding candle. The candle may be specially purchased for this purpose or received as a wedding gift. It may also be the same one that was used in a unity candle ceremony at their wedding. Wedding candles are typically very large, and some are able to burn for as long as 300 hours. Consequently the candle can be expected to last for many years, and the couple may make a ritual of lighting it each year and letting it burn for some time.

Web Site

"Korean Ethnic Minority," Ministry of Culture: People's Republic of China, September 2003. http://www.chinaculture.org/gb/en_aboutchina/2003-09/24/content_23969.htm

Further Reading

Baker, Margaret. *Wedding Customs and Folklore*. Totowa, NJ: Rowman and Littlefield, 1977.

Dresser, Norine. *Multicultural Celebrations: Today's Rules of Etiquette for Life's Special Occasions*. New York: Three Rivers Press, 1999.

Monger, George P. "Anniversaries." In *Marriage Customs of the World*. Santa Barbara, CA: ABC-CLIO, 2004.

Pleck, Elizabeth H. *Celebrating the Family: Ethnicity, Consumer Culture, and Family Rituals.* Cambridge, MA: Harvard University Press, 2000.

Ray, Rayburn W., and Rose Ann Ray. *Wedding Anniversary Idea Book: A Guide to Celebrating Wedding Anniversaries.* Brentwood, TN: J. M. Publications, 1985.

Sowden, Cynthia Lueck. *An Anniversary to Remember.* St. Paul, MN: Brighton Publications, 1992.

RECOMMITMENT CEREMONIES

Alternate Names: Reaffirmation, Renewal Ceremonies, Renewal of Vows

Customs and Symbols: Group Renewals

In a recommitment ceremony, a married couple reaffirms their dedication to marriage and their love for each other. The ceremony typically includes a public renewal of vows and is often followed by a party with family and friends in attendance.

History and Significance

In the early 1950s, the Christian faith-based Marriage Encounter movement began to promote weekend retreats for married couples wishing to reconnect and strengthen their relationships. The practice developed over the next 30 years, with various Christian denominations organizing Marriage Encounter programs tailored for their beliefs. Non-denominational and Jewish Marriage Encounters also developed. In the early 1980s, the Worldwide Marriage Encounter organization adopted and began to promote World Marriage Day. Religious communities were encouraged to offer special services on that day, including renewal of vows for any married couple who wished to participate. As the concept of public renewal of wedding vows grew in popularity, it became increasingly common for any married couple to mark a significant wedding anniversary with a recommitment ceremony. By the late 20th century, the renewal ceremony had become a cultural tradition rather than a religious one, although many recommitment ceremonies continue to emphasize the religious and spiritual aspects of marriage.

Observance

There is tremendous variety in the observance of recommitment ceremonies, which are largely individual affairs designed by the couple who wish to renew their vows. Couples typically choose to renew their vows on the 25th or 50th wedding anniversary, although there are no strict rules concerning when the ceremony may be held or how it may be observed. For example, couples may or may not return to the site of their wedding, may or may not involve the same officiant and **Wedding Party**, and so on.

Generally, recommitment ceremonies take place in the presence of friends and relatives. The couple often acknowledges the challenges, successes, and shared experiences of their marriage, and takes vows to remain committed to each other in the future. The ceremony is considered a romantic gesture that allows a husband and wife to declare publicly their ongoing love for and loyalty to each other.

In some cases, couples have elaborate recommitment ceremonies because they were unable to afford a large wedding when they were originally married. These ceremonies often take on many of the trappings of a first wedding: a white dress for the wife, a tuxedo for the husband, and a reception for guests. Similarly, couples who were married away from home often hold a recommitment ceremony as a kind of wedding to which they can invite family and friends who were not present at the original ceremony. Some people take part in group renewals, where more than one couple renews their wedding vows.

Customs and Symbols

Group Renewals

While many recommitment ceremonies involve just one married couple, many others take place as a group event. For example, some churches schedule yearly recommitment ceremonies including any couples who want to participate. Another form of group renewal takes place at conferences and seminars. These gatherings, typically conducted by clerics, are designed to help couples enhance the spiritual aspect of their marriage, and renewal ceremonies are often part of these events. The growth in popularity of recommitment ceremonies in recent years has prompted hotels, cruise lines, and resort destinations to offer ceremonies as part of group anniversary vacation packages.

Web Sites

"Purpose and History," World Marriage Day, undated.
     http://wmd.wwme.org/purpose-history.html

"We Still Do!," by Caron Chandler Loveless, *Christianity Today: Marriage Partnership*, Summer 2005.
     http://www.christianitytoday.com/mp/2005/002/5.30.html

Further Reading

Ray, Rayburn W., and Rose Ann Ray. *Wedding Anniversary Idea Book: A Guide to Celebrating Wedding Anniversaries.* Brentwood, TN: J. M. Publications, 1985.

Warner, Diane. *Complete Book of Wedding Vows: Hundreds of Ways to Say "I Do."* Franklin Lakes, NJ: Career Press, 1996.

DIVORCE

Customs and Symbols: Annulment, Bet Din, Talaq

Divorce is a fact of life in contemporary America. The conventional wisdom is that about 50 percent of marriages end in divorce. That number appears to have been confirmed by studies examining the marital patterns of Americans. A U.S. Census Bureau study published in 2005 concluded:

> How long do marriages last? . . . First marriages occurring during the peak of the baby-boom years (1955 to 1959) lasted longer than those occurring 20 years later (1975 to 1979). . . . That is to say, a lower percentage of those in this later marriage cohort [group] than baby-boom brides and grooms reached subsequent anniversaries. While 76 percent of men who married in 1955 to 1959 stayed married for at least 20 years, only 58 percent of men who married in 1975 to 1979 stayed married as long. Declines in marital longevity occurred also for men at even shorter anniversaries of 5, 10, or 15 years. Similarly, marital longevity also fell for women in the 1975 to 1979 marriage cohort compared with women married in 1955 to 1959.

If getting married is a major life event for adults, getting unmarried is an equally major event, but one that causes stress and expense. While divorce can be a source of liberation, particularly for those in abusive relationships, for many people divorce leads to great unhappiness as homes and families are broken up, property is divided, children become confused, and old friends the couple had in common disappear.

History and Significance

The Puritans of colonial America saw marriage as a civil contract that could be broken under some circumstances; the most common cause of divorce was adultery, and most such divorces were granted to men. By the 19th century, cruelty (including mental cruelty), intemperance (that is, excessive drinking), and abandonment became common reasons for divorce. By 1900, about two-thirds of divorces were granted to women. Nonetheless, marriage remained relatively stable in the late 19th century, with only one in 20 marriages ending in divorce.

In the 20th century, the divorce rate increased. By 1916, one in nine marriages ended in divorce. The rate rose during the 1920s, then slowed during the Great

While divorce can be a source of liberation, particularly for those in abusive relationships, for many people divorce leads to great unhappiness as homes and families are broken up, property is divided, children become confused, and old friends the couple had in common disappear.

Depression of the 1930s and during the Second World War before reaching a record high level in 1946. The rate slowed during the 1950s and early 1960s before creeping up again in the late 1960s and early 1970s.

Social scientists, legislators, clerics, and others pay close attention to the divorce rate for a variety of reasons. A high divorce rate is an indicator of a breakdown in the structures of society. For government planners, divorce raises a host of social issues. For example, in many families (but by no means all), it is the man who has the greater earning power, making the woman vulnerable to financial hardship after the divorce. Legislatures and the court system struggle to find ways to ensure that alimony payments to women, as well as child support payments, are adequate to ensure some measure of financial equity after a divorce. Social scientists continue to debate the effects of divorce on children; many assert that children from "broken homes" are more likely than those from intact families to experience trouble in school, delinquency, suicide, alcohol and drug abuse, and other problems.

Observance

Divorce laws and procedures vary from state to state. Each state has its own requirements, but in general the civil divorce process goes as follows. It begins when one of the parties, usually after consulting with a lawyer, files a petition for divorce with the court system in the state where the parties live. The divorce petition is then served to the other party, who is required to respond within a certain period of time. Meanwhile, one of the parties can request a separation order that settles a variety of matters until the divorce is finalized: who will live in the couple's residence, who will retain custody of children, and the like.

Many states impose a "cooling-off" period before any legal action can be taken on the divorce petition, hoping that after consideration, the couple decides that they can repair their marriage. A common period is ninety days. In some jurisdictions, one of the parties can request from the court reconciliation counseling, a form of marriage counseling, to explore the possibility of fixing the marriage.

Some divorces, particularly when there are no children, are relatively amicable, although some resentment is hard to avoid when marriage to another person fails to meet a person's needs. Both parties recognize that the marriage is not working, agree to the division of their assets, and go their separate ways. Other divorce proceedings are acrimonious, often because one party feels that the other is making unfair financial demands. Child custody and visitation with children by the non-custodial parent on weekends, on holidays, and during the summer school vacation can also become sources of bitter dispute.

The role of the court (that is, a judge) is to hear each side's point of view, gather information about the financial obligations and earning power of each spouse, determine what kind of custody and visitation arrangement is in the best interests of children, then write a divorce decree that lays out rules the parties will follow in the future. In many states, legal codes determine the amount of alimony and particularly child support the noncustodial parent is required to pay, based on the earning power of each parent.

Among Muslims, divorce proceedings are determined by Islamic law, and the termination of marriage is called *talaq.* Jews often have recourse to a *bet din,* or Jewish religious court, to settle the terms of divorce. Some couples, especially Roman Catholics, obtain annulments in addition to civil divorces.

Customs and Symbols

Annulments

A divorce ends a legally valid marriage. An annulment differs from a divorce by saying in effect that the marriage was invalid to begin with. In the civil courts, marriages can be annulled when the court finds that the marriage failed to meet legal requirements for a valid marriage. A good example is bigamy, where one of the parties is already married.

The Roman Catholic Church, believing that marriage is a sacrament and that vows are binding for life, does not accept divorce. In some instances, though, it grants annulments for reasons that civil courts would not recognize. An annulment then allows the parties to remarry and to remain in good standing with the church. A common ground for annulments is called "defective consent." This means that when the couple was married, one party lacked the ability to fully consent to the marriage because of external pressure (if, for example, the woman was pregnant), immaturity, or sexual impotence. The issue of church annulments has become controversial, for some traditional Catholics believe that the church grants them too freely.

Las Vegas and Other "Quickie" Divorces

For decades a stereotypical divorce in the United States was a divorce in Las Vegas (or Reno), Nevada. Nevada has a short residency requirement—just six weeks—before people can file for a divorce in the state, and the divorce process itself often takes only one to two weeks. With the development of no-fault divorce laws in most states, the Las Vegas divorce has become less popular than it was until the 1970s.

Meanwhile, other options are open to couples who want quick divorces. The Dominican Republic requires essentially no residency, so couples can fly to that county, get divorced quickly, then return home (likely not on the same plane!).

Sources: Nevada State Bar Association, *Divorce* (pamphlet), available online at http://www.nvbar.org/Publications/Publications_Pamphlets/Divorce.htm; Embassy of the United States in Santo Domingo, "Divorce in the Dominican Republic," available online at http://santodomingo.usembassy.gov/Consular/ACS/divorceDR.htm

Bet Din

The bet din is a Jewish religious court. Jewish couples often turn to such a court when they disagree about divorce. The court cannot compel a divorce; all it can do is listen to both parties and make recommendations. Among Orthodox Jews, a husband is required to profer a *get,* or a declaration of divorce.

Talaq

Under Muslim law, a termination of marriage is called a talaq. Islamic law gives a man the right to end a marriage by simply declaring his intention to do so. The law requires him to return his wife dowry, and he remains obligated to support her during a period called *'idda,* or three menstrual periods. Wives do not have the right to talaq, but they can seek a "divorce by mutual consent," usually compensating the husband in return. If the husband does not consent, a woman can turn to an Islamic court, which can force the husband to "pronounce talaq" or can do so for him.

Further Reading

Belli, Melvin, and Mel Krantzler. *Divorcing.* New York: St. Martin's Press, 1988.

Dillon, Michelle. "Annulment." In *Contemporary American Religion.* Edited by Wade Clark Roof. Vol. 1. New York: Macmillan Reference USA, 1999.

Griswold, Robert L. "Divorce." In *The Reader's Companion to American History.* Boston: Houghton Mifflin, 1991.

Gross, David C., and Esther R. Gross. *Under the Wedding Canopy: Love and Marriage in Judaism.* New York: Hippocrene Books, 1996.

Kreider, Rose M. "Number, Timing, and Duration of Marriages and Divorces: 2001." U.S. Census Bureau, Department of Commerce, February 2005. http://www.census.gov/prod/2005pubs/p70-97.pdf

Mir-Hosseini, Ziba Mir-Hosseini. "Divorce." In *Encyclopedia of Islam and the Muslim World.* Edited by Richard C. Martin. Vol. 1. New York: Macmillan Reference USA, 2004.

Photo on facing page: Muslim pilgrims performing the hajj, in Mecca.

Chapter 17: Adult Milestones

INTRODUCTION

This chapter provides an overview of selected milestones of adult life, including home ownership, group reunions, and the completion of the Muslim pilgrimage to Mecca. The meaning and importance attached to each of these events differs among individuals, and can also change with age. For example, attending a school reunion five years after graduation will likely seem very different than attending one after 25 or more years. Similarly, the significance of becoming a homeowner may not be fully realized until many years after the home was purchased. Although these milestone events often have unique—and quite personal—significance, each remains a collective cultural symbol of adulthood in America.

Purchasing a House for the first time is generally seen as a milestone in the life of many Americans. Home ownership is widely considered to be a sign of independence and stability, and is a goal for many adults. The desire to own a home is deeply ingrained in the American character and sometimes referred to as part of the American dream, an idealized wish for a happy and successful life.

Reunions are another significant event in the lives of many Americans. **Class Reunions** are gatherings of those who attended a particular school, usually those who graduated in the same year. Class reunions provide opportunities to renew old friendships and see how classmates have changed over the years. Although the prospect of attending a class reunion can be stressful for some, many look forward to these events with great anticipation. **Family Reunions** bring together people who are related by their connection to one or more common ancestors. Whether held annually or less frequently, contemporary American family reunions provide opportunities for people to explore shared histories, allowing families to reconnect in meaningful ways. **Military Reunions** gather those who served together or had similar experiences serving in the U.S. Armed Forces. For many veterans, reunions provide opportunities not only for social reconnection, but also for the resolution of lingering questions or emotions related to their military service. Children who grew up on U.S. military bases and the spouses of those in military service may also have their own reunions.

One of the most important milestones in the life of observant Muslims is the completion of the pilgrimage to Mecca, a practice known as **Performing the Hajj**. The *hajj* is an annual pilgrimage to Mecca, a city in western Saudi Arabia that is regarded by Muslims as the most holy place in the Islamic world. According to Islamic law, only Muslims may enter the city of Mecca. Every adult Muslim is required to perform the pilgrimage at least once in their lifetime, if they are physically and financially able to make the trip. It is one of the oldest and most important spiritual duties required of Muslims. Many American Muslims experience the pilgrimage to Mecca as a profound spiritual awakening, and the event also strengthens the sense of social and religious unity among Muslims worldwide.

These examples of important events in the lives of American adults are generally interpreted as significant markers of an individual's progress through life. Although not mandatory or universally observed, the majority of Americans can expect to experience at least one of these milestone events over the course of their adult lives.

PURCHASING A HOUSE

Customs and Symbols: House Blessing, Housewarming Party

Purchasing a house is a milestone in the lives of many Americans. Generally considered to be a sign of independence and stability, home ownership may be undertaken by a single person or a married couple.

History and Significance

The desire to own a home is deeply ingrained in the American character. Until about the 1830s, home ownership was beyond the financial reach of most Americans because the materials and technologies used to build homes were expensive. In 1833, however, the so-called balloon-frame home was first developed. Rather than being built with expensive hardwood beams and/or stone by large teams of skilled craftsmen, homes could now be built by smaller teams of carpenters using less expensive two-by-four studs—the same way most modern homes are built. This change brought the possibility of home ownership within reach of a much larger number of Americans.

Home ownership in the United States began to expand rapidly after World War I (1914–18). Contributing to this expansion was the development of a real estate industry, with close associations among builders, real estate brokers, and bankers. The U.S. government also passed laws designed to promote home ownership; very helpful was a 1939 law making home loan interest payments tax deductible. Meanwhile, the development and spread of the automobile allowed people to move farther away from crowded urban areas where living quarters were typically rented. Many people moved into suburbs where they could realize the dream of owning their own home. After World War II (1939–45), many returning soldiers bought homes in new suburban developments, and the size of U.S. suburbs exploded.

Observance

The process of locating and purchasing a house can be both stressful and exciting, including many decisions about location, size, architecture, and cost of the home. A tremendous amount of information and advice for those interested in buying a house has been published in books, newspapers, and magazines, as well as on a variety of Web sites. And al-

The process of locating and purchasing a house can be both stressful and exciting.

315

though home ownership is a major milestone in the life of many adults, there are few celebratory customs surrounding the event. After moving in to their new house, many homeowners host a housewarming party, inviting friends and family to see the property. Others conduct a house blessing ritual to ensure safety, happiness, and prosperity in their new home.

Homes may be purchased by single people or married couples, who generally select and purchase the house together. In traditional Muslim communities, however, a man may buy and furnish a house as a wedding gift for his new wife. This is done as a gesture of appreciation and respect, and to provide her with a comfortable new home in which every detail has been anticipated and arranged for her enjoyment. Among some conservative Muslims, it is considered unseemly to require a new bride to make decisions or arrangements for her new home.

Many Chinese Americans consult almanacs to determine the most favorable day for moving into a new home. Some take occupancy of the home but sleep on the floor until the auspicious date arrives, believing that because they are sleeping on the floor, they have not really moved into the home. Only when the auspicious date arrives do they sleep in a bed.

Customs and Symbols

House Blessing

House blessings can take many forms, depending on the religious tradition of the homeowner. Christians may perform the blessing themselves or with the participation of family, friends, and a priest or pastor. A typical Christian house blessing includes readings from scripture, singing of hymns, or prayers specifically related to the use of each room. There are no specific customs associated with Christian house blessings, and so homeowners are free to create their own meaningful rites.

Wiccans and Neopagans often devise individualized rituals to bless a new house. These ceremonies may be performed alone or with others of the same beliefs. Blessings may acknowledge the differences between the previous living quarters and the new house, express gratitude for good fortune, or celebrate the new home as a personal sanctuary. Some house blessings also include the marking of the home or property boundaries with protective charms.

Hindu homeowners may conduct the *griha pravesh* ceremony before moving into their new house. This ceremony includes rituals and prayers that are intended to remove harmful influences or negativity that may be associated with the property. The homeowners may be assisted by a Hindu priest if one is available. Once the

Feng Shui

*F*eng shui (pronounced *fung shway*) is a Chinese expression meaning "wind and water." It refers to ancient Chinese beliefs having to do with harmonious places to live. The rules of feng shui dictate the flow of positive energy in the home, and thus dictate the placement and design of buildings and rooms. For example, entrances typically face east, for doors facing west are thought to bring bad luck. A front door and a back door should not be aligned directly with each other lest luck and money enter the house through one door and immediately and easily leave through the other. Many Chinese homebuyers consult a feng shui expert before buying a home.

ceremony has been completed, the most opportune moving day is calculated using astrological charts.

Housewarming Party

Housewarming parties are a common American custom whose origins are unclear. These parties are generally hosted by the homeowner shortly after moving in. Guests typically include family members, friends, and sometimes the new neighbors, who come to see the new property and to congratulate the homeowner. Housewarming parties are typically gift-giving occasions, and each guest is likely to bring a small gift that can be used in the new home. Gifts can be anything that the homeowner needs or would enjoy. Salt and bread are traditional gifts that are sometimes still given for housewarmings. This custom, thought to have originated in eastern Europe, signifies a wish that the homeowner never be short of food or good fortune.

Web Sites

"Hindu House Warming Ceremony (Griha Pravesh)," *India Parenting*, undated.
   http://www.indiaparenting.com/articles/data/art54_001.shtml

"House Warming: Plan a Family-Friendly Blessing for Your New Home," by Greg Asimakoupoulos. *Christian Parenting Today*, Fall 2003.
   http://www.christianitytoday.com/cpt/2003/003/3.32.html

"Salting the Bread and the Baby: The Magical Powers of Salt," *Jewish Heritage Online Magazine*, undated.
http://www.jhom.com/topics/salt/magic.htm

Further Reading

"Balloon-Frame House." In *The Reader's Companion to American History*. Boston: Houghton-Mifflin, 1991.

Dresser, Norine. *Multicultural Manners: New Rules of Etiquette for a Changing Society.* New York: John Wiley & Sons, 1996.

Gulevich, Tanya. *Understanding Islam and Muslim Traditions.* Detroit: Omnigraphics, 2004.

Hayden, Dolores. "Housing." In *The Reader's Companion to American History*. Boston: Houghton-Mifflin, 1991.

Starhawk, Diane Baker, and Anne Hill. *Circle Round: Raising Children in Goddess Traditions.* New York: Bantam Books, 1998.

FAMILY REUNIONS

Customs and Symbols: Family Artifacts, Family Tree, Food, Souvenirs, Stories

A family reunion is a gathering of people who are related by their connection to one or more common ancestors. Many families hold reunions annually, while others have reunions on a less regular basis.

History and Significance

Before the 19th century, family reunions were not a common occurrence. Because life expectancy was much shorter, grandparents and even parents were likely to have died by the time children reached adulthood. Extended relations such as nephews, nieces, or cousins, who themselves may have been orphaned, came to live with a family. Further, family members often ended up living far from one another because of migration—both from Europe to North America and within the U.S. as the nation expanded westward. Long-distance travel and communication were difficult, and family members often lost track of one another.

All this began to change with the Industrial Revolution and the modernization that followed. As families began to settle in and around cities, it became easier to stay in contact with one another. Life expectancies increased, so at least two and usually three generations were living at the same time. Advances in long-distance travel and communication also helped people stay in touch, and the concept of family was no longer rooted in place but in time, through common connections. The modern family reunion provides opportunities for people to explore shared histories, and allows families to reconnect with each other in meaningful ways.

Observance

The nature and timing of family reunions varies greatly according to each family's traditions and preferences. Reunions can be simple, informal gatherings that take place on a single afternoon or evening at the home of a family member. They can also be elaborate events held over multiple days, including a wide range of organized events such as cemetery visits, luncheons, community service, scrapbook-making sessions, prayer services, picnics, banquet dinners, speeches and presentations, or trips to local tourist attractions.

Family reunions sometimes coincide with a special event such as the 100th birthday of a grandparent or great-grandparent, or the 60th wedding anniversary of the family's oldest living members. Many reunions celebrate a shared ethnic or cultural heritage, often through the meals served. The family tree is usually a prominent feature of the reunion. At larger family reunions, souvenirs are often sold to help finance the cost of the next reunion.

Reunions are important annual occasions for many African-American families. These reunions tend to be large events held over three or more days, often at a hotel or other facility. The location typically varies each year, allowing different groups of family members to take a turn hosting the event while also attempting to fairly distribute the need for travel. African-American family reunions may also be attended by people who are not related through common ancestry. Many reunions also include long-time friends, neighbors, pastors, former spouses, stepchildren, and others who have established a close relationship with the family.

Customs and Symbols

Family Artifacts

Reunions typically feature displays of items that illustrate some aspect of family history. This can include the family tree as well as photos, scrapbooks, journals and letters, quilts, clothing, personal items, treasured antiques, heirlooms, and other mementos of ancestors. If the reunion takes place at or near an ancestral home, the history of that structure in relation to the family will likely be featured prominently.

Family Tree

A family tree is a graphic representation of a family through the generations. Early ancestors are the "trunk" of the tree, and their descendants are the "branches." In modern American life, interest in genealogy has exploded, and a large number of web sites and organizations help people trace their ancestry. Considerable time, effort, and research are required to assemble a family tree. Consequently, this task is often left to the person who is most interested in the family's history.

Food

At least a portion of any reunion is likely to be organized around a family feast. Such a feast takes on symbolic importance, primarily because mealtime has always been a time when families come together to create a sense of family identity. It is common for family reunions to feature meals that reflect the family's history. Dishes might include those that would have been eaten by the family's distant

Family Histories Lost to Slavery

During a period of approximately 245 years—beginning in about 1619 and lasting until the 13th Amendment to the U.S. Constitution was enacted in 1865—white landowners in some parts of the U.S. were allowed to hold African Americans as slaves. Because the people held as slaves were not given any legal rights or protections, their marriages were not recognized as legally valid and all children born to slaves were considered to be the property of the landowner. Husbands and wives, parents and children, brothers and sisters were commonly separated by slave traders who had no regard for family relationships. When slavery was abolished, many African Americans began to search for their family members. This was no easy task, but some families were reunited. Many more were not, and modern African-American genealogists are consequently faced with untraceable branches of their family trees.

ancestors, as well as those prepared using favorite recipes from more recent ancestors. Many families create and share recipe books for family members.

Souvenirs

It is quite common for larger family reunions to make souvenirs available for purchase by reunion attendees. These items are usually imprinted with the family name(s) and the date of the reunion. Examples of typical family reunion souvenir items are T-shirts, sweatshirts, tote bags, and photo album covers, although a wide variety of personalized items can be used for this purpose.

Stories

Stories and storytelling are important aspects of family reunions. Some of these stories might involve distant ancestors and their perilous trip to the New World. Others might involve the heroism of an ancestor in the Civil War, World War I, World War II, or other conflicts. Still others might celebrate the liberation of African Americans from slavery, or recount the experiences of ancestors who were formerly slaves. These stories create a sense of family identity and are a good way to help children link the history of their family to that of the nation.

At larger family reunions, special events featuring speakers or historical presentations may be arranged. Speakers may be family members who have researched a particular aspect of family history. Non-family members may also be invited to share expert knowledge of a time, place, or event that has significance for the family.

Web Sites

Family Reunion Institute, Temple University, 2001.
http://www.temple.edu/fri/familyreunion

"Family Reunions," by Edith Wagner. *Family Chronicle*, January–February 2000.
http://www.familychronicle.com/FamilyReunions.html

"More Than a Picnic: African American Family Reunions," by Ione D. Vargus Working Paper for the Family Reunion Institute, Temple University, Emory Center for Myth and Ritual in American Life, September 2002.
http://www.marial.emory.edu/pdfs/Vargus022-03.pdf

"Slavery in America: Historical Overview," by Ronald L. F. Davis, undated. Slavery in America (companion web site of PBS series "Slavery and the Making of America").
http://www.slaveryinamerica.org/history/hs_es_overview.htm

Further Reading

Gillis, John R. "Gathering Together: Remembering Memory through Ritual." In *We Are What We Celebrate: Understanding Holidays and Rituals*. Edited by Amitai Etzioni and Jared Bloom. New York: New York University Press, 2004.

Hoffman, Linda Johnson, and Neal Barnett. *The Reunion Planner*. Los Angeles: Goodman Lauren Publishing, 1999.

Neville, Gwen Kennedy. "Reunions." In *Contemporary American Religion*. Edited by Wade Clark Roof. New York: Macmillan Reference USA, 1999.

Pleck, Elizabeth H. *Celebrating the Family: Ethnicity, Consumer Culture, and Family Rituals*. Cambridge, MA: Harvard University Press, 2000.

Wisdom, Emma J. *A Practical Guide to Planning a Family Reunion*. Nashville Post Oak Publications, 1988.

MILITARY REUNIONS

Customs and Symbols: Banquet, Memorial, Militaria

Military reunions gather those who served together or those who had similar experiences serving in the U.S. Armed Forces. Although veterans who served under any conditions might attend a reunion, the close bonds that develop between soldiers in battle make the events particularly popular among those who served during combat.

History and Significance

Serving in the military, particularly in wartime, is a life-altering event for many veterans. Much of the purpose of military training is to make the soldiers part of a team whose members can rely on one another under the most difficult circumstances. Shared experiences are often of a nature that can only be fully understood by other veterans. Accordingly, the bonds that are forged by those who served together tend to be long-lasting and deep. For many veterans, reunions provide opportunities not only for social reconnection, but also for the resolution of lingering questions or emotions related to their military service.

Observance

Military reunions are commonly held for any group of servicepersons who share a common experience. This can include members of a particular unit, those who were stationed on the same base or ship, those who performed the same or similar functions while in the military, or those who served in a specific battle, military conflict, or war. One reunion might include a particular Army platoon whose members fought together in World War II, while another includes all of the nurses who have ever served in air evacuation units in any U.S. military operation.

Reunions may be attended by veterans, active-duty personnel, reservists, and the families of servicepersons. The spouses of those serving in the same unit or on the same ship often form their own bonds. They may attend the reunion or arrange one of their own. Consequently, the event is likely to include a mix of veterans and people who are currently serving as well as their families.

Children who grew up on U.S. military bases may also have their own reunions. Sometimes known as "military brats," they usually moved frequently as their parent was transferred to various posts in the U.S. and abroad. With these often challenging childhood experiences in common, many enjoy attending reunions to swap their own "war stories," including adventures living overseas or changing schools every one or two years. The Military Brats Registry was founded in 1997 to connect children of military parents, and many reunions are facilitated by the organization's web site. Established in 1998, Overseas Brats serves those whose childhood years were spent on U.S. military bases abroad.

> *The bonds that are forged by those who served together tend to be long-lasting and deep. Reunions provide opportunities not only for social reconnection, but also for the resolution of lingering questions or emotions related to their military service.*

Many reunions are held in conjunction with a conference featuring speakers and programs on topics of interest to veterans. Larger reunions typically offer a variety of events that allow attendees to renew old friendships and update each other on life after the military. Reunion memorial services are usually held to honor and remember those who have died. Most reunions include a formal banquet, and some also feature a display of militaria for viewing or purchase.

A large collective military reunion is held each year in Pigeon Forge, Tennessee. The event usually includes a variety of keynote speakers and discussion forums, a military book fair, parades, and social activities including dances and group tours.

Customs and Symbols

Banquet

The focal point of many reunions is the banquet dinner, which may feature speakers or a presentation related to the shared military experience of those assembled. Sometimes a dance follows the banquet, often set to the music that was popular during the attendees' time of service.

Memorial

Memorial services are an important part of most military reunions. Attendees may organize a service as part of another reunion event, or they may go as a group to visit a military cemetery or monument dedicated to those who died in service. Some reunions are held near the sites of important events involving attendees, such as the battlefield where they fought together. Many military groups have visited the beaches of Normandy, France, which was the site of one of the largest military actions of World War II. Some U.S. battleships have become museums, and veterans who were stationed there may go as a group to revisit their time on board.

Militaria

Artifacts and collectibles related to the armed forces of any country or time period are known as militaria. This can include Civil War photographs, service awards and medals, historic newspaper clippings, uniforms, antique firearms, and other items. Military reunions often display a collection of militaria related to the shared experience of attendees.

Web Sites

"Celebrate Freedom: Pigeon Forge Salutes America's Veterans," Celebrate-Freedom.com, undated.
http://www.celebrate-freedom.com

Military Brats Registry, undated.
http://www.military-brats.com

"Military Reunion Articles," *Reunions Magazine*, undated.
http://www.reunionsmag.com/reunionarticles/military.html

Military Reunion Center, Military.com, undated.
http://www.military.com/Resources/ReunionList

Overseas Brats, undated.
http://www.overseasbrats.com

Further Reading

Hoffman, Linda Johnson, and Neal Barnett. *The Reunion Planner*. Los Angeles: Goodman Lauren Publishing, 1999.

Keenan, Alex. "It's the Season to Plan Your Unit's Reunion." *Army Times,* January 23, 2006.

CLASS REUNIONS

Alternate Names: College Reunions, High School Reunions, Homecoming

Customs and Symbols: Awards, Football Classics, Fundraising, Homecoming

Class reunions are gatherings of alumni who graduated from a particular school in the same year. Reunions provide former classmates with an opportunity to renew old friendships and share memories. Most reunions are held at periodic intervals although some are annual events.

History and Significance

American colleges and universities have been holding alumni reunions since the 1800s, and the tradition has grown to include an estimated 150,000 class reunions now held each year. Classmates often form special bonds during high school and college years, and reunions offer a chance to reconnect and reminisce about the experiences in school. Class reunions have become an important and highly anticipated cultural ritual, often causing attendees to reflect on their lives and accomplishments since graduation (*see* **High School Graduation**).

Observance

High school and college reunions are commonly held on the 10th, 20th or 25th, and 50th anniversary of graduation. Some individual classes hold reunions at five-year intervals, and some schools hold multi-class reunions every year as part of homecoming celebrations. Most reunions take place on one evening, but some are weekend affairs that include many different events for classmates and their families. At the minimum, weekend events typically include a welcoming reception on Friday evening, a dinner dance on Saturday evening, and a good-bye brunch on Sunday afternoon.

Class reunions provide opportunities to renew old friendships and see how classmates have changed over the years. Activities are usually structured around shared memories and allow attendees to reminisce and revisit familiar places. The focal point of most class reunions is typically a dinner dance during which awards may be given out and fundraising activities may be conducted.

Historically black colleges and universities, commonly referred to as HBCUs, often hold alumni reunions in conjunction with football classics. The focal point of these weekends is normally the football game and associated tailgate parties. The annual Black College Reunion, also known as Black Beach Week or Black Spring Break, originated as a reunion of alumni of Bethune-Cookman College and Florida A&M University. This three-day event, held on the second weekend in April in Daytona Beach, Florida, is attended each year by an estimated 100,000 African-American students and alumni from all HBCUs.

Customs and Symbols

Awards

During some reunions, classmates acknowledge each other with awards for various "achievements" such as Most Gray Hair, Best-Kept Figure, Most Children, Best Dressed, or Most Times Married. These awards are an updated version of the common yearbook tradition of naming the Most Popular person in the class, or the Most Likely to Succeed.

Football Classics

Multi-class HBCU reunions are often scheduled in conjunction with annual football games known as Classics, which are held at various locations throughout the country. Most Classics take place as part of a weekend of social activities including class reunions, parades, marching band competitions, tailgate parties, step shows, pep rallies, concerts, and special luncheons or dinners. These events are heavily attended by HBCU alumni and their families.

Fundraising

Reunions often include fundraising programs to benefit the school or its students. Private high schools, colleges, and universities have come to depend upon donations from alumni, but fundraising can also be conducted for publicly funded schools. Alumni of a particular class sometimes fund a special scholarship or support a particular program such as theater or athletics, and reunions are often the time when large donations are solicited.

Homecoming

Many schools hold annual homecoming weekends, featuring a variety of events for current students as well as alumni. Homecoming is often a time for informal reunions of alumni united by course of study or membership in a Greek letter society, rather than year of graduation.

Web Site

Moore, Eric. "Black College Football Classic Games: A Taste of the HBCU Athletic Experience." CollegeView.com, undated.
http://www.collegeview.com/articles/CV/hbcu/classic_games.html

Further Reading

Gay, Kathlyn. "Football Classics." In *African-American Holidays, Festivals, and Celebrations.* Detroit: Omnigraphics, 2007.

Lamb, Douglas, and Glenn D. Reeder. "Reliving Golden Days." *Psychology Today,* June 1986.

Lehman, Katherine. "Reunions." In *Encyclopedia of Recreation and Leisure in America.* Edited by Gary S. Cross. Farmington Hills, MI: Charles Scribner's Sons, 2004.

Spratling, Cassandra. "How to Plan a Class Reunion." *Detroit Free Press,* July 15, 2005.

PERFORMING THE HAJJ

Alternate Names: Great Pilgrimage to Mecca, al-Hajj al-Akbar, The Sacred Journey

Customs and Symbols: Circumambulation, Consecration, Deconsecration, Eid al-Adha, Hurrying to Muzdalifah, Running Between the Hills, Standing at Arafat, Throwing Pebbles

The hajj is an annual pilgrimage to Mecca, a city in western Saudi Arabia that is regarded by Muslims as the holiest place in the Islamic world. Every adult Muslim is required to perform the pilgrimage at least once in their lifetime, if they are physically and financially able to make the trip. Muslim men who have successfully completed the hajj (pronounced *HADGE*, literally "to set out for a place") are permitted to use the honorary title hajji or hajj, while Muslim women who complete the pilgrimage may use the honorary title hajjah or hajjiyah.

History and Significance

As one of the most ancient cities in the world, by the sixth century Mecca was already an established center of commerce as well as a religious sanctuary and pilgrimage site for the followers of many pre-Islamic faiths. Islam was established in the 600s C.E., and the hajj pilgrimage to Mecca is one of the Five Pillars of Islam outlined by Muhammad and described in the Qu'ran. The hajj is one of the oldest and most important spiritual duties required of Muslims, and the intricate ceremonies of the pilgrimage memorialize significant events in ancient Islamic history. Although the pilgrimage has been performed for many centuries, the specific rites and rituals that form the hajj have remained virtually unchanged. At various locations in and around Mecca, pilgrims symbolically recreate specific actions of the prophet Abraham (Ibrahim), his wife Hagar, and their son Ishmael (Isma'il), as well as the prophet Muhammad, the founder of Islam. Many Muslims experience the pilgrimage to Mecca as a profound spiritual awakening, and the event also strengthens the sense of social and religious unity among Muslims worldwide.

Many Muslims experience the pilgrimage to Mecca as a profound spiritual awakening, and the event also strengthens the sense of social and religious unity among Muslims worldwide.

From Ancient Caravans to the Jet Age

Faithful Muslims have undertaken the Great Pilgrimage to Mecca for many centuries. From the Middle Ages until early modern times, groups of pilgrims traveled to Mecca in caravans organized from cities in Egypt and other locations, following trade routes and unmarked hajj paths through the desert. Some walked on foot while others rode camels, horses, donkeys, or mules. The most fortunate pilgrims were carried in special cushioned platforms that were enclosed in cloth. One pilgrimage that took place in 1876 included nearly 6,000 people and 10,000 animals traveling across the desert in two long columns.

Before the widespread availability of speedy travel by air or sea, it was not unusual for a pilgrim to take several years to reach Mecca. For centuries, the fastest route for the final leg of the journey to Mecca departed from Damascus, Syria, and took 34 days by caravan under the harshest

Observance

The pilgrimage to Mecca is always performed during the first 10 days of *Dhu al-Hijja,* the last month of the Islamic lunar calendar year. Muslims who intend to undertake the pilgrimage usually begin preparing for the trip several months in advance. In addition to making arrangements for travel and accommodations, many pilgrims prepare themselves spiritually and physically for the journey. Common preparations include focused study of the ritual requirements and various prayers that are to be recited at specific times throughout the journey. Many people also begin a physical conditioning regimen to prepare themselves for the demands of the pilgrimage, which include walking, running, and standing for several hours at a time in a desert climate.

On the day or night before departure for Mecca, family members and friends usually gather at the pilgrim's home for special prayers and readings from the Qu'ran. Usually a meal is shared, and there may be recitation of poetry or songs related to the pilgrimage. Sometimes the atmosphere is somber, with respect for the magnitude of the journey about to begin. Other times it is a celebration, with happiness for the fortunate pilgrim about to set off for Mecca, and in gratitude for the opportunity to undertake the journey.

conditions. However, any pilgrim who ran out of money or provisions would have to stop in the nearest city or town and try to earn enough money to continue the journey. And the road to Mecca was so dangerous that even the most well-planned caravan faced such challenges as illness, injury, or attack by thieves. Over the years, Muslim countries along the route to Mecca began to provide safe stopping places and guarded water supplies for pilgrims. Many of these now-abandoned locations have become important archaeological sites.

By contrast, most pilgrims today can expect to leave home and arrive in Mecca within two days. A large number of hajj travel agencies cater to the needs of pilgrims, handling every detail of the trip. The Internet provides a wealth of information for potential pilgrims. The official sites of the Kingdom of Saudi Arabia ease the way of pilgrims and offer Muslims around the world a virtual hajj experience.

Before arriving in Mecca, pilgrims must be in a sacred state of consecration. Once the consecrated state is achieved, pilgrims may enter the city of Mecca. Most pilgrims perform both the Lesser Pilgrimage (*'umrah*) and the Greater Pilgrimage (hajj), although only the rites of the Greater Pilgrimage are required. The Lesser Pilgrimage begins at the Sacred Mosque of Mecca, *al-Masjid al-Haram*. Here pilgrims perform the rites of circumambulation, meaning to walk in a circle around something) and running between the hills. After these rites are complete, pilgrims ready themselves for the Greater Pilgrimage.

The Greater Pilgrimage begins on the eighth day of Dhu al-Hijja when pilgrims travel to Mount Arafat, located approximately 15.5 miles east of Mecca. Pilgrims must reach Mount Arafat by noon on the ninth day of Dhu al-Hijja. From noon until sunset on that day, pilgrims perform the ritual of standing at Arafat. At sunset, pilgrims leave Arafat in a ritual known as hurrying to Muzdalifah. Pilgrims spend either a few hours or the entire night at Muzdalifah before proceeding on to Mina, where the ritual throwing pebbles and the festival of Eid al-Adha are held over the next three days.

After the Eid, pilgrims perform a rite of partial deconsecration. They will not be fully deconsecrated until they return to Mecca and complete another circumambulation known as *tawaf al-ifadah*. Most then return to Mina for a few days of relaxing and socializing, while some choose to spend more time in Mecca. All pilgrims must make a final circumambulation known as *tawaf al-qudum* before beginning the journey home. Many Muslims who perform the Hajj return home with a renewed commitment to Islam, and feeling more connected to the global Islamic community. Returning pilgrims are usually greeted enthusiastically by family members and friends, and a homecoming celebration is held.

Customs and Symbols

Circumambulation (Tawaf, Tawaf al-Ifadah, Tawaf al-Qudum)

Inside the Sacred Mosque of Mecca is the *Ka'bah*, a cube-shaped building that is believed to be the first house of worship and the site of Muhammad's revelation of God's final instruction to humanity. The Ka'bah symbolizes the sacred foundation of the Islamic faith, and as such, it represents the center of the Islamic universe. It is the point at which all Muslim prayers are directed and the place from which all prayers are believed to be the most effective.

Circumambulation is the ritual of walking in a circle around the Ka'bah, moving in a counterclockwise direction. To begin the ritual, pilgrims move to a position east of the Ka'bah and step forward with their right foot. Each circuit around the Ka'bah has particular significance and is associated with specific prayers. The rites of tawaf and tawaf al-ifadah include seven circuits around the Ka'bah. Tawaf al-qudum includes just one circuit.

Consecration (Ihram)

Ihram is a state of ritual purity and consecration (dedication to the service and worship of Allah) which pilgrims must preserve while performing the rites of the pilgrimage. Special markers are in place several miles outside of Mecca, indicating the points of entry into the sacred area surrounding the city. Muslims who intend to perform the pilgrimage must achieve a consecrated state before passing these markers. At any other time when they do not intend to participate in the pilgrimage, Muslims may enter Mecca and the surrounding area without being consecrated. Non-Muslims are not permitted to enter Mecca or the surrounding area at any time.

To enter the consecrated state, pilgrims cleanse themselves through ritual bathing, declare their intention to undertake the pilgrimage through the recitation of specific prayers, and change from their regular clothes into the special garments of ihram. For men this includes two seamless white cloths, one to be wound around the waist, covering the lower body to the knee, and the other to be wrapped around the torso with one end worn over the left shoulder, leaving the right shoulder and arm exposed. These cloths are secured around the waist with a belt, but otherwise there can be no knots or fasteners of any kind. Men keep their heads bare and wear sandals that expose the backs of their feet. Women wear plain dresses or garments that cover the body from the neckline to the ankles, and completely cover both arms. Women must cover their heads with a cloth, but leave their faces uncovered. The garments worn during the consecrated state symbolize the ultimate unity and equality of all Muslims in the eyes of God.

Certain restrictions apply to pilgrims in the consecrated state. For example, pilgrims are forbidden to wear perfume or jewelry, display any symbol of personal wealth, pick flowers or otherwise uproot plants, kill any animal or insect, or engage in any violent activity, such as fighting or arguing.

Deconsecration (Tahallul)

Pilgrims intentionally deconsecrate themselves through the process of *tahallul,* which includes changing from ihram garments back into regular clothing as well as a ritual haircut. Deconsecration requires the cutting of only three hairs, although many men observe the tradition of completely shaving their heads, beards, and mustaches. Most women cut only a small amount off the end of their hair.

Eid al-Adha (Festival of the Major Sacrifice)

On the third day in Mina, pilgrims celebrate Eid al-Adha, one of the most significant observances of the Islamic year. In gratitude to God for allowing Abraham to sacrifice a ram instead of his son, each individual or family sacrifices a lamb, goat, or camel (or pays a sum of money for the sacrifice to be done on their behalf). Portions of the meat are consumed by the pilgrims and the rest is given to the poor. This festival is also celebrated at the same time by Muslims all over the world.

Hurrying to Muzdalifah (Ifadah, Nafrah)

The ritual of hurrying to Muzdalifah begins at sunset of the day of standing at Arafat. In a practice known as *ifadah* (literally "pouring forth") or *nafrah* (literally "the rush"), pilgrims travel as quickly as possible from Arafat to Mina, a distance of approximately 10.5 miles. Traditionally, pilgrims stop to say evening prayers at Muzdalifah on the way to Mina, and some spend the night there. They then continue on to Mina, where they will spend the next several days observing Eid al-Adha and performing the ritual of throwing pebbles.

From "Of Being Woven" by Jelaluddin Rumi

Rushes and reeds must be *woven*
To be useful as a mat. If they weren't interlaced,
The wind would blow them away.
        Like that, God paired up
Creatures, and gave them friendship.

—Excerpt from a poem composed by the 13th-century Sufi mystical poet Jelaluddin Rumi; translated by Coleman Barks in *The Essential Rumi* (1995).

Running Between the Hills (Sa'y)

After completion of the Lesser Pilgrimage circumambulation, pilgrims immediately begin the rite of *sa'y*. This symbolic reenactment of Hagar's desperate search for water for her young son Ishmael requires pilgrims to run seven times between the hills of al-Safa and al-Marwah, located next to the Sacred Mosque and approximately 437 yards apart. Muslims believe that Hagar's prayers during her search were answered when water began to gush from a natural spring that miraculously formed in the Meccan desert. Water from this spring, known as *zamzam*, is prized by Muslims around the world.

Standing at Arafat (Wuquf)

Standing at Arafat is viewed as the most important event of the pilgrimage. Pilgrims spend the morning praying in the open land near Mount Arafat. They then begin climbing the rocky hillside; by noon the mountain is covered with people. The time from noon until sunset is spent deep in prayer, meditation, and reflection focusing on repentance for sins.

Throwing Pebbles (Rajm)

Muslims believe that Abraham was commanded by God to sacrifice his son Ishmael, and that Satan tempted Abraham three times to disobey the command. Abraham is said to have driven Satan away by throwing stones at him. The ritual of throwing pebbles recreates Abraham's victory over temptation and symbolizes the effort to cast away evil and vice. For three consecutive days, pilgrims throw seven pebbles at each of the three large pillars located in the center of Mina.

Web Sites

"Hajj: The Essential Journey." CNN.com, 2006.
http://www.cnn.com/SPECIALS/2006/hajj

IslamiCity.
http://www.IslamiCity.com

Kingdom of Saudi, Arabia. Ministry of Hajj.
http://www.hajinformation.com

Kingdom of Saudi, Ministry of Islamic Affairs, Endowments, Da'wah and Guidance, undated.
http://www.al-islam.com

"Muhammad: Legacy of a Prophet." PBS.org, 2002.
http://www.pbs.org/muhammad/virtualhajj.shtml

Further Reading

Gulevich, Tanya. *Understanding Islam and Muslim Traditions*. Detroit: Omnigraphics, 2004.

Hammoudi, Abdellah. *A Season in Mecca: Narrative of a Pilgrimage*. New York: Hill and Wang, 2006.

Kueny, Kathryn. "Pilgrimage." In *Encyclopedia of Islam and the Muslim World*. Edited by Richard C. Martin. New York: Macmillan Reference USA, 2003.

Martin, Richard C. "Pilgrimage: Muslim Pilgrimage." In *Encyclopedia of Religion*. Edited by Lindsay Jones. 2nd ed. New York: Macmillan Reference USA, 2005.

Wolfe, Michael. *One Thousand Roads to Mecca: Ten Centuries of Travelers Writing about the Muslim Pilgrimage*. New York: Grove Press, 1997.

Photo on facing page: Retirement can be an opportunity to spend extra time with the grandkids.

Chapter 18: Later Adulthood

INTRODUCTION

The concept and meaning of later adulthood shifted during the 1900s, particularly with the maturity of American Baby Boomers and subsequent generations (collectively, those born after 1945). Life expectancy for Americans increased by more than 30 years during this time, rising from 47.3 years in 1900 to 77.3 years in 2002, with the most dramatic change occurring after about 1950. The U.S. National Center for Health Statistics notes that the majority of this increase can be attributed to medical advances, citing an unprecedented reduction of age-related illness beginning in the late 1960s. Future projections indicate that American life expectancies could reasonably reach 83 years by 2075.

As the average American life expectancy increases, and with advancements in modern health care and preventative treatment, many Americans are living longer, healthier, more active lives than previous generations. During the years that were once thought to be nearing the end of life, Americans are transforming what it means to be a senior citizen. By embarking on new careers, pursuing higher education, making significant contributions in business, politics, education, and philanthropy, and even excelling in athletic endeavors, older Americans are living with more vitality than ever before. This chapter explores selected rites of passage of older adults, including milestone birthdays, **Retirement**, and the range of **New Living Arrangements** available to contemporary senior citizens in the U.S.

Milestone birthdays have become celebratory events for many older Americans. The importance of any specific birthday is naturally related to the outlook and attitude of the celebrant, however birthdays in five- or 10-year increments after about age 50 typically take on special significance. These birthdays are often associated with personal reflection, evaluation of past years, and plans for the years to come. Many social benefits are also often made available to older Americans, such as "senior discounts" at restaurants, shops, and other businesses.

According to ancient beliefs based on the Chinese astrological calendar, the occasion of one's 60th birthday is cause for celebration of longevity and good fortune. Because this calendar runs in 60-year cycles, **Asian-American 60th Birthday** observances are focused on symbolic rebirth and the beginning of a new life cycle. The birthday celebrant usually dresses in special clothing that is fashioned after traditional outfits worn by infants, typically colored red and including a red hat and red slippers. Entertainment at the birthday party is customarily lighthearted and may feature games and performances normally associated with childhood. The entire 60th year is considered to be a lucky time for beginning any new ventures.

Similarly, retirement from full-time employment is viewed as a turning point that signifies a fresh start in life, whether in leisure, volunteerism, or some other pursuit. Many Americans retire around age 65, although a growing number are choosing to retire earlier, later, or not at all. Prior to the 1980s, American retirees generally spent time traveling or pursuing hobbies. In more recent years, retirement has become a highly individualized stage of life in which the retiree may re-engage in work for pay or begin any type of new endeavor. The social expectation that retirees are limited to lives of leisure has fallen away, and many American retirees find themselves busier than when they were fully immersed in their original career.

For many older Americans, housing situations also change with advancing age. Although most continue to live independently in their own homes, other options are available for those requiring dedicated health care or assistance with daily activities. Some seniors progress through a number of different living situations as they age, depending on changing health conditions, level of personal independence, and the ability of family members to provide adequate care.

The options and activities available to contemporary American senior citizens vary widely and are vastly different from the opportunities of previous generations. At the beginning of the 20th century, a 45-year-old American was regarded as old. By the beginning of the 21st, American perceptions of the age at which one becomes old have advanced significantly. Supported by a growing number of older Americans who are involved in every aspect of modern life, attitudes about aging and what it means to be old continue to evolve.

ASIAN-AMERICAN 60TH BIRTHDAY

Alternate Names: Kanreki, Honke-gaeri, Hwangap

Customs and Symbols: Cranes, Food, Gifts, Red Items

For many Asian Americans, the 60th birthday signifies the beginning of a new phase of life. The occasion is a celebration of longevity, and the day also has important astrological symbolism.

History and Significance

> *Many Asian Americans observe the 60th birthday with large parties including special food, music and dancing or other entertainment, and symbolic gifts for the birthday celebrant.*

Many ancient Asian cultures tracked the passage of time with systems based on the Chinese astrological calendar, which runs in cycles of 60 years. According to this calendar, completion of any 60-year cycle results in a phase of rebirth or new beginning. A person celebrating their 60th birthday had therefore lived through one complete life cycle, and was thought to be beginning a second cycle. In Japan, 60th birthdays are called *kanreki* (pronounced *kahn-reh-kee*), meaning "return" and "calendar," or *honke-gaeri* (pronounced *hohn-keh gaah-ree*), meaning "return to the original cycle." The 60th birthday in Korea is known as *hwangap* (pronounced *hwahn-gahp*), meaning "returning to the first year." The occasion is celebrated both for its symbolism as a time of renewal as well as its importance as a sign of longevity. In ancient times, people generally did not live as long as they do today, and reaching the age of 60 was considered to be a great achievement.

Observance

The importance of the 60th birthday has decreased somewhat in modern times because people are generally living longer, but the occasion still has powerful astrological meaning. Many Asian Americans observe the 60th birthday with large parties including special food, music and dancing or other entertainment, and symbolic gifts for the birthday celebrant. The birthday party is usually organized by the celebrant's children with help from other relatives. At the party, the celebrant is honored by their children, grandchildren, and any other young person who has benefited from their support or guidance. The younger people shower the birthday celebrant with thanks, praise, and gifts. According to Korean tradition, the birthday celebrant is seated in front of a special table called a *mangsang*, and each young person approaches to bow deeply in honor of the celebrant. Because the birthday celebrant is thought to be entering a second childhood, entertainment sometimes includes lighthearted activities normally associated with children.

Customs and Symbols

Cranes

The crane is a bird that has long been associated with good fortune, peace, fidelity, and longevity in Japan. Japanese folklore says that cranes live for 1,000 years, and so cranes are often featured in birthday celebrations. Cranes may be used to decorate the birthday cake, and the birthday celebrant is sometimes presented with 1,000 white cranes made of folded paper.

Food

The 60th birthday feast is attended by the celebrant's friends and family. Many special types of food are served, including dishes with particular symbolism for the birthday celebrant, such as eggs and any food that is red in color. According to Chinese custom, the person observing their 60th birthday should eat a bowl of extra-long noodles, which represent long life.

Gifts

The person celebrating a 60th birthday is presented with special gifts, typically including things that symbolize long life or good fortune. Japanese custom dictates that red items should be given as gifts, while Chinese tradition includes gifts of eggs, long noodles, peaches, wine, and money wrapped in red paper. Korean tradition calls for gifts of money wrapped in white paper.

Red Items

Japanese Americans observe the 60th birthday as the beginning of a second childhood due to the beginning of a new calendar cycle. The birthday celebrant normally wears a red cap that is similar to those worn by newborn babies in Japan. A red vest, coat, or socks may also be worn. Gifts given in honor of a 60th birthday normally include anything that is red.

Web Sites

"Birthday Customs of the Elderly in China," by Ye Qinfa. CCTV.com, China Central Television, undated.
  http://www.cctv.com/english/TouchChina/School/Culture/20030225/100336.html

"Celebrating a Full Life," by Heidi Kim. *SkyNews,* January 17, 2003.
  http://www.skynews.co.kr/article_view.asp?ltype=&mcd=70&ccd=6&scd=2&ano=26

"Family Rituals." Korea.net, Korean Overseas Information Service, undated.
  http://www.korea.net/search/contents/tar_work_soci_Family.htm

"Japanese Traditions." Japanese Cultural Center of Hawaii, undated.
  http://www.jcch.com/TRADITIONS_2003_0624.htm

Further Reading

Clark, Donald N. *Culture and Customs of Korea.* Westport, CT: Greenwood Press, 2000.

RETIREMENT

Customs and Symbols: Bridge Employment, Early Retirement, Later Stages of Life (Ashramas) in Hinduism, Pensions, Phased Retirement, Retirement Party, Temporary Theravadin Buddhist Monkhood

Retirement signifies the end of employment and the beginning of a new phase of life. Many people retire around age 65, although a growing number are choosing to retire earlier, later, or not at all. Life after retirement varies tremendously according to individual circumstances.

History and Significance

In colonial America, retirement described the contractual transfer of land or other assets to an heir. Although essentially an inheritance process, retirement usually began before the death of the original landowner. With the rise of American industrialism, retirement indicated an end to working life and the beginning of relatively idle years. After World War II, retirement became standard after an individual worked a set number of years or reached a certain age, usually the early 60s. Retirement then usually meant time spent traveling or pursuing hobbies. By the 1980s, however, workers began retiring much earlier. These younger retirees changed the common understanding of what it meant to be retired, often beginning second careers or pursuing higher education. Over time, retirement has become a turning point in life that signifies something different for each individual, depending on retirement age, personal interests, financial situation, and many other factors.

Observance

Retirement is observed as the departure from a particular type of employment, meaning a specific job, participation in a certain industry, or the abandonment of an entire career. Generally seen as the beginning of a new phase in life, the occasion is usually celebrated with a retirement party organized by coworkers or friends and family members. Followers of Theravada Buddhism sometimes choose to be ordained for a period of temporary Theravadin Buddhist monkhood as a way of marking the passage into retirement.

> *Retirement has become a turning point in life that signifies something different for each individual, depending on retirement age, personal interests, financial situation, and many other factors.*

343

Individual circumstances can heavily influence the decision of when or whether to retire. Workers who are eligible to receive pensions are usually able to do so around age 65, and consequently many choose to retire at that time. However, an increasing number of workers are opting for early retirement. Many retirees begin new careers, work part time, or volunteer, often doing jobs unrelated to the work from which they retired. Some retirees spend less time working for pay, while others seek bridge employment out of necessity or desire. Some choose an alternative work schedule called phased retirement, while many others decide to continue working well into their senior years. Around the time of retirement, observant Hindus will likely be in *vanaprastha*, one of the later stages of life (ashramas) in Hinduism, which requires a significant amount of time to be spent on charitable works.

Customs and Symbols

Bridge Employment

Bridge employment refers to jobs taken by retirees who need extra income to bridge the gap between pension earnings and the cost of living. These jobs are typically low-paying part-time or temporary work.

Early Retirement

Because there is no mandatory retirement age for American workers, early retirement is difficult to define. However, it is generally agreed that choosing to retire before age 65 constitutes an early retirement. Most individuals who retire early do not stop working, instead transitioning to self-employment or new careers.

Later Stages of Life (Ashramas) in Hinduism

Traditional Hindu belief divides life into four stages called *ashramas*. The first two stages are dedicated to study, work, and family life. The third stage, known as vanaprastha, occurs from age 50-75 and usually coincides with the beginning of retirement. It is generally assumed that by age 50, a person will have achieved valuable knowledge and life experience that can benefit younger people. Observant Hindus in this stage of life are expected to focus on charitable works and volunteerism to serve humanity. The final stage of life, known as *sanyasa*, occurs after age 75. During this stage, Hindus strive to practice meditation and contemplation to prepare for a peaceful death.

Pensions

A pension is income provided by a former employer or the U.S. Social Security Administration. Pensions are typically fixed amounts paid at regular intervals, based on the individual's past employment, age, or other factors.

Phased Retirement

Some individuals manage retirement as a gradual process, taking part-time positions or reduced responsibilities before completely leaving a job. Phased retirement is common among older workers who have been with the same employer for a long time. A gradual retirement process allows the transfer of knowledge to successors, and enables the retiree to slowly prepare for complete retirement.

Retirement Party

Retirement is usually celebrated as the start of the leisure years, even if the retiree intends to continue working in some capacity. Parties organized by coworkers traditionally include a meal, gifts, and speeches in honor of the retiree, typically focusing on their career achievements and contributions to the organization. However, these speeches often jokingly focus on mishaps, mistakes, or amusing episodes involving the new retiree. This custom is known as a "roast" and is usually delivered and received in a spirit of friendship and good will.

Temporary Theravadin Buddhist Monkhood

According to the traditions of Theravada Buddhism, lay people may choose temporary ordination to mark a major life event or a status change, such as retirement. During this time, they live at the temple or monastery and receive instruction in the monastic way of life and the principles of wisdom, compassion, and self-discipline. Temporary ordination may be as brief as a few days or as long as several years. This practice is normally undertaken by Buddhist immigrants from Laos, Cambodia, China, Vietnam, Thailand, and other parts of Asia, although some temples also allow American converts to be temporarily ordained.

Web Sites

AARP (American Association of Retired Persons), undated.
    http://www.aarp.org

"Four Stages of Life," Hindu Temple and Cultural Center of Kansas City, August 2003.
    http://www.htccofkc.org/silvernet/four_stages_of_life.htm

Further Reading

Adams, Gary A., and Kenneth S. Shultz. "Retirement." In *Encyclopedia of Industrial and Organization Psychology.* Edited by Steven Rogelberg. Thousand Oaks, CA: Sage Reference, 2007.

Collins, Gerald. "Retirement." In *Encyclopedia of Career Development.* Edited by Jeffrey Greenhaus and Gerard Callanan. Thousand Oaks, CA: Sage Reference, 2006.

Mann, Gurinder Singh, Paul David Numrich, and Raymond B. Williams. *Buddhists, Hindus, and Sikhs in America.* New York: Oxford University Press, 2001.

Seager, Richard Hughes. *Buddhism in America.* New York: Columbia University Press, 1999.

"Working and Retirement: New Options for Older Adults." *Growing Old in America.* Detroit: Thomson Gale, 2006.

NEW LIVING ARRANGEMENTS

Alternate Names: Elder Care, Retirement Living

Customs and Symbols: Adult Day Care, Assisted Living, Home Health Care, Multigenerational Households, Nursing Homes, Retirement Communities, Shared Housing

Various living situations and housing arrangements exist for older Americans. Although most continue to live independently in their own homes, other options are available for those requiring assistance with daily activities or dedicated health care.

History and Significance

As the average life expectancy for Americans increases, housing arrangements for senior citizens continue to evolve. Until the early 1900s, older people who were unable to live independently were looked after by their families. Communal residences known as almshouses were operated by religious and charitable organizations to care for those without families. Since the mid-20th century, many new options have become available for the care of senior citizens, ranging from long-term medical care facilities to the provision of in-home support services. Choosing the right living situation is a significant and difficult process for seniors and their families, who often must balance the need for focused medical care with the desire for continued independence.

Observance

The majority of older Americans live independently in their own homes or in retirement communities, although various alternative living situations exist for senior citizens. Depending on health care requirements, seniors may need assisted living or traditional nursing homes. Those who need minimal support to continue living on their own may choose home health care, while others opt for shared housing arrangements. Many older Americans live in multigenerational households, sometimes with the support of adult day care services. Some seniors progress through a number of different living situations as they age, depending on changing health conditions and the ability of family members to provide adequate care.

Choosing the right living situation is a significant and difficult process for seniors and their families, who often must balance the need for focused medical care with the desire for independence.

Customs and Symbols

Adult Day Care

Older Americans who require intensive medical care or supervision often cannot be left alone for long periods of time. In these situations, adult day care services can assist caregivers who work outside the home during the day. Adult day care facilities generally provide social activities, meals, and health care supervision during normal working hours; participants return to their homes in the evenings. This arrangement allows seniors to continue living at home with their families while ensuring appropriate care.

Assisted Living

Assisted living communities generally support independence and individual privacy within a residential facility setting. Seniors live in private or shared apartments, with a range of basic care services available as needed. Meals, house cleaning, transportation, and other personal care services are usually offered, as well as assistance in arranging any necessary health care.

Home Health Care

Elderly people who live independently but require some assistance with daily activities often hire home health care workers. These personal aides can provide help with shopping, transportation, and basic health needs.

Multigenerational Households

In multigenerational households, extended families live together in one home. This can include any combination of grandparents, parents, children, grandchildren, uncles, aunts, cousins, and other relatives. In some cases, older Americans have assumed parenting responsibilities for their grandchildren or other younger relatives. These intergenerational living arrangements are most often found among Asian-American, Hispanic-American, and African-American families. Traditional Hindu, Muslim, and Jewish families may also include multiple generations living together.

Nursing Homes

Nursing homes are residential facilities that provide intensive health care and rehabilitation services, usually in a communal or semi-private environment. Seniors who need constant supervision or advanced medical care often live in these facilities.

Retirement Communities

Residential developments specifically designed for independent older Americans are known as retirement communities. These include single apartment buildings, residential subdivisions, and communities of freestanding homes. Some retirement communities offer a variety of amenities related to special interests such as sports or hobbies. Others are built around the shared life experience of residents, for example, veterans of military service. Many retirement communities have been established in resorts or areas with warm climates, such as Arizona and Florida.

Shared Housing

Seniors who want to continue living independently sometimes choose shared housing, also known as cohousing. In these situations, the homeowner shares living expenses with one or more roommates.

Web Sites

American Association of Homes and Services for the Aging, undated.
http://www.aahsa.org

"Living with the In-Laws: Multigenerational Households, Though Still Uncommon, Seem to Be Growing in Popularity," by Sarah Max CNN.com, April 22, 2004.
http://money.cnn.com/2004/02/18/pf/yourhome/grannyflats

Further Reading

"Assisted Living Facilities." In *Gale Encyclopedia of Everyday Law.* Edited by Jeffrey Wilson. 2nd ed. Detroit: Thomson Gale, 2006.

Kemper, Robert. "Retirement Communities." In *Encyclopedia of American Urban History.* Edited by David Goldfield. Thousand Oaks, CA: Sage Reference, 2007.

"Nursing Homes." In *Gale Encyclopedia of Everyday Law.* Edited by Jeffrey Wilson. 2nd ed. Detroit: Thomson Gale, 2006.

Wexler, Barbara. "Living Arrangements of the Older Population." *Growing Old in America.* Detroit: Thomson Gale, 2006.

PART 4

Death and Mourning

The Buddhist Obon Festival is a time to honor
ancestors and remember the dead.

Death and Mourning

INTRODUCTION

Throughout human history, death has inspired tremendous fear, insatiable curiosity, intense spiritual questioning, and focused scientific study. The social development of humanity naturally included the formation and evolution of collective ideas about death, along with the emergence of specific rites for burial and grief expression. Discoveries of Neanderthal burial sites provide evidence of organized cultural practices surrounding death and mourning even in the earliest human societies. Ancient Egyptians built elaborate tombs and are thought to be the first to preserve the bodies of the dead before burial. In contrast, early Hindu and Nordic peoples used cremation to destroy the body, releasing the spirits of the dead from physical confines. Such diverse beliefs and practices arose from centuries of human efforts to understand death, its meaning, and what happens after death. Many of these beliefs continue to shape and influence current attitudes and behaviors around death in modern American society.

This part provides an overview of selected beliefs about death and mourning, and describes various rites and customs observed by cultural and religious groups in the U.S. Preparations for an imminent death, readying the body for burial or cremation, ways of mourning and comforting those who grieve, and remembrance of the dead are a direct reflection of collective beliefs about death and the possibility of an afterlife. Some Americans believe that death is a transition to a new life, either by rejoining the living in a new physical form or by reunion with others who have died but continue to exist in spiritual form. Others hold that the spirits of the dead continue to interact with the living, requiring ongoing care and attention and influencing events in the lives of loved ones. Still others view death as a passage to divine judgment, when the life of the deceased will be evaluated and the soul granted the eternal rewards of heaven or sentenced to the punishments of hell. The examples that follow illustrate the influence of these different beliefs and social customs of dying, death, and mourning.

For American Roman Catholics who believe that the souls of the dead will face divine judgment, the **Last Rites** are a critical step in preparing for death. Last rites include a final opportunity for the dying person to repent for their sins, as well as prayers and blessings intended to provide comfort and ease their passing. Because early Christians were often reluctant to acknowledge or speak of the taboo subject of death, the last rites were once viewed with trepidation and a great sense of foreboding. As social attitudes and old superstitions about death slowly changed, and due in large part to the modernization of official Roman Catholic doctrine in the 1960s, the last rites have become much less fearsome.

Preparing the body for burial or cremation is another important part of the process of death for many Americans. For most, washing and **Dressing the Body** are tasks performed by a funeral director. However, Muslim and Jewish traditions call for these preparations to be done by relatives or members of the religious community. In a similar fashion, American Hindus also often prepare the bodies of their deceased loved ones. These practices demonstrate a belief that death is a natural part of life, and the deceased should be cared for by loved ones in death just as they were in life.

American funerals, memorial services, **Burial Practices**, and **Cremation Rituals** vary widely according to religious and cultural traditions. Native American customs continue to be observed in rituals such as the **Iroquois Family Condolence Rite** and the **Shawnee Death Feast**. American Hindus and Buddhists often conduct special rites prior to cremation, which can include prayers, chanting, meditating, and burning incense. Some Jewish and Muslim Americans adhere to traditional rules pertaining to burial positions and burial times, although most burials are governed by the policies and practices of the cemetery. Funeral processions, **Wakes**, and **Repasts** can be celebratory, such as in the case of the **New Orleans Jazz Funeral**, or more somber in tone.

Many Americans remember the dead on special days, sometimes on a specific day after the death of a loved one or as part of an annual memorial event. In recent years, the appearance of **Sidewalk and Other Public Shrines** has become more common as Americans are moved to memorialize unexpected or sudden deaths at the site of tragedy. Once solely a personal act of grief over an individual death, these public shrines have evolved to include expressions of communal mourning. For American Buddhists, the **Forty-Ninth Day Memorial** service is thought to encourage a fortunate reincarnation of the deceased's soul. The first anniversary of the death of a loved one is observed by many American Christians and Jews during the

One-Year Memorial. On **All Souls Day**, American Catholics pray for the souls of deceased loved ones as well as all those who have died.

Two of the more public annual days of remembrance are the Mexican-American **Día de los Muertos**, or Day of the Dead, and the Chinese-American **Ching Ming**. These days are set aside each year to remember those who have died, whether in the preceding year or long ago. Both days demonstrate cultural beliefs that the spirits of the dead continue to interact with the living in positive or negative ways. Día de los Muertos tradition holds that the spirits of the deceased will return to visit their loved ones on this day, and special food and offerings are laid out at home and at the grave site to welcome them. Similarly, Ching Ming illustrates an old Chinese belief that those who continue to properly care for deceased ancestors will benefit from increased happiness, success, and good fortune. Ching Ming observers commonly burn paper representations of items offered for the welfare of the departed. Both of these memorial days allow mourners to continue to feel connected to deceased loved ones, and provide ways of ensuring that the memories of those who have died are preserved.

The wide range of customs observed around death and mourning illustrate the diversity of modern American culture. Many Americans continue to practice the rites and rituals passed down through families, with such traditions often brought to the U.S. by relatives who emigrated generations earlier. The impact of these various practices can be seen in the changing nature of mainstream American society. For example, funeral homes and cemeteries serving large communities of Chinese Americans have recently begun to accommodate the needs of those who observe Ching Ming. Meanwhile, cities with significant Mexican-American populations often hold public celebrations for Día de los Muertos. And some crematoriums are beginning to offer facilities that allow the observance of Hindu and Buddhist cremation rites. In these ways, American social customs continue to be shaped by the specific practices of many different cultures and faiths.

Photo on facing page: A priest performs last rites.

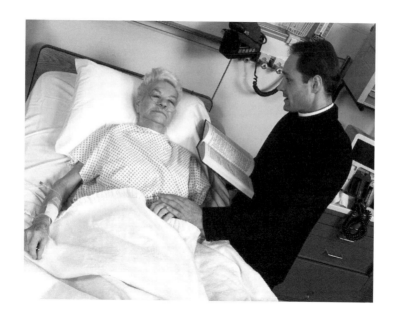

Chapter 19: Preparing the Body

INTRODUCTION

As with other customs surrounding death, special methods of preparing a body for burial or cremation have been practiced by even the most ancient human civilizations. Archaeologists have uncovered evidence that early tribal nations such as the South American Inca performed rituals including the removal of certain internal organs or bones prior to burial. It is also known that ancient Greek, Roman, and Hindu peoples often performed elaborate, multi-step processes to prepare a body for entombment or cremation. Perhaps the most well known burial preparations were those of the ancient Egyptians, whose process of mummification has preserved bodies for many centuries.

In early human cultures, burial preparations varied according to the relative social status and rank of the deceased. Egyptian pharaohs were given the most ornate burials, with body preparation taking days or weeks to complete. Ancient Native American burial customs among tribes such as the Pawnee sometimes included the painting of the body with a red ochre pigment, indicating high social status of the deceased. More recently, during the Victorian era of the 19th century, the bodies of deceased members of the wealthy upper class were prepared with more elaborate ceremony than the common man. This tradition is still observed today, as socially or politically important individuals generally receive more care and attention during preparation for burial than does the average person.

This chapter discusses the pre-burial customs of **Last Rites** and **Dressing the Body**, including specific cultural and religious practices of washing and purifying the body as performed in the U.S. Last rites are religious ceremonies observed primarily by American Catholics and Orthodox Christians as a way of providing comfort to those who are seriously ill or dying. For most Americans, dressing the body of a deceased person is an important part of the preparations for burial or cremation. These tasks are most often performed by a funeral director or mortician, although the body is sometimes prepared by family or community members according to religious traditions.

In some American Jewish communities, preparing the body for burial is a task undertaken by a volunteer organization known as a *chevra kadisha* (burial society). This organization performs ritual washing and dressing of the deceased while reciting prayers over the body. Islamic law also requires burial preparations to be carried out by close relatives or members of the religious community. The body of the deceased is ritually washed and wrapped in shrouds, followed by prayers offered over the body.

The modern practice of embalming bodies prior to burial originated in the Netherlands during the 17th century. The embalming procedure involves draining the blood and other body fluids and replacing them with a mixture of chemicals intended to prevent the spread of disease by killing bacteria. Embalming also slows down the process of decomposition. The first embalming methods included the use of highly toxic and poisonous chemicals, which successfully preserved bodies but were harmful to those who performed the embalming or handled the bodies afterward. The use of formaldehyde, which is considered a safer and less toxic chemical blend, gained popularity around 1900, and quickly became the standard which is still used today. When burial preparations are performed by funeral directors or morticians, embalming is generally done unless the family of the deceased specifies otherwise.

In addition to embalming, cosmetic enhancements are usually also included as part of the burial preparations provided by funeral directors. This may include the application of makeup to the face, hands, and neck as well as styling of the hair to make the body appear lifelike and in peaceful repose. Cosmetic enhancement is most often performed when the body will be viewed by those attending the funeral. Embalming and the use of cosmetics are not required by U.S. law, although the majority of Americans allow both to be done. However, both customs are prohibited by some religious traditions, including the Jewish and Islamic faiths.

LAST RITES

Alternate Names: Anointing of the Sick, Blessing of the Sick, Extreme Unction, Holy Unction

Customs and Symbols: Anointing, Oil, Prayer

Last rites are religious ceremonies performed by a member of the clergy on behalf of a dying person. Although most religions include some form of prayer or blessing for the dying, the term "last rites" generally refers to the Roman Catholic and Orthodox Christian sacrament of Anointing of the Sick (formerly known as Extreme Unction).

History and Significance

For early Christians, Extreme Unction was originally a healing sacrament that could be performed on its own or included in last rites. As the practice gradually became associated only with the final preparation for death, superstitious beliefs developed. Fearing that the ceremony might hasten death instead of healing, many people were reluctant to request last rites until death was a certainty. During the Second Vatican Council (1962-65) the Roman Catholic Church refocused its belief in the original healing nature of the sacrament and officially changed the name to Anointing of the Sick. Catholic leaders clarified that Anointing of the Sick is appropriate for anyone who is seriously ill, facing a life-threatening event such as surgery, suffering from mental or spiritual illness or struggling with addiction, and those at the point of death. This change allowed Catholics to benefit from the sacrament before health conditions became severe and also provided the opportunity for individuals to receive the sacrament more than once over the course of their lives.

Observance

Roman Catholics and Orthodox Christians observe last rites by performing the three sacraments of Anointing of the Sick, Reconciliation (confession of sins), and Holy Communion (*see* **First Communion and Reconciliation**). Last rites can be performed in any location, such as a home, hospital, ambulance, accident scene, or battlefield. Last rites are specifically performed for those who are dying, although any seriously ill or suffering person can receive the sacrament of Anointing of the Sick.

Last rites can be performed in any location, such as a home, hospital, ambulance, accident scene, or battlefield. Last rites are specifically performed for those who are dying, although any seriously ill or suffering person can receive the Anointing of the Sick.

Some individual churches periodically offer the Anointing of the Sick as part of regular services.

Catholic observance of last rites varies according to circumstances. In general, the priest begins by offering a prayer and reading from scripture, sometimes sprinkling holy water over the recipient. He then places his hands on the recipient's head and prays silently. The priest then anoints the recipient with holy oil. At this time, the recipient may confess sins and/or receive Communion. The ceremony can be as brief as a few minutes or as long as desired.

Traditional Orthodox Christian observance requires seven priests and includes seven readings from scripture, seven prayers, and seven anointings. A shortened version of the sacrament is normally performed, including as many priests as are available and witnessed by as many faithful as possible.

Last rites are intended to prepare the recipient for death. However, many believe that the Anointing of the Sick will result in some form of healing. It is generally not expected that an immediate physical healing will occur, thus individuals are encouraged not to wait until the moment of death to receive the rites in order to allow as much time as possible for healing to take place.

Customs and Symbols

Anointing

The priest rubs a small amount of oil on the recipient's forehead and the palms of the recipient's hands. Alternatively, the recipient may receive a small amount of oil on the forehead and on each of the sensory organs, including the eyes, ears, nose, mouth, and hands.

Oil

Sacramental oil known as unction is used to anoint the recipient. The oil is made holy during a special mass that must be conducted by a bishop.

Prayer

Catholic and Orthodox priests offer prayers for the recipient's healing, asking God to bless the recipient and restore their health and strength.

Web Site

"Unction of the Sick." Orthodox Church in America, undated.
    http://www.oca.org/OCchapter.asp?SID=2&ID=55

Further Reading

Donohue, J. M. "Anointing of the Sick II: Liturgy of." In *New Catholic Encyclopedia.* 2nd ed. Detroit: Gale, 2003.

Koenig-Bricker, Woodene. "For Our Healing: The Sacrament of the Anointing of the Sick." *Youth Update Newsletter*, undated.
    http://www.americancatholic.org/Newsletters/YU/ay1292.asp

DRESSING THE BODY

Alternate Names: Ghusl, Laying Out, Taharah

Customs and Symbols: Blankets, Clothing, Shroud

Dressing the body of a deceased person is an almost universal custom in preparation for burial or cremation. Most often performed by a funeral director, the body is also sometimes prepared by family or community members.

History and Significance

Ritual burial preparation can be traced back to the earliest civilizations. The burial customs of the ancient Egyptians are perhaps the most well known, with many published descriptions of the ways in which bodies were dressed for entombment. Historically, great significance was placed on burial clothing that symbolized the status of the deceased in life. While modern burial customs are often far less extravagant, many religious and cultural traditions are still applied to the dressing of the deceased.

Observance

The bodies of the deceased are usually dressed for burial or cremation by secular funeral directors, although some religions have specific rites that must be performed at this time. Funeral directors who serve particular religious communities are often well versed in the appropriate customs. In some religious traditions, the body is dressed by family or community members instead of a funeral director. For observant Jews, this work is known as *taharah* and is performed by a *Chevra Kadisha* (burial society) composed of volunteers from the local synagogue. The Muslim process of preparing a body for burial is called *ghusl* (*see* **Salat al-Janaza**).

Dressing the body of a deceased person is an almost universal custom in preparation for burial or cremation.

Washing or ritual bathing of the body is generally the first step in the dressing process. In some religious traditions, the body is washed by family or community members of the same gender as the deceased. The body is treated with the utmost respect during the bathing process. After the body has been washed, spices, oils, or perfumes are sometimes applied to the skin. In most cases, the body is then dressed in specially chosen clothing. Sometimes the body is wrapped in a shroud. Chinese Americans may also choose to observe the old tradition of wrapping the body in cotton blankets in various significant colors.

Customs and Symbols

Blankets

Some Chinese Americans prepare loved ones for burial by wrapping the body in cotton blankets called *pei*. The blankets are intended to comfort and protect the spirit of the departed, and are wrapped around the body in a particular order. The first blanket is usually solid white, to represent the color of heaven. The second blanket is usually solid red, representing life and happiness. Subsequent blankets may be any color or pattern, with each folded to reveal the blanket below. The second-to-last blanket is the *shau pie* (longevity blanket) and is usually heavier than the others. The final blanket is the *fut pei* (blanket of spirituality) and bears a special design. For observant Chinese Buddhists, the fut pei is usually gold with prayers printed in red. Practicing Chinese Christians may receive a white fut pei featuring a large gold cross.

Clothing

Most people are buried in clothing that typically represents what they may have worn in life. Burial clothing is usually chosen by the family of the deceased, although many people leave specific instructions regarding the clothing in which they want to be buried. Burial clothing varies widely and generally depends upon individual taste and preference.

Some Jewish burial customs allow the deceased to be dressed in typical clothing either underneath or instead of a shroud. Men are generally dressed with a *tallit* (prayer shawl) over their clothing, and may also wear a *kittel* (a white jacket worn for religious ceremonies). Women who normally wore a tallit during prayer may also be wrapped in one for burial.

Some Chinese Americans observe the traditional burial custom of dressing the body in a longevity robe, which symbolizes long life and happiness. If regular clothing is chosen, the body must be dressed in a complete outfit including undergarments. The body may not be buried in any clothing that has been cut or torn.

Shroud

Observant Jews are often buried in shrouds called *takhrikhim*. These are plain white cotton garments that are generally hand-sewn and made without buttons, zippers, or fasteners of any kind. The shroud is the same for men and women, and includes a shirt, pants, head covering, and belt. The shroud covers the entire body, including the face.

Traditional Muslim burial custom requires the body to be dressed in several seamless white shrouds. If the deceased completed the pilgrimage to Mecca, the body is dressed in the same garments worn while **Performing the Hajj**. Shrouds for men are generally composed of three pieces of cloth, while women's shrouds include five pieces.

The bodies of observant Hindus are sometimes wrapped before cremation in a shroud made of new cloth.

Web Sites

"Burial Society," by Jon Kalish. *Weekend All Things Considered*, National Public Radio, March 8, 1998.
   http://www.npr.org/programs/death/980308.death.html

"Fingers Will Twitch . . . ," by Jenn Shreve. Salon.com, May 23, 1999.
   http://www.salon.com/people/story/1999/05/23/mortician/index.html

Further Reading

Diamant, Anita. *Saying Kaddish: How to Comfort the Dying, Bury the Dead, and Mourn As a Jew.* New York: Schocken Books, 1998.

Gong, Rosemary. *Good Luck Life: The Essential Guide to Chinese American Celebrations and Culture.* New York: Harper Collins, 2005.

Gulevich, Tanya. *Understanding Islam and Muslim Traditions.* Detroit: Omnigraphics, 2004.

Photo on facing page: This New Orleans Jazz Funeral was held to honor the victims of Hurricane Katrina.

DEATH AND MOURNING

Chapter 20: Funerals and Other Immediate Mourning Rituals

INTRODUCTION

Until the early 20th century, American funerals and mourning rituals were heavily influenced by practices in western Europe, particularly the traditions of British royalty. Elaborate funerals were customary for those whose families could afford them, and shame fell upon any family who could not. Being laid to rest in a pauper's grave was thought to be one of life's greatest indignities.

Throughout the 19th century, middle- and upper-class Americans emulated the European tradition of strict periods of mourning which were often enforced by intense social pressure. Anyone who did not adhere to the appropriate standards of dress, grooming, and conduct of mourning was thought to be callous, uncaring, lacking in virtue, and even immoral. Although these expectations generally did not apply to working-class Americans, many tried to adhere to the structured mourning customs of the high society in order to publicly demonstrate the depth of their grief.

Mourning jewelry was commonly worn from the 1700s through the early 1900s, primarily by women. This jewelry usually included necklaces, bracelets, brooches, and earrings made of black stones such as jet or beads made of black glass, and sometimes featured a lock of the deceased's hair. Around 1850, some mourning jewelry began to be composed entirely of hair, which was customarily braided into bracelets, necklaces, or brooches for ladies and watch chains for men. Queen Victoria's public mourning of the 1861 death of her husband Prince Albert further popularized the customs of wearing special mourning clothes and jewelry. Following the style preferred by Queen Victoria, mourning jewelry became larger and heavier—and thus more noticeable—during the late 1800s. By the early 1900s, mourning jewelry and clothing had fallen out of fashion in the U.S.

Until the early 20th century it was the norm for funerals to be conducted at home. The body was often laid in a coffin in the parlor of the family home, where the bereaved received visitors before the burial services. The coffin would then be carried in a procession to the church grave yard or cemetery. This procession was generally somber, although the traditional **New Orleans Jazz Funeral** was, and is, a raucous affair featuring music, singing, and dancing. **Wakes** and/or **Repasts** would be held after interment, giving friends and relatives a chance to memorialize the deceased and comfort the bereaved.

Each of these traditions has influenced mainstream American funerals, memorial services, and burial rites to some degree, while specific religious and cultural groups maintain certain traditions uniquely their own. This chapter presents an overview of funeral and mourning customs as practiced by various communities in the U.S., including Native American rituals such as the **Iroquois Family Condolence Rite** and the **Shawnee Death Feast**. The Islamic **Salat al-Janaza** is described along with the Jewish tradition of mourning known as **Aninut**. The fairly recent custom of creating **Sidewalk and Other Public Shrines** enables the expression of communal grief over unexpected, violent deaths while helping to comfort the friends and relatives of the deceased.

Contemporary American ways of grieving continue to be influenced by historical precedents. Strict codes of mourning are no longer enforced, but black clothing is still customary for funerals and wakes. Mourning jewelry may have fallen out of fashion, but those grieving the loss of a loved one may still cherish a particular piece such as a wedding band or other sentimental item. Funeral customs and ritualized expressions of grief help to form connections among those in mourning, transforming personal experiences of death into opportunities for community support.

ANINUT

Customs and Symbols: Keriah, Saying Kaddish, Shiva

In Judaism, the news of the death of a loved one begins aninut, the time of mourning between death and burial. Children, parents, spouses, and siblings of the dead become mourners, or *onen*. Jewish tradition excuses mourners from usual religious observances. Their sole duty is the care of the dead, the washing and preparation of the body for burial, and arrangements for a proper burial.

The Jewish mourner does not eat meat, drink wine, or engage in earthly pleasures or amusements, such as concerts, plays, movies, parties, or festivities. The mourner is also discouraged from studying the Torah—considered to be a source of pleasure—except for instruction in mourning and conducting the burial ceremony, *leviah*. On the Jewish Sabbath, however, mourners carry out all traditional observances and rituals.

History and Significance

The laws of Judaism regarding funerals are detailed and specific, part of the *Halakha*, or body of laws that include the 613 *mitzvot* and rabbinical laws set down by Jewish leaders over centuries. The body of the deceased retains its sanctity. The customs of mourning and burial are designed to afford the dead respect and assist the mourners to keep and strengthen their faith. It is the most solemn of occasions, when display, ostentation, and any kind of celebration are strongly discouraged. The immediate family of the dead is enjoined to remain home and disregard their usual work and pleasures for a certain period of time. Afterward, out of respect for the deceased, they carry out regular memorials and repeat a mourning prayer known as the Kaddish as consolation and a profession of faith.

Observance

Upon hearing of the death of a loved one, mourners tear their clothing in the act of *keriah*. Jewish tradition does not permit the body to be left alone after death, so guardians known as *shomerim* stay with the body to ensure proper observance and respect. In some communities, volunteers from a *chevra kaddisha* (burial society) care for the dead, assisting the bereaved and supervising the funeral and ceremonies.

> *The Jewish customs of mourning and burial are designed to afford the dead respect and assist the mourners to keep and strengthen their faith. It is the most solemn of occasions, when display, ostentation, and any kind of celebration are strongly discouraged.*

Jewish law does not permit autopsies or cremation of the body, although Reform Judaism may permit cremation. Organ donation is allowed, for it makes the body of a living person whole. There is no tradition of embalming the body, or of viewing the body, which would be perceived as an act of disrespect and mockery of the dead. There is no visitation, in which people come to console the bereaved, until after the funeral. There are also no flowers and no music, no social gatherings of any kind. The period of aninut is the most solemn of Jewish occasions, and the mourners are simply left alone.

To prepare for burial, the body is cleaned and wrapped in a shroud. The burial takes place as soon as possible, as a sign of respect to the dead, who are to be helped to the afterlife without delay. Jewish burials do not take place on the Sabbath, or any other holy day. At the graveside service the *hesped*, or eulogy, and the kaddish are said. Saying kaddish is an integral part of the mourning process.

The leviah, which roughly translated means "accompaniment," is the burial ceremony itself. The entire community of relatives, friends, and acquaintances of the deceased attend. The family of the deceased typically casts the first shovelfuls of earth over the coffin or shrouded body. A rabbi presiding at the service recites a prayer for mourning known as *El Molai Rachamim*. As a sign of respect for the dead, visitors to the ceremony leave pebbles on the grave in remembrance of their visit.

The burial service ends the period of aninut and signals the beginning of *shiva*, or shivah, the seven-day period following the burial.

Customs and Symbols

Keriah

Keriah is the first ritual associated with mourning, as it occurs almost immediately following the death of a loved one. By tearing their clothes, mourners physically express the extent of their grief. Some Jews follow this custom in spirit, if not in practice, by pinning a shredded ribbon to their clothing. The tradition of keriah stems from a story in the Torah, in which David tears his clothes when he hears of the death of Saul and Jonathan. The torn garment (or substitute ribbon) is worn for the duration of shiva.

Saying Kaddish

The Kaddish is spoken in Aramaic, although most Jewish prayers are spoken in Hebrew. Orthodox or other strict sects of Judaism allow only males to say the prayer. The mourners, in particular the son or daughter of the deceased, continue to recite the Kaddish for extended periods of time, a tradition that brings them closer to the dead and provides them with a time for remembrance.

For the mourner, the Kaddish is an affirmation of their faith in God. The prayer also serves as a public affirmation of the mourner's love and respect for the deceased. The prayer, in translation in Leo Trepp's *The Complete Book of Jewish Observance*, reads as follows:

> Magnified and sanctified be His Great Name throughout the world, which He has created according to His will. May He establish His Kingdom during your lifetime and during your days, and during the lifetime of the entire House of Israel. To this say ye: Amen [so be it].

> Blessed, praised, exalted, elevated and lauded in every way be His Holy Name. Blessed be He!

> He is above all blessings, hymns, and praises that can be spoken in the world. To this say ye: Amen.

> May there be abundant peace from heaven and life unto us and unto all of Israel. To this say ye: Amen.

> May He, who makes peace in His [heavenly] heights, make peace for us and for all Israel. To this say ye: Amen.

Shiva

For one week after the death of a parent, sibling, child, or spouse, many Jews observe an intense period of mourning. During shiva, mourners refrain from working and normally do not leave the house. Visitors come to offer support and comfort, usually bringing gifts of food as those sitting shiva are restricted from cooking. A special shiva candle is lit and left to burn for the entire week. On the morning of the seventh day after the funeral, the shiva candle is blown out to signify an end to the initial mourning period. At this time, mourners often go for a short walk outside to symbolize their re-entrance into normal daily activities.

Further Reading

Brener, Anne. *Mourning and Mitzvah: A Guided Journal for Walking the Mourner's Path Through Grief to Healing.* Woodstock, VT: Jewish Lights Publishing, 2001.

Diamant, Anita. *Saying Kaddish: How to Comfort the Dying, Bury the Dead, and Mourn as a Jew.* New York: Schocken Books, 1998.

Lamm, Maurice. *The Jewish Way in Death and Mourning.* Middle Village, NY: Jonathan David Publishers, 2000.

Trepp, Leo. *The Complete Book of Jewish Observance.* New York: Behrman House/Summit Books, 1980.

IROQUOIS FAMILY CONDOLENCE RITE

Alternate Name: Condolence Ceremony

Customs and Symbols: Cane, Condoling Party, Wampum, Words of Condolence

The family condolence rite is offered to those who are grieving the death of a family member or loved one. It is considered to be one of the most important rituals practiced by the Iroquois people.

History and Significance

The Iroquois people trace the origin of the condolence rite to Hiawatha, a great chief who was overcome by grief after the death of his family. Iroquois legend tells the story of Hiawatha wandering alone through the forest and coming to a stand of stiff marsh plants with hollow stems. He cut several of these and formed them into strings of beads called *wampum*, which he then hung between two forked sticks. As he hung each string, Hiawatha spoke words of condolence to himself. Hiawatha said that if he ever encountered anyone who was grieving as much as he was then, he would speak the same words to them in order to ease their pain. Hiawatha continued wandering in his sorrow until he met another chief, who took the wampum strings and spoke words of condolence to Hiawatha. The Iroquois believe that this act soothed Hiawatha's grief so that he could once again lead his people, and the rite is now practiced to help those who are grieving to return to their normal activities.

Observance

The family condolence rite is conducted for Iroquois people who are grieving the death of a loved one. A condoling party visits the home of the bereaved and offers ceremonial words of condolence, using strings of wampum that symbolize the various effects of grief. A member of the condoling party hangs the wampum strings over a cane that has been placed across two chairs. One by one, the wampum strings are removed from the cane and passed to the bereaved as specific words of condolence are spoken. When all of the wampum strings have been removed from the cane, a member of the bereaved family repeats the rite to acknowl-

> The family condolence rite is conducted for Iroquois people who are grieving the death of a loved one.

371

edge that the condoling party has also suffered a loss and is grieving. As the grieving person speaks the words of condolence, the wampum strings are placed one by one into a pouch. Once all of the wampum has been placed in the pouch, it is returned to the leader of the condoling party. Everyone then shares a meal provided by the grieving family.

In addition to private condolence ceremonies held for individual families, public condolence rites are often conducted on Memorial Day or Veterans Day in cemeteries where Native American military veterans are buried. In 2003, a large condolence ceremony was held in Arlington National Cemetery near Washington, D.C.

Customs and Symbols

Cane

A cane is used to hold the wampum strings used in the family condolence rite. Placed horizontally between two chairs or other supports, wampum strings are draped over the cane and removed one at a time as specific words of condolence are spoken.

Condoling Party

The condoling party is the group of people who visit the bereaved family in order to offer the condolence rite. Normally the condoling party includes tribal elders and their assistants, but it can also include any member of the tribe.

Wampum

Wampum strings made of colored beads or shells are used in the condolence rite to symbolically remove grief from those who have lost a family member. Wampum is typically woven with certain designs which also serve as a memory aid for those who will say the words of condolence. Iroquois legend says that Hiawatha used three strings of wampum, but some Iroquois tribes now use as many as 13 strings.

Words of Condolence

The Iroquois believe that grief affects people in many ways. The words of condolence offered in the family condolence rite are intended to remove the obstructions and obstacles of grief so that normal activities can resume. Each wampum string is associated with a specific aspect of grief, such as clouded vision, physical discomfort, sleeplessness, loss of appetite, mental distraction, and despair. As each string is taken from the cane and passed to the mourners, it is believed that a specific grief will be relieved.

Further Reading

Graymont, Barbara. *The Iroquois*. Philadelphia: Chelsea House Publishers, 2005.

"Iroqouis Condolence Ceremony." *Indian Country Today*, June 12, 2003.
    http://www.indiancountry.com/content.cfm?id=1055438183

Speck, Frank G., with Alexander General. *Midwinter Rites of the Cayuga Long House*. 1949.
    Reprint, Lincoln: University of Nebraska Press, 1995.

SALAT AL-JANAZA

Customs and Symbols: Ghusl, Surah Ya Sin

The salat al-janaza is the Muslim funeral prayer service. For Muslims, the deceased has left earthly life behind and begun preparation for Judgment Day, the time when the faithful will be conducted to Paradise. On the occasion of a death, it is customary for Muslims to console each other with a quote from the Qu'ran, the holy book of Islam: "To Allah we belong and to Him is our return."

History and Significance

The funeral tradition of Islam arises from the teachings of the prophet Muhammad, who established the faith in the seventh century C.E. The Prophet, as he is known to Muslims, gave instructions for preparing the body, reciting prayers, and presiding at the burial of the deceased. These instructions have been passed down via the Qu'ran as well as scholars' interpretations of its verses.

Mourners repeat prayers to beseech Allah's mercy and understanding for those who have passed away, and to prepare the dead for the final judgment that will allow him or her to enter Paradise. The prescribed prayers to bring this about begin with the dying individuals' profession of faith, the shahada: "There is no God but Allah, and Muhammad is His messenger." The shahada also often comprises the first words a Muslim newborn hears from his or her parents (*see* **Whispering the Shahada**). Thus, life may end with the same expression of faith with which it began.

Observance

After death, Muslims gather in the home of the deceased to grieve. The eyes of the dead are carefully closed. The body must be prepared and buried as soon as possible, but in any case within three days of the death. Islam does not permit autopsies, embalming, or cremation. In some communities, volunteer groups aid families with preparations for the funeral and burial.

After a *ghusl*, or ritual washing, the prayer service takes place, usually in a mosque or funeral home. Traditionally, the deceased is then carried to the gravesite in a procession, in which mourners walk beside or behind the body in silence. Carrying the bier is an honor reserved for close relatives, all of whom are offered a turn to bear the burden of the dead to its final resting place.

At the gravesite the members of the funeral form rows, standing to face the holy city of Mecca. The body is positioned so that it rests on its right side, with the face turned in the direction of Mecca, and buried.

There is no casket, unless it is required by local laws, in which case it is to be as simple as possible and always of wood—never metal. Nothing is put into the grave with the body.

During the burial, the mourners recite prayers and verses from the Qu'ran. All share in the responsibility of filling in the grave, reciting a passage from the Qu'ran with each of the three lumps of earth they throw into the grave. The grave is then marked as simply as possible, with no memorials or carved markers, preferably with a simple stone. The opening chapter of the Qu'ran is then recited by the imam leading the service. Weeping for the dead is permitted, but public displays of grief such as wailing are not.

A period of mourning begins, lasting three days. Visitors come to offer their condolences, while friends prepare food and bring it to the house of the mourners, who are thus relieved of the necessity of preparing their meals. At the home of the deceased, prayers are recited. At the end of the period of mourning, visitors and the family visit the gravesite with offerings of flowers and scented oil, which is poured out over the grave. The funeral is commemorated again on the 40th day after the burial, and then at intervals throughout the year. On the 40th day, a dinner is held at which the deceased is remembered; this ceremony takes place again a year later.

> *A period of mourning begins, lasting three days. At the home of the deceased, prayers are recited. At the end of the period of mourning, visitors and the family visit the gravesite with offerings of flowers and scented oil, which is poured out over the grave.*

Customs and Symbols

Ghusl

The members of the family have the responsibility for ghusl, the ritual washing of the body. The ghusl is performed by a man for a man, a woman for a woman, or by a spouse. Either a man or a woman may perform the same duty for a child. In some Muslim communities, a local mosque or funeral home offers this service to the families of the deceased should they want or need it.

The body is laid out on a table and, with gloved hands, washed carefully, first on the right side and then on the left, at least three times (but always an odd number of times). Scents and oils are added to the final bathing. The body is covered with a white cotton kafan or shroud, to lend it dignity and to protect it from curious onlookers. Three layers of the kafan are used to cover a man, five for a woman. Perfume or camphor is placed on the kafan, which is tied at the head and feet.

Surah Ya Sin

At the moment of death or immediately before it, a funeral prayer is said, Surah Ya Sin, or surah 36 of the Quran. This prayer is intended to make death and its passage into another life easier for the dying person. This particular surah conveys the essence of revelation and the doctrine of faith in Islam. It is also appropriate to recite to a dying person to help them prepare for death.

Web Site

"A Guide for the Muslim Funeral." Islamic Society of North America, undated.
   http://www.isna.net/services/casc/guide.html

Further Reading

Al-Jibaly, Muhammad. *Funerals: Regulations and Exhortations (The Inevitable Journey, Part 3)*. Al-Kitaab and As Sunnah Publishing, 2003.

Esposito, John L., ed. *The Oxford Dictionary of Islam*. New York: Oxford University Press, 2003.

Gulevich, Tanya. *Understanding Islam and Muslim Traditions*. Detroit: Omnigraphics, 2004.

NEW ORLEANS JAZZ FUNERAL

Customs and Symbols: Grand Marshal and the Second Line, "When the Saints Go Marching In"

The unique jazz funeral of New Orleans arose from the confluence of many sources and has developed many of its own customs and institutions, which have survived and adapted to a changing society.

History and Significance

In New Orleans, a lively funeral tradition evolved from a merging of various cultural strands: funeral customs from Africa and the diaspora in the West Indies, the custom of public marching on important occasions, the rise of African-American benevolent societies in the late 18th century, the birth of jazz, and the city's love of celebration and ceremony.

In early New Orleans, bands often marched in the streets for holidays, festivities, and special occasions. To honor the deceased during a funeral ceremony, bands accompanied the coffin to the cemetery with appropriately slow and mournful music. Across the Atlantic Ocean, in west Africa, it was also a tradition to accompany the dead to their burial places with chanting, dancing, and the beating of drums. The men and women brought to New Orleans as slaves also brought their funeral customs. In west Africa, secret societies took care of death rites. After the Civil War and emancipation, these societies were revived in New Orleans as social clubs, with part of their mission being the guarantee of a proper funeral for fellow members. The funeral was the chance for the social clubs to make their style public, their way of advertising themselves to the city and to prospective new members. The members wore matching clothes, and carried the name of the club on a banner and on sashes worn across their bodies.

Observance

A church service takes place, while mourners view the open coffin. Outside the church, a band assembles, its members dressed in somber black. The band leads the funeral procession away from the church, playing slow hymns such as "Just a Closer Walk with Thee" and "Nearer My God to Thee." The musicians play the music note for note, allowing themselves no improvisation or display, no embellishment to make light of the most serious of occasions.

> *In a jazz funeral, onlookers begin walking and dancing and strutting behind the band, and the music turns joyful. The dead have passed to the afterlife, and the living celebrate the life that remains.*

The band waits again as the body is interred and the last words to honor the dead are spoken in the cemetery. The internment takes place above ground—the city of New Orleans lies below sea level and the high water table prevents underground burial. The mourners walk from the gravesite in silence, and band members hold their instruments quietly at their sides before a respectful distance is reached. At a gesture from the grand marshal, the trumpeter gives the signal and the drummers begin to beat time.

A great crowd may form, with people dancing, singing, and shouting, as the music grows raucous. The band breaks out in vigorous song—a traditional favorite is "Didn't He Ramble?"—in order to mark the gusto and well-lived life of the deceased. The musicians begin to improvise, allowing their emotions free play, adapting and embellishing the music. Members of the second line wear hats or white handkerchiefs, and wave them in the air in time to the music while they sing and dance. The handkerchiefs, no longer needed to wipe away the tears, are used instead for a happy celebration.

The New Orleans funeral has survived and adapted. In some of these celebrations, newer music is heard, including popular songs, current dance music, and even rap songs. The quiet and somber march to the grave is also sometimes forgotten, with the dancing and liveliness taking over as soon as the church services finish. While the "jazz funeral" of the past usually took place to honor a jazz musician, in modern times anyone can have such a funeral arranged.

The jazz funeral has also been performed for non-human dead, such as funerals for Hurricane Katrina. The storm devastated New Orleans in the late summer of 2005, shutting down the city, closing many funeral homes and churches, and scattering many of its residents. The observance was meant to usher the deadly storm away from the city permanently.

Customs and Symbols

The Grand Marshal and the Second Line

The grand marshal may be the band leader, or the head of the social club which has made arrangements for the funeral. During the funeral, he is dressed in fine clothes, sometimes wearing white gloves, holding an umbrella to signal those who follow. As he leads the band, onlookers join a second line behind the musicians. Anyone may take part; onlookers begin walking and dancing and strutting behind the band, and the music turns joyful. The dead have passed to the afterlife, and the living celebrate the life that remains. On the occasion of a famous or widely respected figure, thousands may take part, clogging the city's streets.

"When the Saints Go Marching In"

The traditional finale of the New Orleans funeral is "When the Saints Go Marching In." This song began as a traditional spiritual, sung and played in a slow tempo. The lyrics below were collected by Alan Lomax in *The Folk Songs of North America* (1960):

> O when the saints go marchin' in,
> O when the saints go marching in,
> O Lord I want to be in that number,
> O when the saints go marching in.
>
> O when the sun refuse to shine,
> O when the sun refuse to shine,
> O Lord I want to be in that number,
> When the sun refuse to shine.
>
> O when the moon goes down in blood,
> O when the moon goes down in blood,
> O Lord I want to be in that number
> When the moon goes down in blood.
>
> O when the stars have disappeared,
> O when the stars have disappeared,
> O Lord I want to be in that number
> When the stars have disappeared,
>
> O when they crown Him Lord of all,
> O when they crown Him Lord of all,
> O Lord I want to be in that number
> When they crown Him Lord of all.
>
> O when the day of judgment comes,
> O when the day of judgment comes,
> O Lord I want to be in that number
> When the day of judgment comes.

At one time, "When the Saints Go Marching In" was only heard at Sunday church services. According to a New Orleans legend, one day a jazz band was performing

A Holiday for the Dead

On All Saints Day, November 1, the people of New Orleans tend to their famous cemeteries. The above-ground tombs get a coat of whitewash and garlands of "immortelles" (immortals) which are permanent wreaths made of metal wire or plastic, glass beads, and artificial flowers and fruit. People come to pay their respects to the dead, leaving white candles and bouquets of chrysanthemums, and tidying up the photographs, flower vases, plaques, and other objects used to decorate the tomb and mark it as a place of permanent rest. (See **All Souls Day.**)

it while returning from a funeral. Played quickly, the music caught the ear of those inside a church, who rose from their seats and walked out the front door to listen. It was never sung again as a part of their church services.

Further Reading

Florence, Robert. *New Orleans Cemeteries: Life in the Cities of the Dead.* New Orleans: Batture Press, 1997.

Southern, Eileen. *The Music of Black Americans: A History.* New York: W. W. Norton, 1997.

Touchet, Leo, and Vernel Bagneris. *Rejoice When You Die: The New Orleans Jazz Funerals.* Louisiana State University Press, 1998.

WAKES

Alternate Names: Vigil, Visitation

Customs and Symbols: Memorial Service, Offerings, Visitation

A wake is the time set aside before or after a funeral service to provide an informal opportunity for mourners to pay their final respects to the departed and offer support to the immediate family and close friends of the deceased. Wakes are primarily Christian practices, although they are commonly held as part of non-religious funerals as well. The Jewish custom of *shiva* also bears certain similarities to a wake (*see* **Aninut**).

History and Significance

Throughout history, wakes have allowed mourners to participate in communal grieving and remembrance of the dead. First popularized in colonial America by immigrants from western Europe, wakes became closely associated with traditional Irish culture. As Irish immigrants settled in the U.S. and built close-knit communities, the Irish wake became famous for its resemblance to a large, chaotic party. Irish wakes gained a reputation for loud wailing and other public displays of grief, as well as for spirited arguments about various attributes of the deceased and fervent prayers for the soul of the departed. Generally more sedate and restrained by comparison, wakes are now held by mourners of many different cultures and religions. The wake is widely regarded as a necessary part of grieving, and critical to the mourners' healing process.

At a wake, mourners are often encouraged to speak about the deceased or share stories and memories of time spent together. The wake typically provides a more personal expression of mourning than the funeral service.

Observance

Wakes can take many different forms depending on local customs and the religious tradition of the deceased. Some people define the wake as the visitation at the funeral home, while others use the term to describe the **Repast** or meal shared after the funeral. Sometimes the family of the deceased plan a party or gathering in honor of the departed at a later date, and this event can also be called a wake. For many Christian denominations, the wake is a prayer vigil before the funeral. Most often, however, the memorial service held at the funeral home during visitation is thought of as the wake.

The wake is essentially an opportunity for family and friends to gather and talk about the deceased. Mourners are often encouraged to speak about the deceased or share stories and memories of time spent together. In this way, the wake typically provides a more personal expression of mourning than the funeral service. The wake's atmosphere of community grieving, support, and shared memories of the deceased is closely related to the Jewish custom of sitting shiva.

In addition to or instead of a public wake, Chinese Americans often choose to hold a private gathering attended only by the family of the deceased on the evening before the funeral. Depending on whether the deceased was Buddhist, Taoist, or Christian, either of these events might include prayers, chanting, the playing of chimes or drums, the burning of incense or red candles, and sacrificial offerings. Traditionally, each family member pays final respects to the deceased by bowing three times before the casket.

Customs and Symbols

Memorial Service

Memorial services are commonly held at a funeral home. These services often include music, prayers, and/or readings from scripture or an appropriate secular source, which can include favorite passages enjoyed by the deceased in life.

Offerings

Traditional Chinese-American family wakes sometimes include offerings for the spirit of the deceased, similar to those used in **Ching Ming** observances. Food offerings normally include *saam soong*, or "three dishes," which traditionally are roast suckling pig's head, a whole white chicken, and a sautéed vegetable dish called *jai choy*. Saam soong is usually accompanied by three bowls of rice, three cups of wine, and three cups of tea.

Visitation

Visitation, sometimes also referred to as viewing, is the time when the family of the deceased receives visitors at a funeral home. Usually held one to three days before the funeral, visitation allows friends and acquaintances to spend time with the family and offer support or comfort. A brief memorial or prayer service is held during visitation if desired by the bereaved family.

Web Site

"A Parish Guide to Planning When Death Occurs." The Church of St. William, Fridley, MN, undated.
http://www.stwilliams.com/ContactUs/funeral_planning.htm

Further Reading

Gong, Rosemary. *Good Luck Life: The Essential Guide to Chinese American Celebrations and Culture*. New York: Harper Collins, 2005.

Lysaght, Patricia. "Death and Burial." In *Encyclopedia of Food and Culture*. Edited by Solomon H. Katz. New York: Charles Scribner's Sons, 2003.

O'Gorman, Thomas J. "Sorry for Your Troubles." *World of Hibernia*, Winter 1998.

REPASTS

Alternate Names: Funeral Feast, Funeral Meal, Longevity Dinner, *Makaria*, Meal of Condolence, Seudat Havra'ah, Shau Chaan

Customs and Symbols: Charitable Acts, Food

A repast is a meal shared by mourners after a funeral. The communal post-funeral meal takes many forms across cultures and religious traditions in the U.S., but is widely valued for its ability to comfort those suffering the pain of a loved one's death.

History and Significance

The custom of sharing a meal after funeral services is common to nearly all cultures and religions worldwide. The hours immediately after the burial or cremation of a loved one are generally a time of intense sorrow and grief, and bereaved family often benefit from the company of friends and relations. Familiar food brings comfort to those in mourning, and the shared repast offers spiritual sustenance by emphasizing the bonds of family and community.

Observance

There is tremendous variation in the provision of funeral repasts, depending on local custom, cultural background, and religious tradition. Repasts are sometimes held as potluck luncheons at the home of the deceased or in a community room of the deceased's church. Catered meals may also be provided at a restaurant or other facility. Although most localities in the U.S. enforce laws prohibiting the preparation or distribution of food in a funeral home, it is permissible in some states. Where possible, some funeral homes have banquet rooms in which a catered repast may be provided immediately after funeral or cemetery services.

> *Familiar food brings comfort to those in mourning, and the shared repast offers spiritual sustenance by emphasizing the bonds of family and community.*

Tradition dictates the location and type of repast that will be held. After the burial service has been completed, Muslims, Jews, and Hindus generally return to the home of the deceased or the deceased's family to share a feast. Chinese Americans often hold a longevity dinner called *shau chaan* at a favorite restaurant. Buddhists and Muslims view the funeral meal as an opportunity to perform charitable acts on behalf of the deceased. The repast generally provides further opportunity for the sharing of stories and memories of the deceased, and for this reason it is sometimes referred to as a wake. However, some Native American traditions call for a somber funeral meal during which little conversation takes place, and mourners avoid speaking of the deceased.

Customs and Symbols

Charitable Acts

The Muslim funeral meal is provided by the family of the departed as a charitable act that blesses the soul of the deceased. Similarly, Buddhists provide food to monks after the funeral services to confer merit upon the soul of the deceased in the hopes of affecting a positive reincarnation.

Food

Repasts commonly include dishes that were favored by the deceased as well as regional delicacies. Cultural comfort foods and family recipes are also popular choices for these meals. African-American funeral repasts often include southern dishes and traditional soul food, such as fried chicken, baked ham, and other specialties. The Chinese-American shau chaan is a simple meal of *jai choy* (sautéed vegetables), tofu, fish, and steamed rice. Greek Americans often share *makaria*, a traditional funeral meal including *paximathia* (hard, dry toasted bread), baked fish, and brandy. *Mansaf*, a traditional layered dish of flatbread, rice, fried nuts and lamb, is usually served after Muslim funerals. The Jewish funeral repast is called *seudat havra'ah* (the meal of condolence) and generally includes foods such as lentils and boiled eggs, which symbolize the cycle of life.

Desserts and other sweets play a large part in most funeral meals, especially in the Hindu tradition. Three special desserts are usually served after Hindu funeral services: *appam* (a rice-flour pancake), *vada* (a type of donut), and *payasam* (rice pudding). Sweets are particularly important for Hindus because they signify that the bereaved are able to carry on with life after the loss of a loved one.

Further Reading

Eickelman, Dale F. "Rites of Passage: Muslim Rites." In *Encyclopedia of Religion*. Edited by Lindsay Jones. 2nd ed. New York: Macmillan Reference USA, 2005.

Gong, Rosemary. *Good Luck Life: The Essential Guide to Chinese American Celebrations and Culture*. New York: Harper Collins, 2005.

Jurgens, Jane. "Greek Americans." In *Gale Encyclopedia of Multicultural America.* Edited by Jeffrey Lehman. Vol. 2. 2nd ed. Detroit: Gale, 2000.

Opincar, Abe. "He Would've Wanted Everyone to Eat." *New York Times,* August 10, 2005.

Rogak, Lisa. *Death Warmed Over: Funeral Food, Rituals, and Customs From Around the World.* Berkeley, CA: Ten Speed Press, 2004.

Thursby, Jacqueline S. *Funeral Festivals in America: Rituals for the Living.* Lexington: University Press of Kentucky, 2006.
http://www.kentuckypress.com/0813123801excerpt.pdf

Weber, Vicki L., ed. *The Rhythm of Jewish Time: An Introduction to Holidays and Life-Cycle Events.* West Orange, NJ: Behrman House, 1999.

SHAWNEE DEATH FEAST

Customs and Symbols: Darkened Room, Food, Speaking to the Spirits

The Shawnee Death Feast is an annual ceremony held in memory of loved ones who have died. With its focus on caring for the spirits of deceased family members, this simple rite bears similarities to the Mexican **Día de los Muertos** and the Chinese **Ching Ming**.

History and Significance

One of the traditional beliefs of the Shawnee is that the spirits of the dead have the ability to influence the circumstances of the living, for better or worse. The Death Feast is offered to assure the dead that they are remembered fondly and to respectfully request that the living remain undisturbed by their spirits. Although many older Native American religious practices have been overtaken by Christianity, some Shawnee continue to observe the Death Feast as a way of honoring ancestors and other deceased loved ones.

Observance

The Death Feast is normally conducted in private, at the home of the family or friends of the deceased. Special food is prepared and served on a table just as it would be for any guest. This is usually also an opportunity for speaking to the spirits. The food is then left in a darkened room for a period of time. The family and/or friends of the deceased return to the room later to clear away the food, which can then be eaten by the living. It is believed that the spirits of the departed consume the essence (aroma) of the food, although sometimes portions of the food are missing when the family returns.

Customs and Symbols

Darkened Room

The feast is left undisturbed in a darkened room for a few hours or overnight. It is believed that during this time, the spirits of the dead will consume the feast.

Food

The food that is left out for the spirits usually includes traditional Native American dishes, but can include anything that was preferred by the deceased in life.

Speaking to the Spirits

After the feast is set on the table, someone present usually addresses the spirits of the deceased, speaking aloud of fond memories and asking for help, insight, and guidance from the spirits.

Further Reading

Hirschfelder, Arlene B., and Paulette Molin. "Death Feast." In *Encyclopedia of Native American Religions*. New York: Facts on File, 2000.

Hultkrantz, Ake. "North American Indian Religions: An Overview." In *Encyclopedia of Religion*. Edited by Lindsay Jones. 2nd ed. New York: Macmillan Reference USA, 2005.

SIDEWALK AND OTHER PUBLIC SHRINES

Alternate Names: Descansos, Impromptu Shrines, Makeshift Memorials, Spontaneous Shrines

Customs and Symbols: Crosses, Mementos, Online Memorials

Spontaneous shrines are created in response to personal and collective tragedies. These impromptu displays of public grief are established in memory of friends and family members as well as celebrities, public figures, and victims of catastrophic events.

History and Significance

Makeshift shrines have long been created to memorialize unexpected, violent deaths. In medieval Europe, roadside shrines marked the location of an untimely death and the grave of the deceased, who was often buried on the spot. Originally, the shrines were an attempt to appease the angry spirits of the deceased and thereby prevent future hauntings. With the rise of Christianity, the shrines became a reminder for travelers to pray for the souls of the deceased.

In the modern U.S., impromptu memorials provide an outlet for grief surrounding a tragic event and help to form a connection among those in mourning. Once solely a personal act of grief over an individual death, spontaneous shrines have evolved to include expressions of communal mourning.

Although these shrines are an old tradition throughout the southwestern U.S., the transient nature of undocumented memorials makes it impossible to say with any certainty when and where the custom began, and when it began to expand throughout the country.

Observance

Sidewalk memorials are created by those who wish to publicly express sorrow over an unexpected death. Spontaneous shrines are generally created on existing fences, walls, or poles nearest to the death site. Crosses are sometimes erected, and mementos left at these shrines often overflow to cover the nearby sidewalk or street. With the growth of the Internet, online memorials are sometimes created in addition to physical shrines.

Spontaneous shrines for individuals are generally created by the family and friends of the deceased. Usually small in size and composed of significant mementos left by those who knew the deceased well, these shrines become intensely personal manifestations of grief. They are almost always located near the death site, serving as a public reminder of a personal tragedy. These shrines are especially common throughout the southwestern U.S., where they are referred to as *descansos* ("resting places").

Shrines also commonly develop in memory of a celebrity or public figure, especially one who has died suddenly or tragically. These shrines often appear at the death site, but can also be created at the home or grave of the deceased, or another location closely associated with the deceased's life or career. Shrines for public figures are usually established by fans and admirers rather than friends or relatives.

The largest and most extensive spontaneous shrines in the U.S. are those created after public tragedies such as the 1995 bombing of the Alfred P. Murrah Federal Building in Oklahoma City, Oklahoma, the 1999 shootings at Columbine High School in Littleton, Colorado, and the September 11, 2001, terrorist attacks in New York City and Washington, D.C. These shrines included hundreds of thousands of items, many of which were left by concerned individuals with no connection to those who were killed. Impromptu shrines for large-scale tragedies often become pilgrimage sites for mourners.

Impromptu memorials provide an outlet for grief surrounding a tragic event and help to form a connection among those in mourning.

Another pilgrimage site is the Vietnam Veterans Memorial Wall in Washington, D.C., which was dedicated in 1982. Although this planned structure is permanently installed in the nation's capital, it has also become the site of a large, ongoing spontaneous memorial as visitors immediately began leaving mementos at the base of the wall. This unexpected phenomenon quickly captured the attention and imagination of Americans, resulting in even more items being left at the memorial. In 1984, the U.S. National Park Service began collecting and cataloging these items, which are now part of a museum exhibit known as the Vietnam Veterans Memorial Collection.

Customs and Symbols

Crosses

Roadside shrines near fatal accident scenes are often built around a cross, which provides a focal point for the memorial and is sometimes inscribed with the name of the deceased. Mementos may be included along with religious symbols, such as angels or crucifixes.

Mementos

Spontaneous shrines are composed of all manner of items associated with the memory of the deceased, including photos, flowers, candles, stuffed animals, letters, drawings, poems, and other significant personal items.

Online Memorials

Online memorials, sometimes referred to as cybershrines, are web sites created to remember and honor someone who has died. These sites commonly include photos of the deceased and a memorial message. Sometimes an online guest book is included, providing visitors with the opportunity to leave a message of condolence. Many online memorials exist in memory of deceased individuals, along with several "online cemetery" sites that memorialize many individuals at once. Countless web sites were created in remembrance of those who died in the September 11, 2001, terrorist attacks on the U.S.

Web Sites

"Collection Overview," Vietnam Veterans Memorial Collection, June 5, 1997.
   http://www.nps.gov/mrc/indexvvm.htm

"9-11 Memorial Poems and Pictures." 9-11 Heroes, undated.
   http://www.9-11heroes.us/911-memorial-poem.php

"Offerings," Vietnam Veterans Memorial Fund, undated.
   http://vvmf.org/index.cfm?SectionID=84

September 11, 2001, Documentary Project, Library of Congress, undated.
   http://memory.loc.gov/ammem/collections/911_archive

World Gardens Online Memorials and Virtual Cemetery, undated.
   http://www.worldgardens.com

World Wide Cemetery, 2007.
   http://www.cemetery.org

Further Reading

Foote, Kenneth E. *Shadowed Ground: America's Landscapes of Violence and Tragedy*. Austin: University of Texas Press, 2003.

Montgomery, Christine. "Impromptu Memorials Salve Communal Grief: On-Site Tributes the Trend as Pain, Tragedy Hit Home." *Washington Times*, August 5. 1997.

Reid, Jon. "Impromptu Memorials to the Dead." In *Handbook of Death and Dying*. Edited by Clifton Bryant. Thousand Oaks, CA: Sage Reference, 2003.

Chapter 21: Burials

INTRODUCTION

Archaeological discoveries all over the world have revealed that even the earliest humans performed intentional burial of the dead. From the Alpine mountains of Europe to the deepest South American caves, from African deserts to Pacific islands, all manner of human burial sites have been identified. Scientists have located the remains of human burials in underground graves, above-ground tombs, earthen mounds, wooden canoes, burial houses, and glacial ice caps. As ancient peoples developed ideas about death, burial customs evolved to support those beliefs. How and where the dead are buried, and the objects with which the dead are laid to rest, are all a reflection of humankind's diverse ideas about the role of the dead in living societies as well as collective expectations about a possible life after death.

Ancient burials often included material items such as cloth, animal skins, tools, beads, weapons, animal bones, bowls or plates, primitive figurines or drawings, and evidence of organic matter such as food or flowers. It is believed that this practice indicated a level of respect for the dead and a wish to provide items that would be needed in the afterlife. Burial sites found in colder climates might include furs or animal skins, while burials of those in hunting societies might include spears or arrows. Based on these connections, evaluated in combination with what is known about early human societies, modern scientists assert that the inclusion of material goods with a burial clearly indicates a belief in some sort of life after death. The careful arrangement of items around the body also shows a purposeful caring for the dead by those who performed the burial.

Prehistoric burial sites also reveal that bodies were sometimes tied with ropes or the sinews of animals, bound in textiles, or wrapped in animal skins. It is known that some tribal societies in North America and parts of Asia, Africa, and Europe performed double burials, moving the body to its final resting place only after some time in a preliminary location. Advanced burial practices such as these provide evidence of developing cultural attitudes and systematic planning with regard to the dead. Although some of the reasons behind these early burial practices remain unclear, it is believed that corpse binding and double burials may have been intended to affect the movement of the spirit of the deceased. For some, binding the body for burial may have been an attempt to protect the living by preventing the spirit from wandering after death. Conversely, it is thought that for others, binding was done to protect the dead from harassment or harm from evil spirits.

As cultures evolved, burial customs slowly shifted to commonly position the body lying flat on its back, generally unbound, and laid to rest in a single location. Jewelry, gems, personal belongings, decorative items, and household utensils continued to be buried with the dead, although this practice became less common in cultures observing Judeo-Christian religions. Because these faiths held the belief that the dead would be rewarded—or punished—after divine judgment, no material items were thought to be necessary in the afterlife.

Along with the evolution of burial rites and customs, some early societies used cremation to lay the dead to rest. Although the origins of cremation cannot be accurately traced, there is historical evidence that cremations were performed by ancient Viking, Greek, and Roman civilizations, as well as many Native American societies and peoples of India and Asia. Hindu scriptures dating from the second millennium B.C.E. indicate that cremation was viewed as an integral step in the process of death and rebirth. For many centuries cremation was not widely practiced outside of Hindu and Buddhist cultures. The practice began to gain acceptance in North America and Europe only as recently as the 1960s.

The vast diversity of burial practices and customs from the dawn of humanity to modern times continues to shape and inform funeral rites in contemporary American society. Although burials and cremations are generally governed by U.S. civil law, some latitude may be allowed by individual cemeteries and crematoriums for the practice of traditional observances. This chapter briefly describes selected rites, rituals, and customs associated with physical interment, time and position of burial, and cremation as practiced by various religious and cultural groups in the U.S.

BURIAL PRACTICES

Alternate Name: Interment

Customs and Symbols: Arms and Hands, Burial Positions, Burial Times, Cemetery Services, Face

Most cultural and religious burial traditions have been abandoned or adapted to fit the restrictions and customs of burial in modern U.S. society, where civil laws govern the proper burial of the dead. As a result, the vast majority of burials are performed in cemeteries which generally have policies regarding interment. Within these restrictions, some religious traditions are still upheld.

History and Significance

Societies throughout the world have historically performed double or secondary burials, a custom which was fairly common among Native Americans as well as ancient peoples in parts of Asia, Africa, and Europe. The initial burial took place fairly soon after death, with the body buried in the ground or left exposed to the elements in an elevated location such as a mountaintop or in a tree, a practice sometimes referred to as sky burial. The body was left in this initial burial place for a period of time, often until all flesh had decomposed. The bones were then collected from the initial grave and moved to the final grave. Over time, the custom of double burial became less common, eventually being replaced by the custom of burying the deceased just once.

Prehistoric peoples are known to have buried the dead in a fetal position, with the knees drawn up closely to the chest. Sometimes bodies were tightly bound for burial in this position. Similarly, early burial customs in many Native American societies included the binding of the legs, or hands and feet. Sometimes bodies were buried with the legs folded over the upper half of the body. The reasons behind these early burial practices are unclear, although it is believed to have been done as an attempt to prevent the spirit of the deceased from wandering after death. As cultures evolved, burial customs shifted to commonly position the body lying flat and generally unbound. Early Christian cemeteries sometimes arranged gravesites with all the heads aligned in a particular direction. Variances in the chosen direction seem to have been dependent upon local custom.

Observance

Civil law controls burial practices in the U.S., largely requiring the dead to be buried in a cemetery. Cemeteries normally implement policies requiring burials to conform to the established customs of that cemetery, which in most cases include restrictions on burial times and burial positions. Some religious traditions regarding the position of arms and hands and the orientation of the face of the deceased may still be observed within these restrictions. In addition to a funeral or memorial service held elsewhere, cemetery services are sometimes performed at the grave site just before burial.

Customs and Symbols

Arms and Hands

For the majority of burials, arms are placed alongside the body and bent at the elbow to fold naturally across the chest or abdomen. Hands are generally placed one over the other. Muslim tradition requires the right hand to be placed over the left and positioned as if in prayer. Roman Catholic burials often include a rosary placed between the hands.

Burial Positions

In most cases, the deceased are buried in a supine position (lying on the back, face upward). Because gravesites are arranged according to the layout of the individual cemetery for the best use of available space, bodies are not usually oriented in any particular direction.

Burial Times

Most religious and secular communities in the U.S. do not hold specific rules pertaining to the time of burial, however it is usually arranged as quickly as is reasonably possible. Within most religious traditions, burial on holy days or holidays is generally prohibited. Jewish custom encourages burial on the same day as death if at all possible, although it is acceptable to delay the burial in certain circumstances. Jewish burials are not performed on the Sabbath (sunset Friday to sunset Saturday) or on any of the major Jewish holidays. If death occurs just before the Sabbath or a holiday, burial is normally delayed until after the day's observance is complete. Burial may also be delayed for any civil legal reason or if close relatives must travel to be present for funeral services. Similarly, Islamic law specifies that burials occur without any unnecessary delay. Muslims strive to bury the deceased within 24 hours of death, although burial may be delayed for certain reasonable circumstances according to Islamic law.

Cemetery Services

Many families choose to conduct a service at the cemetery, either in a chapel or at the grave site. This service can be held instead of or in addition to a memorial or funeral service held elsewhere. Graveside services vary greatly according to personal preference, religious tradition, and the customs of the cemetery. Most cemetery services include prayers or readings, and some also include music. If the service will be brief, attendees usually stand near the grave; for longer services, chairs and a tent may be provided. Some services conclude with the lowering of the coffin into the grave, followed by family members dropping flowers or a small amount of dirt into the open grave. After the coffin has been placed in the grave, those attending a Jewish burial traditionally stand in two lines facing each other. The mourning family leaves the grave site by walking between these two rows of people, receiving words of comfort as they pass by each person. Those in attendance usually offer the traditional words of consolation, "May you be comforted among all the mourners of Zion and Jerusalem."

Face

Supine burial normally positions the face forward in natural alignment with the body. Muslims prefer to lay the body on its right side, facing Mecca. However, if this is not possible, Muslims are often buried supine with just the head turned to face Mecca.

Web Sites

"Graveside Services," Wyuka Funeral Home, Cemetery, and Park (Lincoln, NE), undated.
http://www.wyuka.com/FuneralHome/Gravesideservice.asp

"Guide to Jewish Funeral Practice." United Synagogue of Conservative Judaism, 2006.
http://www.uscj.org/Guide_to_Jewish_Fune6211.html

"Jewish Burial Customs," Star of David Memorial Chapel (West Babylon, NY), 2006.
http://www.starofdavidmemorialchapel.com/jbc.html#_Toc68663326

"Sacred Burial Practices of Hawaii," by Betty Fullard-Leo, *Coffee Times*, February 1998.
http://www.coffeetimes.com/feb98.htm

"Town Creek Indian Mound: Burial Hut Exhibit." North Carolina Historic Sites, undated.
htttp://www.ah.dcr.state.nc.us/sections/hs/town/burial-hut.htm

Further Reading

Breuilly, Elizabeth. *Religions of the World: The Illustrated Guide to Origins, Beliefs, Traditions, and Festivals*. New York: Facts on File, 1997.

Denny, Frederick. "Postures and Gestures." In *Encyclopedia of Religion*. Edited by Lindsay Jones. 2nd ed. New York: Macmillan Reference USA, 2005.

Gulevich, Tanya. *Understanding Islam and Muslim Traditions*. Detroit: Omnigraphics, 2004.

Hillers, Delbert, and Reuben Kashina. "Burial." In *Encyclopaedia Judaica*. Edited by Michael Berenbaum and Fred Skolnik. 2nd ed. Detroit: Macmillan Reference USA, 2007.

Rutherford, R. "Funeral Rites." *New Catholic Encyclopedia*. 2nd ed. Detroit: Gale, 2003.

CREMATION RITUALS

Customs and Symbols: Ashes, Interment, Scattering, Urn

Cremation is the reduction of a dead body to ash by burning. Cremation occurs at a special facility known as a crematorium and may be done before, after, or instead of a funeral or memorial service. Ashes resulting from a cremation are normally placed in an urn and returned to the family of the deceased for interment, scattering, or another form of preservation.

History and Significance

Cremation is an ancient practice whose origins cannot be accurately traced. There is historical evidence that cremations were performed by ancient Viking, Greek, and Roman civilizations, as well as many Native American societies. Early Hindu scriptures include cremation hymns dating from the second millennium B.C.E., and cremation is an integral part of Buddhist beliefs about death and rebirth. In these societies, cremations have historically been done outdoors without the use of a coffin or casket. For example, coastal or seafaring societies such as the ancient Vikings generally placed the body in a wooden boat which would be ignited and floated out over the water, where it was left to burn until it sank. In India and Nepal, ancient cremation customs are still observed today, with the body being placed atop a pyre (a large pile of wood and other flammable material) which is ignited and left to burn itself out.

The rise of Christianity caused cremation to become less popular in western Europe and North America. However, by the late 19th century, cremation was being encouraged in Europe's larger cities, primarily for public health and sanitation reasons. Despite this, the Roman Catholic Church held a strict ban on the practice until 1963, when the Second Vatican Council allowed Catholics to choose cremation as an alternative to traditional burial. Cremation was once widely condemned in the U.S., although an estimated one quarter of Americans now choose to be cremated. Cremation has become a common practice in the western states, as well as Alaska and Hawaii. In southern states such as Alabama, Mississippi, and Louisiana, cremation is not widely chosen.

Observance

When a traditional funeral is planned before the cremation, the body is embalmed, dressed, and placed in a casket for the memorial service. If services will not be held or are planned for a later time, the body is taken directly to the crematorium, which houses the special furnaces used in cremation. After cremation is complete, the ashes are returned to the family of the deceased.

Final disposition of the ashes varies tremendously according to personal preference and any instructions that may have been left by the deceased. Some bereaved choose to keep the ashes in an urn displayed in their home. Others store the ashes in another location such as a safe-deposit box. Ashes may also be scattered in a favorite location or interred in a cemetery, and sometimes separated for disposition in a number of different ways, for example some being scattered or preserved while the rest are interred. Some modern options include novel approaches such as having a portion of the ashes compressed into artificial gems and worn as jewelry, or mixed with concrete, formed into a special shape, and dropped into the ocean to serve as an artificial reef. Another unusual option is to have the ashes placed in a capsule that is launched into space, where the remains will be sent into orbit around the earth.

Hinduism has a long history of ritual outdoor cremation that is still practiced today in some parts of the world. However, cremation in the U.S. is governed by strict laws and regulations, and so American Hindus normally perform modified indoor versions of the traditional rituals. The body is cremated in a casket with sacred wood and *ghee* (a type of clarified butter) placed inside. If the crematorium permits, family members carry the casket in a final procession to the cremation chamber and then light a small fire inside the casket before it is sent into the chamber. The chief mourner, usually the eldest son of the deceased, operates the controls that start the cremation. When the cremation begins, the family recites prayers to give the soul peace. Ashes are usually scattered over a body of water such as a river, large lake, or the ocean. Some Hindus travel to India to scatter the ashes in the sacred Ganges River.

Buddhists observe cremation by burning incense, chanting, or meditating for the benefit of the soul's next incarnation. After cremation, ashes are often scattered in the air to symbolically represent the Buddhist belief in the impermanence of life.

Customs and Symbols

Ashes

The ashes resulting from cremation are sometimes referred to as cremains, a combination of the words "cremation" and "remains." Normally light grey or white in color, the ashes resemble finely ground sand.

Interment

Ashes are often interred at a cemetery, either by being buried in a traditional grave or stored in a crypt above ground. Many cemeteries have a structure known as a columbarium, which contains many niches or compartments for the above-ground interment of ashes. The Catholic Church requires ashes to be interred in a cemetery, and not scattered or kept at home.

Scattering

Many people choose to scatter the ashes of their loved one in a favorite place that had personal significance to the deceased. Depending on laws that apply to each location, ashes may be scattered over water, in the air, or over land.

Urn

The container that holds cremation ashes is called an urn. The urn can take many forms, with designs as unique as each individual. Urns can be buried or interred with the ashes, or kept in a location that holds meaning either to the deceased or to the bereaved family.

Web Sites

The Cremation Process: Step by Step. Cremation Association of North America, undated.
http://www.cremationassociation.org/docs/stepbystep.pdf

"Death and Dying." *Hinduism Today*, January 1997.
http://www.hinduismtoday.com/archives/1997/1/1997-1-03.shtml

Further Reading

Breuilly, Elizabeth. *Religions of the World: The Illustrated Guide to Origins, Beliefs, Traditions, and Festivals.* New York: Facts on File, 1997.

Davies, Douglas, and Lewis H. Mates, eds. *Encyclopedia of Cremation.* Burlington, VT: Ashgate Publishing, 2005.

Prothero, Stephen. *Purified by Fire: A History of Cremation in America.* Berkeley: University of California Press, 2001.

Photo on facing page: During Día de los Muertos, when people remember deceased loved ones, celebrations can include traditional dancing.

Chapter 22: Memorials and Later Commemorations

INTRODUCTION

Grief over the loss of a loved one can seem overwhelming, especially in the days immediately after a death. As time passes and a sense of normalcy gradually returns to the lives of the bereaved, many find that the pain of grief is not lessened. Sometimes grieving seems even more intense as each "first" is encountered—the first birthday, anniversary, or holiday without the deceased. Memorial rituals can help people come to terms with death through the sharing of grief with others and the opportunities for community support in times of mourning. The diversity of commemorative events practiced by contemporary Americans illustrates the different attitudes about death among various cultures and religious groups. This chapter provides an overview of selected memorial practices as observed in the U.S.

For most Americans, it is natural to remember the dead on special days. These may be informal memorials associated with the deceased's birthday or the anniversary of an event that was important to both the deceased and the bereaved, such as a wedding date. Some memorial services are held on specific dates each year, or to coincide with a particular number of days after the death occurred. The circumstance of each memorial event varies according to religious beliefs, cultural traditions, and local custom.

American Buddhists often hold a memorial service on the forty-ninth day after the death of a loved one. Because traditional Buddhist beliefs about death and rebirth are focused on the intermediate state of the soul during this time, the **Forty-Ninth Day Memorial** is thought to ensure a fortunate reincarnation of the deceased's soul. Christians and Jews in the U.S. often conduct memorials one year after the date of death. These **One-Year Memorials** are held to mark the end of the first year without the deceased. These traditions echo the 19th-century observance of a one-year period of mourning, after which the bereaved could be expected to fully return to normal social activities.

Along with the U.S. Memorial Day holiday, which is intended to remember those who have died in service to the country, some Americans observe special annual days of remembrance of all the deceased. These include the Mexican-American **Día de los Muertos**, the Roman Catholic **All Souls Day**, the Chinese-American **Ching Ming**, and the Japanese-American **Obon Festival**. Annual memorials provide an opportunity for reflection and recollection of memories of those who have died, while allowing mourners to continue to feel connected to deceased loved ones. In general, these recurring memorial events include the offering of special prayers for the benefit of the soul of the departed, visits to the cemetery or grave site, and sometimes the offering of food or other items for the enjoyment of the spirits of the dead.

Día de los Muertos and Ching Ming may be thought of as more than standard memorial services, as both demonstrate a belief that the spirits of the departed can continue to interact with the living. Día de los Muertos is a festive annual occasion celebrated by Mexican Americans, with a growing number of others also taking part. Traditionally, it is believed that the spirits of the dead return to visit their loved ones during Día de los Muertos, and special efforts are undertaken to welcome them. According to traditional Chinese beliefs, those who properly observe Ching Ming will receive help from the spirits and benefit from increased happiness, success, and good fortune. By contrast, neglected spirits can take revenge on the living, bringing bad luck and misfortune. Thus many Chinese Americans make offerings to ensure that spirits are happy and well cared for.

Commemorative ceremonies that encourage remembrance of the deceased are important cultural rituals. Acknowledging the loss of a loved one allows those in mourning to move through grief and eventually return to normal life. Although contemporary American society no longer upholds the strictly regulated mourning customs of past centuries, collective memorial ceremonies continue to benefit those who grieve.

ALL SOULS DAY

Alternate Names: Feast of All Souls, Día de los Muertos, Day of the Dead

Customs and Symbols: Colors, Prayers, Requiem Mass, Visiting the Cemetery

All Souls Day is the annual Roman Catholic day of remembrance of those who have died. Catholics offer prayers for the souls of deceased loved ones, and visiting the cemetery where loved ones are buried is traditional on All Souls Day. Among Mexican Americans, All Souls Day is celebrated as **Día de los Muertos**.

History and Significance

As early as the seventh century, Christian monasteries were dedicating prayers in memory of the deceased. By the late 10th century, the monastery of Cluny in France was observing November 2 in honor of the dead. This date was chosen because it was the day after All Saints Day, a Roman Catholic holy day that honors the saints of the church. The custom of praying for the dead on November 2 gained popularity and the practice began to spread throughout Europe. Church leaders officially recognized All Souls Day by the 14th century, when the day was added to the church calendar.

Observance

On All Souls Day, the whole Catholic community prays for the souls of all the dead, particularly those who may have been forgotten or had no one to pray for them at the time of their death.

All Souls Day is observed on November 2, except when that date falls on a Sunday. In that case, it is observed on November 3. While primarily a Roman Catholic holy day, All Souls Day is sometimes informally observed by Protestants.

Roman Catholic doctrine teaches that after death, the souls of those who were faithful to the church are granted eternal life. However, a soul must be free from sin to gain entrance into heaven. At the time of death, very few souls are completely free of all sin. Most souls must wait in purgatory until they are purified. Only then will they be able to enter heaven and join the full community of saints and faithful deceased.

It is believed that time spent in purgatory can be shortened by prayers offered on behalf of the souls of the deceased. For this reason, Catholics are encouraged to pray throughout the year for the souls of their departed friends and family. On All Souls Day, the whole Catholic community prays for the souls of all the dead, particularly those who may have been forgotten or had no one to pray for them at the time of their death.

The general tone of All Souls Day is very somber. The day focuses on souls in purgatory and the desire to help loved ones into heaven. Although it is not required for Catholics to attend church services on this day, many choose to do so. Visiting the cemetery is also commonly done on All Souls Day.

Customs and Symbols

Colors

The Catholic Church uses special liturgical colors on All Souls Day. The inside of the church may be draped in black, symbolizing grief and death. In addition, the priest may wear black vestments when saying mass. Purple, signifying humility and repentance, is also associated with All Souls Day.

Prayers

Praying for the souls of the departed is thought to shorten their time in purgatory. Traditionally, Catholics offer one set of 18 prayers for the souls of each of their deceased loved ones. This set includes six each of the Catholic Our Father, Hail Mary, and Glory Be prayers. Many Catholics choose to pray the rosary, either in whole or in part, for the benefit of departed souls. Additional unstructured prayers dedicated to the souls of the departed may also be offered.

Requiem Mass

The Requiem Mass is sometimes called the Funeral Mass, the Mass for the Dead, or the Mass of Christian Burial. Offered at funerals, on the anniversary of a loved one's death, and on All Souls Day, the Requiem Mass is thought to assist souls on their journey from purgatory to heaven. The Requiem Mass includes the chanting, singing, or recitation of the Office of the Dead, a special cycle of prayers for the deceased.

Normally, Catholic priests are only allowed to offer one mass each day. On All Souls Day, however, each priest can preside over three Requiem Masses. One is offered for any particular intention, another for the souls of all the faithful departed, and the last in support of the intentions of the pope.

Visiting the Cemetery

Catholics normally visit the graves of deceased loved ones on All Souls Day or on the evening before. At the gravesite, they offer prayers for the deceased and often place candles or flowers on the grave.

Web Sites

"All Saints and All Souls," by Fr. William Saunders, CatholicEducation.org, 2002.
    http://www.catholiceducation.org/articles/religion/re0199.html

"Feast of All Souls." AmericanCatholic.org, undated.
    http://www.americancatholic.org/Features/SaintOfDay/default.asp?id=1187

Further Reading

"All Souls Day." *The Columbia Electronic Encyclopedia*. 6th ed. New York: Columbia University Press, 2006.

Thompson, Sue Ellen, ed. "All Souls Day." In *Holiday Symbols and Customs*. 3rd ed. Detroit: Omnigraphics, 2003.

CHING MING

Alternate Names: Qing Ming, Grave Sweeping Day, Tomb Sweeping Day, Spring Remembrance

Customs and Symbols: Food, Offerings, Visiting the Cemetery, Willow

Ching Ming is the annual Chinese day of remembrance of the dead. It is similar in purpose to the Mexican **Día de los Muertos** and the Roman Catholic **All Souls Day**. Families observe Ching Ming by visiting the cemetery and making offerings of food and other items for the enjoyment of the spirits of deceased loved ones.

History and Significance

Ching Ming is a national holiday in China that can be traced back as early as the Han Dynasty (206 B.C.E. to 220 C.E.) The day began as a celebration of the arrival of spring and originally included kite flying, picnics, and other outdoor activities. Over time the day became more focused on honoring deceased ancestors, and it has grown to be one of the most important annual Chinese cultural and religious events.

Observance

Ching Ming is observed early in the third lunar month of the Chinese calendar, usually on April 5. The name Ching Ming, meaning "clear brightness," refers to the mild weather in China at this time of year. For this reason, Ching Ming is sometimes also known as Spring Remembrance.

According to traditional Chinese beliefs, the spirits of the deceased pass into the underworld where they experience life in much the same way as they did on earth. Spirits continue to interact with living family members, and the nature of this interaction depends on how well the family continues to care for the deceased. Those who properly observe Ching Ming will receive help from the spirits and benefit from increased happiness, success, and good fortune. By contrast, neglected spirits can take revenge on the living, bringing bad luck and misfortune.

> Over time Ching Ming became more focused on honoring deceased ancestors, and it has grown to be one of the most important annual Chinese cultural and religious events.

Many Chinese Americans observe Ching Ming, particularly those of older generations. Families visit the cemetery to care for the gravesite and make offerings in honor of deceased ancestors. Depending on the size of the Chinese-American community and the policies of the local cemetery, there may be a ceremonial procession or public prayer service. The atmosphere is normally one of respect, remembrance, and community.

In parts of the U.S. with large Chinese-American communities, cemeteries offer special services for Ching Ming. Rose Hills Memorial Park in Los Angeles, California, estimates an average of 15,000 visitors for Ching Ming each year. The Historic Chinese American Cemetery of San Jose, California, also hosts a heavily attended Ching Ming ceremony.

Customs and Symbols

Food

Families arrange offerings of food on the grave for the spirit's enjoyment. This can be any kind of food that was preferred by the deceased in life, but often includes fruit, rice, roast chicken or pork, cakes, wine, and tea. Once the spirits have had a chance to enjoy the "essence," or aroma, of the food, family members may share the food in a gravesite picnic.

Offerings

Although spirits live in the underworld, it is believed that they still need the necessities and comforts of life, and they depend on the living to provide these. Families make offerings to ensure that spirits are happy. Offerings are made by burning paper representations of common items such as cars, houses, and clothing, and the smoke carries the items to the underworld. Paper models are made for everything imaginable, even luxuries such as widescreen televisions and swimming pools. Some of these models are extremely detailed and can measure up to six feet high. A common offering is special paper money for the spirits to spend in the afterlife, sometimes known as "Heaven Money."

Visiting the Cemetery

Because families visit the cemetery primarily to clean and maintain the graves of deceased loved ones, Ching Ming is sometimes known as Grave Sweeping Day or Tomb Sweeping Day. After any weeds are removed and grass is neatly trimmed, grave markers may be repainted. Family members lay out offerings of food and fresh flowers and incense is burned. Traditionally, family members then take turns bowing in front of the grave, three times each, cupping their right fist in their left hand in front of themselves.

Willow

Because neglected spirits sometimes become angry that no one has come to honor them during Ching Ming, some people use the branches of a willow tree to keep these evil spirits away. Traditionally, willow sprigs are hung over doorways, placed next to graves and tombs, or worn in the hair. One old belief is that anyone who chooses not to wear a willow sprig on Ching Ming can expect to be reborn as a yellow dog in their next life.

Web Sites

"Celebration of Tomb Sweeping Day (Qing Ming Jie)." Chinese Culture Center of San Francisco, 2000.
    http://www.c-c-c.org/chineseculture/festival/qingming/qingming.html

Historic Chinese American Cemetery of San Jose, undated.
    http://chinesehistoriccemetery.org

Rose Hills Memorial Park (Los Angeles, California), undated.
    http://www.rosehills.com

Further Reading

Khanh, Truong Phuoc. "Chinese Observe Day of Dead Today: Ching Ming Ceremony Took Place at Once-Segregated S.J. Burial Plot." *San Jose Mercury News*, April 5, 2006.

Ramirez, Marc. "Ching Ming Celebration Honors Chinese Ancestors." *Seattle Times*, April 2, 2006.

Vo, Kim. "Cemeteries Increasingly Accommodate Different Cultures." *San Jose Mercury News*, April 13, 2004.

DÍA DE LOS MUERTOS

Alternate Name: Todos Santos

Customs and Symbols: Altars, Flowers, Food, Offerings, Parade, Skeletons and Skulls, Vigil, Visiting the Cemetery

Día de los Muertos, or Day of the Dead, is an annual holiday observed primarily by Mexican Americans. It is a festive time of remembering and celebrating the lives of those who have died, whether in the preceding year or long ago. Typical Día de los Muertos activities include constructing an altar to honor the deceased, preparing special food, visiting the cemetery where loved ones are buried, and laying out offerings (*ofrendas*).

History and Significance

The origins of Día de los Muertos (pronounced *DEE-ah day los MWAIR-tose*) can be traced back nearly 3,000 years to the ancient Aztec people, who observed a month-long festival that included memorials for the deceased. When the Aztecs were conquered by Spain in the early 1500s, Aztec beliefs began to blend with those of Roman Catholicism. Día de los Muertos eventually overlapped with the Catholic All Saints Day and **All Souls Day** (normally November 1 and 2, respectively). Although Spanish missionaries tried to stifle the Aztec culture and way of life, Día de los Muertos celebrations continued. Many of the old Aztec customs, such as decorating gravesites and making offerings to the dead, are still practiced by Mexican Americans today.

Observance

Observance of Día de los Muertos varies widely according to geographic location, community and family traditions, and individual preference. Parades are sometimes held, public or community altars are built, and there may be prayer ceremonies in the cemetery or other public space. Regardless of these differences, nearly all Día de los Muertos celebrations include these important elements: building an altar, making offerings, and, if possible, visiting the cemetery.

Even the dates for Día de los Muertos can vary. In some areas, Día de los Muertos is a three-day holiday beginning October 31 and ending November 2. Some celebrations last for a week or more, while others are held only on November 2.

However, most observances occur on November 1 and 2, with preparations, such as the building of an altar, begun well in advance.

It is generally believed that the spirits of those who have died will return to visit their loved ones during Día de los Muertos. The exact day and time of a spirit's expected return varies according to the dates for observing the holiday. Those who observe Día de los Muertos only on November 2 believe that all spirits return home on that day. Those who observe Día de los Muertos over three days believe that spirits of deceased children (*los angelitos,* or little angels) return to their families beginning in the afternoon of October 31. This day is sometimes known as *Día de los Angelitos* (Day of the Little Angels) or *Día de los Niños* (Day of the Children). Adult spirits are then thought to return to their loved ones beginning in the afternoon of November 1. The night of November 1 is sometimes called *Noche de los Muertos* (Night of the Dead) while November 2 is sometimes known as *Día de los Difuntos* (Day of the Faithful Dead).

In anticipation of the spirits' return, families prepare special food and offerings to welcome them. When spirits arrive at the gravesite or at the home altar, they may enjoy the offerings as well as the company of their loved ones for a short time.

In anticipation of the spirits' return, families prepare special food and offerings to welcome them. The evening of November 1 is a popular time for visiting the cemetery, and those who do this normally bring along offerings to place on the grave. Depending on geographic location and local custom, people may keep a vigil at the cemetery, waiting all night for the spirits of their loved ones to arrive. Some stay at the cemetery only until midnight, and some who leave may return to the gravesite before sunrise on November 2. Still others may keep a vigil at home. When spirits arrive at the gravesite or at the home altar, they may enjoy the offerings as well as the company of their loved ones for a short time. Visiting spirits are believed to return to their graves on November 3.

Día de los Muertos is publicly observed in areas with large Hispanic communities, particularly throughout the southwestern U.S. Many public events are held each year in the city of Phoenix, Arizona, with an annual calendar of festivities published by AZCentral.com. The Museum of Northern Arizona in Flagstaff also sponsors public events in observance of the day. The Mexic-Arte Museum in Austin, Texas, offers special programming for the day each year. The city of Albuquerque, New Mexico, also hosts many Día de los Muertos events, with an events calendar published each year by the *Albuquerque Tribune.*

Customs and Symbols

Altars

Most Día de los Muertos celebrants build at least one altar at home to honor deceased loved ones. Communities sometimes create public altars in remembrance of all those who have died in the past year, such as soldiers at war, police officers and fire fighters who died in the line of duty, or victims of natural disasters.

Home altars are usually made on a table, on top of another piece of furniture such as a chest of drawers, or on a shelf. Some elaborate altars are constructed with three tiers that represent heaven, earth, and purgatory (a place where it is believed that souls are purified before entrance into heaven; *see* **All Souls Day**). Each altar is an intensely personal expression of its creator's memories of the deceased, and as a result, every altar is unique. The altar is usually, but not always, covered with a white cloth, and offerings are then placed on the altar.

Flowers

Marigolds are the traditional flower of the dead and are used liberally in Día de los Muertos celebrations. They are woven into garlands and necklaces, placed on altars and gravesites, and thrown from floats in parades. Marigolds are also strewn on the ground to mark a path that guides spirits on their journey home. The particular scent of marigolds is thought to attract the spirits of the deceased.

Other flowers that are used during Día de los Muertos include cockscomb, white gypsophila, gladioli, and carnations. Decorative flowers are also made out of crepe paper or tissue paper and used to adorn altars and graves.

Food

Certain special foods are prepared and eaten only during Día de los Muertos, most notably *pan de muerto* (bread of the dead). Pan de muerto is sweet egg bread that is normally round and often baked with bits of dough placed on top to form skeletons or skulls and crossed bones. Pan de muerto can also be made in the shape of bones, people, or animals. Sometimes the loaves are decorated with colored sugar on top.

Sugar candies in the shape of skulls or skeletons are another popular food reserved for Día de los Muertos. These sweet treats are a particular favorite of children, and are often included in offerings.

Other traditional Mexican holiday foods are also enjoyed during Día de los Muertos. These include *mole* (chicken or turkey in a sauce made with chocolate, chile peppers, and sesame seeds), *tamales* (corn dough stuffed with meat or vegetables and wrapped in corn husks), pumpkin candy, chocolate, and fruit. *Atole*, a thick beverage made of corn cooked with milk or water and spices, is sometimes also served.

Offerings (Ofrendas)

Offerings are gifts to the spirits that are placed on altars or at gravesites. (Some people use the term "offerings" to refer to the altar itself as well as the items on the altar.) Just as each altar is unique, offerings also vary according to the tastes, interests, and personality of the deceased. Offerings include anything that was loved and enjoyed by the deceased in life, such as music, toys, personal items, clothing, or jewelry. In addition, offerings usually include items that represent the deceased in some way, for example symbols of a beloved hobby or occupation. Candles, flowers, incense, *papeles picados* (colored paper with elaborate designs cut out), favorite food and drinks, and photos of the deceased are common offerings.

The Meaning of Offerings

Some offerings have a particular meaning when included on an altar:

Candles provide light to guide the spirit and heat to warm them when they arrive.

Empty chairs placed next to the altar welcome spirits.

Incense guides the spirits.

Pan de muerto or other food nourishes spirits.

Salt purifies the spirits.

Sugar skulls represent the sweetness of life and the sadness of death.

A washbasin or clean hand towel allow spirits to refresh themselves.

Water quenches the spirit's thirst and also cleanses the spirit.

A woven mat, or *patate*, gives spirits a place to rest.

A figure of a dog represents the belief that when a person dies, he or she is met at the edge of a river by a dog that dances with them, and then swims them across the river to the land of the dead.

Parade

A Día de Los Muertos parade may be held in places with a large Mexican-American population. These parades include dancers, musicians, marchers carrying portable altars, floats displaying huge coffins or skeletons, and other images of the dead. People in the parade and also those watching often dress in costumes representing those they have lost in the past year. Parades may be a procession through town to the local cemetery, or they may lead to a public space where a communal altar has been constructed.

Skeletons and Skulls

The skeleton and the skull are perhaps the most widely recognized symbols of Día de Los Muertos, and they appear in every imaginable size and shape. There are dancing skeletons made with bouncing arms and legs, edible skulls made out of bread or sugar, life-sized and miniature skeletons, and skulls that can be worn as a mask. Especially popular are the handmade figurines called *calacas*, which are skeletons posed in activities such as taking a bath, riding a horse, playing a piano, performing surgery, typing, reading, and anything else that a living person might do. Calacas are commonly used on altars and as gravesite decorations to represent the deceased.

Vigil

People waiting for the spiritual return of their loved ones often keep a vigil, meaning they stay up all night to watch for the spirit's arrival. Offerings are laid out to welcome the spirits. Flowers are sometimes strewn along a path to the home altar or gravesite in order to help the spirit find its way. Whether the vigil is held in the cemetery or at home, it is usually not a somber occasion. People normally use the time to share stories and memories of the deceased person. They may also choose to sing, dance, listen to music, play games, or engage in some activity that the deceased person enjoyed in life. Some people tell stories of events that occurred in the previous year, in order to keep the deceased informed of family news. A meal dedicated to the deceased is usually shared by those keeping watch, and special food is set out for the deceased to enjoy. It is believed that spirits consume only the "essence," or aroma, of the food. The actual food is either disposed of in a special ceremony or it is eaten later by the deceased person's loved ones.

Visiting the Cemetery

A visit to the gravesite is one of the most universal customs of Día de los Muertos. Family members tend to the gravesite by cleaning grave markers and making any necessary repairs. Weeds are removed and grass is cut if needed. The gravesite is then decorated with a variety of objects intended to please the deceased. These decorations might include streamers made of ribbons or colored paper, flags, flowers, candles, or artwork such as colored paper with elaborate designs cut out. Some people choose to paint grave markers or crypts in bright colors, usually some combination of blue, yellow, and pink. When the gravesite is sufficiently cleaned and decorated, offerings are placed on the grave. The amount of time spent at the gravesite varies according to geographic location, family tradition, and individual preference.

Web Sites

"Día de los Muertos, Day of the Dead." Azcentral.com, 2005.
http://www.azcentral.com/ent/dead

Mexic-Arte Museum, Austin, Texas, undated.
http://www.mexic-artemuseum.org/index.html

Museum of Northern Arizona, Flagstaff, undated.
http://www.musnaz.org

Further Reading

Barol, J. M. "Embracing One's Fears: Día de los Muertos Could Change Your Relationship with Death." *Albuquerque (NM) Tribune*, October 21, 2005.

Carmichael, Elizabeth, and Chloe Sayer. *The Skeleton at the Feast: The Day of the Dead in Mexico.* Austin: University of Texas Press, 1992.

"Halloween and Festivals of the Dead in Mexico." In *Junior Worldmark Encyclopedia of World Holidays.* Edited by Robert H. Griffin and Ann H. Shurgin. Vol. 2. Detroit: U*X*L, 2000.

Hoang, Vivi. "Spirits Live on Day of the Dead: Mexican Tradition of Dia de los Muertos Pays Respect to Deceased through Offerings, Communion." *Tennessean*, October 27, 2006.

Jacobs, Andrew. "As Joyous as It Is Macabre; A Mexican Holiday Ensures the Dead Have Their Day." *New York Times*, November 3, 1999.

Menard, Valerie. *The Latino Holiday Book: From Cinco de Mayo to Día de los Muertos—The Celebrations and Traditions of Hispanic-Americans.* New York: Marlowe and Co., 2004.

FORTY-NINTH DAY MEMORIAL

Alternate Name: Sanghika Dana

Customs and Symbols: Altar, Charity toward Monks

Buddhists believe that the circumstances of each soul's rebirth are determined during an intermediate state beginning immediately after death. The forty-ninth day memorial service is thought to facilitate a fortunate reincarnation of the deceased's soul.

History and Significance

Buddhism teaches that immediately upon death, the souls of deceased persons enter into a phase called the *Bardo* (intermediate state) of Becoming. This phase, lasting no longer than forty-nine days, is the critical time in which the soul's rebirth is determined. Buddhists believe that rebirth can be influenced through spiritual practice performed by relatives and friends of the deceased. During the first three weeks after death, it is believed that the dead can more easily benefit from practice done on their behalf. However, the most powerful time to influence the soul's future is on the forty-ninth day after death, when the intermediate state comes to an end and rebirth occurs.

Observance

The family members and/or Buddhist friends of the deceased normally arrange for the forty-ninth day service to take place either at home or at the temple or monastery. Monks and other practitioners are invited to participate in special prayers, chants, and meditations done for the benefit of the deceased, along with a ceremony of charity toward monks called *sanghika dana*.

Customs and Symbols

Altar

During the forty-nine days after death, some Buddhists maintain a home altar in memory of their deceased loved one. The altar is usually taken down after the forty-nine day period is complete, as it is believed that the deceased has by that time been reborn into another existence.

Charity toward Monks (Sanghika Dana)

In performing sanghika dana, the family of the deceased offers gifts of goods or money to the monastery in the name of the deceased. It is believed that by assigning merits to the deceased through this act of giving, the deceased may quickly experience a fortunate rebirth.

Web Sites

His Holiness the Fourteenth Dalai Lama. "Death, Intermediate State, and Rebirth." Amitabha Hospice Service, undated.
> http://www.amitabhahospice.org/hospice/Death-interm_rebirth.php

"When to Practice for Someone Who Has Died." Spiritual Care Program, 2006.
> http://www.spcare.org/practices/suddendeath/afterdeath-whentopractice.html

Further Reading

Erricker, Clive. *Buddhism.* Lincolnwood, IL: NTC Publishing Group, 1995.

Khadro, Sangye. *Preparing for Death and Helping the Dying: A Buddhist Perspective.* Singapore: Kong Meng San Phor Kark See Monastery, 2003.
> http://www.buddhanet.net/pdf_file/death_dying.pdf

OBON FESTIVAL

Alternate Names: Bon Festival, Feast of Lanterns, Urabon

Customs and Symbols: Lanterns, Obon Dancing

Obon is a Buddhist holiday in which the dead are remembered, honored, and welcomed back for a visit to their homes and families. It is traditionally celebrated from the 15th to the 17th days of the seventh month of the year, which coincides with July and August in the Gregorian calendar used in the U.S.

History and Significance

The word obon is an abbreviation of *urabon,* a Japanese version of the Sanskrit word *ullambana,* or "hanging upside down," symbolic of the grief that comes to the household on the death of one of its members. The Obon Festival has its origins in the story of Mokuren, contained in a Buddhist text known as the Ullambana Sutra. In a vision, Mokuren sees his dead mother in the afterlife, where she is suspended in a purgatory of hunger and shadowy ghosts. Dismayed by the vision, Mokuren seeks advice from the Buddha, who admonishes him that his mother lived a life of greed and selfishness and now is paying for her mistakes. In order to release her, the Buddha advises, Mokuren must provide a celebration for the soul of his mother; the feast and the offering of food and dancing performed out of filial piety has its intended effect, and his mother attains her ultimate freedom.

Observance

The Obon holiday emphasizes respect for ancestors and the repaying of one's obligations to them.

In preparation for the return of those who have passed away, families thoroughly clean and sweep their homes. Offerings of food are made at the *abutsudan,* or family altar inside the home. The food offering may include rice, vegetables, fruit, cakes, and sweets. The altar is decorated with flowers and small lanterns, or *chouchin.* The families visit the graves of their ancestors. The graves are swept clean and given offerings of fruit and flowers. If someone in the household has died within the past year, a special *hatsubon* observance is carried out.

By tradition this is a time when people return to their hometowns for a few days to honor their ancestors. At the home, lamps are lit and placed in the doorway to guide the souls of the dead back to their homes. A monk may arrive to perform a chant, while neighbors and friends come by the house to pay their respects.

In the U.S., observances may last up to a week. The holiday emphasizes respect for ancestors and the repaying of one's obligations to them. At the end of the festival, in the ritual known as *Toro Nagashi,* lanterns are set adrift in streams, lakes, and the sea to guide the spirits back to the afterlife.

Customs and Symbols

Lanterns

Lanterns are an important part of Obon observances, used symbolically to light the way for the spirits of ancestors. Usually bright red in color, they shine outside temples, homes, cemeteries, and wherever public festivities are held.

Obon Dancing

The custom of public dancing during the Obon Festival dates back several centuries. The dancers may include men, women, and children, who wear kimonos and dance to music in a great circle around a *yagura* or wooden platform decorated with paper lanterns. While the Obon dance is an important public event in Japan, in the U.S. it may take place within a Buddhist temple or sanctuary as well as during a street festival.

Web Sites

"Belief and Practice: Buddhist Obon Festival." Religion & Ethics Newsweekly, PBS, July 18, 2003.
    http://www.pbs.org/wnet/religionandethics/week646/belief.html

"Obon." Buddhist Church of Sacramento, CA, undated.
    http://www.buddhistchurch.com/events/Obon.htm

"2006 Obon Festival—July 8 and 9." San Jose Buddhist Church Betsuin, CA, undated.
    http://www.sjbetsuin.com/events%20pages/events_obon2006.htm

Further Reading

Matsunami, Kodo. *International Handbook of Funeral Customs.* Westport, CT: Greenwood Press, 1998.

Thompson, Sue Ellen, ed. "Obon Festival." In *Holiday Symbols and Customs.* 3rd ed. Detroit: Omnigraphics, 2003.

ONE-YEAR MEMORIALS

Alternate Names: Panikhidas, Requiem, Shraddha, Yahrzeit

Customs and Symbols: Charitable Acts, Prayers, Requiem Mass, Visiting the Cemetery

The first anniversary of the death of a loved one is given special remembrance in many religious traditions. One-year memorials commonly include prayers or special services offered in memory of the deceased.

History and Significance

Throughout history, people of many different faiths and cultures have observed a one-year mourning period after the death of a loved one. During this year, mourners were often expected to wear special clothing, usually in black or other dark colors, and to refrain from participating in social or recreational activities. The end of the mourning period was marked by a special memorial service.

The first year after a loved one's death can be especially difficult for the bereaved. In many cases, the one-year memorial signals an end to the initial period of intense mourning and can assist the bereaved in returning to normal life.

Although these formalized mourning customs are no longer widely observed, it is generally accepted that the first year after a loved one's death can be especially difficult for the bereaved. In many cases, the one-year memorial signals an end to the initial period of intense mourning and can assist the bereaved in returning to normal life.

Observance

Orthodox Christian Memorial services are held at several points after a loved one's death, including on the first anniversary of the death and every year thereafter. Known as *Panikhidas*, these memorials are usually held in conjunction with or immediately after regular Sunday church services. Roman Catholics offer Requiem Masses for the dead, including prayers for the souls of deceased loved ones. Visiting the cemetery where a loved one is buried is also commonly done on the anniversary day or the evening before. The Jewish ceremony of *Yahrzeit* (literally, "one year's time") includes the recitation of prayers and the lighting of a memorial candle that is left to burn itself out.

The Hindu one-year memorial ceremony is called *shraddha*. Performed to honor the memory of the departed, the ceremony includes prayers and a ritual meal. Priests are invited to the shraddha to represent the deceased, and in that capacity they are treated as honored guests. Many Hindus strive to observe the first shraddha at a holy place such as a shrine or pilgrimage site in India. Subsequent annual shraddha ceremonies are then performed at home.

Customs and Symbols

Charitable Acts

For the one-year memorial of a loved one's death, Hindus and Buddhists commonly perform charitable acts for the benefit of the soul of the departed. The Hindu priests who attend the shraddha ceremony are usually given cash gifts at the end of the meal. Buddhists observe a similar custom by offering alms or gifts at a temple or monastery. These acts of charity are done to confer merit upon the soul of the deceased in the hope of affecting a positive reincarnation.

Prayers

Many Christian denominations emphasize the importance of praying for the souls of the departed on the first anniversary of the death. Many Catholics choose to pray the rosary, either in whole or in part, for the benefit of departed souls. Jewish Yahrzeit tradition includes the recitation of the *Kaddish*, a special prayer for peace and comfort for those in mourning (*see* **Aninut**). During shraddha, Hindus recite prayers from the *Shraddha-Kalpa*, a book of instructions for conducting the shraddha ceremony.

Requiem Mass

The Requiem Mass is thought to assist souls on their journey from purgatory to heaven, and is offered as a one-year memorial and also on Catholic holy days such as **All Souls Day**. The Requiem Mass includes the chanting, singing, or recitation of the Office of the Dead, a special cycle of prayers for the deceased.

Visiting the Cemetery

People of all faiths often visit the graves of deceased loved ones in observance of the first anniversary of death. At the gravesite, they offer prayers for the deceased and often place candles or flowers on the grave.

Web Sites

"Prayers for the Departed." Orthodox Church in America, undated. http://www.oca.org/QA.asp?ID=170&SID=3

Zinner, Ellen. "A Year Is a Relative Thing." Hospice Foundation of America, undated. http://www.hospicefoundation.org/griefAndLoss/year.asp

Further Reading

Erricker, Clive. *Buddhism.* Lincolnwood, IL: NTC Publishing Group, 1995.

Kanitkar, V. P., and W. Owen Cole. *Hinduism.* Lincolnwood, IL: NTC Publishing Group, 1995.

Weber, Vicki L., ed. *The Rhythm of Jewish Time: An Introduction to Holidays and Life-Cycle Events.* West Orange, NJ: Behrman House, 1999.

ORTHODOX CHRISTIAN MEMORIALS

Alternate Names: Trisagion Prayers for the Dead, Panikhidas

Customs and Symbols: Boiled Wheat (Koliva), Candles, Mourning, Prayers

Orthodox Christian churches hold memorials for deceased individuals at significant intervals following the date of death. Memorial services for all of the faithful departed are held periodically throughout the church year.

History and Significance

Orthodox churches teach that the souls of the deceased are subject to a partial judgment by God immediately after death occurs. During this time, souls experience a preview of heaven or hell, depending on the deceased's general behavior and level of communion with God in life. It is believed that full judgment of all souls will occur on the final judgment day for all humanity, known as the Second Coming of Christ. Orthodox Christians believe that on judgment day, all the souls of the departed will be resurrected and ascend into heaven or descend into hell.

Observance

Deceased individuals are remembered at special memorial services held during the period of mourning, on the Sunday closest to the third, ninth, and 40th day after death. The memorial of the third day is a commemoration of the resurrection of Christ, while the ninth-day memorial is intended as a traditional reminder of the deceased. The 40th-day memorial commemorates Christ's ascension into heaven. After the 40th day, services are held on the yearly anniversary of the individual's death. These memorials are usually held in conjunction with or immediately after regular Sunday church services.

Memorial services are offered for all departed souls on four Saturdays during the Orthodox Church year. Known as the Saturdays of the Souls, these days include the two Saturdays before the beginning of Lent, the first Saturday of Lent, and the Saturday before Pentecost. Orthodox churches in the U.S. usually also hold a special service on the Memorial Day holiday.

Traditionally, the family of the deceased individual prepares a boiled wheat dish known as *koliva* and brings this to the

> *Orthodox Christian churches hold memorials for deceased individuals at significant intervals following the date of death.*

425

memorial service as an offering. Prayers are offered for the comfort of the departed soul, and candles may be distributed to those attending the service.

Customs and Symbols

Boiled Wheat (Koliva)

Koliva is a traditional mixture of boiled hulled wheat or barley, sugar, and other ingredients, such as honey, dried fruit, nuts, and spices. This dish originated in the early days of the Orthodox Church, when St. Theodore of Tyre instructed the faithful to prepare it in order to avoid consuming food that had been deliberately tainted by Julian the Apostate, the pagan emperor of Constantinople.

Over time, koliva came to be associated with memorials and belief in the resurrection of the dead. The Bible reports that Jesus explained resurrection by saying, "Truly, truly, I say to you, unless a grain of wheat falls into the earth and dies, it re-

---

A Recipe for Koliva

4 cups hulled wheat
1–2 cups chopped walnuts
2 cups raisins
2 teaspoons cinnamon

For the topping:
2 cups zwieback or graham cracker crumbs
2 cups powdered sugar
white almonds

Two days before the memorial, soak the wheat overnight in enough water to cover it. Drain and rinse it, then cover with water and bring to a boil. Turn down the heat and let it simmer for several hours, making sure to keep enough water in the pot to cover the wheat. Cook until the wheat becomes tender. Drain and rinse twice, then spread the wheat out on a towel to dry overnight.

On the morning of the memorial, mix the wheat with the walnuts, raisins, and cinnamon. Transfer mixture to a large tray and mold unto a mound. Spread the zwieback or graham crackers to cover the top surface of the mound. Sprinkle powdered sugar over the top of the mound, then make a cross with the almonds.

---

mains alone, but if it dies it bears much fruit" (John 12:24, 12:31-35). After the memorial service, the boiled wheat is eaten by the mourners in remembrance of the deceased.

Candles

Lit candles customarily symbolize the resurrection of the dead, as Orthodox Christians view Christ as the light of the world. The bereaved family sometimes gives candles to the clergy and members of the congregation who attend the memorial service.

Mourning

Orthodox Christians observe a period of mourning for the first 40 days after the death of a loved one. During this time, mourners often avoid social gatherings and sometimes wear only black clothing.

Prayers

Orthodox Christians believe that the fate of departed souls in the afterlife is determined by the actions and behaviors of individuals during their lives on earth. Although there is no expectation that prayers offered for the deceased will change the final judgment, it is believed that prayers will comfort the souls of those who have died. The Orthodox Church encourages the faithful to pray for the dead in part because by doing so, the faithful are reminded of their own eventual death and the need to prepare for their own judgment.

Web Sites

"Death, Funeral, Requiem—Orthodox Christian Traditions, Customs, and Practice," by Archpriest Victor Sokolov, Holy Trinity Orthodox Cathedral (San Francisco, CA), 1997.

http://www.holy-trinity.org/liturgics/sokolov-death.html

"The Funeral Service of the Orthodox Church," by Fr. Nektarios Morrow, Greek Orthodox Archdiocese of America, 2005.

http://www.goarch.org/print/en/ourfaith/article9218.asp

"Praying for the Dead," by Phyllis Meshel Onest, *Orthodox Family Life*, undated.

http://www.theologic.com/oflweb/inhome/prydead.htm

"Special Services and Blessings," by Rev. Thomas Fitzgerald, Greek Orthodox Archdiocese of America, 1996.

http://www.goarch.org/en/ourfaith/articles/article7113.asp

Further Reading

Constantelos, Demetrios J. *Understanding the Greek Orthodox Church: Its Faith, History, and Practice.* New York: The Seabury Press, 1982.

Harakas, Stanley S. *The Orthodox Church: 455 Questions and Answers.* Minneapolis, MN: Light and Life Publishing Co., 1987.

Matlins, Stuart M. *The Perfect Stranger's Guide to Funerals and Grieving Practices.* Woodstock, VT: Skylight Paths Publishing, 2000.

Rouvelas, Marilyn. *A Guide to Greek Traditions and Customs in America.* Bethesda, MD: Nea Attiki Press, 1993.

Bibliography

Bibliography

This bibliography lists books, articles, and web sites consulted in the preparation of this volume.

Abiff, I. C. "The History and Uses of Henna." IslamOnline.net, 2001.
http://www.islamonline.net/english/Science/2001/10/article3.shtml

"About Unitarian Universalism." Unitarian Universalist Association, 1995.
http://www.uua.org/aboutuu

Adams, Gary A. and Kenneth S. Shultz. "Retirement." In *Encyclopedia of Industrial and Organization Psychology.* Edited by Steven Rogelberg. Thousand Oaks, CA: Sage Reference, 2007.

"African Gifts for Life Rights of Passage Program." Asomdwee Fie, Shrine of the Abosom and Nsamanfo, Inc. (AFSANI), undated.
http://www.afsani.org/agfl.htm

"African-American Wedding Guide: Rites of Passage." WeddingChannel.com, 1998.
http://www.weddingchannel.com/ui/buildArticle.action?assetUID=3805&c=3805&s=84&t=71&p=5630936

Al-Jibaly, Muhammad. *The Quest for Love and Mercy: Regulations for Marriage and Wedding in Islam.* Beirut, Lebanon: Al-Maktab Al-Islaami, 2000.

"All about Sikhs," undated.
http://allaboutsikhs.com

"All Souls Day." *The Columbia Electronic Encyclopedia.* 6th ed. Columbia University Press, 2006.

al-Misri, Ahmad Ibn Naqib. *Reliance of the Traveller: The Classic Manual of Islamic Sacred Law.* Edited by Nuh Ha Mim Keller. Brentwood, MD: Amana Corporation, 1997.

Ancelet, Barry Jean, Jay Dearborn Edwards, and Glen Pitre. *Cajun Country.* Jackson, MS: University Press of Mississippi, 1991.

"Anointing of the Sick." Catholic Answers, undated.
http://www.catholic.com/library/Anointing_of_the_Sick.asp

"Anointing of the Sick." *The Columbia Electronic Encyclopedia.* 6th ed. Columbia University Press, 2006.

"The Aqiqah for Newborns." The Message of Islam for People Who Think, March 6, 1999.
  http://www.geocities.com/forpeoplewhothink/Answers/Aqiqah.html

Arenz, Kathleen. "Debutantes Come Out at Annual Balls." JS Online *(Milwaukee Journal-Sentinel),* December 8, 2002.
  http://www.jsonline.com/story/index.aspx?id=101319

"Article 2: The Sacrament of Confirmation." United States Conference of Catholic Bishops, undated.
  http://www.usccb.org/catechism/text/pt2sect2chpt1art2.htm

"Attendants: A Glossary of Who's Who in the Wedding Party," The Knot, undated.
  http://www.theknot.com/ch_article.html?Object=AI91217122324&keywordID
  =163&keywordType=2&parentID=527

"Aum" or "Om." Hindunet, undated.
  http://www.hindunet.org/aum

"Background of Selective Service." Selective Service System. April 18, 2007.
  http://www.sss.gov/backgr.htm

Bailey, Beth L. *From Front Porch to Back Seat: Courtship in Twentieth-Century America.* Baltimore, MD: Johns Hopkins University Press, 1988.

Baker, Margaret. *Wedding Customs and Folklore.* Totowa, NJ: Rowman and Littlefield, 1977.

Ball, Joanne Dubbs, and Caroline Torem-Craig. *Wedding Traditions: Here Comes the Bride.* Dubuque, IA: Antique Trader Books, 1997.

Bamberger, Michael. Wonderland: *A Year in the Life of an American High School.* New York: Atlantic Monthly Press, 2004.

Bankhead, Donna, and Lynnette Blas. *Last Minute Weddings.* Franklin Lakes, NJ: Career Press, 1999.

"Baptism," "Catechumen," "Chrism," "Holy Oils," and "Holy Water." *The Catholic Encyclopedia.* Available online at New Advent.
  http://www.newadvent.org/cathen

"Baptism Integrity," undated.
  http://www.baptism.org.uk

"Baptism Preparation." St. Francis of Assisi Parish, undated.
  http://stfrancisa2.com/baptism.htm

Barks, Coleman, trans. *The Essential Rumi.* New York: HarperCollins, 1995.

Barol, J.M. "Embracing One's Fears: Día de los Muertos Could Change Your Relationship with Death." *Albuquerque (NM) Tribune,* October 21, 2005.

Bartos, Patricia. "Remember the Faithful Departed." *Pittsburgh Catholic,* October 20, 2006. http://www.pittsburghcatholic.org/newsarticles_more.phtml?id=1788

Bautista, Edna. *Viva el amor: The Latino Wedding Planner, a Practical Guide for Arranging a Traditional Ceremony and a Fabulous Fiesta.* New York: Fireside, 2001.

Becher, Mordechai. *The Gateway to Judaism: The What, How, and Why of Jewish Life.* Brooklyn, NY: Artscroll Mesorah, 2005. http://www.artscroll.com/Gateway%20to%20Judaism.pdf

Bennett, Roger, Jules Shell, and Nick Kroll. *Bar Mitzvah Disco: The Music May Have Stopped, but the Party's Never Over.* New York: Crown, 2005.

Best, Amy L. *Prom Night: Youth, Schools, and Popular Culture.* New York: Routledge, 2000.

"Bird Myths." Massachusetts Audubon Society, undated. http://www.massaudubon.org/Nature_Connection/wildlife/index.php?subject=Birds:%20General%20Info&id=40

"Birthday Traditions around the World." CyberKisses, undated. http://www.cyberkisses.com/Birthday/birth-traditions.html

"Birthday Trends and Statistics." Hallmark, March 2005. http://pressroom.hallmark.com/birthday_trends_stats.html

"Black College Reunion 2007." *Daytona Beach News-Journal Online,* 2007. http://www.news-journalonline.com/special/bcr

"Black College Reunion Brings Millions to Daytona Area, Expert Says." *Black Issues in Higher Education,* October 25, 2001.

Blum, Mark L. "Death." In *Encyclopedia of Buddhism.* Edited by Robert E. Buswell, Jr. New York: Macmillan Reference USA, 2004.

Boehm, Yohanan. "Horah." In *Encyclopaedia Judaica.* Edited by Michael Berenbaum and Fred Skolnik. Detroit: Macmillan Reference USA, 2007.

Bonvillan, Nancy. *Native American Religion.* New York: Chelsea House, 1996.

Borgatta Edgar F., and Rhonda J. V. Montgomery, eds. *Encyclopedia of Sociology.* New York: Macmillan Reference USA, 2000.

Bose, Sharbari. "The Muslim Wedding Celebration," Brides, undated. http://www.brides.com/weddingstyle/traditions/feature/article/105565

Bradley, Robert. *Husband-Coached Childbirth.* New York: Harper & Row, 1965.

Breuilly, Elizabeth. *Religions of the World: The Illustrated Guide to Origins, Beliefs, Traditions, and Festivals.* New York: Facts on File, 1997.

Bride's magazine. *The Bride's Book of Etiquette.* New York: Penguin, 1999.

"A Brief History of Confirmation." St. James Lutheran Church and School, undated. http://www.stjameslaf.org/confirmation.htm

Brown, Joseph Epes, ed. *The Sacred Pipe: Black Elk's Account of the Seven Rites of the Oglala Sioux.* Norman: University of Oklahoma Press, 1953.

Brownfield, Beth. "Coming of Age/Rites of Passage Programs." Notes prepared for a workshop presented at the Unitarian Universalist General Assembly. N.p., n.d.

Bulcroft, Kris, Linda Smeins, and Richard Bulcroft. *Romancing the Honeymoon: Consummating Marriage in Modern Society.* Thousand Oaks, CA: Sage Publications, 1999.

"Butter and Ghee in India." WebExhibits, undated.
http://webexhibits.org/butter/countries-india.html

"Cambodia: Buddhism." Country Studies (Federal Research Division of the Library of Congress), undated.
http://countrystudies.us/cambodia/48.htm.

Campbell, Carolyn. "Speed Dating: A New Form of Matchmaking," Discovery Health, undated.
http://health.discovery.com/centers/loverelationships/articles/speed_dating.html

Campbell, Joy. "The Dating Scene: Teen Board Panelists Say Group Dating Less Stressful," *Owensboro (KY) Messenger-Inquirer,* October 24, 2006.

Campbell, Richard C. *Two Eagles in the Sun: Your Questions Answered about Mexican Hispanics in the Border Southwest and Other Hispanics in the United States.* Las Cruces, NM: EDITTS Publishing, 1995.

Cantú, Norma Elia. "La Quinceañera: Towards an Ethnographic Analysis of a Life-Cycle Ritual." *Southern Folklore* 56, no. 1 (1999).

Carmichael, Elizabeth and Chloe Sayer. *The Skeleton at the Feast: The Day of the Dead in Mexico.* Austin, TX: University of Texas Press, 1992.

"Case Study: Unyago." Rites of Passage in America: A Traveling Exhibition Organized by the Balch Institute for Ethnic Studies, June 22, 1992-January 2, 1995.
http://www2.hsp.org/exhibits/Balch%20exhibits/rites/afam.html

"A Catholic Confirmation." Request, undated.
http://www.request.org.uk/main/dowhat/confirmation/confirmation05.htm

"Catholic Practices." Catholic Q&A, March 3, 2002.
http://www.catholicqanda.org/FAQ_Library/Other%20Sacraments/Catholic_Baptism_vs_Protestant_Baptism.htm

"Celebrate Freedom: Pigeon Forge Salutes America's Veterans," Celebrate-Freedom.com, undated.
http://www.celebrate-freedom.com

"Celebration of Chinese New Year." Chinese Culture Center of San Francisco, undated.
http://www.c-c-c.org/chineseculture/festival/newyear/newyear.html

"Celebration of Tomb Sweeping Day (Qing Ming Jie)." Chinese Culture Center of San Francisco, 2000.
http://www.c-c-c.org/chineseculture/festival/qingming/qingming.html

"Celtic/Neopagan Handfasting" by B. A. Robinson. Ontario Consultants on Religious Tolerance, April 5, 2005.
http://www.religioustolerance.org/mar_hand.htm

Chick, Garry. "Rites of Passage." In Encyclopedia *of Recreation and Leisure in America.* Edited by Gary S. Cross. Detroit: Charles Scribner's Sons, 2004.

Chidester, David. *Christianity: A Global History.* New York: HarperSanFrancisco, 2000.

"Child's First Birthday (Tol)." Life in Korea, undated.
http://www.lifeinkorea.com/culture/tol/tol.cfm

Chill, Abraham. *The Minhagim: The Customs and Ceremonies of Judaism, Their Origins and Rationale.* New York: Sepher-Hermon Press, 1979.

"Chinese Gender Chart." Baby Gender Prediction, undated.
http://www.babygenderprediction.com/chinese-gender-chart.html

Cho, David. "For Muslims, Courtship Enabled by the Internet." *Washington Post,* June 6, 2004.
http://www.thewashingtonpost.com/wp-dyn/articles/A18646-2004Jun5.html

Clark, Donald N. *Culture and Customs of Korea.* Westport, CT: Greenwood Press, 2000.

Clisby, Heather. "Peach Taffeta Nightmares: The High Price of Being a Bridesmaid," *Santa Barbara Independent,* February 22, 2007.
http://independent.com/news/2007/feb/22/peach-taffeta-nightmares

Cole, Harriette. *Jumping the Broom: The African-American Wedding Planner.* New York: Henry Holt, 2003.

Cole, Harriette. *Vows: The African-American Couples' Guide to Designing a Sacred Ceremony.* New York: Simon and Schuster, 2004.

Cole, Ron. "Learning by Looking to History." The National Rites of Passage Institute, undated.
http://www.ritesofpassage.org/youngstown.htm

Cole, W. Owen, and Piara Singh Sambhi. *The Sikhs: Their Religious Beliefs and Practices.* London: Routledge & Kegan Paul, 1978.

Coleman, James William. *The New Buddhism: The Western Transformation of an Ancient Tradition.* Oxford, U.K.: Oxford University Press, 2001.

Collins, Gerald. "Retirement." In *Encyclopedia of Career Development.* Edited by Jeffrey Greenhaus and Gerard Callanan. Thousand Oaks, CA: Sage Reference, 2006.

"Coming of Age." First Unitarian Church of San José, undated.
http://www.sanjoseuu.org/RE/comingofage.html

"Coming of Age." Web UUs, undated.
http://webuus.com/coa/retreats.shtml

"Coming of Age Programs Include Rewards for All." *InterConnections* 2, No. 4 (August 1999).
http://www.uua.org/interconnections/nourishing/vol2-4-nourishing.html

"Coming of Age 2006." Unitarian Universalist Community Church of Park Forest, Illinois, undated.
http://www.uuccpf.org/coa.htm

"Commencement Program." Oostburg School District, June 2006.
http://www.oostburg.k12.wi.us/ohs/academics/Graduation/Graduation%20Program.htm

"Commencement Program." Patrick Henry High School, June 2006.
http://henry.mpls.k12.mn.us/sites/40ffb804-cceb-41db-92d5-ed0b7a6eb987/uploads/commencement.pdf

"Complete Coverage of Black College Reunion." *Orlando (FL) Sentinel,* 2007.
http://www.orlandosentinel.com/news/local/volusia/orl-bcr-sg,0,3171157.storygallery

Compton, Richard P. "Teen Driver Education." Board on Children, Youth, and Families, May 15, 2006.
http://www.bocyf.org/compton_presentation.pdf

"Confirmation." *The Catholic Encyclopedia,* 1907. Online edition at New Advent.
http://www.newadvent.org/cathen/04215b.htm

"Confirmation." Religious Education Exchange Service, undated.
http://re-xs.ucsm.ac.uk/gcsere/revision/xtianity/ch2/4/2.html

"Confirmation: What's a Parent to Do?" American Catholic.org, undated.
http://www.americancatholic.org/Messenger/May2002/Feature2.asp

Constantelos, Demetrios J. *Understanding the Greek Orthodox Church: Its Faith, History, and Practice.* New York: The Seabury Press, 1982.

"The Constitution of the United States of America: Twenty-Sixth Amendment—Reduction of Voting Age Qualification," U.S. Government Printing Office, November 1, 1996.
http://www.gpoaccess.gov/constitution/html/amdt26.html

Cooper, Susan Lewis, and Ellen Sarasohn Glazer. *Choosing Assisted Reproduction: Social, Emotional, and Ethical Considerations.* Indianapolis, IN: Perspectives Press, 1998.

Cornell, Vincent J. "Integrating the 5 Pillars and Holiest Cities." My School Online, undated.
http://myschoolonline.com/page/0,1871,23327-198473-25-14041,00.html

Craven, Scott. "A Marriage of Aztec, Catholic Cultures." *Hispanic Times Magazine,* Fall 2001.

Craybill, Donald B. "Amish." In *Gale Encyclopedia of Multicultural America.* 2nd ed. Edited by Jeffrey Lehman. Detroit, MI: Gale, 2000.

"Cremation." *New Catholic Encyclopedia.* 2nd ed. Detroit: Gale, 2003.

The Cremation Process: Step by Step. Cremation Association of North America, undated. http://www.cremationassociation.org/docs/stepbystep.pdf

Cripps, Cathy. "History of the Baby Shower." Article City, April 14, 2005. http://www.articlecity.com/articles/women/article_653.shtml

Crouse, Rev. Dr. R. D.. "Baptism, Confirmation, and Holy Communion." The Prayer Book Society of Canada, May 2, 1987. http://www.prayerbook.ca/crouse/writings/baptism_1.htm

"Current Population Survey, 2005 Annual Social and Economic Supplement, Table UC1: Opposite Sex Unmarried Partner Household." U.S. Census Bureau, 2005. http://www.census.gov/population/socdemo/hh-fam/cps2005/tabUC1-all.csv

Daoruang, Nattawud. "I Was a Novice Monk." Gor's World: Life of a Thai Teenager, undated. http://www.gorsworld.com/novice_story.htm.

Daoruang, Panrit "Gor." "I Was a Novice Monk." ThailandLife.com, undated. http://www.thailandlife.com/monk.html

"Dating." Teen Advice Online, undated. http://www.teenadviceonline.org/dating

David, K.C. *The Complete Guide to Gay and Lesbian Weddings.* New York: St. Martin's Griffin, 2005.

Davies, Douglas. "Cremation." In *Handbook of Death and Dying.* Edited by Clifton Bryant. Thousand Oaks, CA: Sage Reference, 2003.

Davies, Douglas and Lewis H. Mates, eds. *Encyclopedia of Cremation.* Burlington, VT: Ashgate Publishing, 2005.

Davis, Ronald L. F. Slavery in America: Historical Overview, undated. http://www.slaveryinamerica.org/history/hs_es_overview.htm

Dawson, Warren R. *The Custom of Couvade.* Manchester, UK: Manchester University Press, 1929.

Dayan, Brigitte. "Pearls, Henna, and Challah: Sephardic Nuptial Customs." *The Jewish News Weekly of Northern California,* November 8, 1996. http://www.jewishsf.com/content/2-0-/module/displaystory/story_id/4886 /edition_id/89/format/html/displaystory.html

"Death and Dying." Hinduism Today, January 1997.
http://www.hinduismtoday.com/archives/1997/1/1997-1-03.shtml

"Dedication of Children." First Baptist Church of Geneva, undated.
http://www.fbcg.com/wwb/child_dedication.htm

DeGidio, Sandra. "The Sacrament of Baptism: Celebrating the Embrace of God."
Catholic Update, undated.
http://www.americancatholic.org/Newsletters/CU/ac0389.asp

Dennis, Wayne. *The Hopi Child.* New York: John Wiley & Sons, 1965.

Denny, Frederick. "Postures and Gestures." In *Encyclopedia of Religion.* 2nd ed. Edited
by Lindsay Jones. New York: Macmillan Reference USA, 2005.

Denny, Frederick Mathewson. *An Introduction to Islam.* 2d ed. New York: Macmillan,
1994.

Desai, V. "Article: Why Do Hindus Not Eat Beef? Or Why is Cow Holy?" The Hindu
Universe, undated.
http://www.hindunet.org/srh_home/1996_10/msg00212.html

"El Día del Santo." Hallmark, February 2003.
http://pressroom.hallmark.com/el_dia_del_santo.html

Diamant, Anita. *The New Jewish Wedding.* New York: Fireside, 2001.

Diamant, Anita. *Saying Kaddish: How to Comfort the Dying, Bury the Dead, and Mourn
As a Jew.* New York: Schocken Books, 1998.

Diamant, Anita, and Howard Cooper. *Living a Jewish Life: Jewish Traditions, Customs
and Values for Today's Families.* New York: HarperCollins, 1991.

Diamant, Anita, and Karen Kushner. *How to Be a Jewish Parent: A Practical Handbook
for Family Life.* New York: Schocken, 2000.

Dineen, Jacqueline. *Births.* Austin, TX: Raintree Steck-Vaughn, 2001.

Dix, Tara K. "What's the Difference Between All Saints and All Souls? Glad You
Asked: Q&A on Church Teaching." *U.S. Catholic,* November 2003.

Donin, Hayim Halevy. *To Be A Jew: A Guide to Jewish Observance in Contemporary Life.*
New York: Basic Books, 1972.

Donohue, J. M. "Anointing of the Sick II: Liturgy of." *New Catholic Encyclopedia.* 2nd
ed. Detroit: Gale, 2003.

Doss, Erika. "Death, Art and Memory in the Public Sphere: The Visual and Material
Culture of Grief in Contemporary America." University of Colorado, 2002.
http://www.colorado.edu/finearts/erikadoss/articles/Doss%20death%20essay.pdf

Douglas, Ann. "Gender Prediction and Heart Rate." SheKnows, undated.
http://sheknows.com/about/look/67.htm

"Drano Test." Snopes.com, July 28, 2004.
http://www.snopes.com/pregnant/drano.htm

Dresser, Norine. *Multicultural Celebrations: Today's Rules of Etiquette for Life's Special Occasion.* New York: Three Rivers Press, 1999.

Dundes, Alan. *The Manner Born: Birth Rites in Cross-cultural Perspective.* Walnut Creek, CA: AltaMira Press, 2003.

Dunham, Carroll, et al. *Mamatoto: A Celebration of Birth.* New York: Penguin, 1991.

Eager, George B. *Love, Dating, and Sex: What Teens Want to Know.* Valdosta, GA: Mailbox Club Books, 1989.

Ebersole, Gary. "Death." In *Encyclopedia of Religion.* 2nd ed. Lindsay Jones. New York: Macmillan Reference USA, 2005.

"The Educational Samskaras: The Upanayana (Initiation). SanathanaDharma.com, undated.
http://www.sanathanadharma.com/samskaras/edu1.htm

"An Egg and a Name," undated.
http://www.csuchico.edu/~cheinz/syllabi/asst001/spring99/wong/wong1.html

Eggan, Fred. *Social Organization of the Western Pueblos.* Chicago: University of Chicago Press, 1950.

Eickelman, Dale F. "Rites of Passage: Muslim Rites." In *Encyclopedia of Religion.* 2nd ed. Lindsay Jones. New York: Macmillan Reference USA, 2005.

Eisner, Jan. "A Rite of Passage That Fills a Need." *Philadelphia Inquirer,* April 11, 2005.
http://www.spokesmanreview.com/breaking/story.asp?ID=3781

"Elijah." Jewish Virtual Library, undated.
http://www.jewishvirtuallibrary.org/jsource/biography/Elijah.html

Elliott, Andrea. "Tending to Muslim Hearts and Islam's Future." *New York Times,* March 7, 2006.

Emrich, Duncan. *The Folklore of Weddings and Marriage: The Traditional Beliefs, Customs, Superstitions, Charms, and Omens of Marriage and Marriage Ceremonies.* New York: American Heritage Press, 1970.

"The End of Life: Exploring Death in America." National Public Radio, undated.
http://www.npr.org/programs/death

Erevia, Angela. *Religious Celebration for the Quinceañera.* San Antonio, TX: Mexican American Cultural Center, 1980.

Erricker, Clive. *Buddhism.* Lincolnwood, IL: NTC Publishing Group, 1995.

Esposito, John L. *What Everyone Needs to Know About Islam.* New York: Oxford University Press, 2002.

"Essential Guide: Receptions." Brides. com, updated.
http://www.brides.com/weddingstyle/receptions/guide

"Essential Questions: Christianity and Lutheranism." Evangelical Lutheran Church in America, undated.
http://www.elca.org/communication/brief.html

Etzioni, Amitai, and Jared Bloom, eds. *We Are What We Celebrate: Understanding Holidays and Rituals.* New York: New York University Press, 2004.

"The Eucharist: Preparation for Holy Communion." St. Michael the Archangel Greek Orthodox Church, undated.
http://www.stmichaelgoc.org/pages/716721

"Fact Sheet: Minimum Drinking Age Laws," U.S. Department of Transportation, December 1999.
http://www.nhtsa.dot.gov/people/injury/alcohol/Community%20Guides%20HTML/PDFs/Public_App7.pdf

"Family Rituals." Korea.net, undated.
http://www.korea.net/search/contents/tar_work_soci_Family.htm

"Feast of All Souls." AmericanCatholic.org, undated.
http://www.americancatholic.org/Features/SaintOfDay/default.asp?id=1187

Fenlon, Amanda. "Collaborative Steps: Paving the Way to Kindergarten for Young Children with Disabilities." *National Association for the Education of Young Children,* March 2005.
http://www.journal.naeyc.org/btj/200503/04fenlon.pdf

Ferrell, Dave. "Life and Death: Inside America's Biggest, Busiest Cemetery. (Rose Hills Memorial Park)." *Los Angeles Magazine,* July 2006.

Fielding, William J. *Strange Customs of Courtship and Marriage.* New York: Permabooks, 1949.

Finch, Christopher. *Highways to Heaven: The Auto Biography of America.* New York: HarperCollins, 1992.

"First Communion at Pilgrim Lutheran." Pilgrim Lutheran Church, undated.
http://www.pilgrimbethesda.org/ministries/firstcommunion.htm

"The First Day of School: Preparing Your Kindergarten or Preschool Student." Chicago Public Schools, undated.
http://www.cps.k12.il.us/Parent/EdChild/First_Day/first_day.html

Fitzgerald, Rev. Thomas. "Special Services and Blessings." Greek Orthodox Archdiocese of America, 1996.
http://www.goarch.org/en/ourfaith/articles/article7113.asp

Flood, Gavin. *An Introduction to Hinduism.* Cambridge, UK: Cambridge University Press, 1996.

"Flowers in Mythology." Encyclopedia of Myths—Fi-Go, 2006.
http://www.mythencyclopedia.com/Fi-Go/Flowers-in-Mythology.html

Fontanel, Béatrice, and Claire d'Harcourt. *Babies: History, Art, and Folklore.* New York:
Henry N. Abrams, 1997.

Foote, Kenneth E. *Shadowed Ground: America's Landscapes of Violence and Tragedy.*
Austin, TX: University of Texas Press, 2003.

"Four Stages of Life," Hindu Temple and Cultural Center of Kansas City, August 2003.
http://www.htccofkc.org/silvernet/four_stages_of_life.htm

Fournier, Catherine. "Celebrating Name Days." Domestic-Church.com, undated.
http://www.domestic-church.com/CONTENT.DCC/19980101/ARTICLES
/NAMEDAYS.HTM

Fox, Annie. *Can You Relate?: Real World Advice for Teens on Guys, Girls, Growing Up,
and Getting Along.* Minneapolis: Free Spirit, 2000.

Foy, Felician A., and Rose M. Avato, eds. *Our Sunday Visitor's Catholic Almanac 1998.*
Huntington, IN: Our Sunday Visitor, 1997.

Frazer, Sir James George. *The Golden Bough: A Study in Magic and Religion.* New York:
Macmillan, 1922, New York: Bartleby.com, 2000.
http://www.bartleby.com/196/5.html

"Frequent Questions." Abingdon Episcopal Church, undated.
http://www.abingdonchurch.org/FrequentQuestions.htm

Fullard-Leo, Betty. "Sacred Burial Practices of Hawaii." *Coffee Times,* February 1998.
http://www.coffeetimes.com/feb98.htm

Ganteaume, Cécile R. "White Mountain Apache Dance: Expressions of Spirituality." In
Native American Dance: Ceremonies and Social Traditions. Edited by Charlotte
Heth. Washington, DC: National Museum of the American Indian, Smithsonian
Institution, 1992.

Garrett, Michael, and J. T. Garrett. *Native American Faith in America.* New York: Facts
on File, 2003.

Garrison, Graham. *Groomed: From Proposal to Vows, Wedding Planning and an Engagement from a Groom's Point of View.* Lincoln, NE: iUniverse, 2005.

Gavazzi, Stephen M., Keith A. Alford, and Patrick C. McHenry. "Culturally Specific
Programs for Foster Care Youth." *Family Relations* 45, no. 2 (April 1996).

Gay, Kathlyn. "Football Classics." In *African-American Holidays, Festivals, and Celebrations.* Detroit: Omnigraphics, 2007.

Geffen, Rela M., ed. *Celebration & Renewal: Rites of Passage in Judaism.* Philadelphia:
Jewish Publication Society, 1993.

Geijbels, M. *An Introduction to Islam: Muslim Beliefs and Practices. Part* 2. Rawalpindi, Pakistan: Christian Study Centre, 1975.

Gelbard, Shmuel Pinchas. *Judaism for the Rite Reasons: Concepts and Customs, Sources and Reasons.* Translated by R. David Derovan. Petach Tikva, Israel: Mifal Rashi Publishing, 2003.

General, Alexander and Frank G. Speck. *Midwinter Rites of the Cayuga Long House.* Lincoln, NE: University of Nebraska Press, 1995.

Gibran, Kahlil. *The Prophet.* 1923. Reprint, New York: Alfred A. Knopf, 2001.

Gifford, Edward S. *The Evil Eye: Studies in the Folklore of Vision.* New York, Macmillan, 1958.

Gillis, John R. "Gathering Together: Remembering Memory through Ritual." In *We Are What We Celebrate: Understanding Holidays and Rituals.* Edited by Amitai Etzioni and Jared Bloom. New York: New York University Press, 2004.

Glinert, Lewis, ed. "Nedavá, pl. Nedavót." In *Joys of Hebrew.* New York: Oxford University Press, 1992.

Goldberg, Harvey E. *Jewish Passages: Cycles of Jewish Life.* Berkeley: University of California Press, 2003.

Goldin, Claudia. "The Human Capital Century." Hoover Institution, Stanford University, 2002.
http://educationnext.org/20031/73.html

Gollaher, David L. *Circumcision: A History of the World's Most Controversial Surgery.* New York: Basic Books, 2000.

Gong, Rosemary. *Good Luck Life: The Essential Guide to Chinese American Celebrations and Culture.* New York: Harper Collins, 2005.

"Goodbye to the Baby Tooth (Various Tooth Fairy Tales around the World)." Multiculturalpedia, undated.
http://www.netlaputa.ne.jp/~tokyo3/e/teeth_e.html

Goravani, Das. "What is Vedic Astrology? What You Need to Know." About.com, undated.
http://hinduism.about.com/library/weekly/aa020502a.htm

Gordis, Daniel. *Becoming a Jewish Parent: How to Explore Spirituality and Tradition with Your Children.* New York: Harmony, 1999.

Gould, Meredith. *The Catholic Home: Celebrations and Traditions for Holidays, Feast Days, and Every Day.* New York: Doubleday, 2004.

Gourse, Leslie. *Native American Courtship and Marriage Traditions.* Summertown, TN: Native Voices, 2005.

"Graduated Driver License—Under Age 18." Florida Department of Highway Safety & Motor Vehicles, undated.
http://www.hsmv.state.fl.us/ddl/teendriv.html

"Graduated Driver Licensing." Centers for Disease Control and Prevention, March 30, 2006.
http://www.cdc.gov/ncipc/duip/spotlite/GradDrvLic.htm

"Graduation 2006." Hallmark Press Room, May 2006.
http://pressroom.hallmark.com/graduation_facts.html

"Graveside Services," Wyuka Funeral Home, Cemetery, and Park, Lincoln, NE, undated.
http://www.wyuka.com/FuneralHome/Gravesideservice.asp

Graymont, Barbara. *The Iroquois.* Philadelphia, PA: Chelsea House Publishers, 2005.

Green, R. H. "Courtly Love." In *New Catholic Encyclopedia.* 2nd ed. Detroit: Gale, 2003.

Grider, Sylvia. "Spontaneous Shrines: A Modern Response to Tragedy and Disaster." *New Directions in Folklore,* October 2001.
http://www.temple.edu/isllc/newfolk/shrines.html

Griffin, Robert H., and Ann H. Shurgin, eds. "China." In *Junior Worldmark Encyclopedia of World Holidays.* Vol. 2. Detroit: U*X*L, 2000.

Griffin, Robert H., and Ann H. Shurgin, eds. "Halloween and Festivals of the Dead." In *Junior Worldmark Encyclopedia of World Holidays.* Vol. 2. Detroit: U*X*L, 2000.

Griffin, Robert H., and Ann H. Shurgin, eds. "Mexico." In *Junior Worldmark Encyclopedia of World Holidays.* Vol. 2. Detroit U*X*L, 2000.

Gross, David C., and Esther R. Gross. *Under the Wedding Canopy: Love and Marriage in Judaism.* New York: Hippocrene Books, 1996.

"Guide to Jewish Funeral Practice." United Synagogue of Conservative Judaism, 2006.
http://www.uscj.org/Guide_to_Jewish_Fune6211.html

"A Guide to Music at Your Wedding." University of Virginia Library, undated.
http://www.lib.virginia.edu/MusicLib/guides/wedding.html

"Guidelines for Preparation and Celebration of the Sacraments of Initiation for the Diocese of Fort Worth." The Catholic Diocese of Fort Worth, undated.
http://www.fwdioc.org/img2/fFormation/SacramentalGuidelines5_29_03.pdf

Gulevich, Tanya. *Understanding Islam and Muslim Traditions.* Detroit: Omnigraphics, 2004.

"Hajj: Pilgrimage to the House of Allah in Mecca." Islam.com, undated.
http://www.islam.com/hajj/hajj.htm

"Hajj: The Essential Journey." CNN.com, 2006.
http://www.cnn.com/SPECIALS/2006/hajj

Hammoudi, Abdellah. *A Season in Mecca: Narrative of a Pilgrimage.* New York: Hill and Wang, 2006.

Hand, Robert. "The History of Astrology: Another View." Zodiacal, undated. http://www.zodiacal.com/articles/hand/history.htm

"Happy Birthday, We'll Sue." Snopes.com, August 11, 2002. http://www.snopes.com/music/songs/birthday.asp

Harakas, Stanley S. *The Orthodox Church: 455 Questions and Answers.* Minneapolis, MN: Light and Life Publishing Co., 1987.

Hardy, Melissa A. and Kim Shuey. "Retirement." In *Encyclopedia of Sociology.* 2nd ed. Edited by Edgar F. Borgatta and Rhonda J. V. Montgomery. New York: Macmillan Reference USA, 2001.

Henderson, Helene, ed. *Holidays, Festivals, and Celebrations of the World Dictionary.* 3rd ed. Detroit: Omnigraphics, 2005.

Higginbotham, Joyce and River. *Paganism: An Introduction to Earth-Centered Religions.* St. Paul, MN: Lewellyn Publications, 2002.

Hightower, Jamake. *Ritual of the Wind: North American Indian Ceremonies, Music, and Dances.* New York: Viking, 1977.

Hill, Paul, Jr. *Coming of Age: African American Male Rites-Of-Passage.* Chicago: African American Images, 1992.

Hillers, Delbert and Reuben Kashina. "Burial." In *Encyclopaedia Judaica.* 2nd ed. Edited by Michael Berenbaum and Fred Skolnik. Detroit: Macmillan Reference USA, 2007.

"Hindu Samskaras." SanathanaDharma.com, undated. http://www.sanathanadharma.com/samskaras

"Hinduism." British Broadcasting Corporation, undated. http://www.bbc.co.uk/religion/religions/hinduism/features/rites/birth

"Hinduism for Schools," undated. Vivekananda Centre London, undated. http://www.btinternet.com/~vivekananda/schools1s4.htm

Hirschfelder, Arlene, and Paulette Molin. *The Encyclopedia of Native American Religions: An Introduction.* New York: Facts on File, 1992.

His Holiness the Fourteenth Dalai Lama. "Death, Intermediate State, and Rebirth." Amitabha Hospice Service, undated. http://www.amitabhahospice.org/hospice/Death-interm_rebirth.php

"History of Baby Showers." Birthday Express, undated. http://www.birthdayexpress.com/bexpress/planning/BabyShowers.asp

"History of Birthday Cake." Tokenz, undated. http://www.tokenz.com/history-of-birthday-cake.html

"History of Graduation." Brownilocks and the Three Bear, undated.
http://www.brownielocks.com/graduation.html

Hoang, Vivi. "Spirits Live on Day of the Dead: Mexican Tradition of Dia de los Muertos Pays Respect to Deceased through Offerings, Communion." *The Tennessean,* October 27, 2006.

Hoffman, Linda Johnson, and Neal Barnett. *The Reunion Planner.* Los Angeles, CA: Goodman Lauren Publishing, 1999.

Holm, Jean, and John Bowker, eds. *Rites of Passage.* London: Pinter, 1994.

Holt, Leann. "A Different View of Death: Diverse Cultures and Neighborhoods Brought Together for Day of the Dead Parade." *Albuquerque (NM) Journal,* November 7, 2005.

The Holy Bible, containing the Old and New Testaments. Dallas: Melton, 1952.

"Holy Water." East Lewis County Catholic Community, undated.
http://landru.i-link-2.net/shnyves/holy_water2.htm

"Host." The Catholic Encyclopedia, 1907. Online edition at New Advent.
http://www.newadvent.org/cathen/07489d.htm

"How Do We Use a Paschal Candle?" Evangelical Lutheran Church in America, December 2002.
http://www.elca.org/dcm/worship/faq/worship_space/paschal_candle.html

Hultkrantz, Ake. *Native Religions of North America: The Power of Visions and Fertility.* San Francisco: Harper & Row, 1987.

Hultkrantz, Ake. "North American Indian Religions: An Overview." In *Encyclopedia of Religion.* 2nd ed. Edited by Lindsay Jones. New York: Macmillan Reference USA, 2005.

Iannelli., Vincent, M.D. "The Tooth Fairy and Losing a First Baby Tooth." About.com, undated.
http://pediatrics.about.com/cs/weeklyquestion/a/041704_ask.htm

"IndiaMystica, Customs and Ceremonies: Upanayanam." Indian Culture Online, undated.
http://www.gurjari.net/ico/Mystica/html/upanayanam.htm

"Iroqouis Condolence Ceremony." Indian Country Today, June 12, 2003.
http://www.indiancountry.com/content.cfm?id=1055438183

Isca, Kay Lynn. *Catholic Etiquette: What You Need to Know about Catholic Rites and Wrongs.* Huntington, IN: Our Sunday Visitor, 1997.

"Islam: Governing Under Sharia" by Sharon Otterman. Council on Foreign Relations, undated.
http://www.cfr.org/publication/8034/islam.html

Jackson, Edgar N. *The Christian Funeral: Its Meaning, Its Purpose, and Its Modern Practice.* New York: Channel Press, 1966.

Jacobs, Andrew. "As Joyous as It Is Macabre; A Mexican Holiday Ensures the Dead Have Their Day." *New York Times,* November 3, 1999.

Jain, Anita. "Is Arranged Marriage Really Any Worse Than Craigslist?" *New York Magazine,* April 4, 2005.

"Japanese Traditions." Japanese Cultural Center of Hawaii, undated.
http://www.jcch.com/TRADITIONS_2003_0624.htm

Jaynes, Gerald, ed. "Funeral Rites." In *Encyclopedia of African American Society.* Thousand Oaks, CA: Sage Reference, 2005.

"Jewish Burial Customs," Star of David Memorial Chapel, West Babylon, NY, 2006.
http://www.starofdavidmemorialchapel.com/jbc.html#_Toc68663326

"Jewish Henna Traditions from Kurdistan." The Henna Page, 2005.
http://www.hennapage.com/henna/encyclopedia/kurdjewish

"Jewish Holy Books." Judaism, undated.
http://scheinerman.net/judaism/holybooks

"Jewish Publication Society Bible." SimpletoRemember.com, undated.
http://www.simpletoremember.com/vitals/TanachSearch.htm

"The Jewish Wedding Guide." Jewish-American History Documentation Foundation, undated.
http://www.jewish-history.com/minhag.htm

"Jewish Wedding 101," Ketubah.com, undated.
http://www.ketubah.com/engine.cfm?i=72

"Jewish Weddings: Reception Rituals." TheKnot.com, undated.
http://www.theknot.com/ch_article.html?Object+A191108165802

John Paul II. "Angelus: Commemoration of All the Faithful Departed (All Souls Day)." November 2, 2003.

Johnson, Judith. *The Wedding Ceremony Planner: The Essential Guide to the Most Important Part of Your Wedding Day.* Naperville, IL: Sourcebooks Casablanca, 2005.

Johnson, Kevin Orlin. "Water: Holy and Plain." In *Why Do Catholics Do That?: A Guide to the Teachings and Practices of the Catholic Church.* New York: Ballantine, 1994.

Jones, Leslie. *Happy Is the Bride the Sun Shines On: Wedding Beliefs, Customs, and Traditions.* Chicago, IL: Contemporary Books, 1995.

Jurgens, Jane. "Greek Americans." Multicultural America, undated.
http://www.everyculture.com/multi/Du-Ha/Greek-Americans.html

Kalavar, Jyotsna M. "Hindu Samskāras: Milestones of Child Development." In *Rituals and Patterns in Children's Lives.* Edited by Kathy Merlock Jackson. Madison: University of Wisconsin Press, 2005.

Kalish, John. "Burial Society." Weekend All Things Considered, National Public Radio, March 8, 1998.
http://www.npr.org/programs/death/980308.death.html

Kamat, Vikas. "Indian Culture: The Sacred Thread." Kamat's Potpourri, June 9, 2004.
http://www.kamat.com/indica/culture/sub-cultures/sacred-thread.htm

Kandell, Leslie. "Reliving the Old Days with the Old Selves." *New York Times,* May 3, 2002.

Kanitkar, V. P. and W. Owen Cole. *Hinduism.* Lincolnwood, IL: NTC Publishing Group, 1995.

Kaplan-Mayer, Gabrielle. *The Creative Jewish Wedding Book: A Hands-On Guide to New and Old Traditions, Ceremonies and Celebrations.* Woodstock, VT: Jewish Lights Publishing, 2004.

Kaplan-Mayer, Gabrielle. "Planning Your Jewish Wedding: Seven Simple Steps," MyJewishLearning.com, undated.
http://www.myjewishlearning.com/lifecycle/Marriage/LiturgyRitualCustom/ModernCustoms/Howto_Wedding.htm

Katz-Stone, Adam. "Jews and Baby Showers: Are They Okay?" Jewish Family.com, undated.
http://www.jewishfamily.com/jc/lifecycle/jews_and_baby.phtml

Kaufman, Michael. *Love, Marriage, and Family in Jewish Law and Tradition.* Northvale, NJ: J. Aronson, 1992.

Keenan, Alex. "It's the Season to Plan Your Unit's Reunion." *Army Times,* January 23, 2006.

Kelleher, Elizabeth. "Day of the Dead: You'll Have Too Much Fun to Be Frightened During this Mexican Holiday." *National Geographic Kids,* October 2005.

Kemper, Robert. "Retirement Communities." In *Encyclopedia of American Urban History.* Edited by David Goldfield. Thousand Oaks, CA: Sage Reference, 2007.

Kett, Joseph F. *Rites of Passage: Adolescence in America, 1790 to the Present.* New York: Basic Books, 1977.

Khadro, Sangye. Preparing for Death and Helping the Dying: A Buddhist Perspective. Singapore: Kong Meng San Phor Kark See Monastery, 2003.
http://www.buddhanet.net/pdf_file/death_dying.pdf

Khanh, Truong Phuoc. "Chinese Observe Day of Dead Today: Ching Ming Ceremony Took Place at Once-Segregated S.J. Burial Plot." *San Jose Mercury News,* April 5, 2006.

Kim, Heidi. "Celebrating a Full Life." *SkyNews,* January 17, 2003.
http://www.skynews.co.kr/article_view.asp?ltype=&mcd=70&ccd=6&scd=2&ano=26

Klausner, Abraham J. *Weddings: A Complete Guide to All Religious and Interfaith Marriage Services.* Columbus, OH: Alpha Publishing, 1986.

Knipe, David M. "Hinduism: Experiments in the Sacred." In *Religious Traditions of the World: A Journey through Africa, North America, Mesoamerica, Judaism, Christianity, Islam, Hinduism, Buddhism, China, and Japan.* Edited H. Byron Earhart. New York: HarperSanFrancisco, 1993. Reprinted online at Hindu Gateway.
http://www.hindugateway.com/library/rituals

Knott, Kim. *Hinduism: A Very Short Introduction.* Oxford, U.K.: Oxford University Press, 1998.

Koenig-Bricker, Woodene. "For Our Healing: The Sacrament of the Anointing of the Sick." *Youth Update Newsletter,* undated.
http://www.americancatholic.org/Newsletters/YU/ay1292.asp

"Korean Ethnic Minority," Ministry of Culture: People's Republic of China, September 2003.
http://www.chinaculture.org/gb/en_aboutchina/2003-09/24/content_23969.htm

Kosofsky, Scott-Martin. *The Book of Customs: A Complete Handbook for the Jewish Year.* New York: HarperSanFrancisco, 2004.

Kuehnelt-Leddihn, Erik R. von. *Faith and Reason.* Fort Royal, VA: Christendom Press, 1996.

Kueny, Kathryn. "Pilgrimage." In *Encyclopedia of Islam and the Muslim World.* Edited by Richard C. Martin. New York: Macmillan Reference USA, 2003.

Kutty, Ahmad. "What is Aqiqah?" Islamic Institute of Toronto, September 28, 2005.
http://www.islam.ca/answers.php?id=833

Kutty, Ahmad. "What is the Islamic Ruling on Aqiqah?" Islamic Institute of Toronto, March 8, 2001.
http://www.islam.ca/answers.php?id=24

"Lag B'Omer." Jewish Outreach Institute, undated.
http://www.joi.org/celebrate/lagbomer/index.shtml

Lamb, Douglas and Glenn D. Reeder. "Reliving Golden Days." *Psychology Today,* June 1986.

Lankford, Mary D. *Quinceañera: A Latina's Journey to Womanhood.* Brookfield, CT: Millbrook Press, 1994.

Leahy, Michael. *Hard Lessons: Senior Year at Beverly Hills High School.* Boston: Little, Brown, 1988.

Leavitt, Judith Walzer. *Brought to Bed: Child-bearing in America.* New York: Oxford University Press, 1986.

Lee, Vera. *Something Old, Something New: What You Didn't Know about Wedding Ceremonies, Celebrations & Customs.* Naperville, IL: Sourcebooks, 1994.

Lehman, Katherine. "Cyber Dating." In *Encyclopedia of Recreation and Leisure in America.* Edited by Gary S. Cross. Detroit, MI: Charles Scribner's Sons, 2004.

Lehman, Katherine. "Reunions." In *Encyclopedia of Recreation and Leisure in America.* Edited by Gary S. Cross. Detroit: Charles Scribner's Sons, 2004.

Leighton, Dorothea, and Clyde Kluckhohn. *Children of the People: The Navajo Individual and His Development.* Cambridge, MA: Harvard University Press, 1947.

"Lent and the Renewal of Our Baptismal Promises." Presentation Ministries, undated. http://www.presentationministries.com/brochures/LentRenewal.asp

Lewis, Linda Rannells. *Birthdays: Their Delights and Disappointments, Past and Present, Worldly, Astrological, and Infamous.* Boston: Little, Brown, 1976.

Lewit, Jane, and Ellen Epstein. *The Bar/Bat Mitzvah Planbook.* Lanham, MD: Scarborough House, 1991.

"Life Advice about Your Child's First Day at School." Federal Citizen Information Center, January 2006.
http://www.pueblo.gsa.gov/cic_text/family/firstday/firstday.htm

"The Life of Baptism." Evangelical Lutheran Church in America, 2005.
http://www.renewingworship.org/about/proposal/pdf_old/03_Holy_Baptism.pdf

Linton, Ralph, and Adelin Linton. *The Lore of Birthdays.* New York: Henry Schuman, 1952. Reprint. Detroit: Omnigraphics, 1998.

"Listening to Mothers: Report of the First National U.S Survey of Women's Childbearing Experiences Issued by Executive Summary and Recommendations." Maternity Center Association, October 2002.
http://www.maternitywise.org/pdfs/LtMrecommendations.pdf

Lochtefeld, James G. "The Japji." Carthage College, undated.
http://personal.carthage.edu/jlochtefeld/sikh/japji.htm

Loftin, John D. *Religion and Hopi Life in the Twentieth Century.* Bloomington: Indiana University Press, 1991

Lomax, Alan. "236. When the Saints Go Marchin' In." In *The Folk Songs of North America in the English Language.* Garden City, NY: Doubleday & Company, 1960.

"Lore and Tradition." WeddingDetails.com, undated.
http://www.weddingdetails.com/lore

Loveless, Caron Chandler. "We Still Do!" Christianity Today: Marriage Partnership, Summer 2005.
http://www.christianitytoday.com/mp/2005/002/5.30.html

Ly, Phuong. "The Karma Kids." The Buddhist Channel, August 14, 2004.
http://www.buddhistnews.tv/current/karma-kids-140803.php

Lysaght, Patricia. "Death and Burial." In *Encyclopedia of Food and Culture*. Edited by Solomon H. Katz. New York: Charles Scribner's Sons, 2003.

Mahoney, Rebecca. "B-CU Gets Back Into the Reunion Business." *Orlando (FL) Sentinel*, March 29, 2007.
http://www.orlandosentinel.com/news/local/volusia/orl-vbcr2907mar29,0,7444840
.story

Malik, Rajiv. "Seeking the Lord of the Seven Hills." *Hinduism Today*, January/February/March 2006.
http://www.hinduismtoday.com/archives/2006/1-3/pdf/section-1_2006-01-01
_p06-36.pdf

"Las Mañanitas." Lucerito's Music, undated.
http://www.lucerito.net/mananitas.htm

Manjul, V.L. "Starting Vedic Studies: Backed by Scripture, Girls Get Their Sacred Thread." *Hinduism Today*, October/November/December 2002.
http://www.hinduismtoday.com/archives/2002/10-12/59-girls_thread.shtml

Mann, Gurinder Singh, Paul David Numrich, and Raymond B. Williams. *Buddhists, Hindus, and Sikhs in America*. New York: Oxford University Press, 2001.

"The Manners of Welcoming the New-Born Child in Islam." TROID: The Reign of Islaamic Da'wah, undated.
http://www.troid.org/articles/sisters/children/newborn.htm

"Mantra—Sacred Fire." Understanding Hinduism, undated.
http://www.hinduism.co.za/mantras-.htm

Marcus, Rabbi Yosef. "I Know it's a Big Holiday, but What Exactly is Lag B'Omer?" Ask Moses.com, undated.
http://www.askmoses.com/qa_detail.html?h=196&o=472

Marling, Karal Ann. *Debutante: Rites and Regalia of American Debdom*. Lawrence: University Press of Kansas, 2004.

"Marriage: Overview: Liturgy, Ritual, and Custom." MyJewishLearning.com.
http://www.myjewishlearning.com/lifecycle/Marriage/LiturgyRitualCustom.htm

Martin, Richard C. "Pilgrimage: Muslim Pilgrimage." In *Encyclopedia of Religion*. 2nd ed. Edited by Lindsay Jones. New York: Macmillan Reference USA, 2005.

Martinez, Rebekah. "The Day of the Dead: Houston Celebrates the Mexican Holiday." *Semana*, October 26, 2003.

Matlins, Stuart M. *The Perfect Stranger's Guide to Funerals and Grieving Practices*. Woodstock, VT: Skylight Paths Publishing, 2000.

Max, Sarah. "Living with the In-Laws: Multigenerational Households, Though Still Uncommon, Seem to Be Growing in Popularity." CNN.com, April 22, 2004. http://money.cnn.com/2004/02/18/pf/yourhome/grannyflats

McBride-Mellinger, Maria. *The Perfect Wedding Reception: Stylish Ideas for Every Season.* New York: HarperResource, 2001.

McBrien, Richard P. *The HarperCollins Encyclopedia of Catholicism.* New York: Harper-SanFrancisco, 1985.

McClain, J. P., and J. M. Donohue, "Anointing of the Sick I: Theology of." *New Catholic Encyclopedia.* 2nd ed. Detroit: Gale, 2003.

McLaren, Angus. *Reproductive Rituals: The Perception of Fertility in England from the Sixteenth Century to the Nineteenth Century.* London: Methuen, 1984.

Mcloughlin, Helen. My Nameday—Come for Dessert. 1962. EWTN Global Catholic Network. http://www.ewtn.com/library/family/namday.txt

"Mehndi." MyBindi.com, 2001. http://www.mybindi.com/weddings/festivities/mehndi.cfm

Meltzer, David, ed. *Birth: An Anthology of Ancient Texts, Songs, Prayers, and Stories.* San Francisco: North Point Press, 1981.

Melwani, Lavina. "Hindu Rituals for Death and Grief." BeliefNet, undated. http://www.beliefnet.com/story/120/story_12093_1.html

Menard, Valerie. *The Latino Holiday Book: From Cinco de Mayo to Día de los Muertos—The Celebrations and Traditions of Hispanic-Americans.* New York: Marlowe and Co., 2004.

"Michigan's Graduated License System." Michigan.gov, undated. http://www.michigan.gov/documents/Michigans_Graduated_Licensing_System_153498_7.pdf

Milgram, Rabbi Goldie. "Lag B'Omer Ecstasy." Reclaiming Judaism as Spiritual Practice, 2004. http://www.rebgoldie.com/lagbomer.htm

Milgram, Rabbi Goldie. "Upsherin: A Coming of Age Ritual for Toddlers and their Families." Reclaiming Judaism as Spiritual Practice, 2004. http://www.rebgoldie.com/upsherin.htm

"Military Reunion Articles," *Reunions Magazine,* undated. http://www.reunionsmag.com/reunionarticles/military.html

Military Reunion Center, Military.com, undated. http://www.military.com/Resources/ReunionList

Miller, G. Wayne. *Coming of Age: The True Adventures of Two American Teens.* New York: Random House, 1995.

Mir-Hosseini, Ziba. "Marriage." In *Encyclopedia of Islam and the Muslim World.* Edited by Richard C. Martin. New York: Macmillan Reference USA, 2004.

Mir-Hosseini, Ziba. "Nikah." In *Encyclopedia of Islam and the Muslim World.* Edited by Richard C. Martin. New York: Macmillan Reference USA, 2004.

Molin, Paulette. "Death Feast, Shawnee," In *Encyclopedia of Native American Religions.* Edited by Arlene B. Hirschfelder. New York: Facts on File, 2000.

Mollica, Kelly A. "Early Retirement." In *Encyclopedia of Career Development.* Edited by Jeffrey Greenhaus and Gerard Callanan. Thousand Oaks, CA: Sage Reference, 2006.

Monger, George P. *Marriage Customs of the World: From Henna to Honeymoons.* Santa Barbara, CA: ABC/CLIO, 2004.

Montgomery, Christine. "Impromptu Memorials Salve Communal Grief: On-Site Tributes the Trend as Pain, Tragedy Hit Home." *Washington Times,* August 5, 1997.

Moore, Eric. "Black College Football Classic Games: A Taste of the HBCU Athletic Experience." CollegeView.com, undated.
http://www.collegeview.com/articles/CV/hbcu/classic_games.html

Moorhead, Joanna. "Christenings and Naming Ceremonies—Which Is Right for You?" Baby World, undated.
http://www.babyworld.co.uk/information/newparents/christenings.asp

Moorhead, Molly. "Yesterday's Sexism in Debutante Balls Today." *St. Petersburg Times,* January 6, 2004.
http://www.sptimes.com/2004/01/06/Columns/Yesterday_s_sexism_in.shtml

Mordecai, Carolyn. *Weddings: Dating and Love Customs of Cultures Worldwide.* Phoenix, AZ: Nittany Publishers, 1999.

Morgenstern, Julian. *Rites of Birth, Marriage, Death and Kindred Occasions among the Semites.* Cincinnati, OH: Hebrew Union College Press, 1966.

Morrow, Fr. Nektarios. "The Funeral Service of the Orthodox Church." Greek Orthodox Archdiocese of America, 2005.
http://www.goarch.org/print/en/ourfaith/article9218.asp

Moskovitz, Patti. *The Complete Bar/Bat Mitzvah Book: Everything You Need to Plan a Meaningful Celebration.* Franklin Lakes, NJ: Career Press, 2000.

"Muhammad: Legacy of a Prophet." PBS.org, 2002.
http://www.pbs.org/muhammad/virtualhajj.shtml

Murillo, Kathy. "Altar Statements: Homemade Shrines Honor Departed Loved Ones for Día de los Muertos." *Arizona Republic,* October 28, 2006.

"Muslim Funeral Guide." Islamic Information Office, undated.
http://www.iio.org/janazah/bur_1299.pdf

"Muslims: Births, Babies and Motherhood." Ethnicity Online, undated.
http://www.ethnicityonline.net/islam_birth.htm

"Namakarana." Astrojyoti, undated.
http://www.astrojyoti.com/namakaran.htm

National Rites of Passage Institute, undated.
http://www.ritesofpassage.org

Neville, Gwen Kennedy. "Reunions." In *Contemporary American Religion.* Edited by Wade Clark Roof. New York: Macmillan Reference USA, 1999.

Nevins, Albert J. *A Saint for Your Name: Saints for Girls.* Huntington, IN: Our Sunday Visitor, 1980.

Newmark, Peter. "Notes on Florigraphy." *The Linguist* 40, no. 5 (2001).

"9-11 Memorial Poems and Pictures." 9-11 Heroes, undated.
http://www.9-11heroes.us/911-memorial-poem.php

Norland, Christina. "Fragile Families Research Brief Number 5." The Fragile Families and Child Wellbeing Study, January 2001.
http://www.fragilefamilies.princeton.edu/briefs/researchbrief5.pdf

Nutini, Hugo. "Day of the Dead." In *Encyclopedia of Religion.* Vol. 4, 2nd ed. Edited by Lindsay Jones. Macmillan Reference USA, 2005.

O'Gorman, Thomas J. "Sorry for Your Troubles." *World of Hibernia,* Winter 1998.

O'Grady, John F. *Catholic Beliefs and Traditions: Ancient and Ever New.* New York: Paulist Press, 2001.

"Old Wives Tales," by Robin Weiss. About: Parenting and Family, undated.
http://pregnancy.about.com/cs/myths/a/aa042299.htm

Onest, Phyllis Meshel. "Celebrating Your Patron's Saint Day." Theologic Systems, undated.
http://www.theologic.com/oflweb/inhome/nameday1.htm

Opincar, Abe. "He Would've Wanted Everyone to Eat." *New York Times,* August 10, 2005.

Opler, Morris Edward. *Childhood and Youth in Jicarilla Apache Society.* Vol. 5 of Publications of the Frederick Webb Hodge Anniversary Publication Fund. Los Angeles: The Southwest Museum, 1964.

"Order of Reception Events." USABride.com, updated
http://usabride.com/wedplan/a_reception?order.html

"Origins of the Bridal Party," Wedding Strategies, undated.
http://www.weddingstrategies.com/ceremony/traditions/origins-bridal-party.htm

Ortiz, Alfonso. *The Tewa World: Space, Time, Being, and Becoming in a Pueblo Society.* Chicago: University of Chicago Press, 1969.

Otnes, Cele C., and Elizabeth H. Pleck. *Cinderella Dreams: The Allure of the Lavish Wedding.* Berkeley: University of California Press, 2003.

Pancrazio, Angela Cara. "Day of the Dead Altars on Display." *Arizona Republic,* November 2, 2006.

"A Parish Guide to Planning When Death Occurs." The Church of St. William, undated. http://www.stwilliams.com/ContactUs/funeral_planning.htm

Parsons, Elsie Clews. *Pueblo Mothers and Children: Essays by Elsie Clews Parsons, 1915-1924.* Edited by Barbara A. Babcock. Santa Fe, NM: Ancient City Press, 1991.

Paul, Pamela. "Calling It Off." *Time,* October 1, 2003.

Pear, Robert. "Social Security Underestimates Future Life Spans, Critics Say." *New York Times,* December 31, 2004.

Pellicer, Metty. "Fil-Am Presents Fourth Triennial Debutantes' Ball." Fil-Am Atlanta, undated. http://www.atl-filam.org/Events/2003/Debutantes/Deb_Post_Story.htm

Perkins, Useni Eugene. *Harvesting Generations: The Positive Development of Black Youth.* Chicago: Third World Press, 1986.

Philip Lief Group. *Going to the Chapel: The Ultimate Wedding Guide for Today's Black Couple.* New York: G.P. Putnam's Sons, 1998.

"Pidyon ha-Bat/ha-Ben (Redemption of the Firstborn)" by Rabbi Rona Shapiro. Ritualwell.org, undated. http://www.ritualwell.org/lifecycles/babieschildren/pidyonhabenhabat/pidyon2.xml

"Pierre Lorillard IV: The Tuxedo." Inventor of the Week Archive, May, 1997. http://web.mit.edu/invent/iow/lorillard.html

Pilcher, Jeffrey M. "Day of the Dead." In *Encyclopedia of Food and Culture.* Vol. 1. Edited by Solomon H. Katz. Charles Scribner's Sons, 2003.

"Pipestone/Catlinite." Rocks and Minerals.com, undated. http://www.rocksandminerals.com/specimens/pipestone.htm

Pleck, Elizabeth H. *Celebrating the Family: Ethnicity, Consumer Culture, and Family Rituals.* Cambridge, MA: Harvard University Press, 2000.

"Pomp and Circumstance: Why Americans Graduate to Elgar." Elgar: Home Page of the Elgar Society and the Elgar Foundation, undated. http://www.elgar.org/3pomp-b.htm

"Popular Wedding Traditions and Superstitions," British Broadcasting Corporation, 2005. http://www.bbc.co.uk/dna/h2g2/A3383633

Post, Peggy. "What Are the Responsibilities of the Wedding Party?" Wedding Channel, undated. http://www.weddingchannel.com/ui/buildArticle.action?assetUID=87490&c=87490&s=84&t=71&p=67479800&l=135864

Powers, William K. *Oglala Religion.* Lincoln: University of Nebraska Press, 1977.

Powers, William K. "Wiping the Tears: Lakota Religion in the Twenty-first Century." In *Native Religions and Cultures of North America.* Edited by Lawrence E. Sullivan. New York: Continuum, 2000.

"Prayers for the Departed." Orthodox Church in America, undated.
http://www.oca.org/QA.asp?ID=170&SID=3

"Pre-license Driver Education." *Countermeasures That Work: A Highway Safety Countermeasure Guide For State Highway Safety.* National Highway Traffic Safety Administration, January 2006.
http://www.nhtsa.dot.gov/people/injury/airbags/Countermeasures/pages/C

Pries, Allison. "Englewood Cliff, NJ, Matchmaking Business Blends Counseling, Astrology," *Hackensack (NJ) Record,* June 12, 2002.

"Prom Advice." The Fashion Institute of Design and Merchandising, undated.
http://www.promadvice.com

"Prom Guide to Proms and After-prom Themes." Party 411, undated.
http://www.party411.com/prom-themes.html

Prothero, Stephen. *Purified by Fire: A History of Cremation in America.* Berkeley, CA: University of California Press, 2001.

Puckle, Bertram S. *Funeral Customs: Their Origin and Development.* Detroit: Singing Tree Press, 1968.

"Purpose and History," World Marriage Day, undated.
http://wmd.wwme.org/purpose-history.html

Qinfa, Ye. "Birthday Customs of the Elderly in China." CCTV.com, undated.
http://www.cctv.com/english/TouchChina/School/Culture/20030225/100336.html

"Question 21.8.2: What is Upsherin?" Internet FAQ Archives, undated.
http://www.faqs.org/faqs/judaism/FAQ/12-Kids/section-43.html

"Quinceañera! A Celebration of Latina Womanhood." *Voices: The Journal of New York Folklore* 28 (Fall-Winter 2002).
http://www.nyfolklore.org/pubs/voic28-3-4/onair.html

Rabinowicz, Harry. "Cremation." In *Encyclopaedia Judaica.* 2nd ed. Edited by Michael Berenbaum and Fred Skolnik. Detroit: Macmillan Reference USA, 2007.

Rajhans, Gayan. "The Gayatri Mantra: What You Need to Know." About.com, undated.
http://hinduism.about.com/library/weekly/aa061003a.htm

Ramirez, Marc. "Ching Ming Celebration Honors Chinese Ancestors." *Seattle Times,* April 2, 2006.

Ray, Rayburn W. and Rose Ann. *Wedding Anniversary Idea Book: A Guide to Celebrating Wedding Anniversaries.* Brentwood, TN: J. M. Publications, 1985.

"The Real Presence of Jesus Christ in the Sacrament of the Eucharist: Basic Questions and Answers." United States Conference of Catholic Bishops: Doctrine and Pastoral Practices, June 15, 2001.
http://www.usccb.org/dpp/realpresence.htm

"Red Egg and Ginger Parties." About.com, undated.
http://chinesefood.about.com/library/weekly/aa012303a.htm

Reed, Richard K. *Birthing Fathers: The Transformation of Men in American Rites of Birth.* New Brunswick, NJ: Rutgers University Press, 2005.

Reid, Jon. "Impromptu Memorials to the Dead." In *Handbook of Death and Dying.* Edited by Clifton Bryant. Thousand Oaks, CA: Sage Reference, 2003.

"Religion and Ethics: Muslim Weddings" by Ruqaiyyah Waris Maqsood. British Broadcasting Corporation, undated.
http://www.bbc.co.uk/religion/religions/islam/features/rites/weddings.shtml

"Religious Growth and Learning." The Unitarian Church of Lincoln, May 21, 2006.
http://www.unitarianlincoln.org/rgl.html

Richstatter, Thomas. "Anointing the Sick: A Parish Sacrament." Catholic Update Newsletter, undated.
http://www.americancatholic.org/Newsletters/CU/ac0196.asp

Rights of Passage Youth Empowerment Foundation, undated.
http://www.ritesofpassageonline.org

Rinehart, Robin. *Contemporary Hinduism: Ritual, Culture, and Practice.* Santa Barbara, CA: ABC-CLIO, 2004.

Roach, John. "Ancient Flowers Found in Egypt Coffin." *National Geographic News,* June 29, 2006.
http://news.nationalgeographic.com/news/2006/06/060629-egypt-flowers.html

"Road Skills Test Study Guide." Michigan.gov, March 2005.
http://www.michigan.gov/documents/ROAD_SKILLS_TEST_STUDY_GUIDE_05-02_21935_7.pdf

Rogak, Lisa. *Death Warmed Over: Funeral Food, Rituals, and Customs From Around the World.* Berkeley, CA: Ten Speed Press, 2004.

Rommelmann, Nancy. "Crying and Digging: Reclaiming the Realities and Rituals of Death." *Los Angeles Times,* February 6, 2005.

Rothman, Ellen K. *Hands and Hearts: A History of Courtship in America.* New York: Basic Books, 1984.

Rouvelas, Marilyn. *A Guide to Greek Traditions and Customs in America.* Bethesda, MD: Nea Attiki Press, 1993.

Rushforth, Scott, and Steadman Upham. *A Hopi Social History: Anthropological Perspectives on Sociocultural Persistence and Change.* Austin: University of Texas Press, 1992.

Rushton, Lucy. *Birth Customs.* New York: Thomson Learning, 1993.

Rutherford, R. "Funeral Rites." In *New Catholic Encyclopedia.* 2nd ed. Detroit: Gale, 2003.

"Sacred Samskaras." *Hinduism Today,* May-June 2001.
   http://www.hinduismtoday.com/archives/2001/5-6/45_insight.shtml

"Samskaras of Childhood: Annaprasana (First Feeding)." SanathanaDharma.com, undated.
   http://www.sanathanadharma.com/samskaras/childhood3.htm#Annaprasana

"Samskaras of Childhood: Chudakarana." SanathanaDharma.com, undated.
   http://www.sanathanadharma.com/samskaras/childhood4.htm#Chudakarana

"Samskaras of Childhood: Jatakarma (Birth Ceremony)." SanathanaDharma.com, undated.
   http://www.sanathanadharma.com/samskaras/childhood.htm

"Samskaras of Childhood: Karnavedha." SanathanaDharma.com, undated.
   http://www.sanathanadharma.com/samskaras/childhood5.htm#Karnavedha

"Samskaras of Childhood: Namakarana." SanathanaDharma.com, undated.
   http://www.sanathanadharma.com/samskaras/childhood1.htm#Namakarana

"Samskaras." *Hinduism Today,* October 1994.
   http://www.hinduismtoday.com/archives/1994/10/1994-10-10.shtml

Sanford, A. Whitney. "The Hindu Ritual Calendar." In *Contemporary Hinduism: Ritual, Culture, and Practice.* Edited by Robin Rinehart. Santa Barbara, CA: ABC-CLIO, 2004.

Saunders, Fr. William. "All Saints and All Souls." CatholicEducation.org, 2002.
   http://www.catholiceducation.org/articles/religion/re0199.html

"Saving Teenage Lives: The Case for Graduated Driver Licensing" and "Traditional Driver Licensing vs. Graduated Driver Licensing." National Highway Traffic Safety Administration, undated.
   http://www.nhtsa.dot.gov/people/injury/newdriver/SaveTeens/toc.html

Scholten, Catherine M. *Childbearing in American Society, 1650-1850.* New York: New York University Press, 1985.

Seager, Richard Hughes. *Buddhism in America.* New York: Columbia University Press, 1999.

Sebora, Jenna. "Preparing for Kindergarten." *Minnesota Herald Journal,* August 22, 2005.
   http://www.herald-journal.com/archives/2005/columns/js082205.html

"The Second Vatican Council Resource Guide." Seattle University, undated.
   http://www.seattleu.edu/lemlib/web_archives/vaticanII/vaticanII.htm

The Seeker's Glossary of Buddhism. 2nd ed. New York: Sutra Translation Committee of the United States and Canada, 1998.
   http://www.buddhanet.net/pdf_file/budglossary.pdf

Setright, L. J. K. *Drive On! A Social History of the Motor Car.* London: Granta Books, 2003.

"Sexual and Reproductive Health: Women and Men." Alan Guttmacher Institute, October 2002.
http://www.guttmacher.org/pubs/fb_10-02.html

Shaw, Kim. *The New Book of Wedding Etiquette: How to Combine the Best Traditions with Today's Flair.* Roseville, CA: Prima Publishing, 2001.

Shettles, Landrum B., and David M. Rorvik. *How to Choose the Sex of Your Baby.* New York: Broadway Books, 2001.

Shorter, Edward. *Women's Bodies: A Social History of Women's Encounters with Health, Ill-Health, and Medicine.* New Brunswick, NJ: Transaction, 1991.

Shreve, Jenn. "Fingers Will Twitch…" Salon.com, May 23, 1999.
http://www.salon.com/people/story/1999/05/23/mortician/index.html

Signature Bride Magazine. *Going to the Chapel.* New York: Putnam, 1998.

Simmons, Rabbi Shraqa. "Upsherin." Aish.com (Aish HaTorah), June 30, 2002.
http://www.aish.com/literacy/lifecycle/Upsherin.asp

Singh, Rajwant, and Georgia Rangel. "Sikhism: A Portrait." In *Sourcebook of the World's Religions: An Interfaith Guide to Religion and Spirituality.* Edited by Joel Beversluis. Novato, CA: New World Library, 2000.

Smith, Richard J. *China's Cultural History: The Qing Dynasty, 1644-1912.* 2nd ed. Boulder, CO: Westview Press, 1994.

"Social Interaction in Islam." Muslim Women's League, September, 1995.
http://www.mwlusa.org/publications/essays/socialinteraction.html

Sokolov, Archpriest Victor. "Death, Funeral, Requiem—Orthodox Christian Traditions, Customs, and Practice." Holy Trinity Orthodox Cathedral (San Francisco, CA), 1997.
http://www.holy-trinity.org/liturgics/sokolov-death.html

Sowden, Cynthia Lueck. *An Anniversary to Remember.* St. Paul, MN: Brighton Publications, 1992.

Spangenberg, Lisl M. *Timeless Traditions: A Couple's Guide to Wedding Customs around the World.* New York: Universe Publishing, 2001.

Spencer, Melanie. "Celebration, Not Sorrow: On Día de los Muertos, Loved Ones Remembered with Candles, Photos and Their Favorite Foods." *Austin American-Statesman,* October 27, 2005.

Spratling, Cassandra. "How to Plan a Class Reunion." *Detroit Free Press,* July 15, 2005.

"St. Francis Youth Confirmation." St. Francis Assisi Catholic Church, undated.
http://www.stfrancisa2.com/yes/confirmation.html

St. John, Kelly. "Sidewalk Shrines of Teddy Bears, Liquor; Memorials for the Fallen of Urban Life Exist as Much for the Living as for the Dead." *San Francisco Chronicle,* August 5, 2002.

Stewart, Arlene. *A Bride's Book of Wedding Traditions.* New York: William Morrow, 1995.

Stockel, H. Henrietta. *Chiricahua Apache Women and Children: Safekeepers of the Heritage.* College Station, TX: Texas A&M University Press, 2000.

Stoppard, Miriam. *Conception, Pregnancy, and Birth.* New York: DK Publishing, 2005.

Stroup, Herbert. *Like a Great River: An Introduction to Hinduism.* New York: Harper & Row, 1972.

Sturgis, Ingrid. *The Nubian Wedding Book: Words and Rituals to Celebrate and Plan an African-American Wedding.* New York: Three Rivers Press, 1997.

"The Sunrise Dance." Peabody Museum of Archaeology and Ethnology, undated. http://www.peabody.harvard.edu/maria/Sunrisedance.html

Swanson, Christopher B. "Who Graduates? Who Doesn't?: A Statistical Portrait of Public High School Graduation, Class of 2001." Urban Institute. February 25, 2004. http://www.urban.org/publications/410934.html

Talamantez, Inés. "In the Space between Earth and Sky: Contemporary Mescalero Apache Ceremonialism." In *Native Religions and Cultures of North America: Anthropology of the Sacred.* Edited by Lawrence E. Sullivan Sullivan. New York: Continuum, 2000.

"Tallit, Tephillin & Kippah." Reclaiming Judaism.org, undated. http://www.reclaimingjudaism.org/bmitzvah/Tallit.htm#The%20Meaning

Tandavan, Dr. Devananda. "Healing—A Contented Cow's Milk: Part 1." *Hinduism Today,* December 1995. http://www.hinduismtoday.com/archives/1995/12/11_healing_cows_milk.shtml

"Teen Driver Fact Sheet." Centers for Disease Control and Prevention, March 30, 2006. http://www.cdc.gov/ncipc/factsheets/teenmvh.htm

"They'll Never Know: Eight Hidden Ways to Cut Wedding Costs." SmartMoney.com, 2006. http://www.smartmoney.com/divorce/marriage/index.cfm?story=wedding-cutcosts

Thomas, Louis-Vincent. "Funeral Rites: An Overview." In *Encyclopedia of Religion.* 2nd ed. Edited by Lindsay Jones. Detroit: Macmillan Reference USA, 2005.

Thompson, Marlena. "Wedding Customs: Old, New, and Renovated." United Jewish Communities: The Federations of North America, undated. http://www.ujc.org/content_display.html?ArticleID=1596

Thompson, Sue Ellen, ed. *Holiday Symbols and Customs.* 3rd ed. Detroit: Omnigraphics, 2003.

Thursby, Jacqueline S. Excerpt from *Funeral Festivals in America: Rituals for the Living*. Lexington, KY: University Press of Kentucky, 2006. http://www.kentuckypress.com/0813123801excerpt.pdf

"Torah." Judaism 101, undated. http://www.jewfaq.org/torah.htm

Touger, Eli. "Upsherinish: A Milestone in a Child's Education." Chabad.org, undated. http://www.chabad.org/library/article.asp?AID=81568

Toussaint, David. *Gay and Lesbian Weddings: Planning the Perfect Same-Sex Ceremony*. New York: Ballantine Books, 2004.

"Town Creek Indian Mound: Burial Hut Exhibit." North Carolina Historic Sites, undated. http://www.ah.dcr.state.nc.us/sections/hs/town/burial-hut.htm

"Transition Rituals: A Faith-By-Faith Guide to Rites for the Deceased." BeliefNet, undated. http://www.beliefnet.com/story/78/story_7894_1.html

Trepp, Leo. *The Complete Book of Jewish Observance*. New York: Behrman House/Summit Books, 1980.

Turkington, Carol, and Michael M. Alper. *Understanding Fertility and Infertility: The Sourcebook for Reproductive Problems*. New York: Checkmark Books, 2003.

Turner, Jeffrey Scott. *Dating and Sexuality in America: A Reference Handbook*. Santa Barbara, CA: ABC-CLIO, 2003.

"2004-2005 Users' Manual." Unitarian Universalist Fellowship of Ames, undated. http://www.uufames.org/users_manual/manual.html

Ulrich, Lorene B. "Bridge Employment." In *Encyclopedia of Career Development*. Edited by Jeffrey Greenhaus and Gerard Callanan. Thousand Oaks, CA: Sage Reference, 2006.

"Unction of the Sick." Orthodox Church in America, undated. http://www.oca.org/OCchapter.asp?SID=2&ID=55

"Unitarian Universalist History." Unitarian Universalist Association, undated. http://www.uua.org/aboutuu/history.html

"Update Your Faith: Questions and Answers, When Should Someone Receive the Anointing of the Sick?" American Catholic, undated. http://www.americancatholic.org/UpdateYourFaith/answers.asp?QC0196a

"Valentine's Day: February 14." U.S. Census Bureau, February 10, 2005. http://www.census.gov/Press-Release/www/releases/archives/facts_for_features_special_editions/003147.html

Vargus, Ione D. "More Than a Picnic: African American Family Reunions." Working

Paper for the Family Reunion Institute, Temple University, Emory Center for Myth and Ritual in American Life. September 2002.
http://www.marial.emory.edu/pdfs/Vargus022-03.pdf

Venkatesananda, Sri Swami. "Pre-Determined Maha Samadhi." The Divine Life Society, undated.
http://www.dlshq.org/saints/siva_samadhi.htm

Vida, Vendela. *Girls on the Verge: Debutante Dips, Gang Drive-bys, and Other Initiations.* New York: St. Martin's, 1999.

Vidrine, Jane. "Cajun Wedding Traditions," Louisiana's Living Traditions, undated.
http://www.louisianafolklife.org/LT/Articles_Essays/cajun_wed.html

Vo, Kim. "Cemeteries Increasingly Accommodate Different Cultures." *San Jose Mercury News,* April 13, 2004.

Wagner, Edith. "Family Reunions." *Family Chronicle,* January–February 2000.
http://www.familychronicle.com/FamilyReunions.html

Waldman, Carl. *Atlas of the North American Indian.* New York: Facts on File, 1985.

Warner, Diane. *Complete Book of Wedding Vows: Hundreds of Ways to Say "I Do."* Franklin Lakes, NJ: Career Press, 1996.

"Wat Lao Buddha Khanti," undated.
http://www.buddhakhanti.org

Waters, Frank. *Book of the Hopi.* New York: Penguin, 1977.

Weber, Vicki L. *The Rhythm of Jewish Time: An Introduction to Holidays and Life-Cycle Events.* West Orange, NJ: Behrman House, 1999.

"Wedding Anniversaries." *World Almanac and Book of Facts.* World Almanac Education Group, 2003.

"Wedding Traditions and Customs Around the World." WorldWeddingTraditions.com, 2004.
http://www.worldweddingtraditions.com

Weiss, Robin. "Old Wives Tales." About.com: Parenting and Family, undated.
http://pregnancy.about.com/cs/myths/a/aa042299.htm

"Welcome to the Sacrament of Baptism in the Eastern Orthodox Church." St. Sophia Greek Orthodox Cathedral, undated.
http://www.stsophia.org/sacraments_baptism.pdf

Wertz, Richard W., and Dorothy C. Wertz. *Lying In: A History of Childbirth in America.* New Haven, Conn.: Yale University Press, 1977.

West, John O. *Mexican-American Folklore: Legends, Songs, Festivals, Proverbs, Crafts, Tales of Saints, of Revolutionaries, and More.* Little Rock, AR: August House, 1988.

Westbrook, Caroline. "Jewish Weddings." British Broadcasting Corporation, undated.

http://www.bbc.co.uk/religion/religions/judaism/features/rites/weddings

Wexler, Barbara. "Living Arrangements of the Older Population." *Growing Old in America.* Detroit: Thomson Gale, 2006.

"What Is the Episcopal Church?" Good Shepard Episcopal Church, undated. http://www.goodshepherdkingwood.org/whatis.htm

"What Is Unitarian Universalist Coming of Age?" Long Island Area Council of Unitarian Universalist Congregations, undated. http://www.liacuu.org/COA/COA_Special_Needs.doc

"What You Should Know about Baby Showers." Blue Bambu, undated. http://www.bluebambu.com/Customer%20Service/party-favors-babyhist.html

"What's the Origin of the Tooth Fairy?" The Straight Dope, July 20, 2004. http://www.straightdope.com/mailbag/mtoothfairy.html

"When Kids Drive." LHJ.com *(Ladies Home Journal),* undated. http://ww4.lhj.com/lhj/story.jhtml?storyid=/templatedata/bhg/story/data/10815.xml&categoryid=/templatedata/lhj/category/data/Teens.xml

"When to Practice for Someone Who Has Died." Spiritual Care Program, 2006. http://www.spcare.org/practices/suddendeath/afterdeath-whentopractice.html

Williams-Wheeler, Dorrie. "Junior Sorority Teaches Girls Skills To Last a Lifetime." ellaOnline: The Voice of Women, 2006. http://www.bellaonline.com/articles/art11834.asp

Wilson, Jeffrey, ed. *Gale Encyclopedia of Everyday Law.* 2nd ed. Detroit: Thomson Gale, 2006.

Winikka, Anja. "Customs: Ancient Wedding Day Traditions." Chinese Weddings by The Knot, undated. http://www.chineseweddingsbytheknot.com/articles/article.aspx?articleid+A609919094253

Wisdom, Emma J. *A Practical Guide to Planning a Family Reunion.* Nashville, TN: Post Oak Publications, 1988.

Wolfe, Michael. *One Thousand Roads to Mecca: Ten Centuries of Travelers Writing about the Muslim Pilgrimage.* New York: Grove Press, 1997.

Wong, Grace. "Ka-ching: Wedding Price Tag Nears $30K." CNN/Money, May 20, 2005. http://money.cnn.com/2005/05/20/pf/weddings

"Working and Retirement: New Options for Older Adults." *Growing Old in America.* Detroit: Thomson Gale, 2006.

Wurtzel, Nancy. "The Tooth Fairy." The Sideroad, undated. http://www.sideroad.com/Legends/tooth_fairy.html

Young, Michael E., and Katie Menzer. "Study: Moms Can Bench Labor Coach." *Dallas Morning News,* December 29, 2005.

http://www.dallasnews.com/sharedcontent/dws/dn/latestnews/stories/123005 dnmetbabypush.1cc9c894.html

Zinner, Ellen. "A Year Is a Relative Thing." Hospice Foundation of America, undated. http://www.hospicefoundation.org/griefAndLoss/year.asp

Photo and Illustration Credits

Photo and Illustration Credits

Index

Index

A

Aaron, 71, 72, 73
Abraham, 64, 69, 70, 329
abutsudan, 420
acîca. *See* aqiqah
Acoma Pueblo, 83
acts of acceptance, 126
Acts of the Apostles, 140
Adam and Eve, 57, 249
adhān, 35, 36
Adi Granth, 53
adult day care, 347, 348
adulthood. *See* adult milestones; courtship;
    engagement; later adulthood; post-wedding
    events; wedding ceremonies; wedding
    preparations; wedding receptions
adult milestones, 313–35. *See also* class
    reunions; family reunions; military
    reunions; performing the hajj; purchasing a
    house
advice and emotional support (baby shower),
    8–9, 257
affirmation ceremony, 203
Africa
  coming-of-age rituals, 197
  double burials, 394, 396
  funeral customs, 377
  henna body painting, 231, 246
  kola nut, 229
  libation, 254
  matchmaking, 218
  pre-wedding gatherings, 237
  queh-queh, 254
  secondary burials, 396
  wedding receptions, 288
Africacentrism, 197, 198, 200, 201

African-American coming-of-age processes. *See*
    African-American rites-of-passage programs
African-American rites-of-passage programs,
    159, 195 (ill.), 195–96, 197–201, 202
African Americans
  benevolent societies, 377
  Black College Reunion, 327
  debutante, 179
  family reunions, 320
  jumping the broom, 266, 271–72
  kola nut, 229
  loading the bride, 210, 231, 238, 256–57
  multigenerational households, 348
  queh-queh, 253, 254
  repast, 385
  second line dance, 279, 287
  slavery, 321
  wedding attire, 241
  wedding ceremonies, 263
  wedding dances, 284
African deserts, 393
African proverbs, 199
Akan/Adrinka people, 198
akïkah. *See* aqiqah
Alabama, 400
Alaska, 400
Albert, Prince, 241, 366
Albuquerque, New Mexico, 413
alcohol, avoidance of, 282
aleph-bet card, 90, 91
al-hajj al-akbar. *See* performing the hajj
alimony, 308
aliyah, 134, 135
Allah, 78, 263, 332, 374
alliance making. *See* matchmaking
All Saints Day, 380, 406, 412

471